THE
ESSENTIAL
PEIRCE

THE
ESSENTIAL
PEIRCE

Selected Philosophical Writings

VOLUME 1
(1867–1893)

▬

edited by

Nathan Houser and Christian Kloesel

Indiana
University
Press

BLOOMINGTON AND INDIANAPOLIS

The paper used in this publication meets the minimum requirements of American National Standard for Information Sciences—Permanence of Paper for Printed Library Materials, ANSI Z39.48-1984.
∞™

MANUFACTURED IN THE UNITED STATES OF AMERICA

Library of Congress Cataloging-in-Publication Data

Peirce, Charles S. (Charles Sanders), 1839–1914.
  [Selections. 1992]
  The essential Peirce : selected philosophical writings / edited by Nathan Houser and Christian Kloesel.
    p.   cm.
  Includes bibliographical references and index.
  Contents: v. 1. 1867–1893.
  ISBN 0-253-32849-7 (alk. paper). — ISBN 0-253-20721-5 (pbk. : alk. paper)
  1. Philosophy. I. Houser, Nathan. II. Kloesel, Christian J. W.
III. Title.
B945.P4125   1991
191—dc20   91-32113

1   2   3   4   5   96   95   94   93   92

The old Sphinx bit her thick lip,—
    Said, "Who taught thee me to name?
I am thy spirit, yoke-fellow,
    Of thine eye I am eyebeam."
                    —Emerson

*Greek sculpture of the Sphinx, in the British Museum,
as reproduced in the Century Dictionary*

Contents

THE *MONIST* METAPHYSICAL SERIES

CHRONOLOGY

1839 Born on 10 Sept. in Cambridge, MA, to Benjamin and Sarah
     Hunt (Mills) Peirce
1855 Entered Harvard College
1859 Graduated (A.B.) from Harvard
     Temporary aide in U.S. Coast Survey, fall to spring '60
1860 Studied classification with Agassiz, summer-fall
1861 Entered Lawrence Scientific School at Harvard
     Appointed regular aide in Coast Survey, 1 July
1862 Married to Harriet Melusina Fay, 16 Oct.
1863 Graduated *summa cum laude* (Sc.B.) in chemistry from Lawrence
     Scientific School
1865 Harvard lectures on "The Logic of Science," spring
     Began Logic Notebook, 12 Nov.; last entry in Nov. '09
1866 Lowell Institute lectures on "The Logic of Science; or Induc-
     tion and Hypothesis," 24 Oct.—1 Dec.
1867 Elected to American Academy of Arts and Sciences, 30 Jan.
1869 First of ca. 300 *Nation* reviews, in Mar.; last in Dec. '08
     Assistant at Harvard Observatory, Oct. '69–Dec. '72
     Harvard lectures on "British Logicians," Dec.—Jan.
1870 First Survey assignment in Europe: 18 June—7 Mar. '71
1872 Founding member of Cambridge Metaphysical Club, Jan.
     In charge of Survey office, spring-summer
     Put in charge of pendulum experiments, beginning in Nov.
     Promoted to rank of Assistant in the Survey, 1 Dec.
1875 Second Survey assignment in Europe: Apr. '75–Aug. '76
     Served as first official American delegate to International Geo-
     detic Association in Paris, 20–29 Sept.
1876 Separated from Melusina in Oct.
1877 Elected to National Academy of Sciences, 20 Apr.
     Third Survey assignment in Europe: 13 Sept.—18 Nov.
     Represented U.S. at International Geodetic Association confer-
     ence in Stuttgart, 27 Sept.—2 Oct.
1878 *Photometric Researches* published in Aug.
1879 Lecturer in Logic (till '84) at Johns Hopkins University
     First meeting of JHU Metaphysical Club, 28 Oct.
1880 Elected to London Mathematical Society, 11 Mar.
     Fourth Survey assignment in Europe: Apr.—Aug.
     French Academy address on value of gravity, 14 June
1881 Elected to American Association for the Advancement of Sci-
     ence in Aug.

1883   *Studies in Logic* published in spring
        Divorced from Melusina, 24 Apr.
        Married to Juliette Froissy (Pourtalès), 30 Apr.
        Fifth and final Survey assignment in Europe: May—Sept.
1884   In charge of Office of Weights and Measures, Oct.—22 Feb. '85
1888   Purchased "Arisbe," outside Milford, PA
1889   Contributor to *Century Dictionary*
1891   Resigned from Coast and Geodetic Survey, 31 Dec.
1892   Lowell lectures on "The History of Science," 28 Nov.—5 Jan.
1893   *Petrus Peregrinus* announced; prospectus only published
        "Search for a Method" announced by Open Court; not completed
1894   "The Principles of Philosophy" (in 12 vols.) announced by Henry Holt Co.; not completed
        "How to Reason" rejected by both Macmillan and Ginn Co.
1895   "New Elements of Mathematics" rejected by Open Court
1896   Consulting chemical engineer (till '02), St. Lawrence Power Co.
1898   Cambridge lectures on "Reasoning and the Logic of Things," 10 Feb.—7 Mar.
        "The History of Science" announced by G. P. Putnam's; not completed
1901   Contributor to *Dictionary of Philosophy and Psychology*
1902   Grant application for "Proposed Memoirs on Minute Logic" rejected by Carnegie Institution
1903   Harvard lectures on "Pragmatism," 26 Mar.—17 May
        Lowell lectures on "Some Topics of Logic," 23 Nov.—17 Dec.
1907   Harvard Philosophy Club lectures on "Logical Methodeutic," 8–13 Apr.
1909   Last published article, "Some Amazing Mazes"
1914   Died on 19 April

FOREWORD

The purpose of this collection of writings by Charles Sanders Peirce is to provide, in a convenient format, those of his most important papers that will enable readers to form a relatively complete impression of the main doctrines of his system of philosophy and to study its development. The present volume covers a period of about twenty-seven years, roughly one-half of Peirce's immensely productive life; the remaining two decades will be covered in the second volume. Limitations of space have forced us to exclude, almost entirely, his mathematical, logical, and scientific writings, as well as his many contributions to such disciplines as history and psychology. (But readers should be forewarned that Peirce's thought, more than that of any other classic American philosopher, is self-consciously related to mathematical, logical, and scientific conceptions. Many of his most significant scientific writings are available in the annual reports of the U.S. Coast and Geodetic Survey and the first six volumes of the *Writings of Charles S. Peirce;* his logical writings in volumes 2–4 of the *Collected Papers of Charles Sanders Peirce;* and his mathematical writings in the four volumes of Carolyn Eisele's *The New Elements of Mathematics.*) The writings in this volume are arranged chronologically from 1867 to 1893, ending with Peirce's first sustained and systematic presentation of his evolutionary metaphysics in the *Monist.*

The Introduction provides a summary account of Peirce's philosophy, which serves as a general background and provides structure for the twenty-five items in the present volume. These begin with Peirce's highly regarded alternative to Kantian philosophy, his "New List of Categories," from which he sets out to develop a new system of thought that will answer many of the perennial questions of philosophy. In the *Journal of Speculative Philosophy* Cognition Series (items 2–4), he attempts to work out a new account of mind and reality based on the results of his "new list" and to provide the foundation for a truly objective and empirical system of philosophy, in which epistemology would be grounded in the representation of external facts; in brief, to unify philosophy and science. In his review of Fraser's *Berkeley* (item 5), Peirce gives an account of his newly embraced "scholastic realism" and develops a common-sense theory of truth and reality that goes far in the direction of his soon-to-be-born pragmatism. Not surprisingly, his pragmatic turn is also apparent in "A New Class of Observations" (item 6); for, by this time, his pragmatism was already five years old. It is noteworthy that in this paper Peirce includes sensations within the class of 'objects' that should be studied scientifically by controlled observation, and there is at least the suggestion that, for philosophical and scientific investigations, he is beginning to consider phenomenology as an alternative to logic. The "Illustrations of the Logic of Science" (items 7–12) contain Peirce's first published account of pragmatism—though the name does not occur. This series, sometimes said to be the lesson of Darwin for philosophy, marks an important stage in Peirce's continuing advance toward a more and more realistic system of thought and, according to Max Fisch, it is "the nineteenth-century *Discourse in the Method of Rightly Conducting the Reason and Searching for the Truth in the Sciences.*" Item 13, the first part of an essay on the algebra of logic, deals with certain affinities between logical, epistemological, psychological, and physiological conceptions, which suggests that Peirce had by this time acquired an architectonic purview. Certainly by 1882, in his outline for his Johns Hopkins logic course (item 14), he is emphasizing the underlying unity of the sciences, for he proclaims that it is in the application of the methods of one science to another that the chief advances of thought will be made in the years to come.

If there is a significant turning-point in the twenty-five papers in this volume, it comes in "Design and Chance" (item 15), where Peirce accepts the doctrine that absolute chance is an active agent in the evolution of the universe and even of the laws of nature, a doctrine that marks his turn toward the evolutionary metaphysics of the latter part of this volume. The next two items represent another important step in Peirce's development, namely his recognition of the need for indices both in logic and in thought, for it is only with indices that reference can be made to *individuals* or to *actual* events and states of affairs. In item 16, Peirce reintroduces his best-known semiotic triad (icon, index, symbol), and in item 17 he proclaims the importance of the *Outward Clash*, the compelling sense of an opposing *other* in all experience: and thus takes an important step toward accepting the reality of secondness. After "Design and Chance," many of the strands of thought that run through the first seventeen papers coalesce, and enough fell into place sometime in 1885 to lead Peirce to his great guess at the riddle of the universe. It was the synthesis of his theory of categories with his new evolutionary cosmology that most directly led to his hypothesis that "three elements are active in the world": first, *chance;* second, *law;* and third, *habit-taking*. This guess is first formulated in item 18, and the remaining seven items fill out the details and ramifications of this guess for philosophy and science. "A Guess at the Riddle" (item 19) constitutes Peirce's first general treatment of his new evolutionary philosophy, a broad and systematic theory based on his guess. His "discovery" that the active elements of the universe are coincident with his categories leads him to accept them as the architectonic key to philosophy. It is the key he proceeds to use to reorganize the different branches of science and philosophy. Peirce projected "A Guess at the Riddle" as a full treatise on his new system of thought, in which all human knowledge would be reorganized according to his architectonic program, but circumstances prevented his completing that work. Item 20 provides, in a somewhat popular form, parts of what would have been included in the unwritten second chapter of the larger treatise, and items 21–25 fill in many of the remaining gaps. Thus, what began in 1867 as an analytical, epistemological philosophy, came to fruition in 1891–93 in the evolutionary and social philosophy of the five papers of the *Monist* Metaphysical Series.

Peirce was fifty-three years old when the final paper in this volume was published in 1893. He would live for another twenty-one years and, during that time, would produce his most fully developed theory of signs and many of his most subtle and profound metaphysical theories. It was also during these later years that his interest in pragmatism was rekindled and that, in an attempt to work out a proof of his pragmatism, he put into service his unique system of graphical logic (his existential graphs) alongside his categories and his theory of signs.

As the present volume ends, Peirce has not yet arrived at many of the views described in the Introduction. Not for another five years would he be what Max Fisch has called "a three-category realist," and he had been "a two-category realist," who accepted the reality of secondness, for only about three years. Most of the papers in the present volume were written while Peirce's realism was limited to a single universe, that of thirdness—or the world of thought. The twenty-five papers should be read with this in mind, but also with the understanding that Peirce is *on his way toward* a more complete realism. But what should be kept in mind, above all, is that Peirce's writings are signs of a great intellect *in the process* of working its way toward the truth.

But these signs are profuse. Peirce's extant writings—and there are many that were lost during his peregrinations for the Coast and Geodetic Survey and on several other occasions after his death—would fill over one hundred (500-page) volumes. A selected edition of some fifty volumes would be necessary to get a comprehensive sense of his work in mathematics, the natural sciences, philosophy and logic, history and psychology, and the several other areas to which he contributed. The most ambitious multi-volume edition, *Writings of Charles S. Peirce: A Chronological Edition,* is now underway at the Peirce Edition Project in Indianapolis; thirty volumes are projected. The first multi-volume edition appeared sixty years ago, when the first six of eight volumes of the *Collected Papers* (1931–35, 1958) were published. Four other major editions have appeared within the last fifteen years. Peirce's *Contributions to THE NATION* was edited by Kenneth Ketner, in four parts, between 1975 and 1988, and his *New Elements of Mathematics,* in four volumes, by Carolyn Eisele in 1976. The following year saw the publication of Peirce's *Complete Published Works*, a 149-microfiche edition accompanied by a printed *Comprehensive Bibliography* (revised and enlarged by 12 fiches in 1986), and in 1985, Carolyn Eisele brought out two volumes of *Historical Perspectives on Peirce's Logic of Science*.

The present two-volume collection is not intended to replace the more comprehensive editions, but to provide an affordable and reliable text that covers the full extent of Peirce's system of philosophy. Its thematic boundaries are more expansive than those of several other one- or two-volume collections; it is arranged chronologically, in two parts, so as to permit study of the development of Peirce's thought; and, importantly, it pays especial attention to the integrity of the edited text of his writings. Although the last few items cannot be said to be fully critical texts, the volume as a whole may be considered reliable from a textual point of view.

Of the twenty-five items included in this volume, nineteen were published during Peirce's lifetime. Since these are among his most important philosophical writings, all have been republished in the different volumes of the *Collected Papers*, and a number of them have reappeared, in whole or in part, in various other anthologies and in the first five volumes of *Writings*. The six remaining items (6, 15, and 17–20) are unpublished manuscripts and typescripts. Only items 17 and 19 are included in the *Collected Papers*, and the remaining four items have appeared for the first time, or will soon appear, in the *Writings:* item 6 in W3, item 15 in W4, item 18 in W5, item 20 in W6. All six manuscripts and typescripts have been edited from the originals in Harvard's Houghton Library. The first eighteen items in the present volume have been adopted directly from their appearance in the *Writings*, volumes 2 through 5 (including some of the corrections in the second printing of volume 2), and as these have been prepared according to the standards of the Modern Language Association's Committee on Scholarly Editions, they represent critical, authoritative texts. (For emendations and textual cruxes in these eighteen items, which are not reproduced in the Notes, readers should consult that edition.) We have attempted to edit items 19–25 according to similar standards, but they cannot be said to have had the benefit of the same intensive, complete sort of historical, bio-bibliographical, and textual/editorial work that is required in the preparation of a critical edition. This is especially true for the five articles in the *Monist* Metaphysical Series (items 21–25), for which there are a number of relevant manuscripts and galleys, and, to a lesser degree, for "A Guess at the Riddle" (item 19), for several chapters of which there are more versions than one; in the latter, we have chosen what seemed most representative and finished.

In all cases, we have corrected typographical errors and other obvious mistakes (and have listed most of the emendations in editorial notes following Peirce's text) but have retained inconsistencies in spelling and punctuation when they reflect acceptable nineteenth-century standards and practices. (Only the word "indispensible" has been permitted to appear in Peirce's idiosyncratic form, for that is how he consistently, and consciously, spelled it throughout his life.) Purely cosmetic changes, such as the italicization of book titles or the indentation of opening paragraphs, have been made silently. We have also supplied titles for the three untitled items (5, 15, 20), and missing words are supplied in italic brackets. For the rest, our editing has been guided by restraint and accuracy, and the texts included here represent what Peirce wrote, not what we think he should have written.

The twenty-five items in the present collection are printed with a minimum of editorial intrusion in the text, although we have used a few editorial symbols to reflect certain physical problems in both published and unpublished papers, and have indicated, in standard form (with superscript arabic numerals), where we have contributed editorial notes. The footnotes appearing at the bottom of their respective pages are Peirce's own and are identified by asterisks, daggers, and so on. (In a few of these footnotes, we have provided, in square brackets, additional information—such as names, dates, page numbers, and references to papers in the *Writings*—which seemed more useful and economical here than in additional entries in the Notes section.) The (editorial) Notes, which are numbered consecutively within each of the twenty-five items, provide various kinds of information (including translations) that Peirce himself did not provide. Preceding this Foreword, there is a brief Chronology listing the most significant dates and events in Peirce's life and work, and the volume concludes with a detailed Index.

Two other features in Peirce's text must be mentioned: the editorial symbols and the headnotes appearing between title and text. The editorial symbols, as indicated, reflect physical problems, whether in published papers or unpublished manuscripts and typescripts, and they include the following: words (or parts of words) appearing in italic brackets indicate that they have been supplied (or reconstructed) by the editors; italic brackets enclosing three ellipsis points indicate one or more lost manuscript pages; and sets of double slashes mark the beginning and end of Peirce's undecided alternate readings, with the single slash dividing the original from the alternative inscription. The headnotes, which appear in reduced type between the title of each item and the text proper, serve several purposes. They identify each item as a published paper or an unpublished manuscript; provide information on its composition or publication (and its later use elsewhere in Peirce's work and its republication in one of the two main editions of his writings); characterize its contents and main arguments; and indicate its place in the overall development of Peirce's system of philosophy. Papers published during Peirce's lifetime are identified by P followed by a number and the bibliographic information provided in the *Comprehensive Bibliography* (2nd rev. ed. [Bowling Green, OH: Philosophy Documentation Center, 1986]). Unpublished papers are identified by MS followed by the number assigned in Richard Robin's *Annotated Catalogue of the Papers of Charles S. Peirce* (Amherst: University of Massachusetts Press, 1967) and his "The Peirce Papers: A Supplementary Catalogue" (*Transactions of the Charles S. Peirce Society* 7 [1971]: 37–57); when the reference is to newly numbered manuscripts in their reassembled and chronologically arranged form as listed in the *Writings,* MS is printed in italic type (and followed by the new Peirce Edition Project number). Republication (or first publication) of each item is indicated by W *(Writings of Charles S. Peirce),* followed by volume and page numbers; CP *(Collected Papers of Charles Sanders Peirce),* followed by volume and paragraph numbers; and, in one instance, HPPLS *(Historical Perspectives on Peirce's Logic of Science),* followed by page numbers. (Some of these identifying letters are used in the Introduction as well, which also includes a reference to NEM, Carolyn Eisele's edition of *The New Elements of Mathematics.*)

Although there are several references, especially in the Introduction, to some of the more important secondary studies on Peirce's philosophy, it might have been helpful, some might say, to have provided a list of "Secondary Studies" or "Further Readings." We decided against such a list for three reasons: (1) the number of secondary studies on Peirce has grown to enormous proportions, especially during the last two decades, and brief articles are sometimes more helpful than whole monographs; (2) whatever selection we might make (with its concomitant exclusions) would be sure to exhibit our biases and critical dispositions; and (3) there are two useful lists of secondary studies, through 1982, in the *Comprehensive Bibliography* and in *The Relevance of Charles Peirce* (La Salle, IL: The Hegeler Institute, 1983), and the improvement in library indexing services and the growing use of bibliographic databases have almost obviated the need for printed bibliographies. If there are two studies with which everyone should be familiar, whether novice or seasoned scholar, they are Christopher Hookway's *Peirce* (London: Routledge & Kegan Paul, 1985), which will shortly be available in paperback, and Max Fisch's *Peirce, Semeiotic, and Pragmatism* (Bloomington: Indiana University Press, 1986), which represents many years of searching scholarship. And we should not neglect to mention that the *Transactions,* the journal of the Peirce Society, is already in its twenty-seventh year.

Nor should we neglect to mention, finally, that we have had some help in the preparation of this first of our two volumes of Peirce's selected philosophical writings. We are grateful, for her invaluable assistance, to Beth Sakaguchi; to our colleagues at the Indiana University Press, for their encouragement and cooperation; to the Indiana University School of Liberal Arts for its continuing support; and to André De Tienne, for his scholarly advice and careful reading of a large part of the whole manuscript.

Indianapolis   Nathan Houser
July 1991   Christian Kloesel

INTRODUCTION

Charles Sanders Peirce was born on 10 September 1839 in Cambridge, Massachusetts—when Darwin was only 30 years old—and he lived until 1914, the year World War I began. His father, Benjamin Peirce, was a distinguished professor at Harvard College and the most respected mathematician in America. The Peirce family was well connected in academic and scientific circles, and Charles grew up on intimate terms with the leading figures. He was regarded as a prodigy in both science and philosophy, and more brilliant in mathematics than even his father. Unfortunately for Peirce, his independence of mind, which was at first so much admired, turned out to be a severe impediment to his success. In part this was due to the times. For as James Feibleman has pointed out, with the expansion of the United States and the rise of the great western cities, New England, and especially Boston and Cambridge, became more and more insular and conservative and grew fearful of genius and originality.[1] As great a thinker as any that America has ever produced, Peirce was thwarted at almost every turn, and only by great effort of will was he able to fulfill some of the promise he exhibited as a young man.

Peirce's importance as a thinker was not entirely lost on his own age. Among his friends and admirers were such respected philosophers as William James, Josiah Royce, and John Dewey, and the renowned mathematician and logician Ernst Schröder. Yet after a short tenure at the Johns Hopkins University as a part-time lecturer in logic (1879–1884), and a premature—and forced—retirement (1891) from the U.S. Coast and Geodetic Survey, where he was in charge of gravity experiments and pendulum research, Peirce was unable to obtain regular employment again. He spent much of the latter third of his life struggling to make ends meet, and many of his writings of those years were done for pay. These include book reviews for newspapers and popular journals, contributions to dictionaries and encyclopedias, and translations (mainly from French and German). There were also a number of philosophical articles composed to satisfy the expectations and instructions of paying editors. For a period, beginning about 1890, Peirce's life was often dominated by one unsuccessful "get rich scheme" after another.[2] By the turn of the century, he began to worry

1. James Feibleman, "The Relation of Peirce to New England Culture," *American Journal of Economics and Sociology* 4 (1944): 99–107.
    2. For an account of some of these "get rich schemes," see Christian J. W. Kloesel, "Charles Peirce and Honoré de Clairefont," *Versus* 49 (1988): 5–18.

about getting his program of philosophy and his discoveries in mathematics and logic into print, but almost all his proposals failed to win support. It was more than twenty years after his death, and only after the Harvard Philosophy Department brought out a collection of his papers, that scholars began more generally to glimpse the importance and profundity of his thought. By 1936 Alfred North Whitehead would describe America as the developing center of worthwhile philosophy, and identify Charles Peirce and William James as the founders of the American renaissance. "Of these men," Whitehead said, "W.J. is the analogue to Plato, and C.P. to Aristotle."[3]

Interest in Peirce has grown enormously in recent years, and estimates of his significance as a thinker continue to run high. His work in logic, algebraical and graphical, has come to be regarded as substantial for both its historical impact and its enduring importance for research. Hilary Putnam expressed his surprise upon discovering "how much that is quite familiar in modern logic actually became known to the logical world through the efforts of Peirce and his students,"[4] and W. V. Quine dates modern logic from "the emergence of general quantification theory at the hands of Frege and Peirce."[5] More recently, John Sowa has demonstrated how Peirce's graphical system of logic (his existential graphs) improves on other logics for the representation of discourse, and the study of language generally, and he has used the existential graphs as the logical foundation for his own conceptual graphs, "which combine Peirce's logic with research on semantic networks in artificial intelligence and computational linguistics."[6] In philosophy more generally, Peirce's work has been the focus of a considerable resurgence of interest throughout the world. This is demonstrated by the growing number of books and articles about Peirce, by increasing references to his ideas, and by the testimony of respected philosophers such as Karl Popper, who regards Peirce as "one of the greatest philosophers of all time."[7] Finally, in the rapidly growing field of study known as semiotics, Peirce is universally acknowledged as one of the founders, even *the* founder, and his theory of signs is among the most frequently studied and systematically examined of all foundational theories. The importance of semiotics for all

3. Whitehead to Charles Hartshorne, 2 Jan. 1936, in Victor Lowe, *Alfred North Whitehead: The Man and His Work*, ed. J. B. Schneewind (Baltimore: Johns Hopkins University Press, 1990), 2:345.

4. Hilary Putnam, "Peirce the Logician," *Historia Mathematica* 9 (1982): 295.

5. W. V. Quine, "In the Logical Vestibule," *Times Literary Supplement*, 12 July 1985, p. 767.

6. John Sowa, "Matching Logical Structure to Linguistic Structure," in *Studies in the Logic of Charles S. Peirce* (Bloomington: Indiana University Press, 1992).

7. Quoted by James Bird, "A Giant's Voice from the Past," *Times Higher Education Supplement*, 8 Sept. 1989.

disciplines that deal crucially with *representation* (among them epistemology, linguistics, anthropology, and cognitive science, and probably
all the fine arts) is only beginning to be recognized. In his 1989 Jefferson
Lecture, Walker Percy argued that modern science is radically inco-
herent—"not when it seeks to understand things and subhuman organisms and the cosmos itself, but when it seeks to understand man, not
man's physiology or neurology or his bloodstream, but man *qua* man,
man when he is peculiarly human"—but that, with his theory of signs,
Peirce laid the groundwork for a coherent science of man that is yet
to be worked out.[8]

Peirce developed an early interest in philosophy, particularly the
writings of Kant, and in formal logic, but his training led him to
experimental science, especially two sciences with a marked mathematical basis: astronomy and geodesy. His first book, *Photometric Researches* (1878), was the result of several years of astronomical observations at the Harvard Observatory. It included Ptolemy's catalogue of
stars, in a translation Peirce made from a manuscript in the Biblio-
thèque Nationale in Paris. He published many papers and monographs on geodesy, and one of these is still considered a classic in the
field. He was a geodesist with the U.S. Coast and Geodetic Survey for
nearly thirty years, and later he worked for a time as a consulting
chemical engineer for the St. Lawrence Power Company.

But throughout his life, committed as it was to science, he maintained a continuing research program in philosophy and logic. He
delivered series of lectures at different institutions from the mid-1860s
until after the turn of the century, and from 1879 to 1884 he taught logic
at the Johns Hopkins University, the first true graduate school in
America. When in the late 1880s he wrote definitions for the *Century
Dictionary*, it was no doubt his enthusiasm for the Hopkins model that
led him to define "university" as "an association of men for the purpose of study, which confers degrees which are acknowledged as valid
throughout Christendom, is endowed, and is privileged by the state,
in order that the people may receive intellectual guidance and that the
theoretical problems which present themselves in the development of
civilization may be resolved." The definition was the subject of an
anecdote by John Jay Chapman:

Charles Peirce wrote the definition of University in the Century Dictionary.
He called it an institution for purposes of study. They wrote to him that their
notion had been that a university was an institution for instruction. He wrote
back that if they had any such notion they were grievously mistaken, that a

8. Walker Percy, "The Fateful Rift: The San Andreas Fault in the Modern Mind,"
18th Jefferson Lecture in the Humanities, delivered 3 May 1989 in Washington, D.C.

university had not and never had had anything to do with instruction and that until we got over this idea we should not have any university in this country.[9]

In his day, Peirce was a more international figure than is generally known. He visited Europe five times between 1870 and 1883, and although he usually traveled as a scientist—to swing pendulums and to compare American weights and measures with European standards—he met prominent mathematicians and logicians as well as scientists, including De Morgan, McColl, Jevons, Clifford, and Herbert Spencer. Peirce corresponded with most of these scholars, and also with Schröder, Cantor, Kempe, Jourdain, Victoria Lady Welby, and others. Through Lady Welby, Peirce's letters on semiotic were occasionally passed on to C. K. Ogden who, with I. A. Richards, published some of them in the classic *The Meaning of Meaning.* Wittgenstein's good friend F. P. Ramsey was much impressed with these letters and, in his review of the *Tractatus,* remarked that Wittgenstein would have profited from Peirce's type-token distinction.[10]

Peirce's systematic philosophy, which is the focus of the present collection of writings, is difficult to characterize in a few words. For one thing, it consists of a number of distinct but interrelated theories and doctrines, any one of which could easily be the subject of whole books—as some, in fact, have been. Among the most characteristic of Peirce's theories are his *pragmatism* (or "pragmaticism," as he later called it), a method of sorting out conceptual confusions by relating meaning to consequences; *semiotic,* his theory of information, representation, communication, and the growth of knowledge; *objective idealism,* his monistic thesis that matter is effete mind (with the corollary that mind is inexplicable in terms of mechanics); *fallibilism,* the thesis that no inquirer can ever claim with full assurance to have reached the truth, for new evidence or information may arise that will reverberate throughout one's system of beliefs affecting even those most entrenched; *tychism,* the thesis that chance is really operative in the universe; *synechism,* the theory that continuity prevails and that the presumption of continuity is of enormous methodological importance for philosophy; and, finally, *agapism,* the thesis that love, or sympathy, has real influence in the world and, in fact, is "the great evolutionary agency of the universe." The last three doctrines are part of Peirce's comprehensive *evolutionary cosmology.*

9. Max H. Fisch, "Peirce at the Johns Hopkins University," in *Peirce, Semeiotic, and Pragmatism* (Bloomington: Indiana University Press, 1986), p. 36.
10. See Charles S. Hardwick, "Peirce's Influence on Some British Philosophers: A Guess at the Riddle," in *Studies in Peirce's Semiotic* (Peirce Studies 1, Lubbock: Institute for Studies in Pragmaticism, 1979), p. 27. Ramsey's review of Wittgenstein appeared in *Mind* 32:128 (1923): 465–78.

Besides this imposing assemblage of theories, there is still another barrier to an easy characterization of Peirce's philosophy, signaled by the reference to Darwin in the opening paragraph. Peirce's philosophy does not consist of a set of static doctrines, thought up and written down once and for all; its development over his more than fifty years of scholarship appropriately represents his Darwinian motivation. Not only did he think of himself as working out an evolutionary philosophy, one that includes humankind as part of the evolving natural world, but his writings illustrate his personal commitment to the principle of evolutionary growth. Peirce was always open to the revelations of experience and was prepared to change his theories accordingly. Some of these changed dramatically over the course of his life; nearly all changed in one way or another. We cannot draw one consistent philosophy from Peirce's writings without ignoring conflicting passages. A tendency by some of Peirce's commentators to overlook this characteristic of his thought has led to much confusion. This point was made rather dramatically by the late Indiana philosopher Arthur F. Bentley:

What one says 20 years from what one says another time, must be studied as Event-in-process. . . . Peirce did not have a modernized post Jamesian vocabulary for behaviors. He floundered and turned. . . . You can show Peirce as all sorts of things. But take the full flow of Peirce's development, his 1869 essays for actuality; his relations logic—his statement about concepts in 187/8/ Sci Monthly; his late effort at a functional logic nobody ever mentions, etc. You have an event in progress. It is, for me, one of the greatest event/s/ among all events.[11]

It is impossible, in a short introduction, to present fully Peirce's most characteristic philosophical doctrines and theories, let alone give serious attention to the development of his thought. It is difficult to give even a satisfactory outline of his philosophical development. Over the years, scholars have described the key steps in his intellectual life in different ways. To give some chronological structure to such studies, Max Fisch has divided Peirce's philosophical activity into three periods: (1) the Cambridge period (1851–1870), from his reading of Whately's *Logic* to his memoir on the logic of relatives; (2) the cosmopolitan period (1870–1887), the time of his most important scientific work, when he traveled extensively in Europe, as well as in the United States and Canada; and (3) the Arisbe period (1887–1914), from his move to Milford, Pennsylvania, until his death—the longest and philosophically most productive period.[12]

11. Arthur F. Bentley to Joseph Ratner, 1 July 1948. This letter is deposited with the Bentley Papers in the Lilly Library, Indiana University.
12. Max H. Fisch, "Peirce's Arisbe: The Greek Influence in His Later Philosophy," in *Peirce, Semeiotic, and Pragmatism*, p. 227.

Gérard Deledalle has associated these periods more directly with Peirce's philosophical activity and has given them more figurative names: (1) "Leaving the Cave" (1851–1870), the period of the evolution of Peirce's thought beginning with his critique of Kantian logic and Cartesianism; (2) "The Eclipse of the Sun" (1870–1887), the period dominated by his discovery of modern logic and pragmatism; and (3) "The Sun Set Free" (1887–1914), the period of his founding of semiotic on a phenomenology based on his logic of relations and of his working out his scientific metaphysics, the crowning-point of his philosophical achievement.[13]

A somewhat different account of the principal stages of Peirce's development is given by Murray Murphey, who associates each of Peirce's key shifts of thought with important discoveries in logic. He identifies four main phases: (1) Peirce's Kantian phase (1857–1865/66); (2) the phase beginning with the discovery of the irreducibility of the three syllogistic figures (1866–1869/70); (3) the phase beginning with the discovery of the logic of relations (1869/70–1884); and (4) the phase beginning with the discovery of quantification and of set theory (1884–1914).[14]

Probably the most significant development in Peirce's intellectual life was the evolution of his thought from its quasi-nominalist and idealist beginnings to its broadly and strongly realist conclusion. Because there are so many variants of these doctrines, a few selections from Peirce's *Century Dictionary* definitions will help reveal his conceptions of these terms:

Nominalism: 1. The doctrine that nothing is general but names; more specifically, the doctrine that common nouns, as *man, horse,* represent in their generality nothing in the real things, but are mere conveniences for speaking of many things at once, or at most necessities of human thought; individualism.

Idealism: 1. The metaphysical doctrine that the real is of the nature of thought; the doctrine that all reality is in its nature psychical.

Realist: 1. A logician who holds that the essences of natural classes have some mode of being in the real things; in this sense distinguished as a scholastic realist; opposed to nominalist. 2. A philosopher who believes in the real existence of the external world as independent of all thought about it, or, at least, of the thought of any individual or any number of individuals.

Peirce also defined "ideal-realism" as "a metaphysical doctrine which combines the principles of idealism and realism." As a variant of this

13. Gérard Deledalle, *Charles S. Peirce: An Intellectual Biography* (Amsterdam: John Benjamins, 1990), p. xxxi.
14. Murray G. Murphey, *The Development of Peirce's Philosophy* (Cambridge: Harvard University Press, 1961), p. 3.

term, he defined the ideal-realism of his father as "the opinion that nature and the mind have such a community as to impart to our guesses a tendency toward the truth, while at the same time they require the confirmation of empirical science."

The lifelong tension between nominalism and realism in Peirce's own intellectual life is testament to the general importance he attached to it; in fact, if any single question can be said to have been viewed by Peirce as the most important philosophical question of his time, it is that of deciding between the two doctrines. Peirce concurred in this with his old schoolmate Francis Ellingwood Abbot, who in 1885 wrote that "so far was the old battle of Nominalism and Realism from being fought out by the end of the fifteenth century that it is to-day the deep, underlying problem of problems, on the right solution of which depends the life of philosophy itself in the ages to come."[15] For Peirce, as for Abbot, the significance of the outcome of this "battle" was not limited to technical philosophy:

Though the question of realism and nominalism has its roots in the technicalities of logic, its branches reach about our life. The question whether the *genus homo* has any existence except as individuals, is the question whether there is anything of any more dignity, worth, and importance than individual happiness, individual aspirations, and individual life. Whether men really have anything in common, so that the *community* is to be considered as an end in itself, and if so, what the relative value of the two factors is, is the most fundamental practical question in regard to every institution the constitution of which we have it in our power to influence. (item 5)

According to Fisch, Peirce's progress toward realism began early and was gradual, but there were key steps that divide it into stages.[16] Peirce took his first deliberate step in 1868 when, in the second paper of his cognition series (item 3), he "declares unobtrusively for realism." Although this step marks only a small shift in Peirce's thought— the introduction of "the long run" into his theory of reality—it is an important one, for it brings to an end his period of avowed nominalism.[17]

Peirce's second deliberate step was taken in 1871, when in his Berkeley review (item 5) he again declared for "the realism of Scotus" and

15. Francis Ellingwood Abbot, *Scientific Theism* (London: Macmillan, 1885), pp. 11–12.
16. The account of Peirce's progress toward realism contained in this and the following eight paragraphs is based on Max Fisch, "Peirce's Progress from Nominalism toward Realism," in *Peirce, Semeiotic, and Pragmatism,* pp. 184–200; unless otherwise noted, quotations are from that essay.
17. Whether Peirce was ever really a thoroughgoing nominalist or only a more nominalistic realist than he would be later is discussed by Don D. Roberts in "On Peirce's Realism" and Fred Michael in "Two Forms of Scholastic Realism in Peirce's Philosophy," *Transactions of the Charles S. Peirce Society* 6 (1970): 67–83 and 24 (1988): 317–48.

recognized that realism is temporally oriented toward the future while nominalism is oriented toward the past. Fisch points out that this second declaration came when, after a period of intensive study of the schoolmen, Peirce had become well acquainted with the writings of Duns Scotus.

Peirce took his third step in mid-1872 when, in the Cambridge Metaphysical Club, he first presented his pragmatism in which the meaning of conceptions is referred to future experience: "So we say that the inkstand upon the table is heavy. And what do we mean by that? We only mean that if its support be removed it will fall to the ground. . . . So that . . . knowledge of the thing which exists all the time, exists only by virtue of the fact that when a certain occasion arises a certain idea will come into the mind" (W3:30–31). A few months later, Peirce wrote that "no cognition . . . has an intellectual significance for what it is in itself, but only for what it is in its effects upon other thoughts. And the existence of a cognition is not something actual, but consists in the fact that under certain circumstances some other cognition will arise" (W3:77). But the best-known statement of the doctrine came in 1878, in the second of his "Illustrations of the Logic of Science," in the now famous version of his pragmatic maxim: "consider what effects, which might conceivably have practical bearings, we conceive the object of our conception to have. Then, our conception of these effects is the whole of our conception of the object."

Fisch stops enumerating the steps toward realism in 1872, and divides the rest of Peirce's development into two periods, the pre-*Monist* period (1872–1890) and the *Monist* period (1891–1914). He summarizes the key factors of the former period as follows:

The chief developments in the pre-*Monist* period whose effects on Peirce's realism will appear in the *Monist* period are his pragmatism; his work on the logic of relations and on truth-tables, indices, and quantification; the resulting reformulation of his categories; his work and that of Cantor and Dedekind on transfinite numbers; the appearance in 1885 of provocative books by Royce and Abbot; and, at the end of the period, a fresh review of the history of philosophy for purposes of defining philosophical terms for the *Century Dictionary*.

In the pre-*Monist* period, a step that had special importance for Peirce's philosophical development was his recognition, with the help of his Johns Hopkins student O. H. Mitchell, of the need for indices in his algebra of logic. Peirce recognized the need for indices in notations adequate for the full representation of reasoning because he had come to understand the importance of pinning down thought to *actual* situations. "The actual world," he said, "cannot be distinguished from a world of imagination by any description. Hence the need of pronouns and indices" (item 16). Fisch points out that Peirce's incorporation of indices into his system of logic called for a reformulation both of his theory of signs and of his general theory of categories. It was then that Peirce reintroduced the familiar icon-index-symbol trichotomy and his reformulated categories denoting three kinds of characters (singular, dual, and plural), which he associated with three kinds of fact: "fact about an object, fact about two objects (relation), fact about several objects (synthetic fact)" (W5:244).

At the end of the pre-*Monist* period, Peirce took a major step toward a more robust realism, a step related to his recognition of the need for indices. This was his acceptance, in about 1890, of Scotus's haecceities—the reality of actuality or of secondness. Peirce could no longer ignore the "Outward Clash," as Hegel had much to the detriment of his system of philosophy. With the acceptance of the reality of seconds, Peirce acknowledged the mode of being that distinguishes the individual from the general, and isolated his categories of fact: qualia, relations, and signs.

The *Monist* period began with the series of five papers that concludes the present volume. It is the first of four series of papers that Peirce contributed to the *Monist*, which, after its founding in 1890, became his chief medium of publication. In each of these series, and in many of his other writings of the period, he continued to weed out the remaining nominalistic and many of the idealistic elements of his philosophy. Peirce took his most decisive step toward realism in 1897. Fisch has nicely illustrated this last great step by contrasting two passages, one from a January 1897 review of the third volume of Schröder's *Algebra und Logik der Relative*, and the other from an 18 March 1897 letter to William James. In January, Peirce wrote: "I formerly [as late as October 1896] defined the possible as that which in a given state of information (real or feigned) we do not know not to be true. But this definition today seems to me only a twisted phrase which, by means of two negatives, conceals an anacoluthon" (CP 3.527). Two months later he wrote to James: "The possible is a positive universe, and the two negations happen to fit it, but that is all" (CP 8.308). Peirce thus added *the possible* as a third mode of being—and, in so doing, gave up his long-held, Mill-inspired frequency theory of probability—and his scheme of categories was fundamentally complete. To his categories in their form of thirdness (feeling, or signs of firstness; sense of action and reaction, or signs of secondness; and sense of learning or mediation, or signs of thirdness) and in their form of secondness (qualia, or facts of firstness; relations, or facts of secondness; and signs, or facts of thirdness), Peirce now added what might be called his ontological categories, his categories in their form of firstness: *firstness*, or the being of positive qualitative possibility; *secondness*, or the being of actual fact; and *thirdness*, or the being of law that will govern facts in the future (CP 1.23).

Peirce was then, in 1897, what Fisch calls a "three-category realist." He had very early accepted the reality of thirds, the universe of thought or signs. This universe was the only reality Peirce the idealist had admitted until about 1890 when he accepted the reality of seconds, the universe of facts (influenced by Scotus). Finally, in 1897 he broadened his evolving realism to accept the reality of firsts, the universe of possibility (influenced by Aristotle). Recognizing the significance of these steps for the growth of his thought, Peirce now characterized himself as "an Aristotelian of the scholastic wing, approaching Scotism, but going much further in the direction of scholastic realism" (CP 5.77n1).

One further step from the *Monist* period should be mentioned, for it brings together two fundamental strands of Peirce's thought: his pragmatism and his semiotic. In his third *Monist* series, beginning in 1905, Peirce sought to *prove* his doctrine of pragmatism (pragmaticism), and in the course of working out his proof, he wove his two great theories into a unified doctrine. He concluded that his semiotic pragmatism entails realism, so that a proof of pragmatism is, at the same time, a proof of realism, and that the pragmatist is "obliged to subscribe to the doctrine of a real Modality, including real Necessity and real Possibility" (CP 5.457).

Although Peirce was aware that at least some of the steps described above were important milestones in his development, he did not regard them as ushering in new *systems* of thought. According to Murphey, Peirce regarded each phase of his thought as merely a *revision* of "a single over-all architectonic system" and always preserved as much as he could from each earlier phase. His philosophy might be likened to "a house which is being continually rebuilt from within."[18]

Some scholars have not accepted the one-system account of Peirce's philosophy. Thomas Goudge, in particular, has argued that "Peirce's ideas fall naturally into two broad groups whose opposite character is a reflection of a deep conflict in his thinking" and that this opposition is the result of his conflicting commitment to both naturalism and transcendentalism.[19] By "naturalism" Goudge has in mind scientific philosophy more or less in the positivist sense, a philosophy that puts logical analysis on a pedestal and eschews speculation and system-building. Transcendentalism, on the other hand, discounts logical analysis in favor of metaphysical construction, embracing both speculation and architectonic. Peirce the naturalist tended to nominalism, while Peirce the transcendentalist tended to realism. It was Peirce the naturalist who was the pragmatist, while Peirce the transcendentalist

18. Murray G. Murphey, *The Development of Peirce's Philosophy*, p. 3.
19. Thomas Goudge, *The Thought of C. S. Peirce* (Toronto: University of Toronto Press, 1950), p. xx.

tended to intuitionism. Goudge finds that Peirce's naturalism was the stronger tendency, which guided him in his researches in formal logic, semiotic, scientific method, phenomenology, and critical metaphysics, while the weaker transcendentalism "is most apparent in his views on cosmology, ethics, and theology."[20]

Goudge has indeed uncovered what may *appear* to be two Peirces, but the finding of most recent scholarship is that the tension is not as great as he thought. Peirce's philosophy is broad and subtle and appears to be able to accommodate results that would be incompatible in narrower systems of thought. It is not possible here to argue for the coherence of the various claims and doctrines that Goudge and others have found to be in conflict. The best that can be done is to outline the basic architecture of Peirce's philosophy and to give a glimpse of its overall unity.

For Peirce, as for Kant, logic was the key to philosophy. He claimed that from the age of twelve, after reading his brother's copy of Whately's *Elements of Logic,* he could no longer think of anything except as an exercise in logic.[21] Peirce's study of logic was not limited to the formal theory of deductive reasoning or to the foundations of mathematics, although he made important contributions to both. When he sought the professorship of physics at the Johns Hopkins (before being appointed part-time lecturer in logic), he wrote to President Daniel C. Gilman that it was as a logician that he sought to head that department and that he had learned physics in his study of logic. "The data for the generalizations of logic are the special methods of the different sciences," he pointed out, and "to penetrate these methods the logician has to study various sciences rather profoundly."

But it was not just as a theory of reasoning or as a critique of methods that logic was important for philosophy. "Philosophy," Peirce said, "seeks to explain the universe at large, and to show what there is intelligible or reasonable in it. It is therefore committed to the notion (a postulate, which however may not be completely true) that the process of nature and the process of thought are alike" (NEM 4:375). Whether completely true or not, if philosophy seeks to *explain* the universe at large, and if our *explanations* presuppose a rational organization of the universe—which, otherwise, would hardly be explicable at all—then we are, in effect, committed to the thesis that the process of nature is (or is like) a rational process. Logic, therefore, has more than heuristic value for philosophy.

It is important to bear in mind that when Peirce called himself a logician—the first and perhaps only person to have his occupation

20. Ibid., pp. 5–7.
21. Max H. Fisch, Introduction to *Writings of Charles S. Peirce* (Bloomington: Indiana University Press, 1982), i:xviii.

listed as "logician" in *Who's Who*—he was not thinking of himself as a logical technician or as a logicist who viewed logic as the deductive foundation for mathematics. Although his many contributions to technical logic—including his 1881 axiomatization of the natural numbers, his 1885 quantification theory and introduction of truth-functional analysis, and his lifelong development of the logic of relations—have considerable importance for the foundations of mathematics, his main concern was to build an adequate theory of science and an objective theory of rationality. His general conception of logic was closer to modern-day philosophy of science, together with epistemology and philosophical logic, than to today's mathematical logic. In his later years, Peirce gave a great deal of attention to the classification and relations of the sciences, and he came to associate much of what we would today call mathematical logic with mathematics; logic, on the other hand, he came to regard as a normative science concerned with intellectual goodness, and, in his most developed view, it is coextensive with semiotic, which constitutes the very heart of philosophy.

Peirce's philosophy is thoroughly systematic—some might say it is systematic to a fault. Central to his system is the idea that certain conceptions are fundamental to others, those to still others, and so on; so that it is possible to analyze our various theoretical systems (our sciences) into a dependency hierarchy. At the top of this hierarchy (or at the *base* if we envision a ladder of conceptions) we find a set of universal categories, an idea Peirce shared with many of the greatest systematic thinkers including Aristotle, Kant, and Hegel. Peirce's universal categories are three: firstness, secondness, and thirdness. Firstness is that which is as it is independently of anything else. Secondness is that which is as it is relative to something else. Thirdness is that which is as it is as mediate between two others. In Peirce's opinion, all conceptions at the most fundamental level can be reduced to these three.

This theory of categories, in its most abstracted form, belongs to mathematics, which stands at the pinnacle of the sciences. Peirce followed his father in defining mathematics as the science which deduces consequences from hypotheses—from what is given—but there is more to it than that. Mathematics is a science of discovery that investigates the realm of abstract forms, the realm of ideal objects (*entia rationis*). It is the mathematician who first discovers the fundamentality of triadicity by finding that monadic, dyadic, and triadic relations are irreducible, while relations of any degree (or adicity) greater than triadic can be expressed in combinations of triadic relations. This is known as Peirce's reduction thesis.

Mathematics presupposes no other science but is presupposed by all other sciences. After mathematics comes philosophy, which has three main branches: phenomenology, normative science, and metaphysics—dependent on each other in reverse order. Not surprisingly, Peirce's categories make their appearance in each of these parts of philosophy (as they must if they are universal categories). He explained this in the fifth of a series of lectures on pragmatism given at Harvard in 1903:

Philosophy has three grand divisions. The first is Phenomenology, which simply contemplates the Universal Phenomenon and discerns its ubiquitous elements, Firstness, Secondness, and Thirdness, together perhaps with other series of categories. The second grand division is Normative Science, which investigates the universal and necessary laws of the relation of Phenomena to *Ends,* that is, perhaps, to Truth, Right, and Beauty. The third grand division is Metaphysics, which endeavors to comprehend the Reality of the Phenomena. (CP 5.121)

Before giving this division, Peirce had warned his audience: "Now I am going to make a series of assertions which will sound wild" (CP 5.120), but he stressed that it was essential to his case for pragmatism.

The three divisions of philosophy are directly related to the categories. In attending to the universal elements of phenomena in their immediate phenomenal character, phenomenology treats of phenomena as firsts. Here the categories appear as fundamental categories of experience (or consciousness): firstness is the monadic element of experience usually identified with feeling, secondness is the dyadic element identified with the sense of action and reaction, and thirdness is the triadic element identified with the sense of learning or mediation as in thought or semiosis.

In attending to the laws of the relation of phenomena to ends, normative science treats of phenomena as seconds. The three normative sciences—esthetics, ethics, logic—were associated with three kinds of goodness: esthetical goodness (esthetics considers "those things whose ends are to embody qualities of feeling"), ethical goodness (ethics considers "those things whose ends lie in action"), and logical goodness (logic considers "those things whose end is to represent something"). The normative sciences correspond to the three categories and are dependent on each other, again in reverse order. Logic (or semiotic), in turn, has three branches: speculative grammar, critic, and speculative rhetoric. (Sometimes Peirce used different names.) Speculative grammar studies what is requisite for representation of any kind; it is the study of the "general conditions of signs being signs" (CP 1.444). Critic is the formal science of the *truth* of representations; it is the study of the reference of signs to their objects. Speculative rhetoric studies how knowledge is transmitted; it might be called the science of interpretation. (These three branches correspond more or less to Carnap's syntactics-semantics-pragmatics triad, which he learned from Charles Morris, who had probably derived it from Peirce.)

The three normative sciences are followed by metaphysics, the third and last branch of philosophy. The general task of metaphysics is "to study the most general features of reality and real objects" (item 21). In attempting to comprehend the reality of phenomena, that is, in treating of phenomena as representing something that is inherently mind-independent, metaphysics treats of phenomena as thirds. Logic (semiotic), the normative science immediately preceding metaphysics, gives structure to metaphysical investigations which are, not surprisingly, replete with triadic divisions. Among these we find possibility, actuality, destiny; chance, law, habit; and mind, matter, evolution.

Most typical of Peirce's metaphysical theories are his objective idealism and his evolutionary cosmology. In "The Architecture of Theories" (item 21), Peirce characterized objective idealism as holding that "matter is effete mind," mind that has become hide-bound with habit. According to this doctrine, matter is mind that has lost so much of the element of spontaneity through the acquisition of habits that it has taken on the dependable law-governed nature we attribute to material substance. It is the one intelligible theory of the universe, according to Peirce, a monism that regards psychical law as primordial, and physical law as derived and special.

Peirce's wide-ranging evolutionary cosmology is more difficult to characterize briefly. Some regard it as the weakest part of his work; W. B. Gallie called it the "white elephant" of Peirce's philosophy.[22] But others hail Peirce's cosmology as the prelude to contemporary cosmological physics.[23] It should be remembered that, according to Peirce, part of the purpose of philosophy is to explain the universe at large. In this he was a follower of the earliest Greek philosophers. In any case, Peirce's cosmological story goes roughly as follows.[24]

In the beginning there was *nothing*. But this primordial nothing was not the nothingness of a void or empty space, it was a *no-thing-ness*, the nothingness characteristic of the absence of any determination. Peirce described this state as "completely undetermined and dimen-

22. W. B. Gallie, *Peirce and Pragmatism* (Harmondsworth: Penguin, 1952), p. 215.

23. For example, see Ilya Prigogine and Isabelle Stengers, *Order Out of Chaos* (New York: Bantam, 1984), pp. 302–03.

24. My account of Peirce's cosmological theory is based, in part, on Peter T. Turley, *Peirce's Cosmology* (New York: Philosophical Library, 1977). Randall R. Dipert, in a review of Turley (*Nature and System* 1 [1979]: 134–41), warned that "by shunning key logical and mathematical issues in Peirce's writing, certain important aspects of his writing, such as his synechism, his theory of relations, and his theory of 'evolving dimensionality' of continua can hardly be discussed at all. . . . Every volume of Peirce's writing should perhaps contain the warning: 'Let no one enter here who is ignorant of logic, mathematics, and the history of science.' " Dipert is no doubt correct; for without such knowledge, it is not possible to penetrate fully the depths of Peirce's metaphysics.

sionless potentiality," which may be characterized by freedom, chance, and spontaneity (CP 6.193, 200).

The first step in the evolution of the world is the transition from undetermined and dimensionless potentiality to *determined* potentiality. The agency in this transition is chance or pure spontaneity. This new state is a Platonic world, a world of pure firsts, a world of qualities that are mere eternal possibilities. We have moved, Peirce says, from a state of absolute nothingness to a state of *chaos*.

Up to this point in the evolution of the world, all we have is real possibility, firstness; nothing is actual yet—there is no secondness. Somehow, the possibility or potentiality of the chaos is self-actualizing, and the second great step in the evolution of the world is that in which the world of actuality emerges from the Platonic world of qualities. The world of secondness is a world of events, or facts, whose being consists in the mutual interaction of actualized qualities. But this world does not yet involve thirdness, or law.

The transition to a world of thirdness, the third great step in cosmic evolution, is the result of a habit-taking tendency inherent in the world of events. Peirce liked to illustrate with dice or playing cards how single random events, if their mere occurrence established a tendency, however slight, for the recurrence of events of that type, could lead to large-scale uniformities. A habit-taking tendency is a generalizing tendency, and the emergence of all uniformities, from time and space to physical matter and even the laws of nature, can be explained as the result of the universe's tendency to take habits. Peirce regarded this surrender of chance and freedom to habit and law as a growth toward concrete reasonableness. Although he at times envisioned an end of history marked by the crystallization of mind that has become completely law-governed and without any residual spontaneity (truly *concrete* reasonableness), he sometimes held that an element of freedom and originality will persist in a universe that has reached a state of equilibrium between chance and law.

This is only a partial sketch of *some* of the characteristic theories and doctrines of Peirce's metaphysics, the third and final division of philosophy. It does not account for the role of semiosis or the power of love in the evolution of the cosmos, nor does it distinguish between the different modes of evolution that characterize Peirce's more developed thought (as in item 25). (In his classification of the sciences, philosophy is followed by the special sciences, such as physics and psychology, then by sciences of review, and, finally, by practical sciences such as pedagogics.)

The preceding summary provides a mere skeletal account of Peirce's system of philosophy, but it should suffice to convey a sense of both its breadth and its unity. When viewed as a whole, Peirce's philosophy may be characterized in different ways but, however char-

acterized, it must be said to be a *scientific* philosophy. This acknowledges both its empirical character and its adherence to scientific, or
experimental, methodology. Certainly it is appropriate to call Peirce's
philosophy an *empirical* philosophy, and he himself thought of his
pragmatism as a "propepositivism." But Peirce should not be regarded, as he sometimes is, as a positivist.

Peirce asserted quite emphatically that "experience is our only
teacher," and thus embraced a fundamental tenet of classical empiricism. Yet he rejected the doctrine of a *tabula rasa*, claiming that there
"is not one drop of principle in the whole vast reservoir of established
scientific theory that has sprung from any other source than the power
of the human mind to *originate* ideas that are true." But this power to
originate ideas is feeble, Peirce said, and "the truths are almost
drowned in a flood of false notions." Experience enables us to "filter
off" the false ideas, "letting the truth pour on in its mighty current"
(CP 5.50).

Peirce's devotion to mathematics and science, his emphasis on the
scientific method, and his pragmatic maxim (which sounds a lot like
a verification principle) certainly suggest an affinity between pragmatism and positivism. As late as 1905, he explained the purpose of his
pragmatism in a way that seems to share significant positivist concerns:

It will serve to show that almost every proposition of ontological metaphysics
is either meaningless gibberish—one word being defined by other words, and
they by still others, without any real conception ever being reached—or else
is downright absurd; so that all such rubbish being swept away, what will
remain of philosophy will be a series of problems capable of investigation by
the observational methods of the true sciences. (CP 5.423)

The pragmatic maxim may thus be taken as a test for whether our
conceptions, and our theories, are indexed to experience, or whether
they are part of a mere language game. But though there are many
points in common between pragmatism and positivism, there are important differences, especially Peirce's insistence on realism and on the
legitimacy of abductive reasoning, and his denial of a sharp demarcation between the language of observation and the language of theory.[25]

Peirce's general philosophy is sometimes called a *pragmatic* philosophy, where pragmatism is taken as more than just a theory of meaning
or a method for analyzing conceptions. It combines Peirce's brand of
empiricism with scientific method and the process orientation of Darwin's evolutionism—together with an Aristotelian teleological twist—

---

25. See David Gruender, "Pragmatism, Science, and Metaphysics," in *The Relevance
of Charles Peirce*, ed. Eugene Freeman (La Salle: The Hegeler Institute, 1983): 271–90.

into a broad philosophical program. It is a philosophy in which *purpose* appears to play the part for Peirce that *intentionality* played for Brentano. The mark of intelligence, on Peirce's view, is purpose, and purpose is always related to action. Peirce's pragmatism may thus be seen as a praxis philosophy: "The elements of every concept enter into logical thought at the gate of perception and make their exit at the gate of purposive action; and whatever cannot show its passports at both those two gates is to be arrested as unauthorized by reason" (CP 5.212).

Pragmatism, however, focuses on *intellectual* purport, which would seem to encompass only part of the range of possible semiosis. Consequently, pragmatism may be narrower than, or apply to only part of, Peirce's general theory of signs. Perhaps it is best to describe his philosophy as a *semiotic* philosophy. But, in that case, is it a semiotic idealism or realism? As either alternative can be supported, the choice seems to depend on who makes it.

According to David Savan, Peirce is a semiotic idealist. Savan distinguishes between two forms of semiotic idealism: a mild variety that holds that any properties, attributes, or characteristics of whatever exists depend upon the system of signs, representations, or interpretations through which they are signified, and a strong variety that holds that the very existence of anything depends upon the system of signs, representations, and interpretations which purport to refer to it. Savan claims that Peirce is a mild semiotic idealist.[26]

According to Thomas Short, on the other hand, Peirce is a semiotic realist.[27] The decision to label Peirce one way or the other seems to reflect the relative importance one attaches to the different elements of the sign relation, and often seems to be a matter of emphasis rather than a divergence of doctrine. Since he explicitly embraced a more and more encompassing realism, it might seem more appropriate to follow Short and call Peirce a semiotic realist—especially as that reflects his pragmatic admonition that our conceptions are meaningless unless they have reference to something outside of intellect: "it is necessary that a method should be found by which our beliefs may be determined by nothing human, but by some external permanency—by something upon which our thinking has no effect" (item 7). Yet one could counter that Peirce's adherence to his doctrine of objective idealism also recommends Savan's viewpoint. It is interesting to consider whether Peirce's philosophy might be best represented in his definition of his father's *ideal-realism*, which "combines the principles of idealism and realism."

26. David Savan, "Toward a Refutation of Semiotic Idealism," *Semiotic Inquiry* 3 (1983): 1–8.

27. Thomas L. Short, "What They Said in Amsterdam: Peirce's Semiotic Today," *Semiotica* 60 (1986): 103–28.

Peirce's theory of signs has, more than any of his other theories, attracted widespread attention in recent years. It was an outgrowth of many factors and influences including, perhaps primarily, his study of and reaction to Schiller but especially Kant; his study of logic, most importantly the logics of De Morgan and Boole (and also those of Aristotle and the medieval logicians); his reaction to Darwin and the idea of evolution; and, finally, the growing abstraction in mathematics, perhaps especially the development of topology and non-Euclidean geometry. Under all these influences Peirce acquired new insights and directions, and was led along paths never before traveled. But, more than anything else, it was his discovery that his sign conception could clear up many theretofore intractable philosophical problems that convinced him of the importance of signs. After rejecting certain Kantian restrictions on what could or could not be represented, he undertook an investigation of the entire range of representability and studied, among other things, conceptions of God, mathematical infinity, totality, immediacy, and necessity. As a result of these investigations Peirce developed and sharpened his semiotic ideas, and with the addition of certain phenomenological conceptions, he arrived at the view that "all consciousness is sign consciousness" and that in studying signs one addresses "whatever could be a subject of philosophic concern and insight."[28] Believing that in semiotic he had a better ground for philosophy than in traditional epistemology, Peirce worked at expanding his findings into a general theory of signs, and later, in considering what the universe must be like for signs (or semiosis) to be possible, he built a semiotic framework for most of his major philosophical work.

In its most abbreviated form, Peirce's theory of signs goes something like this. A sign is anything which stands *for* something *to* something. What the sign stands *for* is its object, what it stands *to* is the interpretant. The sign relation is *fundamentally* triadic: eliminate either the object or the interpretant and you annihilate the sign. This was the key insight of Peirce's semiotic, and one that distinguishes it from most theories of representation that attempt to make sense of signs (representations) that are related only to objects.

As his theory evolved, Peirce came to distinguish between different kinds of objects and interpretants. Every sign has two objects, a dynamic object, "the really efficient but not immediately present object," and an immediate object, "the object as the sign represents it." And every sign has three interpretants, a final (or logical) interpretant, which is the "effect that would be produced on the mind by the sign

---

28. Joseph L. Esposito, "On the Origins and Foundations of Peirce's Semiotic," in *Studies in Peirce's Semiotic* (Peirce Studies 1, Lubbock: Institute for Studies in Pragmaticism, 1979), p. 20. Much of this paragraph is derived from Esposito's paper, which gives a good historical introduction to Peirce's semiotic.

after sufficient development of thought," a dynamic interpretant, which is the "effect actually produced on the mind," and an immediate interpretant, which is the "interpretant represented or signified in the sign" (CP 8.343). Any given sign only partially reveals its dynamic object, and that partial revelation constitutes its immediate object. Similarly, the final interpretant of a sign is the result of (or is what would result from) a history of semiotic interaction with the given dynamic object, while the dynamic interpretant is the effect the sign actually produces (at a given time), and the immediate interpretant is the immediate significance of the sign independent of any previous history involving its object.

Peirce explained that signs can be divided in different ways according to this analysis of the structure of signs. If we consider the nature of any given sign (the ground of the sign), it will be found to be intrinsically either a quality (a qualisign), an existent thing or event (a sinsign), or a law or habit (a legisign). If we consider a sign's relation to its dynamic object, we will find that it is like its object (an icon), that it has an actual, existential connection with its object (an index), or that it is related to its object by convention or habit (a symbol). If we consider the relation of the sign to its final interpretant—how the sign is interpreted—it will appear to be a sign of possibility (a rheme), a sign of actual existence (a dicent), or a sign of law (an argument). Since every sign is something in itself, has a relation to its object, and represents its object in some way or other, the above divisions can be used to yield a classification of signs that makes more distinctions than most rival theories.

Using only these three triadic divisions of signs, as Peirce often did, we derive a ten-fold classification of signs sufficient for most analytical purposes. For example, we can identify a paint chip (as a sign of color) as a rhematic-iconic-qualisign, a weathervane as a dicent-indexical-sinsign, and a proper name as a rhematic-indexical-legisign. But, unfortunately, as anyone knows who has tried to work out examples of Peirce's classes, it is not as easy as we might think—which means either that we do not quite understand Peirce or that his theory is a bit ambiguous.

The fact is, Peirce did not settle exclusively on his ten-fold classification of signs, but developed a more complex classification based on ten rather than three triadic divisions. In this fuller analysis Peirce considered such three-fold divisions as the nature of immediate objects (descriptives, or indefinites; designatives, or singulars; and copulatives, or generals) and the nature of the assurance afforded the interpreter (abducents, or assurance by instinct; inducents, or assurance by experience; and deducents, or assurance by form or habit). With these ten divisions, Peirce was able to isolate sixty-six distinct classes of signs and, thus, to eliminate most of the ambiguity of his more abbreviated classification. But Peirce never completed this part of his general theory, and the precise nature and order of the ten trichotomies remains an important problem for semiotic theorists to work out more fully. Perhaps in our present state of understanding of language and semiosis we have no need for such complexity—just as we once had no need for relativity physics—but where principled distinctions can be made, they should be made, and, in any case, they will probably someday be needed.

So far, this sketch of Peirce's theory of signs has focused on speculative grammar, which considers "in what sense and how there can be any true proposition and false proposition, and what are the general conditions to which thought or signs of any kind must conform in order to assert anything" (CP 2.206). The philosopher who concentrates on this branch of semiotic investigates representation relations (signs), seeks to work out the necessary and sufficient conditions for representing, and classifies the different possible kinds of representation. Speculative grammar is often presented as if it were the whole of Peirce's semiotic, perhaps because that is where we encounter some of his best-known trichotomies.

The second branch of semiotic, critic, is "the science of the necessary conditions of the attainment of truth" (CP 1.445). It is "that part of logic . . . which, setting out with such assumptions as that every assertion is either true or false, and not both, and that some propositions may be recognized to be true, studies the constituent parts of arguments and produces a classification of arguments" (CP 2.205). By means of this classification, arguments "that are bad are thrown into one division, and those which are good into another, these divisions being defined by marks recognizable even if it be not known whether the arguments are good or bad." To complete its task, critic "has to divide good arguments by recognizable marks into those which have different orders of validity, and has to afford means for measuring the strength of arguments" (CP 2.203). Thus, in addition to investigating truth conditions in general, the philosopher who concentrates on critic will investigate Peirce's well-known division of reasoning into abduction, induction, and deduction (and the corresponding theories of abductive, inductive, and deductive logic). Much of what made up the traditional logic curriculum belongs in critic, as does much that is dealt with in philosophical logic, especially topics that concern truth and reference.

The third branch of semiotic, speculative rhetoric, is "the study of the necessary conditions of the transmission of meaning by signs from mind to mind, and from one state of mind to another" (CP 1.445). More succinctly, it studies the conditions for the development and growth of thought. The focus for the philosopher who studies this branch is the relation between representations and interpreting thoughts (or interpretations). Whereas critic is the science of the *necessary* conditions for the attainment of truth, speculative rhetoric is the science of the *general* conditions for the attainment of truth. Peirce often emphasized the study of *methods* of reasoning as a main concern of speculative rhetoric, and he sometimes suggested that this branch of logic might be better named "methodeutic." Questions of meaning and interpretation dominate this branch, and it may be that pragmatism, as a theory of meaning or inquiry, belongs here. So may the contemporary study of hermeneutics, something Peirce himself once suggested, although with reference to Aristotle's hermeneutic. Be that as it may, it would appear that Peirce's theory of signs encompasses much of what lies at the heart of modern philosophy, and it has relevance for many other disciplines.

Peirce's analysis of the sign relation as fundamentally triadic motivated much that is unique in his philosophy. His insistence that every interpretant is related to its object through the mediation of a sign constitutes a denial of intuition; for intuition requires a direct dyadic relation between an interpretant and its object—somehow we just know something about an object (a person, a state of affairs, whatever) *without* the intervention of a sign. There is no good reason to suppose that we have such a faculty, as Peirce argued in the first paper of his cognition series (item 2). (And yet, in a different sense, Peirce gives us a compelling theory of intuition. With an appeal to abduction and to his belief that we are attuned to nature through centuries of evolutionary development—so that we are actual embodiments of natural principles—Peirce argues, following his father, that we have a natural inclination to the truth, a tendency to guess correctly. But this is a semiotic kind of intuition that bears the Peircean sign of the three.)

But how does an object determine its interpretant through the mediation of a sign? According to Peirce, the dynamic object, the really efficient but not immediately present object, is the object that somehow determines the sign and through the sign mediately determines an interpretant. How can an object that is *external* to the sign (the immediate object is the *internal* object) be a determining force in shaping the interpretant? Notice that this amounts to asking how objects (or the external world) can determine mind.

Every sign *represents* an object (in some way or other) to the interpretant. The interpretant is, or helps make up, a habit that "guides" our future (and present) actions or thought with respect to the object in question, or objects *like* the one in question. If the interpretant is untrue to the object, our behavior will not be (or *may* not be) successful—reality will have its way with us. Not until our interpretants (our ideas or intellectual habits) are fully attuned to their objects will we avoid unexpected confrontations with a resistant reality. In this way, the real object determines or shapes our mind, our reservoir of intellectual habits.

Does this make Peirce a semiotic realist? It would seem so. Not only does the mind represent the world, it represents it in a certain way: namely, *the way it is forced to represent the world by the resistance of the world to error.* Surely this is a kind of realism. And it is also a semiotic account of pragmatism which, as Christopher Hookway points out, "is supposed to explain how an independent reality can constrain our opinions through perception."[29]

But this is not the whole story. Our perceptions themselves are, to some extent, constrained by previous opinions, and our thoughts by past thoughts, so that it cannot be said that the only *determining* factor in our lives is a resistant external reality. There are many ways to live in the world, and intellect does not constrain us to a single path. There is far more to an intellect than the mere representation of external objects: there are plans and purposes and ideals, all of which can be infixed in intellectual habits that *predetermine future behavior.* And, of course, future behavior will shape the world that is to come. What is so interesting about Peirce's views is that we as individuals, we as humanity, have some measure of control over our intellectual habits. We have a *choice.* We can deliberately, though with effort, change our intellectual habits—which means that we can *change our minds:* and that means that we have some measure of control over which of the many possible futures will be ours. Perhaps this is semiotic idealism but, if so, it is an idealism compatible with semiotic realism.

Peirce's inclusion of the interpretant as fundamental in the sign relation shows that all thought is *to some degree* a matter of interpretation. All advanced thought uses symbols of one kind or another, and thus rests on convention. On Peirce's view, then, all advanced thinking depends on one's participation in a linguistic or semiotic *community.* Peirce's stress on the importance of community was a common theme throughout his work, and it increased as he came to understand more fully the importance of convention for semiosis. Peirce appealed to a community of inquirers for his theory of truth, and he regarded the *identification with community* as fundamental for the advancement of knowledge (the end of the highest semiosis) and, also, for the advancement of human relations. Peirce's semiotic theory of inquiry is sometimes regarded as a "logical socialism," a view supported by the following provocative remark (in item 25):

Here, then, is the issue. The gospel of Christ says that progress comes from every individual merging his individuality in sympathy with his neighbors.

29. Christopher Hookway, *Peirce* (London: Routledge & Kegan Paul, 1985), p. 246.

On the other side, the conviction of the nineteenth century is that progress takes place by virtue of every individual's striving for himself with all his might and trampling his neighbor under foot whenever he gets a chance to do so. This may accurately be called the Gospel of Greed.

The sentiment expressed here is similar to that in Peirce's statement about the significance of the nominalism-realism question for *life*. Clearly, his brand of realism is opposed not only to nominalism but also to the "gospel of greed" (or what is sometimes referred to as "crass materialism").

This has been, at best, a preliminary sketch of Peirce's system of thought and of some of the more characteristic of his philosophical doctrines, and much has been left out. For example, there has been no discussion of Peirce's opposition to determinism (in item 22), or of the intriguing story of his working his way to his guess at the riddle of the universe that led him to his evolutionary cosmology.[30] Little has been said about his lifelong study of mathematics and his nearly lifelong study and practice of experimental science, or of the importance of these for his philosophy. His phenomenology and his theories of esthetics and ethics have barely been mentioned, even though they offer unique and important insights and perspectives for current research, and provide essential support for other parts of his system of thought. His phenomenology has begun to attract widespread attention, and it may turn out that his phenomenological derivation of his categories is of more importance for philosophy than his mathematico-logical derivation. Finally, some scholars might highlight the evolution of his very profound religious views, which are often thought of as completing his metaphysics. It can only be hoped that what has been said here is enough to give a sense of the breadth and profundity—*and unity*—of Peirce's philosophical thought, and to inspire the reader to the sometimes difficult but always rewarding study of his writings.

Nathan Houser

30. For a brief rendition of this "intriguing story," see Fisch, "Peirce's Arisbe," in *Peirce, Semeiotic, and Pragmatism*, pp. 229–38.

THE
ESSENTIAL
PEIRCE

On a New List of Categories

P 32: Proceedings of the American Academy of Arts
and Sciences *7 (1868):287–98. [Also published in W2:49–59
(with the four other papers in the so-called PAAAS Series and
with references to related manuscripts published in W1) and
in CP1.545–59. Peirce completely rewrote the paper to serve as
the opening chapter of his 1894 "How to Reason" (MS 403).]
Presented to the Academy on 14 May 1867, this paper is,
according to Peirce, "perhaps the least unsatisfactory, from a
logical point of view, that I ever succeeded in producing" and,
with item 3 below, one of his two "strongest philosophical
works." The culmination of a ten-year effort and the keystone
of Peirce's system of philosophy, it argues for a new post-
Kantian set of categories (or univeral conceptions) by demon-
strating that they are required for the unification of experience. Peirce's argument is essentially a logical derivation,
though it depends on a type of mental separation he called
'prescision', which is also required for his later phenomenological derivation of the categories.*

§1. This paper is based upon the theory already established,[1] that
the function of conceptions is to reduce the manifold of sensuous
impressions to unity, and that the validity of a conception consists in
the impossibility of reducing the content of consciousness to unity
without the introduction of it.

§2. This theory gives rise to a conception of gradation among those
conceptions which are universal. For one such conception may unite
the manifold of sense and yet another may be required to unite the
conception and the manifold to which it is applied; and so on.

§3. That universal conception which is nearest to sense is that of
the present, in general. This is a conception, because it is universal. But
as the act of *attention* has no connotation at all, but is the pure denotative power of the mind, that is to say, the power which directs the
mind to an object, in contradistinction to the power of thinking any
predicate of that object,—so the conception of *what is present in general,*
which is nothing but the general recognition of what is contained in

attention, has no connotation, and therefore no proper unity. This conception of the present in general, or IT in general, is rendered in philosophical language by the word "substance" in one of its meanings. Before any comparison or discrimination can be made between what is present, what is present must have been recognized as such, as *it*, and subsequently the metaphysical parts which are recognized by abstraction are attributed to this *it*, but the *it* cannot itself be made a predicate. This *it* is thus neither predicated of a subject, nor in a subject, and accordingly is identical with the conception of substance.

§4. The unity to which the understanding reduces impressions is the unity of a proposition. This unity consists in the connection of the predicate with the subject; and, therefore, that which is implied in the copula, or the conception of *being*, is that which completes the work of conceptions of reducing the manifold to unity. The copula (or rather the verb which is copula in one of its senses) means either *actually is* or *would be*, as in the two propositions, "There *is* no griffin," and "A griffin *is* a winged quadruped." The conception of *being* contains only that junction of predicate to subject wherein these two verbs agree. The conception of being, therefore, plainly has no content.

If we say "The stove is black," the stove is the *substance*, from which its blackness has not been differentiated, and the *is*, while it leaves the substance just as it was seen, explains its confusedness, by the application to it of *blackness* as a predicate.

Though *being* does not affect the subject, it implies an indefinite determinability of the predicate. For if one could know the copula and predicate of any proposition, as " . . . is a tailed-man," he would know the predicate to be applicable to something supposable, at least. Accordingly, we have propositions whose subjects are entirely indefinite, as "There is a beautiful ellipse," where the subject is merely *something actual or potential;* but we have no propositions whose predicate is entirely indeterminate, for it would be quite senseless to say, "*A* has the common characters of all things," inasmuch as there are no such common characters.

Thus substance and being are the beginning and end of all conception. Substance is inapplicable to a predicate, and being is equally so to a subject.

§5. The terms "prescision" and "abstraction," which were formerly applied to every kind of separation, are now limited, not merely to mental separation, but to that which arises from *attention to* one element and *neglect of* the other. Exclusive attention consists in a definite conception or *supposition* of one part of an object, without any supposition of the other. Abstraction or prescision ought to be carefully distinguished from two other modes of mental separation, which may be termed *discrimination* and *dissociation.* Discrimination has to do merely with the essences of terms, and only draws a distinction in meaning.

Dissociation is that separation which, in the absence of a constant association, is permitted by the law of association of images. It is the consciousness of one thing, without the necessary simultaneous consciousness of the other. Abstraction or prescision, therefore, supposes a greater separation than discrimination, but a less separation than dissociation. Thus I can discriminate red from blue, space from color, and color from space, but not red from color. I can prescind red from blue, and space from color (as is manifest from the fact that I actually believe there is an uncolored space between my face and the wall); but I cannot prescind color from space, nor red from color. I can dissociate red from blue, but not space from color, color from space, nor red from color.

Prescision is not a reciprocal process. It is frequently the case, that, while *A* cannot be prescinded from *B*, *B* can be prescinded from *A*. This circumstance is accounted for as follows. Elementary conceptions only arise upon the occasion of experience; that is, they are produced for the first time according to a general law, the condition of which is the existence of certain impressions. Now if a conception does not reduce the impressions upon which it follows to unity, it is a mere arbitrary addition to these latter; and elementary conceptions do not arise thus arbitrarily. But if the impressions could be definitely comprehended without the conception, this latter would not reduce them to unity. Hence, the impressions (or more immediate conceptions) cannot be definitely conceived or attended to, to the neglect of an elementary conception which reduces them to unity. On the other hand, when such a conception has once been obtained, there is, in general, no reason why the premises which have occasioned it should not be neglected, and therefore the explaining conception may frequently be prescinded from the more immediate ones and from the impressions.

§6. The facts now collected afford the basis for a systematic method of searching out whatever universal elementary conceptions there may be intermediate between the manifold of substance and the unity of being. It has been shown that the occasion of the introduction of a universal elementary conception is either the reduction of the manifold of substance to unity, or else the conjunction to substance of another conception. And it has further been shown that the elements conjoined cannot be supposed without the conception, whereas the conception can generally be supposed without these elements. Now, empirical psychology discovers the occasion of the introduction of a conception, and we have only to ascertain what conception already lies in the data which is united to that of substance by the first conception, but which cannot be supposed without this first conception, to have the next conception in order in passing from being to substance.

It may be noticed that, throughout this process, *introspection* is not resorted to. Nothing is assumed respecting the subjective elements of consciousness which cannot be securely inferred from the objective elements.

§7. The conception of *being* arises upon the formation of a proposition. A proposition always has, besides a term to express the substance, another to express the quality of that substance; and the function of the conception of being is to unite the quality to the substance. Quality, therefore, in its very widest sense, is the first conception in order in passing from being to substance.

Quality seems at first sight to be given in the impression. Such results of introspection are untrustworthy. A proposition asserts the applicability of a mediate conception to a more immediate one. Since this is *asserted*, the more mediate conception is clearly regarded independently of this circumstance, for otherwise the two conceptions would not be distinguished, but one would be thought through the other, without this latter being an object of thought, at all. The mediate conception, then, in order to be *asserted* to be applicable to the other, must first be considered without regard to this circumstance, and taken immediately. But, taken immediately, it transcends what is given (the more immediate conception), and its applicability to the latter is hypothetical. Take, for example, the proposition, "This stove is black." Here the conception of *this stove* is the more immediate, that of *black* the more mediate, which latter, to be predicated of the former, must be discriminated from it and considered *in itself*, not as applied to an object, but simply as embodying a quality, *blackness*. Now this *blackness* is a pure species or abstraction, and its application to *this stove* is entirely hypothetical. The same thing is meant by "the stove is black," as by "there is blackness in the stove." *Embodying blackness* is the equivalent of *black*.* The proof is this. These conceptions are applied indifferently to precisely the same facts. If, therefore, they were different, the one which was first applied would fulfil every function of the other; so that one of them would be superfluous. Now a superfluous conception is an arbitrary fiction, whereas elementary conceptions arise only upon the requirement of experience; so that a superfluous elementary conception is impossible. Moreover, the conception of a pure abstraction is indispensible, because we cannot comprehend an agreement of two things, except as an agreement in some *respect*, and this respect is such a pure abstraction as blackness. Such a pure abstraction, reference to which constitutes a *quality* or general attribute, may be termed a *ground*.

Reference to a ground cannot be prescinded from being, but being can be prescinded from it.

---

*This agrees with the author of *De Generibus et Speciebus, Ouvrages Inédits d'Abélard* [Paris, 1836], p. 528.

§8. Empirical psychology has established the fact that we can know a quality only by means of its contrast with or similarity to another.[2] By contrast and agreement a thing is referred to a correlate, if this term may be used in a wider sense than usual. The occasion of the introduction of the conception of reference to a ground is the reference to a correlate, and this is, therefore, the next conception in order.

Reference to a correlate cannot be prescinded from reference to a ground; but reference to a ground may be prescinded from reference to a correlate.

§9. The occasion of reference to a correlate is obviously by comparison. This act has not been sufficiently studied by the psychologists, and it will, therefore, be necessary to adduce some examples to show in what it consists. Suppose we wish to compare the letters p and b. We may imagine one of them to be turned over on the line of writing as an axis, then laid upon the other, and finally to become transparent so that the other can be seen through it. In this way we shall form a new image which mediates between the images of the two letters, inasmuch as it represents one of them to be (when turned over) the likeness of the other. Again, suppose we think of a murderer as being in relation to a murdered person; in this case we conceive the act of the murder, and in this conception it is represented that corresponding to every murderer (as well as to every murder) there is a murdered person; and thus we resort again to a mediating representation which represents the relate as standing for a correlate with which the mediating representation is itself in relation. Again, suppose we look out the word *homme* in a French dictionary; we shall find opposite to it the word *man*, which, so placed, represents *homme* as representing the same two-legged creature which *man* itself represents. By a further accumulation of instances, it would be found that every comparison requires, besides the related thing, the ground, and the correlate, also a *mediating representation which represents the relate to be a representation of the same correlate which this mediating representation itself represents.* Such a mediating representation may be termed an *interpretant,* because it fulfils the office of an interpreter, who says that a foreigner says the same thing which he himself says. The term "representation" is here to be understood in a very extended sense, which can be explained by instances better than by a definition. In this sense, a word represents a thing to the conception in the mind of the hearer, a portrait represents the person for whom it is intended to the conception of recognition, a weathercock represents the direction of the wind to the conception of him who understands it, a barrister represents his client to the judge and jury whom he influences.

Every reference to a correlate, then, conjoins to the substance the conception of a reference to an interpretant; and this is, therefore, the next conception in order in passing from being to substance.

Reference to an interpretant cannot be prescinded from reference to a correlate; but the latter can be prescinded from the former.

§10. Reference to an interpretant is rendered possible and justified by that which renders possible and justifies comparison. But that is clearly the diversity of impressions. If we had but one impression, it would not require to be reduced to unity, and would therefore not need to be thought of as referred to an interpretant, and the conception of reference to an interpretant would not arise. But since there is a manifold of impressions, we have a feeling of complication or confusion, which leads us to differentiate this impression from that, and then, having been differentiated, they require to be brought to unity. Now they are not brought to unity until we conceive them together as being *ours*, that is, until we refer them to a conception as their interpretant. Thus, the reference to an interpretant arises upon the holding together of diverse impressions, and therefore it does not join a conception to the substance, as the other two references do, but unites directly the manifold of the substance itself. It is, therefore, the last conception in order in passing from being to substance.

§11. The five conceptions thus obtained, for reasons which will be sufficiently obvious, may be termed *categories*. That is,

> BEING,
> > Quality (Reference to a Ground),
> > Relation (Reference to a Correlate),
> > Representation (Reference to an Interpretant),
> SUBSTANCE.

The three intermediate conceptions may be termed accidents.

§12. This passage from the many to the one is numerical. The conception of a *third* is that of an object which is so related to two others, that one of these must be related to the other in the same way in which the third is related to that other. Now this coincides with the conception of an interpretant. An *other* is plainly equivalent to a *correlate*. The conception of second differs from that of other, in implying the possibility of a third. In the same way, the conception of *self* implies the possibility of an *other*. The *Ground* is the self abstracted from the concreteness which implies the possibility of an other.

§13. Since no one of the categories can be prescinded from those above it, the list of supposable objects which they afford is,

> What is.
> > Quale—that which refers to a ground,
> > Relate—that which refers to ground and correlate,
> > Representamen—that which refers to ground, correlate,
> > > and interpretant.
> It.

§14. A quality may have a special determination which prevents its being prescinded from reference to a correlate. Hence there are two kinds of relation.

1st. That of relates whose reference to a ground is a prescindible or internal quality.

2d. That of relates whose reference to a ground is an unprescindible or relative quality.

In the former case, the relation is a mere *concurrence* of the correlates in one character, and the relate and correlate are not distinguished. In the latter case the correlate is set over against the relate, and there is in some sense an *opposition*.

Relates of the first kind are brought into relation simply by their agreement. But mere disagreement (unrecognized) does not constitute relation, and therefore relates of the second kind are only brought into relation by correspondence in fact.

A reference to a ground may also be such that it cannot be prescinded from a reference to an interpretant. In this case it may be termed an *imputed* quality. If the reference of a relate to its ground can be prescinded from reference to an interpretant, its relation to its correlate is a mere concurrence or community in the possession of a quality, and therefore the reference to a correlate can be prescinded from reference to an interpretant. It follows that there are three kinds of representations.

1st. Those whose relation to their objects is a mere community in some quality, and these representations may be termed *Likenesses*.

2d. Those whose relation to their objects consists in a correspondence in fact, and these may be termed *Indices* or *Signs*.

3d. Those the ground of whose relation to their objects is an imputed character, which are the same as *general signs,* and these may be termed *Symbols*.

§15. I shall now show how the three conceptions of reference to a ground, reference to an object, and reference to an interpretant are the fundamental ones of at least one universal science, that of logic. Logic is said to treat of second intentions as applied to first. It would lead me too far away from the matter in hand to discuss the truth of this statement; I shall simply adopt it as one which seems to me to afford a good definition of the subject-genus of this science. Now, second intentions are the objects of the understanding considered as representations, and the first intentions to which they apply are the objects of those representations. The objects of the understanding, considered as representations, are symbols, that is, signs which are at least potentially general. But the rules of logic hold good of any symbols, of those which are written or spoken as well as of those which are thought. They have no immediate application to likenesses or indices, because no arguments can be constructed of these alone, but do apply to all symbols. All symbols, indeed, are in one sense relative to the understanding, but only in the sense in which also all things are relative to the understanding. On this account, therefore, the relation to the understanding need not be expressed in the definition of the sphere of logic, since it determines no limitation of that sphere. But a distinction can be made between concepts which are supposed to have no existence except so far as they are actually present to the understanding, and external symbols which still retain their character of symbols so long as they are only *capable* of being understood. And as the rules of logic apply to these latter as much as to the former (and though only through the former, yet this character, since it belongs to all things, is no limitation), it follows that logic has for its subject-genus all symbols and not merely concepts.* We come, therefore, to this, that logic treats of the reference of symbols in general to their objects. In this view it is one of a trivium of conceivable sciences. The first would treat of the formal conditions of symbols having meaning, that is of the reference of symbols in general to their grounds or imputed characters, and this might be called formal grammar; the second, logic, would treat of the formal conditions of the truth of symbols; and the third would treat of the formal conditions of the force of symbols, or their power of appealing to a mind, that is, of their reference in general to interpretants, and this might be called formal rhetoric.

There would be a general division of symbols, common to all these sciences; namely, into,

1°: Symbols which directly determine only their *grounds* or imputed qualities, and are thus but sums of marks or *terms;*

2°: Symbols which also independently determine their *objects* by means of other term or terms, and thus, expressing their own objective validity, become capable of truth or falsehood, that is, are *propositions;* and,

3°: Symbols which also independently determine their *interpretants,* and thus the minds to which they appeal, by premising a proposition or propositions which such a mind is to admit. These are *arguments.*

And it is remarkable that, among all the definitions of the proposition, for example, as the *oratio indicativa,* as the subsumption of an object under a concept, as the expression of the relation of two concepts, and as the indication of the mutable ground of appearance, there is, perhaps, not one in which the conception of reference to an object

---

*Herbart says: "Unsre sämmtlichen Gedanken lassen sich von zwei Seiten betrachten; theils als Thätigkeiten unseres Geistes, theils in Hinsicht dessen, *was* durch sie gedacht wird. In letzterer Beziehung heissen sie *Begriffe,* welches Wort, indem es das *Begriffene* bezeichnet, zu abstrahiren gebietet von der Art und Weise, wie wir den Gedanken empfangen, produciren, oder reproduciren mögen." But the whole difference between a concept and an external sign lies in these respects which logic ought, according to Herbart, to abstract from.[3]

or correlate is not the important one. In the same way, the conception of reference to an interpretant or third, is always prominent in the definitions of argument.

In a proposition, the term which separately indicates the object of the symbol is termed the subject, and that which indicates the ground is termed the predicate. The objects indicated by the subject (which are always potentially a plurality,—at least, of phases or appearances) are therefore stated by the proposition to be related to one another on the ground of the character indicated by the predicate. Now this relation may be either a concurrence or an opposition. Propositions of concurrence are those which are usually considered in logic; but I have shown in a paper upon the classification of arguments that it is also necessary to consider separately propositions of opposition, if we are to take account of such arguments as the following:—

Whatever is the half of anything is less than that of which it is the half;

$$A \text{ is half of } B:$$
$$\therefore A \text{ is less than } B.$$

The subject of such a proposition is separated into two terms, a "subject nominative" and an "object accusative."

In an argument, the premises form a representation of the conclusion, because they indicate the interpretant of the argument, or representation representing it to represent its object. The premises may afford a likeness, index, or symbol of the conclusion. In deductive argument, the conclusion is represented by the premises as by a general sign under which it is contained. In hypotheses, something *like* the conclusion is proved, that is, the premises form a likeness of the conclusion. Take, for example, the following argument:—

$$M \text{ is, for instance, } P', P'', P''', \text{ and } P^{iv};$$
$$S \text{ is } P', P'', P''', \text{ and } P^{iv}:$$
$$\therefore S \text{ is } M.$$

Here the first premise amounts to this, that "P', P'', P''', and P^{iv}" is a likeness of M, and thus the premises are or represent a likeness of the conclusion. That it is different with induction another example will show.

$$S', S'', S''', \text{ and } S^{iv} \text{ are taken as samples of the collection } M;$$
$$S', S'', S''', \text{ and } S^{iv} \text{ are } P:$$
$$\therefore \text{ All } M \text{ is } P.$$

Hence the first premise amounts to saying that "S', S'', S''', and S^{iv}" is an index of M. Hence the premises are an index of the conclusion.

The other divisions of terms, propositions, and arguments arise from the distinction of extension and comprehension. I propose to treat this subject in a subsequent paper.[4] But I will so far anticipate that, as to say that there is, first, the direct reference of a symbol to its objects, or its denotation; second, the reference of the symbol to its ground, through its object, that is, its reference to the common characters of its objects, or its connotation; and third, its reference to its interpretants through its object, that is, its reference to all the synthetical propositions in which its objects in common are subject or predicate, and this I term the information it embodies. And as every addition to what it denotes, or to what it connotes, is effected by means of a distinct proposition of this kind, it follows that the extension and comprehension of a term are in an inverse relation, as long as the information remains the same, and that every increase of information is accompanied by an increase of one or other of these two quantities. It may be observed that extension and comprehension are very often taken in other senses in which this last proposition is not true.

This is an imperfect view of the application which the conceptions which, according to our analysis, are the most fundamental ones find in the sphere of logic. It is believed, however, that it is sufficient to show that at least something may be usefully suggested by considering this science in this light.

2

Questions Concerning Certain Faculties Claimed for Man

P 26: Journal of Speculative Philosophy *2 (1868):103–14.*
[Also published in W2:193–211 (with related letters and earlier
attempts at this article and the two that follow) and in CP
5.213–63.] Item 2 is the first of three articles usually referred
to as the JSP Cognition Series, *in which Peirce develops some*
of the results and consequences of item 1 and attempts "to
prove and to trace the consequences of certain propositions in
epistemology tending toward the recognition of the reality of
continuity and of generality and going to show the absurdity
of individualism and of egoism." (In "The Law of Mind"
[item 23], he indicates that this is an early attempt at develop-
ing his doctrine of synechism.) Peirce's opposition to Carte-
sianism results in the following four denials: (1) we have no
power of introspection, but all knowledge of the internal
world is derived by hypothetical reasoning from our knowl-
edge of external facts, (2) we have no power of intuition, but
every cognition is determined logically by previous cogni-
tions, (3) we have no power of thinking without signs, and
(4) we have no conception of the absolutely incognizable.

QUESTION 1. *Whether by the simple contemplation of a cognition, indepen-*
dently of any previous knowledge and without reasoning from signs, we are
enabled rightly to judge whether that cognition has been determined by a
previous cognition or whether it refers immediately to its object.

Throughout this paper, the term *intuition* will be taken as signifying a cognition not determined by a previous cognition of the same
object, and therefore so determined by something out of the consciousness.* Let me request the reader to note this. *Intuition* here will be

---

*The word *intuitus* first occurs as a technical term in St. Anselm's *Monologium.* He
wished to distinguish between our knowledge of God and our knowledge of finite things
(and, in the next world, of God, also); and thinking of the saying of St. Paul, *Videmus*
nunc per speculum in ænigmate: tunc autem facie ad faciem, he called the former *speculation*
and the latter *intuition.* [1] This use of "speculation" did not take root, because that word

nearly the same as "premise not itself a conclusion"; the only difference being that premises and conclusions are judgments, whereas an
intuition may, as far as its definition states, be any kind of cognition
whatever. But just as a conclusion (good or bad) is determined in the
mind of the reasoner by its premise, so cognitions not judgments may
be determined by previous cognitions; and a cognition not so determined, and therefore determined directly by the transcendental object, is to be termed an *intuition.*

Now, it is plainly one thing to have an intuition and another to
know intuitively that it is an intuition, and the question is whether
these two things, distinguishable in thought, are, in fact, invariably
connected, so that we can always intuitively distinguish between an
intuition and a cognition determined by another. Every cognition, as
something present, is, of course, an intuition of itself. But the determination of a cognition by another cognition or by a transcendental
object is not, at least so far as appears obviously at first, a part of the
immediate content of that cognition, although it would appear to be
an element of the action or passion of the transcendental *ego,* which
is not, perhaps, in consciousness immediately; and yet this transcendental action or passion may invariably determine a cognition of itself,
so that, in fact, the determination or non-determination of the cognition by another may be a part of the cognition. In this case, I should
say that we had an intuitive power of distinguishing an intuition from
another cognition.

There is no evidence that we have this faculty, except that we seem
to *feel* that we have it. But the weight of that testimony depends
entirely on our being supposed to have the power of distinguishing in
this feeling whether the feeling be the result of education, old associations, etc., or whether it is an intuitive cognition; or, in other words,
it depends on presupposing the very matter testified to. Is this feeling
infallible? And is this judgment concerning it infallible and so on, *ad
infinitum?* Supposing that a man really could shut himself up in such
a faith, he would be, of course, impervious to the truth, "evidence-
proof."

But let us compare the theory with the historic facts. The power

---

already had another exact and widely different meaning. In the middle ages, the term
"intuitive cognition" had two principal senses, 1st, as opposed to abstractive cognition,
it meant the knowledge of the present as present, and this is its meaning in Anselm; but
2d, as no intuitive cognition was allowed to be determined by a previous cognition, it
came to be used as the opposite of discursive cognition (see Scotus, *In sententias,* lib. 2,
dist. 3, qu. 9), and this is nearly the sense in which I employ it. This is also nearly the
sense in which Kant uses it, the former distinction being expressed by his *sensuous* and
non-sensuous. (See *Werke,* herausg. Rosenkrantz, Thl. 2, S. 713, 31, 41, 100, u. s. w.) An
enumeration of six meanings of intuition may be found in Hamilton's *Reid,* p. 759.

of intuitively distinguishing intuitions from other cognitions has not prevented men from disputing very warmly as to which cognitions are intuitive. In the middle ages, reason and external authority were regarded as two coördinate sources of knowledge, just as reason and the authority of intuition are now; only the happy device of considering the enunciations of authority to be essentially indemonstrable had not yet been hit upon. All authorities were not considered as infallible, any more than all reasons; but when Berengarius said that the authoritativeness of any particular authority must rest upon reason, the proposition was scouted as opinionated, impious, and absurd. Thus, the credibility of authority was regarded by men of that time simply as an ultimate premise, as a cognition not determined by a previous cognition of the same object, or, in our terms, as an intuition. It is strange that they should have thought so, if, as the theory now under discussion supposes, by merely contemplating the credibility of the authority, as a Fakir does his God, they could have seen that it was not an ultimate premise! Now, what if our *internal* authority should meet the same fate, in the history of opinions, as that external authority has met? Can that be said to be absolutely certain which many sane, well-informed, and thoughtful men already doubt?*

Every lawyer knows how difficult it is for witnesses to distinguish between what they have seen and what they have inferred. This is

---

*The proposition of Berengarius is contained in the following quotation from his *De Sacra Cœna:* *"Maximi plane cordis est, per omnia ad dialecticam confugere, quia confugere ad eam ad rationem est confugere, quo qui non confugit, cum secundum rationem sit factus ad imaginem dei, suum honorem reliquit, nec potest renovari de die in diem ad imaginem dei."*[2] The most striking characteristic of medieval reasoning, in general, is the perpetual resort to authority. When Fredegisus[3] and others wish to prove that darkness is a thing, although they have evidently derived the opinion from nominalistic-Platonistic meditations, they argue the matter thus: "God called the darkness, night"; then, certainly, it is a thing, for otherwise before it had a name, there would have been nothing, not even a fiction to name. Abelard thinks it worth while to cite Boëthius, when he says that space has three dimensions, and when he says that an individual cannot be in two places at once.[4] The author of *De Generibus et Speciebus,* a work of a superior order, in arguing against a Platonic doctrine, says that if whatever is universal is eternal, the *form* and matter of Socrates, being severally universal, are both eternal, and that, therefore, Socrates was not created by God, but only put together, *"quod quantum a vero deviet, palam est."* The authority is the final court of appeal. The same author, where in one place he doubts a statement of Boëthius, finds it necessary to assign a special reason why in this case it is not absurd to do so. *Exceptio probat regulam in casibus non exceptis.*[5] Recognized authorities were certainly sometimes disputed in the twelfth century; their mutual contradictions insured that; and the authority of philosophers was regarded as inferior to that of theologians. Still, it would be impossible to find a passage where the authority of Aristotle is directly denied upon any logical question. *"Sunt et multi errores eius,"* says John of Salisbury, *"qui in scripturis tam Ethnicis, quam fidelibus poterunt inveniri: verum in logica parem habuisse non legitur."*[6] *"Sed nihil adversus Aristotelem,"* says Abelard, and in another place, *"Sed si Aristotelem Peripateticorum principem culpare possumus, quam amplius in hac arte recepimus?"*[7] The idea of going without an authority, or of subordinating authority to reason, does not occur to him.

particularly noticeable in the case of a person who is describing the performances of a spiritual medium or of a professed juggler. The difficulty is so great that the juggler himself is often astonished at the discrepancy between the actual facts and the statement of an intelligent witness who has not understood the trick. A part of the very complicated trick of the Chinese rings consists in taking two solid rings linked together, talking about them as though they were separate—taking it for granted, as it were—then pretending to put them together, and handing them immediately to the spectator that he may see that they are solid. The art of this consists in raising, at first, the strong suspicion that one is broken. I have seen McAlister[8] do this with such success, that a person sitting close to him, with all his faculties straining to detect the illusion, would have been ready to swear that he saw the rings put together, and, perhaps, if the juggler had not professedly practised deception, would have considered a doubt of it as a doubt of his own veracity. This certainly seems to show that it is not always very easy to distinguish between a premise and a conclusion, that we have no infallible power of doing so, and that in fact our only security in difficult cases is in some signs from which we can infer that a given fact must have been seen or must have been inferred. In trying to give an account of a dream, every accurate person must often have felt that it was a hopeless undertaking to attempt to disentangle waking interpretations and fillings out from the fragmentary images of the dream itself.

The mention of dreams suggests another argument. A dream, as far as its own content goes, is exactly like an actual experience. It is mistaken for one. And yet all the world believes that dreams are determined, according to the laws of the association of ideas, &c., by previous cognitions. If it be said that the faculty of intuitively recognizing intuitions is asleep, I reply that this is a mere supposition, without other support. Besides, even when we wake up, we do not find that the dream differed from reality, except by certain *marks*, darkness and fragmentariness. Not unfrequently a dream is so vivid that the memory of it is mistaken for the memory of an actual occurrence.

A child has, as far as we know, all the perceptive powers of a man. Yet question him a little as to *how* he knows what he does. In many cases, he will tell you that he never learned his mother-tongue; he always knew it, or he knew it as soon as he came to have sense. It appears, then, that *he* does not possess the faculty of distinguishing, by simple contemplation, between an intuition and a cognition determined by others.

There can be no doubt that before the publication of Berkeley's book on Vision,[9] it had generally been believed that the third dimension of space was immediately intuited, although, at present, nearly all admit that it is known by inference. We had been *contemplating* the object since the very creation of man, but this discovery was not made until we began to *reason* about it.

Does the reader know of the blind spot on the retina? Take a number of this journal, turn over the cover so as to expose the white paper, lay it sideways upon the table before which you must sit, and put two cents upon it, one near the left-hand edge, and the other to the right. Put your left hand over your left eye, and with the right eye look *steadily* at the left-hand cent. Then, with your right hand, move the right-hand cent (which is now plainly seen) *towards* the left hand. When it comes to a place near the middle of the page it will disappear—you cannot see it without turning your eye. Bring it nearer to the other cent, or carry it further away, and it will reappear; but at that particular spot it cannot be seen. Thus it appears that there is a blind spot nearly in the middle of the retina; and this is confirmed by anatomy. It follows that the space we immediately see (when one eye is closed) is not, as we had imagined, a continuous oval, but is a ring, the filling up of which must be the work of the intellect. What more striking example could be desired of the impossibility of distinguishing intellectual results from intuitional data, by mere contemplation?

A man can distinguish different textures of cloth by feeling; but not immediately, for he requires to move his fingers over the cloth, which shows that he is obliged to compare the sensations of one instant with those of another.

The pitch of a tone depends upon the rapidity of the succession of the vibrations which reach the ear. Each of those vibrations produces an impulse upon the ear. Let a single such impulse be made upon the ear, and we know, experimentally, that it is perceived. There is, therefore, good reason to believe that each of the impulses forming a tone is perceived. Nor is there any reason to the contrary. So that this is the only admissible supposition. Therefore, the pitch of a tone depends upon the rapidity with which certain impressions are successively conveyed to the mind. These impressions must exist previously to any tone; hence, the sensation of pitch is determined by previous cognitions. Nevertheless, this would never have been discovered by the mere contemplation of that feeling.

A similar argument may be urged in reference to the perception of two dimensions of space. This appears to be an immediate intuition. But if we were to *see* immediately an extended surface, our retinas must be spread out in an extended surface. Instead of that, the retina consists of innumerable needles pointing towards the light, and whose distances from one another are decidedly greater than the *minimum visibile*.[10] Suppose each of those nerve-points conveys the sensation of a little colored surface. Still, what we immediately see must even then be, not a continuous surface, but a collection of spots. Who could discover this by mere intuition? But all the analogies of the nervous system are against the supposition that the excitation of a single nerve can produce an idea as complicated as that of a space, however small. If the excitation of no one of these nerve-points can immediately convey the impression of space, the excitation of all cannot do so. For, the excitation of each produces some impression (according to the analogies of the nervous system), hence, the sum of these impressions is a necessary condition of any perception produced by the excitation of all; or, in other terms, a perception produced by the excitation of all is determined by the mental impressions produced by the excitation of every one. This argument is confirmed by the fact that the existence of the perception of space can be fully accounted for by the action of faculties known to exist, without supposing it to be an immediate impression. For this purpose, we must bear in mind the following facts of physio-psychology: 1. The excitation of a nerve does not of itself inform us where the extremity of it is situated. If, by a surgical operation, certain nerves are displaced, our sensations from those nerves do not inform us of the displacement. 2. A single sensation does not inform us how many nerves or nerve-points are excited. 3. We can distinguish between the impressions produced by the excitations of different nerve-points. 4. The differences of impressions produced by different excitations of similar nerve-points are similar. Let a momentary image be made upon the retina. By No. 2, the impression thereby produced will be indistinguishable from what might be produced by the excitation of some conceivable single nerve. It is not conceivable that the momentary excitation of a single nerve should give the sensation of space. Therefore, the momentary excitation of all the nerve-points of the retina cannot, immediately or mediately, produce the sensation of space. The same argument would apply to any unchanging image on the retina. Suppose, however, that the image moves over the retina. Then the peculiar excitation which at one instant affects one nerve-point, at a later instant will affect another. These will convey impressions which are very similar by 4, and yet which are distinguishable by 3. Hence, the conditions for the recognition of a relation between these impressions are present. There being, however, a very great number of nerve-points affected by a very great number of successive excitations, the relations of the resulting impressions will be almost inconceivably complicated. Now, it is a known law of mind, that when phenomena of an extreme complexity are presented, which yet would be reduced to *order* or mediate simplicity by the application of a certain conception, that conception sooner or later arises in application to those phenomena. In the case under consideration, the conception of extension would reduce the phenomena to unity, and, therefore, its genesis is fully accounted for. It remains only to explain why the previous cognitions which determine it are not more clearly apprehended. For this explanation, I shall refer to a paper upon a new list of categories, §5,* merely adding that just as we are able to recognize our friends by certain appearances, although we cannot possibly say what those appearances are and are quite unconscious of any process of reasoning, so in any case when the reasoning is easy and natural to us, however complex may be the premises, they sink into insignificance and oblivion proportionately to the satisfactoriness of the theory based upon them. This theory of space is confirmed by the circumstance that an exactly similar theory is imperatively demanded by the facts in reference to time. That the course of time should be immediately felt is obviously impossible. For, in that case, there must be an element of this feeling at each instant. But in an instant there is no duration and hence no immediate feeling of duration. Hence, no one of these elementary feelings is an immediate feeling of duration; and, hence the sum of all is not. On the other hand, the impressions of any moment are very complicated,—containing all the images (or the elements of the images) of sense and memory, which complexity is reducible to mediate simplicity by means of the conception of time.†

Proceedings of the American Academy, May 14, 1867. [Item 1 above, pp. 1–10.]

†The above theory of space and time does not conflict with that of Kant so much as it appears to do. They are in fact the solutions of different questions. Kant, it is true, makes space and time intuitions, or rather forms of intuition, but it is not essential to his theory that intuition should mean more than "individual representation." The apprehension of space and time results, according to him, from a mental *process,*—the "Synthesis der Apprehension in der Anschauung." (See *Critik d. reinen Vernunft.* Ed. 1781, pp. 98 *et seq.*) My theory is merely an account of this synthesis.

The gist of Kant's "Transcendental Æsthetic" is contained in two principles. First, that universal and necessary propositions are not given in experience. Second, that universal and necessary facts are determined by the conditions of experience in general. By a universal proposition is meant merely, one which asserts something of *all* of a sphere,—not necessarily one which all men believe. By a necessary proposition, is meant one which asserts what it does, not merely of the actual condition of things, but of every possible state of things; it is not meant that the proposition is one which we cannot help believing. Experience, in Kant's first principle, cannot be used for a product of the objective understanding, but must be taken for the first impressions of sense with consciousness conjoined and worked up by the imagination into images, together with all which is logically deducible therefrom. In this sense, it may be admitted that universal and necessary propositions are not given in experience. But, in that case, neither are any inductive conclusions which might be drawn from experience, given in it. In fact, it is the peculiar function of induction to produce universal and necessary propositions. Kant points out, indeed, that the universality and necessity of scientific inductions are but the analogues of philosophic universality and necessity; and this is true, in so far as it is never allowable to accept a scientific conclusion without a certain indefinite drawback. But this is owing to the insufficiency in the number of the instances; and whenever instances may be had in as large numbers as we please, *ad infinitum,* a truly universal and necessary proposition is inferable. As for Kant's second principle, that the truth of universal and necessary propositions is dependent upon the conditions of the general experience, it is no more nor less than the principle of Induction. I go to a fair and draw from the "grab-bag" twelve packages. Upon opening them, I find that every one contains a red ball. Here is a universal fact. It depends, then, on the condition of the experience. What is the condition of the experience? It is solely that the balls are the contents of packages drawn from that bag, that is, the only thing which determined the experience, was the drawing from the bag. I infer, then, according to the principle

We have, therefore, a variety of facts, all of which are most readily explained on the supposition that we have no intuitive faculty of distinguishing intuitive from mediate cognitions. Some arbitrary hypothesis may otherwise explain any one of these facts; this is the only theory which brings them to support one another. Moreover, no facts require the supposition of the faculty in question. Whoever has studied the nature of proof will see, then, that there are here very strong reasons for disbelieving the existence of this faculty. These will become still stronger when the consequences of rejecting it have, in this paper and in a following one, been more fully traced out.

QUESTION 2. *Whether we have an intuitive self-consciousness.*

Self-consciousness, as the term is here used, is to be distinguished both from consciousness generally, from the internal sense, and from pure apperception. Any cognition is a consciousness of the object as represented; by self-consciousness is meant a knowledge of ourselves. Not a mere feeling of subjective conditions of consciousness, but of our personal selves. Pure apperception is the self-assertion of THE *ego;* the self-consciousness here meant is the recognition of my *private* self. I know that *I* (not merely *the* I) exist. The question is, how do I know it; by a special intuitive faculty, or is it determined by previous cognitions?

Now, it is not self-evident that we have such an intuitive faculty, for it has just been shown that we have no intuitive power of distinguishing an intuition from a cognition determined by others. Therefore, the existence or non-existence of this power is to be determined upon evidence, and the question is whether self-consciousness can be explained by the action of known faculties under conditions known to exist, or whether it is necessary to suppose an unknown cause for this cognition, and, in the latter case, whether an intuitive faculty of self-consciousness is the most probable cause which can be supposed.

It is first to be observed that there is no known self-consciousness to be accounted for in extremely young children. It has already been pointed out by Kant* that the late use of the very common word "I" with children indicates an imperfect self-consciousness in them, and that, therefore, so far as it is admissible for us to draw any conclusion

---

of Kant, that what is drawn from the bag will contain a red ball. This is induction. Apply induction not to any limited experience but to all human experience and you have the Kantian philosophy, so far as it is correctly developed.

Kant's successors, however, have not been content with his doctrine. Nor ought they to have been. For, there is this third principle: "Absolutely universal propositions must be analytic." For whatever is absolutely universal is devoid of all content or determination, for all determination is by negation. The problem, therefore, is not how universal propositions can be synthetical, but how universal propositions appearing to be synthetical can be evolved by thought alone from the purely indeterminate.

Werke, vii (2), 11.

in regard to the mental state of those who are still younger, it must be against the existence of any self-consciousness in them.

On the other hand, children manifest powers of thought much earlier. Indeed, it is almost impossible to assign a period at which children do not already exhibit decided intellectual activity in directions in which thought is indispensable to their well-being. The complicated trigonometry of vision, and the delicate adjustments of coördinated movement, are plainly mastered very early. There is no reason to question a similar degree of thought in reference to themselves.

A very young child may always be observed to watch its own body with great attention. There is every reason why this should be so, for from the child's point of view this body is the most important thing in the universe. Only what it touches has any actual and present feeling; only what it faces has any actual color; only what is on its tongue has any actual taste.

No one questions that, when a sound is heard by a child, he thinks, not of himself as hearing, but of the bell or other object as sounding. How when he wills to move a table? Does he then think of himself as desiring, or only of the table as fit to be moved? That he has the latter thought, is beyond question; that he has the former, must, until the existence of an intuitive self-consciousness is proved, remain an arbitrary and baseless supposition. There is no good reason for thinking that he is less ignorant of his own peculiar condition than the angry adult who denies that he is in a passion.

The child, however, must soon discover by observation that things which are thus fit to be changed are apt actually to undergo this change, after a contact with that peculiarly important body called Willy or Johnny. This consideration makes this body still more important and central, since it establishes a connection between the fitness of a thing to be changed and a tendency in this body to touch it before it is changed.

The child learns to understand the language; that is to say, a connection between certain sounds and certain facts becomes established in his mind. He has previously noticed the connection between these sounds and the motions of the lips of bodies somewhat similar to the central one, and has tried the experiment of putting his hand on those lips and has found the sound in that case to be smothered. He thus connects that language with bodies somewhat similar to the central one. By efforts, so unenergetic that they should be called rather instinctive, perhaps, than tentative, he learns to produce those sounds. So he begins to converse.

It must be about this time that he begins to find that what these people about him say is the very best evidence of fact. So much so, that testimony is even a stronger mark of fact than *the facts themselves*, or rather than what must now be thought of as the *appearances* themselves.

(I may remark, by the way, that this remains so through life; testimony will convince a man that he himself is mad.) A child hears it said that the stove is hot. But it is not, he says; and, indeed, that central body is not touching it, and only what that touches is hot or cold. But he touches it, and finds the testimony confirmed in a striking way. Thus, he becomes aware of ignorance, and it is necessary to suppose a *self* in which this ignorance can inhere. So testimony gives the first dawning of self-consciousness.

But, further, although usually appearances are either only confirmed or merely supplemented by testimony, yet there is a certain remarkable class of appearances which are continually contradicted by testimony. These are those predicates which *we* know to be emotional, but which *he* distinguishes by their connection with the movements of that central person, himself (that the table wants moving, etc.). These judgments are generally denied by others. Moreover, he has reason to think that others, also, have such judgments which are quite denied by all the rest. Thus, he adds to the conception of appearance as the actualization of fact, the conception of it as something *private* and valid only for one body. In short, *error* appears, and it can be explained only by supposing a *self* which is fallible.

Ignorance and error are all that distinguish our private selves from the absolute *ego* of pure apperception.

Now, the theory which, for the sake of perspicuity, has thus been stated in a specific form, may be summed up as follows: At the age at which we know children to be self-conscious, we know that they have been made aware of ignorance and error; and we know them to possess at that age powers of understanding sufficient to enable them then to infer from ignorance and error their own existence. Thus we find that known faculties, acting under conditions known to exist, would rise to self-consciousness. The only essential defect in this account of the matter is, that while we know that children exercise *as much* understanding as is here supposed, we do not know that they exercise it in precisely this way. Still the supposition that they do so is infinitely more supported by facts, than the supposition of a wholly peculiar faculty of the mind.

The only argument worth noticing for the existence of an intuitive self-consciousness is this. We are more certain of our own existence than of any other fact; a premise cannot determine a conclusion to be more certain than it is itself; hence, our own existence cannot have been inferred from any other fact. The first premise must be admitted, but the second premise is founded on an exploded theory of logic. A conclusion cannot be more certain than that some one of the facts which support it is true, but it may easily be more certain than any one of those facts. Let us suppose, for example, that a dozen witnesses testify to an occurrence. Then my belief in that occurrence rests on the belief that each of those men is generally to be believed upon oath. Yet the fact testified to is made more certain than that any one of those men is generally to be believed. In the same way, to the developed mind of man, his own existence is supported by *every other fact,* and is, therefore, incomparably more certain than any one of these facts. But it cannot be said to be more certain than that there is another fact, since there is no doubt perceptible in either case.

It is to be concluded, then, that there is no necessity of supposing an intuitive self-consciousness, since self-consciousness may easily be the result of inference.

QUESTION 3. *Whether we have an intuitive power of distinguishing between the subjective elements of different kinds of cognitions.*

Every cognition involves something represented, or that of which we are conscious, and some action or passion of the self whereby it becomes represented. The former shall be termed the objective, the latter the subjective, element of the cognition. The cognition itself is an intuition of its objective element, which may therefore be called, also, the immediate object. The subjective element is not necessarily immediately known, but it is possible that such an intuition of the subjective element of a cognition of its character, whether that of dreaming, imagining, conceiving, believing, etc., should accompany every cognition. The question is whether this is so.

It would appear, at first sight, that there is an overwhelming array of evidence in favor of the existence of such a power. The difference between seeing a color and imagining it is immense. There is a vast difference between the most vivid dream and reality. And if we had no intuitive power of distinguishing between what we believe and what we merely conceive, we never, it would seem, could in any way distinguish them; since if we did so by reasoning, the question would arise whether the argument itself was believed or conceived, and this must be answered before the conclusion could have any force. And thus there would be a *regressus ad infinitum.* Besides, if we do not know that we believe, then, from the nature of the case, we do not believe.

But be it noted that we do not intuitively know the existence of this faculty. For it is an intuitive one, and we cannot intuitively know that a cognition is intuitive. The question is, therefore, whether it is necessary to suppose the existence of this faculty, or whether then the facts can be explained without this supposition.

In the first place, then, the difference between what is imagined or dreamed and what is actually experienced, is no argument in favor of the existence of such a faculty. For it is not questioned that there are distinctions in what is present to the mind, but the question is, whether independently of any such distinctions in the immediate *objects* of consciousness, we have any immediate power of distinguishing different modes of consciousness. Now, the very fact of the immense difference in the immediate objects of sense and imagination, sufficiently accounts for our distinguishing those faculties; and instead of being an argument in favor of the existence of an intuitive power of distinguishing the subjective elements of consciousness, it is a powerful reply to any such argument, so far as the distinction of sense and imagination is concerned.

Passing to the distinction of belief and conception, we meet the statement that the knowledge of belief is essential to its existence. Now, we can unquestionably distinguish a belief from a conception, in most cases, by means of a peculiar feeling of conviction; and it is a mere question of words whether we define belief as that judgment which is accompanied by this feeling, or as that judgment from which a man will act. We may conveniently call the former *sensational*, the latter *active* belief. That neither of these necessarily involves the other, will surely be admitted without any recital of facts. Taking belief in the sensational sense, the intuitive power of reorganizing it will amount simply to the capacity for the sensation which accompanies the judgment. This sensation, like any other, is an object of consciousness; and therefore the capacity for it implies no intuitive recognition of subjective elements of consciousness. If belief is taken in the active sense, it may be discovered by the observation of external facts and by inference from the sensation of conviction which usually accompanies it.

Thus, the arguments in favor of this peculiar power of consciousness disappear, and the presumption is again against such a hypothesis. Moreover, as the immediate objects of any two faculties must be admitted to be different, the facts do not render such a supposition in any degree necessary.

QUESTION 4. *Whether we have any power of introspection, or whether our whole knowledge of the internal world is derived from the observation of external facts.*

It is not intended here to assume the reality of the external world. Only, there is a certain set of facts which are ordinarily regarded as external, while others are regarded as internal. The question is whether the latter are known otherwise than by inference from the former. By introspection, I mean a direct perception of the internal world, but not necessarily a perception of it *as* internal. Nor do I mean to limit the signification of the word to intuition, but would extend it to any knowledge of the internal world not derived from external observation.

There is one sense in which any perception has an internal object, namely, that every sensation is partly determined by internal conditions. Thus, the sensation of redness is as it is, owing to the constitution of the mind; and in this sense it is a sensation of something internal. Hence, we may derive a knowledge of the mind from a consideration of this sensation, but that knowledge would, in fact, be an inference from redness as a predicate of something external. On the other hand, there are certain other feelings—the emotions, for example—which appear to arise in the first place, not as predicates at all, and to be referable to the mind alone. It would seem, then, that by means of these, a knowledge of the mind may be obtained, which is not inferred from any character of outward things. The question is whether this is really so.

Although introspection is not necessarily intuitive, it is not self-evident that we possess this capacity; for we have no intuitive faculty of distinguishing different subjective modes of consciousness. The power, if it exists, must be known by the circumstance that the facts cannot be explained without it.

In reference to the above argument from the emotions, it must be admitted that if a man is angry, his anger implies, in general, no determinate and constant character in its object. But, on the other hand, it can hardly be questioned that there is some relative character in the outward thing which makes him angry, and a little reflection will serve to show that his anger consists in his saying to himself, "this thing is vile, abominable, etc.," and that it is rather a mark of returning reason to say, "I am angry." In the same way any emotion is a predication concerning some object, and the chief difference between this and an objective intellectual judgment is that while the latter is relative to human nature or to mind in general, the former is relative to the particular circumstances and disposition of a particular man at a particular time. What is here said of emotions in general, is true in particular of the sense of beauty and of the moral sense. Good and bad are feelings which first arise as predicates, and therefore are either predicates of the not-I, or are determined by previous cognitions (there being no intuitive power of distinguishing subjective elements of consciousness).

It remains, then, only to inquire whether it is necessary to suppose a particular power of introspection for the sake of accounting for the sense of willing. Now, volition, as distinguished from desire, is nothing but the power of concentrating the attention, of abstracting. Hence, the knowledge of the power of abstracting may be inferred from abstract objects, just as the knowledge of the power of seeing is inferred from colored objects.

It appears, therefore, that there is no reason for supposing a power of introspection; and, consequently, the only way of investigating a psychological question is by inference from external facts.

QUESTION 5. *Whether we can think without signs.*

This is a familiar question, but there is, to this day, no better argument in the affirmative than that thought must precede every sign. This assumes the impossibility of an infinite series. But Achilles, as a fact, will overtake the tortoise. *How* this happens, is a question not necessary to be answered at present, as long as it certainly does happen.

If we seek the light of external facts, the only cases of thought which we can find are of thought in signs. Plainly, no other thought can be evidenced by external facts. But we have seen that only by external facts can thought be known at all. The only thought, then, which can possibly be cognized is thought in signs. But thought which cannot be cognized does not exist. All thought, therefore, must necessarily be in signs.

A man says to himself, "Aristotle is a man; *therefore,* he is fallible." Has he not, then, thought what he has not said to himself, that all men are fallible? The answer is, that he has done so, so far as this is said in his *therefore.* According to this, our question does not relate to *fact*, but is a mere asking for distinctness of thought.

From the proposition that every thought is a sign, it follows that every thought must address itself to some other, must determine some other, since that is the essence of a sign. This, after all, is but another form of the familiar axiom, that in intuition, i.e. in the immediate present, there is no thought, or, that all which is reflected upon has past. *Hinc loquor inde est.* That, since any thought, there must have been a thought, has its analogue in the fact that, since any past time, there must have been an infinite series of times. To say, therefore, that thought cannot happen in an instant, but requires a time, is but another way of saying that every thought must be interpreted in another, or that all thought is in signs.

QUESTION 6. *Whether a sign can have any meaning, if by its definition it is the sign of something absolutely incognizable.*

It would seem that it can, and that universal and hypothetical propositions are instances of it. Thus, the universal proposition, "all ruminants are cloven-hoofed," speaks of a possible infinity of animals, and no matter how many ruminants may have been examined, the possibility must remain that there are others which have not been examined. In the case of a hypothetical proposition, the same thing is still more manifest; for such a proposition speaks not merely of the actual state of things, but of every possible state of things, all of which are not knowable, inasmuch as only one can so much as exist.

On the other hand, all our conceptions are obtained by abstractions and combinations of cognitions first occurring in judgments of experience. Accordingly, there can be no conception of the absolutely incognizable, since nothing of that sort occurs in experience. But the meaning of a term is the conception which it conveys. Hence, a term can have no such meaning.

If it be said that the incognizable is a concept compounded of the concept *not* and *cognizable,* it may be replied that *not* is a mere syn-categorematic term and not a concept by itself.

If I think "white," I will not go so far as Berkeley and say that I think of a person seeing,[11] but I will say that what I think is of the nature of a cognition, and so of anything else which can be experienced. Consequently, the highest concept which can be reached by abstractions from judgments of experience—and therefore, the highest concept which can be reached at all—is the concept of something of the nature of a cognition. *Not,* then, or *what is other than,* if a concept, is a concept of the cognizable. Hence, not-cognizable, if a concept, is a concept of the form "*A,* not-*A,*" and is, at least, self-contradictory. Thus, ignorance and error can only be conceived as correlative to a real knowledge and truth, which latter are of the nature of cognitions. Over against any cognition, there is an unknown but knowable reality; but over against all possible cognition, there is only the self-contradictory. In short, *cognizability* (in its widest sense) and *being* are not merely metaphysically the same, but are synonymous terms.

To the argument from universal and hypothetical propositions, the reply is, that though their truth cannot be cognized with absolute certainty, it may be probably known by induction.

QUESTION 7. *Whether there is any cognition not determined by a previous cognition.*

It would seem that there is or has been; for since we are in posses-sion of cognitions, which are all determined by previous ones, and these by cognitions earlier still, there must have been a *first* in this series or else our state of cognition at any time is completely determined, according to logical laws, by our state at any previous time. But there are many facts against the last supposition, and therefore in favor of intuitive cognitions.

On the other hand, since it is impossible to know intuitively that a given cognition is not determined by a previous one, the only way in which this can be known is by hypothetic inference from observed facts. But to adduce the cognition by which a given cognition has been determined is to explain the determinations of that cognition. And it is the only way of explaining them. For something entirely out of consciousness which may be supposed to determine it, can, as such, only be known and only adduced in the determinate cognition in question. So, that to suppose that a cognition is determined solely by something absolutely external, is to suppose its determinations incapable of explanation. Now, this is a hypothesis which is warranted under no circumstances, inasmuch as the only possible justification for a hypothesis is that it explains the facts, and to say that they are explained and at the same time to suppose them inexplicable is self-contradictory.

If it be objected that the peculiar character of *red* is not determined by any previous cognition, I reply that that character is not a character of red as a cognition; for if there be a man to whom red things look as blue ones do to me and *vice versa,* that man's eyes teach him the same facts that they would if he were like me.

Moreover, we know of no power by which an intuition could be known. For, as the cognition is beginning, and therefore in a state of change, at only the first instant would it be intuition. And, therefore, the apprehension of it must take place in no time and be an event occupying no time.* Besides, all the cognitive faculties we know of are relative, and consequently their products are relations. But the cognition of a relation is determined by previous cognitions. No cognition not determined by a previous cognition, then, can be known. It does not exist, then, first, because it is absolutely incognizable, and second, because a cognition only exists so far as it is known.

The reply to the argument that there must be a first is as follows: In retracing our way from conclusions to premises, or from determined cognitions to those which determine them, we finally reach, in all cases, a point beyond which the consciousness in the determined cognition is more lively than in the cognition which determines it. We have a less lively consciousness in the cognition which determines our cognition of the third dimension than in the latter cognition itself; a less lively consciousness in the cognition which determines our cognition of a continuous surface (without a blind spot) than in this latter cognition itself; and a less lively consciousness of the impressions which determine the sensation of tone than of that sensation itself. Indeed, when we get near enough to the external this is the universal rule. Now let any horizontal line represent a cognition, and let the length of the line serve to measure (so to speak) the liveliness of consciousness in that cognition. A point, having no length, will, on this principle, represent an object quite out of consciousness. Let one horizontal line below another represent a cognition which determines the cognition represented by that other and which has the same object as the latter. Let the finite distance between two such lines represent that they are two different cognitions. With this aid to thinking, let us see whether "there must be a first." Suppose an inverted triangle ▽ to be gradually dipped into water. At any date or instant, the surface of the water makes a horizontal line across that triangle. This line represents a cognition. At a subsequent date, there is a sectional line so made, higher upon the triangle. This represents another cognition of the same object determined by the former, and having a livelier consciousness. The apex of the triangle represents the object external to the

---

*This argument, however, only covers a part of the question. It does not go to show that there is no cognition undetermined except by another like it.

mind which determines both these cognitions. The state of the triangle before it reaches the water, represents a state of cognition which contains nothing which determines these subsequent cognitions. To say, then, that if there be a state of cognition by which all subsequent cognitions of a certain object are not determined, there must subsequently be some cognition of that object not determined by previous cognitions of the same object, is to say that when that triangle is dipped into the water there must be a sectional line made by the surface of the water lower than which no surface line had been made in that way. But draw the horizontal line where you will, as many horizontal lines as you please can be assigned at finite distances below it and below one another. For any such section is at some distance above the apex, otherwise it is not a line. Let this distance be a. Then there have been similar sections at the distances $\frac{1}{2}a$, $\frac{1}{4}a$, $\frac{1}{8}a$, $\frac{1}{16}a$, above the apex, and so on as far as you please. So that it is not true that there must be a first. Explicate the logical difficulties of this paradox (they are identical with those of the Achilles) in whatever way you may. I am content with the result, as long as your principles are fully applied to the particular case of cognitions determining one another. Deny motion, if it seems proper to do so; only then deny the process of determination of one cognition by another. Say that instants and lines are fictions; only say, also, that states of cognition and judgments are fictions. The point here insisted on is not this or that logical solution of the difficulty, but merely that cognition arises by a *process* of beginning, as any other change comes to pass.

In a subsequent paper, I shall trace the consequences of these principles, in reference to the questions of reality, of individuality, and of the validity of the laws of logic.

3

Some Consequences of Four Incapacities

P 27: Journal of Speculative Philosophy 2 (1868):140–57.
*[Also published in W2:211–42 and in CP 5.264–317.] With item
1 above, one of Peirce's two "strongest philosophical works,"
this article develops an account of mind and reality from the
ground prepared in item 2. Peirce asserts that all mental
events are valid inferences, and claims that as every thought
is a sign, so man himself is a sign. He also gives a fairly
detailed account of his theory of signs as of 1868, and makes
his first published declaration for scholastic realism. (Peirce's
philosophy of mind as developed here is, according to Christopher Hookway, a type of functionalism.)*

Descartes is the father of modern philosophy, and the spirit of
Cartesianism—that which principally distinguishes it from the scholasticism which it displaced—may be compendiously stated as follows:

1. It teaches that philosophy must begin with universal doubt;
whereas scholasticism had never questioned fundamentals.

2. It teaches that the ultimate test of certainty is to be found in the
individual consciousness; whereas scholasticism had rested on the testimony of sages and of the Catholic Church.

3. The multiform argumentation of the middle ages is replaced by
a single thread of inference depending often upon inconspicuous
premises.

4. Scholasticism had its mysteries of faith, but undertook to explain
all created things. But there are many facts which Cartesianism not
only does not explain, but renders absolutely inexplicable, unless to
say that "God makes them so" is to be regarded as an explanation.

In some, or all of these respects, most modern philosophers have
been, in effect, Cartesians. Now without wishing to return to scholasticism, it seems to me that modern science and modern logic require us
to stand upon a very different platform from this.

1. We cannot begin with complete doubt. We must begin with all
the prejudices which we actually have when we enter upon the study

of philosophy. These prejudices are not to be dispelled by a maxim, for they are things which it does not occur to us *can* be questioned. Hence this initial scepticism will be a mere self-deception, and not real doubt; and no one who follows the Cartesian method will ever be satisfied until he has formally recovered all those beliefs which in form he has given up. It is, therefore, as useless a preliminary as going to the North Pole would be in order to get to Constantinople by coming down regularly upon a meridian. A person may, it is true, in the course of his studies, find reason to doubt what he began by believing; but in that case he doubts because he has a positive reason for it, and not on account of the Cartesian maxim. Let us not pretend to doubt in philosophy what we do not doubt in our hearts.

2. The same formalism appears in the Cartesian criterion, which amounts to this: "Whatever I am clearly convinced of, is true." If I were really convinced, I should have done with reasoning, and should require no test of certainty. But thus to make single individuals absolute judges of truth is most pernicious. The result is that metaphysicians will all agree that metaphysics has reached a pitch of certainty far beyond that of the physical sciences;—only they can agree upon nothing else. In sciences in which men come to agreement, when a theory has been broached, it is considered to be on probation until this agreement is reached. After it is reached, the question of certainty becomes an idle one, because there is no one left who doubts it. We individually cannot reasonably hope to attain the ultimate philosophy which we pursue; we can only seek it, therefore, for the *community* of philosophers. Hence, if disciplined and candid minds carefully examine a theory and refuse to accept it, this ought to create doubts in the mind of the author of the theory himself.

3. Philosophy ought to imitate the successful sciences in its methods, so far as to proceed only from tangible premises which can be subjected to careful scrutiny, and to trust rather to the multitude and variety of its arguments than to the conclusiveness of any one. Its reasoning should not form a chain which is no stronger than its weakest link, but a cable whose fibres may be ever so slender, provided they are sufficiently numerous and intimately connected.

4. Every unidealistic philosophy supposes some absolutely inexplicable, unanalyzable ultimate; in short, something resulting from mediation itself not susceptible of mediation. Now that anything *is* thus inexplicable can only be known by reasoning from signs. But the only justification of an inference from signs is that the conclusion explains the fact. To suppose the fact absolutely inexplicable, is not to explain it, and hence this supposition is never allowable.

In the last number of this journal will be found a piece entitled "Questions concerning certain Faculties claimed for Man," which has been written in this spirit of opposition to Cartesianism. That criticism of certain faculties resulted in four denials, which for convenience may here be repeated:

1. We have no power of Introspection, but all knowledge of the internal world is derived by hypothetical reasoning from our knowledge of external facts.

2. We have no power of Intuition, but every cognition is determined logically by previous cognitions.

3. We have no power of thinking without signs.

4. We have no conception of the absolutely incognizable.

These propositions cannot be regarded as certain; and, in order to bring them to a further test, it is now proposed to trace them out to their consequences. We may first consider the first alone; then trace the consequences of the first and second; then see what else will result from assuming the third also; and, finally, add the fourth to our hypothetical premises.

In accepting the first proposition, we must put aside all prejudices derived from a philosophy which bases our knowledge of the external world on our self-consciousness. We can admit no statement concerning what passes within us except as a hypothesis necessary to explain what takes place in what we commonly call the external world. Moreover when we have upon such grounds assumed one faculty or mode of action of the mind, we cannot, of course, adopt any other hypothesis for the purpose of explaining any fact which can be explained by our first supposition, but must carry the latter as far as it will go. In other words, we must, as far as we can do so without additional hypotheses, reduce all kinds of mental action to one general type.

The class of modifications of consciousness with which we must commence our inquiry must be one whose existence is indubitable, and whose laws are best known, and, therefore (since this knowledge comes from the outside), which most closely follows external facts; that is, it must be some kind of cognition. Here we may hypothetically admit the second proposition of the former paper, according to which there is no absolutely first cognition of any object, but cognition arises by a continuous process. We must begin, then, with a *process* of cognition, and with that process whose laws are best understood and most closely follow external facts. This is no other than the process of valid inference, which proceeds from its premise, *A*, to its conclusion, *B*, only if, as a matter of fact, such a proposition as *B* is always or usually true when such a proposition as *A* is true. It is a consequence, then, of the first two principles whose results we are to trace out, that we must, as far as we can, without any other supposition than that the mind reasons, reduce all mental action to the formula of valid reasoning.

But does the mind in fact go through the syllogistic process? It is certainly very doubtful whether a conclusion—as something existing in the mind independently, like an image—suddenly displaces two premises existing in the mind in a similar way. But it is a matter of constant experience, that if a man is made to believe in the premises, in the sense that he will act from them and will say that they are true, under favorable conditions he will also be ready to act from the conclusion and to say that that is true. Something, therefore, takes place within the organism which is equivalent to the syllogistic process.

A valid inference is either *complete* or *incomplete*. An incomplete inference is one whose validity depends upon some matter of fact not contained in the premises. This implied fact might have been stated as a premise, and its relation to the conclusion is the same whether it is explicitly posited or not, since it is at least virtually taken for granted; so that every valid incomplete argument is virtually complete. Complete arguments are divided into *simple* and *complex*. A complex argument is one which from three or more premises concludes what might have been concluded by successive steps in reasonings each of which is simple. Thus, a complex inference comes to the same thing in the end as a succession of simple inferences.

A complete, simple, and valid argument, or syllogism, is either *apodictic* or *probable*. An apodictic or deductive syllogism is one whose validity depends unconditionally upon the relation of the fact inferred to the facts posited in the premises. A syllogism whose validity should depend not merely upon its premises, but upon the existence of some other knowledge, would be impossible; for either this other knowledge would be posited, in which case it would be a part of the premises, or it would be implicitly assumed, in which case the inference would be incomplete. But a syllogism whose validity depends partly upon the *non-existence* of some other knowledge, is a *probable* syllogism.

A few examples will render this plain. The two following arguments are apodictic or deductive:

1. No series of days of which the first and last are different days of the week exceeds by one a multiple of seven days; now the first and last days of any leap-year are different days of the week, and therefore no leap-year consists of a number of days one greater than a multiple of seven.

2. Among the vowels there are no double letters; but one of the double letters (*w*) is compounded of two vowels: hence, a letter compounded of two vowels is not necessarily itself a vowel.

In both these cases, it is plain that as long as the premises are true, however other facts may be, the conclusions will be true. On the other hand, suppose that we reason as follows:—"A certain man had the Asiatic cholera. He was in a state of collapse, livid, quite cold, and without perceptible pulse. He was bled copiously. During the process he came out of collapse, and the next morning was well enough to be about. Therefore, bleeding tends to cure the cholera." This is a fair probable inference, provided that the premises represent our whole knowledge of the matter. But if we knew, for example, that recoveries from cholera were apt to be sudden, and that the physician who had reported this case had known of a hundred other trials of the remedy without communicating the result, then the inference would lose all its validity.

The absence of knowledge which is essential to the validity of any probable argument relates to some question which is determined by the argument itself. This question, like every other, is whether certain objects have certain characters. Hence, the absence of knowledge is either whether besides the objects which, according to the premises, possess certain characters, any other objects possess them; or, whether besides the characters which, according to the premises, belong to certain objects, any other characters not necessarily involved in these belong to the same objects. In the former case, the reasoning proceeds as though all the objects which have certain characters were known, and this is *induction;* in the latter case, the inference proceeds as though all the characters requisite to the determination of a certain object or class were known, and this is *hypothesis.* This distinction, also, may be made more plain by examples.

Suppose we count the number of occurrences of the different letters in a certain English book, which we may call *A.* Of course, every new letter which we add to our count will alter the relative number of occurrences of the different letters; but as we proceed with our counting, this change will be less and less. Suppose that we find that as we increase the number of letters counted, the relative number of *e*'s approaches nearly 11¼ *per cent* of the whole, that of the *t*'s 8½ *per cent,* that of the *a*'s 8 *per cent,* that of the *s*'s 7½ *per cent,* &c. Suppose we repeat the same observations with half a dozen other English writings (which we may designate as *B, C, D, E, F, G*) with the like result. Then we may infer that in every English writing of some length, the different letters occur with nearly those relative frequencies.

Now this argument depends for its validity upon our *not* knowing the proportion of letters in any English writing besides *A, B, C, D, E, F,* and *G.* For if we know it in respect to *H,* and it is not nearly the same as in the others, our conclusion is destroyed at once; if it is the same, then the legitimate inference is from *A, B, C, D, E, F, G,* and *H,* and not from the first seven alone. This, therefore, is an *induction.*

Suppose, next, that a piece of writing in cypher is presented to us, without the key. Suppose we find that it contains something less than 26 characters, one of which occurs about 11 *per cent* of all the times, another 8½ *per cent,* another 8 *per cent,* and another 7½ *per cent.* Suppose that when we substitute for these *e, t, a,* and *s,* respectively, we are able to see how single letters may be substituted for each of the other characters so as to make sense in English, provided, however, that we allow the spelling to be wrong in some cases. If the writing is of any considerable length, we may infer with great probability that this is the meaning of the cipher.

The validity of this argument depends upon there being no other known characters of the writing in cipher which would have any weight in the matter; for if there are—if we know, for example, whether or not there is any other solution of it—this must be allowed its effect in supporting or weakening the conclusion. This, then, is *hypothesis*.

All valid reasoning is either deductive, inductive, or hypothetic; or else it combines two or more of these characters. Deduction is pretty well treated in most logical text-books; but it will be necessary to say a few words about induction and hypothesis in order to render what follows more intelligible.

Induction may be defined as an argument which proceeds upon the assumption that all the members of a class or aggregate have all the characters which are common to all those members of this class concerning which it is known, whether they have these characters or not; or, in other words, which assumes that that is true of a whole collection which is true of a number of instances taken from it at random. This might be called statistical argument. In the long run, it must generally afford pretty correct conclusions from true premises. If we have a bag of beans partly black and partly white, by counting the relative proportions of the two colors in several different handfuls, we can approximate more or less to the relative proportions in the whole bag, since a sufficient number of handfuls would constitute all the beans in the bag. The central characteristic and key to induction is, that by taking the conclusion so reached as major premise of a syllogism, and the proposition stating that such and such objects are taken from the class in question as the minor premise, the other premise of the induction will follow from them deductively. Thus, in the above example we concluded that all books in English have about $11\frac{1}{4}$ *per cent* of their letters *e*'s. From that as major premise, together with the proposition that *A, B, C, D, E, F,* and *G* are books in English, it follows deductively that *A, B, C, D, E, F,* and *G* have about $11\frac{1}{4}$ *per cent* of their letters *e*'s. Accordingly, induction has been defined by Aristotle as the inference of the major premise of a syllogism from its minor premise and conclusion.[1] The function of an induction is to substitute for a series of many subjects, a single one which embraces them and an indefinite number of others. Thus it is a species of "reduction of the manifold to unity."

Hypothesis may be defined as an argument which proceeds upon the assumption that a character which is known necessarily to involve a certain number of others, may be probably predicated of any object which has all the characters which this character is known to involve. Just as induction may be regarded as the inference of the major premise of a syllogism, so hypothesis may be regarded as the inference of the minor premise, from the other two propositions. Thus, the example taken above consists of two such inferences of the minor premises of the following syllogisms:

1. Every English writing of some length in which such and such characters denote *e, t, a,* and *s,* has about 11¼ *per cent* of the first sort of marks, 8½ of the second, 8 of the third, and 7½ of the fourth;
This secret writing is an English writing of some length, in which such and such characters denote *e, t, a,* and *s,* respectively:
∴ This secret writing has about 11¼ *per cent* of its characters of the first kind, 8½ of the second, 8 of the third, and 7½ of the fourth.

2. A passage written with such an alphabet makes sense when such and such letters are severally substituted for such and such characters.
This secret writing is written with such an alphabet.
∴ This secret writing makes sense when such and such substitutions are made.

The function of hypothesis is to substitute for a great series of predicates forming no unity in themselves, a single one (or small number) which involves them all, together (perhaps) with an indefinite number of others. It is, therefore, also a reduction of a manifold to unity.* Every deductive syllogism may be put into the form

*Several persons versed in logic have objected that I have here quite misapplied the term *hypothesis,* and that what I so designate is an argument from *analogy.*[2] It is a sufficient reply to say that the example of the cipher has been given as an apt illustration of hypothesis by Descartes (Rule 10, *Œuvres choisies:* Paris, 1865, page 334), by Leibniz (*Nouveaux Essais,* lib. 4, ch. 12, §13, Ed. Erdmann, p. 383 *b*), and (as I learn from D. Stewart; *Works,* vol. 3, pp. 305 et seqq.)[3] by Gravesande, Boscovich, Hartley, and G. L. Le Sage. The term *Hypothesis* has been used in the following senses:—1. For the theme or proposition forming the subject of discourse. 2. For an assumption. Aristotle divides *theses* or propositions adopted without any reason into definitions and hypotheses.[4] The latter are propositions stating the existence of something. Thus the geometer says, "Let there be a triangle." 3. For a condition in a general sense. We are said to seek other things than happiness ἐξ ὑποθέσεως, conditionally. The best republic is the ideally perfect, the second the best on earth, the third the best ἐξ ὑποθέσεως, under the circumstances. Freedom is the ὑπόθεσις or condition of democracy. 4. For the antecedent of a hypothetical proposition. 5. For an oratorical question which assumes facts. 6. In the *Synopsis* of Psellus,[5] for the reference of a subject to the things it denotes. 7. Most commonly in modern times, for the conclusion of an argument from consequence and consequent to antecedent. This is my use of the term. 8. For such a conclusion when too weak to be a theory accepted into the body of a science.
  I give a few authorities to support the seventh use:
  Chauvin.—*Lexicon Rationale,* 1st Ed.—"Hypothesis est propositio, quæ assumitur ad probandam aliam veritatem incognitam. Requirunt multi, ut hæc hypothesis vera esse cognoscatur, etiam antequam appareat, an alia ex eâ deduci possint. Verum aiunt alii, hoc unum desiderari, ut hypothesis pro vera admittatur, quod nempe ex hac talia deducitur, quæ respondent phænomenis, et satisfaciunt omnibus difficultatibus, quæ hac parte in re, et in iis quæ de ea apparent, occurrebant."[6]
  Newton.—"Hactenus phænomena cœlorum et maris nostri per vim gravitatis exposui, sed causam gravitatis nondum assignavi. . . . Rationem vero harum gravitatis

If *A*, then *B*;
But *A*:
∴ *B*.

And as the minor premise in this form appears as antecedent or reason of a hypothetical proposition, hypothetic inference may be called reasoning from consequent to antecedent.

The argument from analogy, which a popular writer upon logic[9] calls reasoning from particulars to particulars, derives its validity from its combining the characters of induction and hypothesis, being analyzable either into a deduction or an induction, or a deduction and a hypothesis.

But though inference is thus of three essentially different species, it also belongs to one genus. We have seen that no conclusion can be legitimately derived which could not have been reached by successions

---

proprietatum ex phænomenis nondum potui deducere, et hypotheses non fingo. Quicquid enim ex phænomenis non deducitur, *hypothesis* vocanda est. . . . In hâc Philosophiâ Propositiones deducuntur ex phænomenis, et redduntur generales per inductionem." *Principia. Ad fin.*[7]

Sir Wm. Hamilton.—"*Hypotheses*, that is, propositions which are assumed with probability, in order to explain or prove something else which cannot otherwise be explained or proved."—*Lectures on Logic* (Am. Ed.), p. 188.

"The name of *hypothesis* is more emphatically given to provisory suppositions, which serve to explain the phenomena in so far as observed, but which are only asserted to be true, if ultimately confirmed by a complete induction."—Ibid., p. 364.

"When a phenomenon is presented which can be explained by no principle afforded through experience, we feel discontented and uneasy; and there arises an effort to discover some cause which may, at least provisionally, account for the outstanding phenomenon; and this cause is finally recognized as valid and true, if, through it, the given phenomenon is found to obtain a full and perfect explanation. The judgment in which a phenomenon is referred to such a problematic cause, is called a *Hypothesis.*"—Ibid., pp. 449, 450. See also *Lectures on Metaphysics*, p. 117.

J. S. Mill.—"An hypothesis is any supposition which we make (either without actual evidence, or on evidence avowedly insufficient), in order to endeavor to deduce from it conclusions in accordance with facts which are known to be real; under the idea that if the conclusions to which the hypothesis leads are known truths, the hypothesis itself either must be, or at least is likely to be true."—*Logic* (6th Ed.), vol. 2, p. 8.

Kant.—"*If all the consequents of a cognition are true, the cognition itself is true.* . . . It is allowable, therefore, to conclude from consequent to *a* reason, but without being able to determine this reason. From the complexus of all consequents alone can we conclude the truth of a determinate reason. . . . The difficulty with this *positive* and *direct* mode of inference *(modus ponens)* is that the totality of the consequents cannot be apodeictically recognized, and that we are therefore led by this mode of inference only to a probable and *hypothetically* true cognition *(Hypotheses).* "—*Logik* by Jäsche, *Werke*, ed. Rosenkranz and Schubert, vol. 3, p. 221.

"A hypothesis is the judgment of the truth of a reason on account of the sufficiency of the consequents."—Ibid., p. 262.

Herbart.—"We can make hypotheses, thence deduce consequents, and afterwards see whether the latter accord with experience. Such suppositions are termed hypotheses."—*Einleitung; Werke*, vol. 1, p. 53.[8]

Beneke.—"Affirmative inferences from consequent to antecedent, or hypotheses."—*System der Logik*, vol. 2, p. 103.

There would be no difficulty in greatly multiplying these citations.

of arguments having two premises each, and implying no fact not asserted.

Either of these premises is a proposition asserting that certain objects have certain characters. Every term of such a proposition stands either for certain objects or for certain characters. The conclusion may be regarded as a proposition substituted in place of either premise, the substitution being justified by the fact stated in the other premise. The conclusion is accordingly derived from either premise by substituting either a new subject for the subject of the premise, or a new predicate for the predicate of the premise, or by both substitutions. Now the substitution of one term for another can be justified only so far as the term substituted represents only what is represented in the term replaced. If, therefore, the conclusion be denoted by the formula,

$$S \text{ is } P;$$

and this conclusion be derived, by a change of subject, from a premise which may on this account be expressed by the formula,

$$M \text{ is } P,$$

then the other premise must assert that whatever thing is represented by S is represented by M, or that

$$\text{Every } S \text{ is an } M;$$

while, if the conclusion, S is P, is derived from either premise by a change of predicate, that premise may be written

$$S \text{ is } M;$$

and the other premise must assert that whatever characters are implied in P are implied in M, or that

$$\text{Whatever is } M \text{ is } P.$$

In either case, therefore, the syllogism must be capable of expression in the form,

$$S \text{ is } M; M \text{ is } P:$$
$$\therefore S \text{ is } P.$$

Finally, if the conclusion differs from either of its premises, both in subject and predicate, the form of statement of conclusion and premise may be so altered that they shall have a common term. This can always be done, for if P is the premise and C the conclusion, they may be stated thus:

$$\text{The state of things represented in } P \text{ is real,}$$
$$\text{and}$$
$$\text{The state of things represented in } C \text{ is real.}$$

In this case the other premise must in some form virtually assert that every state of things such as is represented by C is the state of things represented in P.

All valid reasoning, therefore, is of one general form; and in seeking to reduce all mental action to the formulæ of valid inference, we seek to reduce it to one single type.

An apparent obstacle to the reduction of all mental action to the type of valid inferences is the existence of fallacious reasoning. Every argument implies the truth of a general principle of inferential procedure (whether involving some matter of fact concerning the subject of argument, or merely a maxim relating to a system of signs), according to which it is a valid argument. If this principle is false, the argument is a fallacy; but neither a valid argument from false premises, nor an exceedingly weak, but not altogether illegitimate, induction or hypothesis, however its force may be over-estimated, however false its conclusion, is a fallacy.

Now words, taken just as they stand, if in the form of an argument, thereby do imply whatever fact may be necessary to make the argument conclusive; so that to the formal logician, who has to do only with the meaning of the words according to the proper principles of interpretation, and not with the intention of the speaker as guessed at from other indications, the only fallacies should be such as are simply absurd and contradictory, either because their conclusions are absolutely inconsistent with their premises, or because they connect propositions by a species of illative conjunction, by which they cannot under any circumstances be validly connected.

But to the psychologist an argument is valid only if the premises from which the mental conclusion is derived would be sufficient, if true, to justify it, either by themselves, or by the aid of other propositions which had previously been held for true. But it is easy to show that all inferences made by man, which are not valid in this sense, belong to four classes, viz.: 1. Those whose premises are false; 2. Those which have some little force, though only a little; 3. Those which result from confusion of one proposition with another; 4. Those which result from the indistinct apprehension, wrong application, or falsity, of a rule of inference. For, if a man were to commit a fallacy not of either of these classes, he would, from true premises conceived with perfect distinctness, without being led astray by any prejudice or other judgment serving as a rule of inference, draw a conclusion which had really not the least relevancy. If this could happen, calm consideration and care could be of little use in thinking, for caution only serves to insure our taking all the facts into account, and to make those which we do take account of, distinct; nor can coolness do anything more than to enable us to be cautious, and also to prevent our being affected by a passion in inferring that to be true which we wish were true, or which we fear may be true, or in following some other wrong rule of inference. But experience shows that the calm and careful consideration of the same distinctly conceived premises (including prejudices) will insure the pronouncement of the same judgment by all men. Now if a fallacy belongs to the first of these four classes and its premises are false, it is to be presumed that the procedure of the mind from these premises to the conclusion is either correct, or errs in one of the other three ways; for it cannot be supposed that the mere falsity of the premises should affect the procedure of reason when that falsity is not known to reason. If the fallacy belongs to the second class and has some force, however little, it is a legitimate probable argument, and belongs to the type of valid inference. If it is of the third class and results from the confusion of one proposition with another, this confusion must be owing to a resemblance between the two propositions; that is to say, the person reasoning, seeing that one proposition has some of the characters which belong to the other, concludes that it has all the essential characters of the other, and is equivalent to it. Now this is a hypothetic inference, which though it may be weak, and though its conclusion happens to be false, belongs to the type of valid inferences; and, therefore, as the *nodus* of the fallacy lies in this confusion, the procedure of the mind in these fallacies of the third class conforms to the formula of valid inference. If the fallacy belongs to the fourth class, it either results from wrongly applying or misapprehending a rule of inference, and so is a fallacy of confusion, or it results from adopting a wrong rule of inference. In this latter case, this rule is in fact taken as a premise, and therefore the false conclusion is owing merely to the falsity of a premise. In every fallacy, therefore, possible to the mind of man, the procedure of the mind conforms to the formula of valid inference.

The third principle whose consequences we have to deduce is, that, whenever we think, we have present to the consciousness some feeling, image, conception, or other representation, which serves as a sign. But it follows from our own existence (which is proved by the occurrence of ignorance and error) that everything which is present to us is a phenomenal manifestation of ourselves. This does not prevent its being a phenomenon of something without us, just as a rainbow is at once a manifestation both of the sun and of the rain. When we think, then, we ourselves, as we are at that moment, appear as a sign. Now a sign has, as such, three references: 1st, it is a sign *to* some thought which interprets it; 2d, it is a sign *for* some object to which in that thought it is equivalent; 3d, it is a sign, *in* some respect or quality, which brings it into connection with its object. Let us ask what the three correlates are to which a thought-sign refers.

  1. When we think, to what thought does that thought-sign which

is ourself address itself? It may, through the medium of outward expression, which it reaches perhaps only after considerable internal development, come to address itself to thought of another person. But whether this happens or not, it is always interpreted by a subsequent thought of our own. If, after any thought, the current of ideas flows on freely, it follows the law of mental association. In that case, each former thought suggests something to the thought which follows it, i.e. is the sign of something to this latter. Our train of thought may, it is true, be interrupted. But we must remember that, in addition to the principal element of thought at any moment, there are a hundred things in our mind to which but a small fraction of attention or consciousness is conceded. It does not, therefore, follow, because a new constituent of thought gets the uppermost, that the train of thought which it displaces is broken off altogether. On the contrary, from our second principle, that there is no intuition or cognition not determined by previous cognitions, it follows that the striking in of a new experience is never an instantaneous affair, but is an *event* occupying time, and coming to pass by a continuous process. Its prominence in consciousness, therefore, must probably be the consummation of a growing process; and if so, there is no sufficient cause for the thought which had been the leading one just before, to cease abruptly and instantaneously. But if a train of thought ceases by gradually dying out, it freely follows its own law of association as long as it lasts, and there is no moment at which there is a thought belonging to this series, subsequently to which there is not a thought which interprets or repeats it. There is no exception, therefore, to the law that every thought-sign is translated or interpreted in a subsequent one, unless it be that all thought comes to an abrupt and final end in death.

2. The next question is: For what does the thought-sign stand— what does it name—what is its *suppositum?* The outward thing, undoubtedly, when a real outward thing is thought of. But still, as the thought is determined by a previous thought of the same object, it only refers to the thing through denoting this previous thought. Let us suppose, for example, that Toussaint is thought of, and first thought of as a *Negro,* but not distinctly as a man. If this distinctness is afterwards added, it is through the thought that a *Negro* is a *man;* that is to say, the subsequent thought, *man,* refers to the outward thing by being predicated of that previous thought, *Negro,* which has been had of that thing. If we afterwards think of Toussaint as a general, then we think that this Negro, this man, was a general. And so in every case the subsequent thought denotes what was thought in the previous thought.

3. The thought-sign stands for its object in the respect which is thought; that is to say, this respect is the immediate object of conscious-

ness in the thought, or, in other words, it is the thought itself, or at least what the thought is thought to be in the subsequent thought to which it is a sign.

We must now consider two other properties of signs which are of great importance in the theory of cognition. Since a sign is not identical with the thing signified, but differs from the latter in some respects, it must plainly have some characters which belong to it in itself, and have nothing to do with its representative function. These I call the *material* qualities of the sign. As examples of such qualities, take in the word "man" its consisting of three letters—in a picture, its being flat and without relief. In the second place, a sign must be capable of being connected (not in the reason but really) with another sign of the same object, or with the object itself. Thus, words would be of no value at all unless they could be connected into sentences by means of a real copula which joins signs of the same thing. The usefulness of some signs—as a weathercock, a tally, &c.—consists wholly in their being really connected with the very things they signify. In the case of a picture such a connection is not evident, but it exists in the power of association which connects the picture with the brain-sign which labels it. This real, physical connection of a sign with its object, either immediately or by its connection with another sign, I call the *pure demonstrative application* of the sign. Now the representative function of a sign lies neither in its material quality nor in its pure demonstrative application; because it is something which the sign is, not in itself or in a real relation to its object, but which it is *to a thought*, while both of the characters just defined belong to the sign independently of its addressing any thought. And yet if I take all the things which have certain qualities and physically connect them with another series of things, each to each, they become fit to be signs. If they are not regarded as such they are not actually signs, but they are so in the same sense, for example, in which an unseen flower can be said to be *red*, this being also a term relative to a mental affection.

Consider a state of mind which is a conception. It is a conception by virtue of having a *meaning*, a logical comprehension; and if it is applicable to any object, it is because that object has the characters contained in the comprehension of this conception. Now the logical comprehension of a thought is usually said to consist of the thoughts contained in it; but thoughts are events, acts of the mind. Two thoughts are two events separated in time, and one cannot literally be contained in the other. It may be said that all thoughts exactly similar are regarded as one; and that to say that one thought contains another, means that it contains one exactly similar to that other. But how can two thoughts be similar? Two objects can only be *regarded* as similar if they are compared and brought together in the mind. Thoughts have no existence except in the mind; only as they are regarded do they exist. Hence, two thoughts cannot *be* similar unless they are brought together in the mind. But, as to their existence, two thoughts are separated by an interval of time. We are too apt to imagine that we can frame a thought similar to a past thought, by matching it with the latter, as though this past thought were still present to us. But it is plain that the knowledge that one thought is similar to or in any way truly representative of another, cannot be derived from immediate perception, but must be an hypothesis (unquestionably fully justifiable by facts), and that therefore the formation of such a representing thought must be dependent upon a real effective force behind consciousness, and not merely upon a mental comparison. What we must mean, therefore, by saying that one concept is contained in another, is that we normally represent one to be in the other; that is, that we form a particular kind of judgment,* of which the subject signifies one concept and the predicate the other.

No thought in itself, then, no feeling in itself, contains any others, but is absolutely simple and unanalyzable; and to say that it is composed of other thoughts and feelings, is like saying that a movement upon a straight line is composed of the two movements of which it is the resultant; that is to say, it is a metaphor, or fiction, parallel to the truth. Every thought, however artificial and complex, is, so far as it is immediately present, a mere sensation without parts, and therefore, in itself, without similarity to any other, but incomparable with any other and absolutely *sui generis.* † Whatever is wholly incomparable with anything else is wholly inexplicable, because explanation consists in bringing things under general laws or under natural classes. Hence every thought, in so far as it is a feeling of a peculiar sort, is simply an ultimate, inexplicable fact. Yet this does not conflict with my postulate that no fact should be allowed to stand as inexplicable; for, on the one hand, we never can think, "This is present to me," since, before we have time to make the reflection, the sensation is past, and, on the other hand, when once past, we can never bring back the quality of the feeling as it was *in and for itself,* or know what it was like *in itself,* or even discover the existence of this quality except by a corollary from our general theory of ourselves, and then not in its idiosyncrasy, but only as something present. But, as something present, feelings are all alike and require no explanation, since they contain only what is universal. So that nothing which we can truly predicate of feelings is

---

*A judgment concerning a minimum of information, for the theory of which see my paper on Comprehension and Extension, in the *Proceedings of the American Academy of Arts and Sciences,* vol. 7, p. 426. [W2:70–86.]

†Observe that I say *in itself.* I am not so wild as to deny that my sensation of red to-day is like my sensation of red yesterday. I only say that the similarity can *consist* only in the physiological force behind consciousness,—which leads me to say, I recognize this feeling the same as the former one, and so does not consist in a community of sensation.

left inexplicable, but only something which we cannot reflectively know. So that we do not fall into the contradiction of making the Mediate immediate. Finally, no present actual thought (which is a mere feeling) has any meaning, any intellectual value; for this lies not in what is actually thought, but in what this thought may be connected with in representation by subsequent thoughts; so that the meaning of a thought is altogether something virtual. It may be objected, that if no thought has any meaning, all thought is without meaning. But this is a fallacy similar to saying, that, if in no one of the successive spaces which a body fills there is room for motion, there is no room for motion throughout the whole. At no one instant in my state of mind is there cognition or representation, but in the relation of my states of mind at different instants there is.* In short, the Immediate (and therefore in itself unsusceptible of mediation—the Unanalyzable, the Inexplicable, the Unintellectual) runs in a continuous stream through our lives; it is the sum total of consciousness, whose mediation, which is the continuity of it, is brought about by a real effective force behind consciousness.

Thus, we have in thought three elements: 1st, the representative function which makes it a *representation;* 2d, the pure denotative application, or real connection, which brings one thought into *relation* with another; and 3d, the material quality, or how it feels, which gives thought its *quality.* †

That a sensation is not necessarily an intuition, or first impression of sense, is very evident in the case of the sense of beauty; and has been shown, upon page 15, in the case of sound. When the sensation beautiful is determined by previous cognitions, it always arises as a predicate; that is, we think that something is beautiful. Whenever a sensation thus arises in consequence of others, induction shows that those others are more or less complicated. Thus, the sensation of a particular kind of sound arises in consequence of impressions upon the various nerves of the ear being combined in a particular way, and following one another with a certain rapidity. A sensation of color depends upon impressions upon the eye following one another in a regular manner, and with a certain rapidity. The sensation of beauty arises upon a manifold of other impressions. And this will be found to hold good in all cases. Secondly, all these sensations are in themselves simple, or more so than the sensations which give rise to them. Accordingly, a sensation is a simple predicate taken in place of a complex predicate; in other words, it fulfils the function of an hypothesis. But the general

---

*Accordingly, just as we say that a body is in motion, and not that motion is in a body we ought to say that we are in thought, and not that thoughts are in us.

†On quality, relation, and representation, see *Proceedings of the American Academy of Arts and Sciences,* vol. 7, p. 293. [Item 1 above, pp. 1–10.]

principle that every thing to which such and such a sensation belongs, has such and such a complicated series of predicates, is not one determined by reason (as we have seen), but is of an arbitrary nature. Hence, the class of hypothetic inferences which the arising of a sensation resembles, is that of reasoning from definition to definitum, in which the major premise is of an arbitrary nature. Only in this mode of reasoning, this premise is determined by the conventions of language, and expresses the occasion upon which a word is to be used; and in the formation of a sensation, it is determined by the constitution of our nature, and expresses the occasions upon which sensation, or a natural mental sign, arises. Thus, the sensation, so far as it represents something, is determined, according to a logical law, by previous cognitions; that is to say, these cognitions determine that there shall be a sensation. But so far as the sensation is a mere feeling of a particular sort, it is determined only by an inexplicable, occult power; and so far, it is not a representation, but only the material quality of a representation. For just as in reasoning from definition to definitum, it is indifferent to the logician how the defined word shall sound, or how many letters it shall contain, so in the case of this constitutional word, it is not determined by an inward law how it shall feel in itself. A feeling, therefore, as a feeling, is merely the *material quality* of a mental sign.

But there is no feeling which is not also a representation, a predicate of something determined logically by the feelings which precede it. For if there are any such feelings not predicates, they are the emotions. Now every emotion has a subject. If a man is angry, he is saying to himself that this or that is vile and outrageous. If he is in joy, he is saying "this is delicious." If he is wondering, he is saying "this is strange." In short, whenever a man feels, he is thinking of *something*. Even those passions which have no definite object—as melancholy— only come to consciousness through tinging the *objects of thought*. That which makes us look upon the emotions more as affections of self than other cognitions, is that we have found them more dependent upon our accidental situation at the moment than other cognitions; but that is only to say that they are cognitions too narrow to be useful. The emotions, as a little observation will show, arise when our attention is strongly drawn to complex and inconceivable circumstances. Fear arises when we cannot predict our fate; joy, in the case of certain indescribable and peculiarly complex sensations. If there are some indications that something greatly for my interest, and which I have anticipated would happen, may not happen; and if, after weighing probabilities, and inventing safeguards, and straining for further information, I find myself unable to come to any fixed conclusion in reference to the future, in the place of that intellectual hypothetic inference which I seek, the feeling of *anxiety* arises. When something happens for which I cannot account, I *wonder*. When I endeavor to realize to myself what I never can do, a pleasure in the future, I *hope*. "I do not understand you," is the phrase of an angry man. The indescribable, the ineffable, the incomprehensible, commonly excite emotion; but nothing is so chilling as a scientific explanation. Thus an emotion is always a simple predicate substituted by an operation of the mind for a highly complicated predicate. Now if we consider that a very complex predicate demands explanation by means of an hypothesis, that that hypothesis must be a simpler predicate substituted for that complex one; and that when we have an emotion, an hypothesis, strictly speaking, is hardly possible—the analogy of the parts played by emotion and hypothesis is very striking. There is, it is true, this difference between an emotion and an intellectual hypothesis, that we have reason to say in the case of the latter, that to whatever the simple hypothetic predicate can be applied, of that the complex predicate is true; whereas, in the case of an emotion this is a proposition for which no reason can be given, but which is determined merely by our emotional constitution. But this corresponds precisely to the difference between hypothesis and reasoning from definition to definitum, and thus it would appear that emotion is nothing but sensation. There appears to be a difference, however, between emotion and sensation, and I would state it as follows:

There is some reason to think that, corresponding to every feeling within us, some motion takes place in our bodies. This property of the thought-sign, since it has no rational dependence upon the meaning of the sign, may be compared with what I have called the material quality of the sign; but it differs from the latter inasmuch as it is not essentially necessary that it should be felt in order that there should be any thought-sign. In the case of a sensation, the manifold of impressions which precede and determine it are not of a kind, the bodily motion corresponding to which comes from any large ganglion or from the brain, and probably for this reason the sensation produces no great commotion in the bodily organism; and the sensation itself is not a thought which has a very strong influence upon the current of thought except by virtue of the information it may serve to afford. An emotion, on the other hand, comes much later in the development of thought—I mean, further from the first beginning of the cognition of its object—and the thoughts which determine it already have motions corresponding to them in the brain, or the chief ganglion; consequently, it produces large movements in the body, and independently of its representative value, strongly affects the current of thought. The animal motions to which I allude, are, in the first place and obviously, blushing, blenching, staring, smiling, scowling, pouting, laughing, weeping, sobbing, wriggling, flinching, trembling, being petrified, sighing, sniffing, shrugging, groaning, heartsinking, trepidation, swelling of the heart, etc., etc. To these may, perhaps, be added, in the second place, other more complicated actions, which nevertheless spring from a direct impulse and not from deliberation.

That which distinguishes both sensations proper and emotions from the feeling of a thought, is that in the case of the two former the material quality is made prominent, because the thought has no relation of reason to the thoughts which determine it, which exists in the last case and detracts from the attention given to the mere feeling. By there being no relation of reason to the determining thoughts, I mean that there is nothing in the content of the thought which explains why it should arise only on occasion of these determining thoughts. If there is such a relation of reason, if the thought is essentially limited in its application to these objects, then the thought comprehends a thought other than itself; in other words, it is then a complex thought. An incomplex thought can, therefore, be nothing but a sensation or emotion, having no rational character. This is very different from the ordinary doctrine, according to which the very highest and most metaphysical conceptions are absolutely simple. I shall be asked how such a conception of a *being* is to be analyzed, or whether I can ever define *one*, *two*, and *three*, without a diallele. Now I shall admit at once that neither of these conceptions can be separated into two others higher than itself; and in that sense, therefore, I fully admit that certain very metaphysical and eminently intellectual notions are absolutely simple. But though these concepts cannot be defined by genus and difference, there is another way in which they can be defined. All determination is by negation; we can first recognize any character only by putting an object which possesses it into comparison with an object which possesses it not. A conception, therefore, which was quite universal in every respect would be unrecognizable and impossible. We do not obtain the conception of Being, in the sense implied in the copula, by observing that all the things which we can think of have something in common, for there is no such thing to be observed. We get it by reflecting upon signs—words or thoughts;—we observe that different predicates may be attached to the same subject, and that each makes some conception applicable to the subject; then we imagine that a subject has something true of it merely because a predicate (no matter what) is attached to it,—and that we call Being. The conception of being is, therefore, a conception about a sign—a thought, or word;—and since it is not applicable to every sign, it is not primarily universal, although it is so in its mediate application to things. Being, therefore, may be defined; it may be defined, for example, as that which is common to the objects included in any class, and to the objects not included in the same class. But it is nothing new to say that metaphysical conceptions are primarily and at bottom thoughts about words, or thoughts about thoughts; it is the doctrine both of Aristotle (whose categories are parts of speech) and of Kant (whose categories are the characters of different kinds of propositions).

Sensation and the power of abstraction or attention may be regarded as, in one sense, the sole constituents of all thought. Having considered the former, let us now attempt some analysis of the latter. By the force of attention, an emphasis is put upon one of the objective elements of consciousness. This emphasis is, therefore, not itself an object of immediate consciousness; and in this respect it differs entirely from a feeling. Therefore, since the emphasis, nevertheless, consists in some effect upon consciousness, and so can exist only so far as it affects our knowledge; and since an act cannot be supposed to determine that which precedes it in time, this act can consist only in the capacity which the cognition emphasized has for producing an effect upon memory, or otherwise influencing subsequent thought. This is confirmed by the fact that attention is a matter of continuous quantity; for continuous quantity, so far as we know it, reduces itself in the last analysis to time. Accordingly, we find that attention does, in fact, produce a very great effect upon subsequent thought. In the first place, it strongly affects memory, a thought being remembered for a longer time the greater the attention originally paid to it. In the second place, the greater the attention, the closer the connection and the more accurate the logical sequence of thought. In the third place, by attention a thought may be recovered which has been forgotten. From these facts, we gather that attention is the power by which thought at one time is connected with and made to relate to thought at another time; or, to apply the conception of thought as a sign, that it is the *pure demonstrative application* of a thought-sign.

Attention is roused when the same phenomenon presents itself repeatedly on different occasions, or the same predicate in different subjects. We see that A has a certain character, that B has the same, C has the same; and this excites our attention, so that we say, "*These* have this character." Thus attention is an act of induction; but it is an induction which does not increase our knowledge, because our "these" covers nothing but the instances experienced. It is, in short, an argument from enumeration.

Attention produces effects upon the nervous system. These effects are habits, or nervous associations. A habit arises, when, having had the sensation of performing a certain act, m, on several occasions a, b, c, we come to do it upon every occurrence of the general event, l, of which a, b, and c are special cases. That is to say, by the cognition that

Every case of a, b, or c, is a case of m,

is determined the cognition that

Every case of l is a case of m.

Thus the formation of a habit is an induction, and is therefore necessarily connected with attention or abstraction. Voluntary actions result from the sensations produced by habits, as instinctive actions result from our original nature.

We have thus seen that every sort of modification of consciousness—Attention, Sensation, and Understanding—is an inference. But the objection may be made that inference deals only with general terms, and that an image, or absolutely singular representation, cannot therefore be inferred.

"Singular" and "individual" are equivocal terms. A singular may mean that which can be but in one place at one time. In this sense it is not opposed to general. *The sun* is a singular in this sense, but, as is explained in every good treatise on logic, it is a general term. I may have a very general conception of Hermolaus Barbarus,[10] but still I conceive him only as able to be in one place at one time. When an image is said to be singular, it is meant that it is absolutely determinate in all respects. Every possible character, or the negative thereof, must be true of such an image. In the words of the most eminent expounder of the doctrine, the image of a man "must be either of a white, or a black, or a tawny; a straight, or a crooked; a tall, or a low, or a middle-sized man."[11] It must be of a man with his mouth open or his mouth shut, whose hair is precisely of such and such a shade, and whose figure has precisely such and such proportions. No statement of Locke has been so scouted by all friends of images as his denial that the "idea" of a triangle must be either of an obtuse-angled, right-angled, or acute-angled triangle.[12] In fact, the image of a triangle must be of one, each of whose angles is of a certain number of degrees, minutes, and seconds.

This being so, it is apparent that no man has a *true* image of the road to his office, or of any other real thing. Indeed he has no image of it at all unless he can not only recognize it, but imagines it (truly or falsely) in all its infinite details. This being the case, it becomes very doubtful whether we ever have any such thing as an image in our imagination. Please, reader, to look at a bright red book, or other brightly colored object, and then to shut your eyes and say whether you *see* that color, whether brightly or faintly—whether, indeed, there is anything like sight there. Hume and the other followers of Berkeley maintain that there is no difference between the sight and the memory of the red book except in "their different degrees of force and vivacity." "The colors which the memory employs," says Hume, "are faint and dull compared with those in which our original perceptions are clothed."[13] If this were a correct statement of the difference, we should remember the book as being less red than it is; whereas, in fact, we remember the color with very great precision for a few moments [please to test this point, reader], although we do not see any thing like it. We carry away absolutely nothing of the color except the *consciousness that we could recognize it.* As a further proof of this, I will request the reader to try a little experiment. Let him call up, if he can, the image of a horse—not of one which he has ever seen, but of an imaginary one,—and before reading further let him by contemplation* fix the image in his memory . . . . . Has the reader done as requested? for I protest that it is not fair play to read further without doing so.— Now, the reader can say in general of what color that horse was, whether grey, bay, or black. But he probably cannot say *precisely* of what shade it was. He cannot state this as exactly as he could just after having *seen* such a horse. But why, if he had an image in his mind which no more had the general color than it had the particular shade, has the latter vanished so instantaneously from his memory while the former still remains? It may be replied, that we always forget the details before we do the more general characters; but that this answer is insufficient is, I think, shown by the extreme disproportion between the length of time that the exact shade of something looked at is remembered as compared with that instantaneous oblivion to the exact shade of the thing imagined, and the but slightly superior vividness of the memory of the thing seen as compared with the memory of the thing imagined.

The nominalists, I suspect, confound together thinking a triangle without thinking that it is either equilateral, isosceles, or scalene, and thinking a triangle without thinking whether it is equilateral, isosceles, or scalene.

It is important to remember that we have no intuitive power of

*No person whose native tongue is English will need to be informed that contemplation is essentially (1) protracted (2) voluntary, and (3) an action, and that it is never used for that which is set forth to the mind in this act. A foreigner can convince himself of this by the proper study of English writers. Thus, Locke (*Essay concerning Human Understanding*, Book II, chap. 19, §1) says, "If it [an idea] be held there [in view] long under attentive consideration, 'tis *Contemplation*"; and again (*Ibid.*, Book II, chap. 10, §1), "Keeping the *Idea,* which is brought into it [the mind] for some time actually in view, which is called *Contemplation.*" This term is therefore unfitted to translate *Anschauung*; for this latter does not imply an act which is necessarily protracted or voluntary, and denotes most usually a mental presentation, sometimes a faculty, less often the reception of an impression in the mind, and seldom, if ever, an action. To the translation of *Anschauung* by intuition, there is, at least, no such insuperable objection. Etymologically the two words precisely correspond. The original philosophical meaning of intuition was a cognition of the present manifold in that character; and it is now commonly used, as a modern writer says, "to include all the products of the perceptive (external or internal) and imaginative faculties; every act of consciousness, in short, of which the immediate object is an *individual,* thing, act, or state of mind, presented under the condition of distinct existence in space and time."[14] Finally, we have the authority of Kant's own example for translating his *Anschauung* by *Intuitus*;[15] and, indeed, this is the common usage of Germans writing Latin. Moreover, *intuitiv* frequently replaces *anschauend* or *anschaulich.* If this constitutes a misunderstanding of Kant, it is one which is shared by himself and nearly all his countrymen.

distinguishing between one subjective mode of cognition and another; and hence often think that something is presented to us as a picture, while it is really constructed from slight data by the understanding. This is the case with dreams, as is shown by the frequent impossibility of giving an intelligible account of one without adding something which we feel was not in the dream itself. Many dreams, of which the waking memory makes elaborate and consistent stories, must probably have been in fact mere jumbles of these feelings of the ability to recognize this and that which I have just alluded to.

I will now go so far as to say that we have no images even in actual perception. It will be sufficient to prove this in the case of vision; for if no picture is seen when we look at an object, it will not be claimed that hearing, touch, and the other senses, are superior to sight in this respect. That the picture is not painted on the nerves of the retina is absolutely certain, if, as physiologists inform us, these nerves are needle-points pointing to the light and at distances considerably greater than the *minimum visibile.* [16] The same thing is shown by our not being able to perceive that there is a large blind spot near the middle of the retina. If, then, we have a picture before us when we see, it is one constructed by the mind at the suggestion of previous sensations. Supposing these sensations to be signs, the understanding by reasoning from them could attain all the knowledge of outward things which we derive from sight, while the sensations are quite inadequate to forming an image or representation absolutely determinate. If we have such an image or picture, we must have in our minds a representation of a surface which is only a part of every surface we see, and we must see that each part, however small, has such and such a color. If we look from some distance at a speckled surface, it seems as if we did not see whether it were speckled or not; but if we have an image before us, it must appear to us either as speckled, or as not speckled. Again, the eye by education comes to distinguish minute differences of color; but if we see only absolutely determinate images, we must, no less before our eyes are trained than afterwards, see each color as particularly such and such a shade. Thus to suppose that we have an image before us when we see, is not only a hypothesis which explains nothing whatever, but is one which actually creates difficulties which require new hypotheses in order to explain them away.

One of these difficulties arises from the fact that the details are less easily distinguished than, and forgotten before, the general circumstances. Upon this theory, the general features exist in the details: the details are, in fact, the whole picture. It seems, then, very strange that that which exists only secondarily in the picture should make more impression than the picture itself. It is true that in an old painting the details are not easily made out; but this is because we know that the blackness is the result of time, and is no part of the picture itself. There is no difficulty in making out the details of the picture as it looks at present; the only difficulty is in guessing what it used to be. But if we have a picture on the retina, the minutest details are there as much as, nay, more than, the general outline and significancy of it. Yet that which must actually be seen, it is extremely difficult to recognize; while that which is only abstracted from what is seen is very obvious.

But the conclusive argument against our having any images, or absolutely determinate representations in perception, is that in that case we have the materials in each such representation for an infinite amount of conscious cognition, which we yet never become aware of. Now there is no meaning in saying that we have something in our minds which never has the least effect on what we are conscious of knowing. The most that can be said is, that when we see we are put in a condition in which we are able to get a very large and perhaps indefinitely great amount of knowledge of the visible qualities of objects.

Moreover, that perceptions are not absolutely determinate and singular is obvious from the fact that each sense is an abstracting mechanism. Sight by itself informs us only of colors and forms. No one can pretend that the images of sight are determinate in reference to taste. They are, therefore, so far general that they are neither sweet nor non-sweet, bitter nor non-bitter, having savor or insipid.

The next question is whether we have any general conceptions except in judgments. In perception, where we know a thing as existing, it is plain that there is a judgment that the thing exists, since a mere general concept of a thing is in no case a cognition of it as existing. It has usually been said, however, that we can call up any concept without making any judgment; but it seems that in this case we only arbitrarily suppose ourselves to have an experience. In order to conceive the number 7, I suppose, that is, I arbitrarily make the hypothesis or judgment, that there are certain points before my eyes, and I judge that these are seven. This seems to be the most simple and rational view of the matter, and I may add that it is the one which has been adopted by the best logicians. If this be the case, what goes by the name of the association of images is in reality an association of judgments. The association of ideas is said to proceed according to three principles—those of resemblance, of contiguity, and of causality. But it would be equally true to say that signs denote what they do on the three principles of resemblance, contiguity, and causality. There can be no question that anything *is* a sign of whatever is associated with it by resemblance, by contiguity, or by causality: nor can there be any doubt that any sign recalls the thing signified. So, then, the association of ideas consists in this, that a judgment occasions another judgment, of which it is the sign. Now this is nothing less nor more than inference.

Everything in which we take the least interest creates in us its own particular emotion, however slight this may be. This emotion is a sign and a predicate of the thing. Now, when a thing resembling this thing is presented to us, a similar emotion arises; hence, we immediately infer that the latter is like the former. A formal logician of the old school may say, that in logic no term can enter into the conclusion which had not been contained in the premises, and that therefore the suggestion of something new must be essentially different from inference. But I reply that that rule of logic applies only to those arguments which are technically called completed. We can and do reason—

> Elias was a man;
> ∴ He was mortal.

And this argument is just as valid as the full syllogism, although it is so only because the major premise of the latter happens to be true. If to pass from the judgment "Elias was a man" to the judgment "Elias was mortal," without actually saying to one's self that "All men are mortal," is not inference, then the term "inference" is used in so restricted a sense that inferences hardly occur outside of a logic-book.

What is here said of association by resemblance is true of all association. All association is by signs. Everything has its subjective or emotional qualities, which are attributed either absolutely or relatively, or by conventional imputation to anything which is a sign of it. And so we reason,

> The sign is such and such;
> ∴ The sign is that thing.

This conclusion receiving, however, a modification, owing to other considerations, so as to become—

> The sign is almost (is representative of) that thing.

We come now to the consideration of the last of the four principles whose consequences we were to trace; namely, that the absolutely incognizable is absolutely inconceivable. That upon Cartesian principles the very realities of things can never be known in the least, most competent persons must long ago have been convinced. Hence the breaking forth of idealism, which is essentially anti-Cartesian, in every direction, whether among empiricists (Berkeley, Hume), or among noologists (Hegel, Fichte). The principle now brought under discussion is directly idealistic; for, since the meaning of a word is the conception it conveys, the absolutely incognizable has no meaning because no conception attaches to it. It is, therefore, a meaningless word; and, consequently, whatever is meant by any term as "the real" is cognizable in some degree, and so is of the nature of a cognition, in the objective sense of that term.

At any moment we are in possession of certain information, that is, of cognitions which have been logically derived by induction and hypothesis from previous cognitions which are less general, less distinct, and of which we have a less lively consciousness. These in their turn have been derived from others still less general, less distinct, and less vivid; and so on back to the ideal* first, which is quite singular, and quite out of consciousness. This ideal first is the particular thing-in-itself. It does not exist *as such.* That is, there is no thing which is in-itself in the sense of not being relative to the mind, though things which are relative to the mind doubtless are, apart from that relation. The cognitions which thus reach us by this infinite series of inductions and hypotheses (which though infinite *a parte ante logice,* is yet as one continuous process not without a beginning *in time*) are of two kinds, the true and the untrue, or cognitions whose objects are *real* and those whose objects are *unreal.* And what do we mean by the real? It is a conception which we must first have had when we discovered that there was an unreal, an illusion; that is, when we first corrected ourselves. Now the distinction for which alone this fact logically called, was between an *ens* relative to private inward determinations, to the negations belonging to idiosyncrasy, and an *ens* such as would stand in the long run. The real, then, is that which, sooner or later, information and reasoning would finally result in, and which is therefore independent of the vagaries of me and you. Thus, the very origin of the conception of reality shows that this conception essentially involves the notion of a COMMUNITY, without definite limits, and capable of an indefinite increase of knowledge. And so those two series of cognitions—the real and the unreal—consist of those which, at a time sufficiently future, the community will always continue to reaffirm; and of those which, under the same conditions, will ever after be denied. Now, a proposition whose falsity can never be discovered, and the error of which therefore is absolutely incognizable, contains, upon our principle, absolutely no error. Consequently, that which is thought in these cognitions is the real, as it really is. There is nothing, then, to prevent our knowing outward things as they really are, and it is most likely that we do thus know them in numberless cases, although we can never be absolutely certain of doing so in any special case.

---

*By an ideal, I mean the limit which the possible cannot attain.

But it follows that since no cognition of ours is absolutely determinate, generals must have a real existence. Now this scholastic realism is usually set down as a belief in metaphysical fictions. But, in fact, a realist is simply one who knows no more recondite reality than that which is represented in a true representation. Since, therefore, the word "man" is true of something, that which "man" means is real. The nominalist must admit that man is truly applicable to something; but he believes that there is beneath this a thing in itself, an incognizable reality. His is the metaphysical figment. Modern nominalists are mostly superficial men, who do not know, as the more thorough Roscellinus and Occam did, that a reality which has no representation is one which has no relation and no quality. The great argument for nominalism is that there is no man unless there is some particular man. That, however, does not affect the realism of Scotus; for although there is no man of whom all further determination can be denied, yet there is a man, abstraction being made of all further determination. There is a real difference between man irrespective of what the other determinations may be, and man with this or that particular series of determinations, although undoubtedly this difference is only relative to the mind and not *in re.* Such is the position of Scotus.* Occam's great objection is, there can be no real distinction which is not *in re,* in the thing-in-itself; but this begs the question, for it is itself based only on the notion that reality is something independent of representative relation.†

Such being the nature of reality in general, in what does the reality of the mind consist? We have seen that the content of consciousness, the entire phenomenal manifestation of mind, is a sign resulting from inference. Upon our principle, therefore, that the absolutely incognizable does not exist, so that the phenomenal manifestation of a substance is the substance, we must conclude that the mind is a sign developing according to the laws of inference. What distinguishes a man from a word? There is a distinction doubtless. The material qualities, the forces which constitute the pure denotative application, and the meaning of the human sign, are all exceedingly complicated in comparison with those of the word. But these differences are only relative. What other is there? It may be said that man is conscious, while a word is not. But consciousness is a very vague term. It may mean that emotion which accompanies the reflection that we have animal life. This is a consciousness which is dimmed

---

*"Eadem natura est, quæ in existentia per gradum singularitatis est determinata, et in intellectu, hoc est ut habet relationem ad intellectum ut cognitum ad cognoscens, est indeterminata."—*Quæstiones Subtillissimæ,* lib. 7, qu. 18.[17]

†See his argument *Summa logices,* part i, cap. 16.[18]

when animal life is at its ebb in old age, or sleep, but which is not dimmed when the spiritual life is at its ebb; which is the more lively the better *animal* a man is, but which is not so, the better *man* he is. We do not attribute this sensation to words, because we have reason to believe that it is dependent upon the possession of an animal body. But this consciousness, being a mere sensation, is only a part of the *material quality* of the man-sign. Again, consciousness is sometimes used to signify the *I think,* or unity in thought; but this unity is nothing but consistency, or the recognition of it. Consistency belongs to every sign, so far as it is a sign; and therefore every sign, since it signifies primarily that it is a sign, signifies its own consistency. The man-sign acquires information, and comes to mean more than he did before. But so do words. Does not electricity mean more now than it did in the days of Franklin? Man makes the word, and the word means nothing which the man has not made it mean, and that only to some man. But since man can think only by means of words or other external symbols, these might turn round and say: "You mean nothing which we have not taught you, and then only so far as you address some word as the interpretant of your thought." In fact, therefore, men and words reciprocally educate each other; each increase of a man's information involves and is involved by, a corresponding increase of a word's information.

Without fatiguing the reader by stretching this parallelism too far, it is sufficient to say that there is no element whatever of man's consciousness which has not something corresponding to it in the word; and the reason is obvious. It is that the word or sign which man uses *is* the man himself. For, as the fact that every thought is a sign, taken in conjunction with the fact that life is a train of thought, proves that man is a sign; so, that every thought is an *external* sign, proves that man is an external sign. That is to say, the man and the external sign are identical, in the same sense in which the words *homo* and *man* are identical. Thus my language is the sum total of myself; for the man is the thought.

It is hard for man to understand this, because he persists in identifying himself with his will, his power over the animal organism, with brute force. Now the organism is only an instrument of thought. But the identity of a man consists in the *consistency* of what he does and thinks, and consistency is the intellectual character of a thing; that is, is its expressing something.

Finally, as what anything really is, is what it may finally come to be known to be in the ideal state of complete information, so that reality depends on the ultimate decision of the community; so thought is what it is, only by virtue of its addressing a future thought which is in its value as thought identical with it, though more developed. In this way, the existence of thought now, depends on what is to be hereafter; so that it has only a potential existence, dependent on the future thought of the community.

The individual man, since his separate existence is manifested only by ignorance and error, so far as he is anything apart from his fellows, and from what he and they are to be, is only a negation. This is man,

> proud man,
> Most ignorant of what he's most assured,
> His glassy essence.[19]

4

Grounds of Validity of the Laws of Logic: Further Consequences of Four Incapacities

P 41: Journal of Speculative Philosophy *2 (1869):193–208. [Also published in W2:242–72 and in CP 5.318–57. Changes in an offprint (MS 593), prepared as essay 6 of his 1893 "Search for a Method," are recorded in the Notes.] In this article, the culmination of the Cognition Series, Peirce works out a rationale for the objective validity of the laws of logic and, by linking epistemology with a social theory of logic, grounds induction in altruistic sentiments. He also discusses a version of the liar paradox and offers a solution based on the supposition that "every proposition asserts its own truth," and he makes his first published reference to De Morgan's work on the logic of relations.*

If, as I maintained in an article in the last number of this Journal,[1] every judgment results from inference, to doubt every inference is to doubt everything. It has often been argued that absolute scepticism is self-contradictory; but this is a mistake: and even if it were not so, it would be no argument against the absolute sceptic, inasmuch as he does not admit that no contradictory propositions are true. Indeed, it would be impossible to move such a man, for his scepticism consists in considering every argument and never deciding upon its validity; he would, therefore, act in this way in reference to the arguments brought against him.

But then there are no such beings as absolute sceptics. Every exercise of the mind consists in inference, and so, though there are inanimate objects without beliefs, there are[2] no intelligent beings in that condition.

Yet it is quite possible that a person should doubt every principle of inference. He may not have studied logic, and though a logical formula may sound very obviously true to him, he may feel a little uncertain whether some subtle deception may not lurk in it. Indeed,

I certainly shall have, among the most cultivated and respected of my readers, those who deny that those laws of logic which men generally admit have universal validity. But I address myself, also, to those who have no such doubts, for even to them it may be interesting to consider how it is that these principles come to be true. Finally, having put forth in former numbers of this Journal[3] some rather heretical principles of philosophical research, one of which is that nothing can be admitted to be absolutely inexplicable, it behooves me to take up a challenge which has been given me to show how upon my principles the validity of the laws of logic can be other than inexplicable.

I shall be arrested, at the outset, by a sweeping objection to my whole undertaking. It will be said that my deduction of logical principles, being itself an argument, depends for its whole virtue upon the truth of the very principles in question; so that whatever my proof may be, it must take for granted the very things to be proved. But to this I reply, that I am neither addressing absolute sceptics, nor men in any state of fictitious doubt whatever. I require the reader to be candid; and if he becomes convinced of a conclusion, to admit it. There is nothing to prevent a man's perceiving the force of certain special arguments, although he does not yet know that a certain general law of arguments holds good; for the general rule may hold good in some cases and not in others. A man may reason well without understanding the principles of reasoning, just as he may play billiards well without understanding analytical mechanics. If you, the reader, actually find that my arguments have a convincing force with you, it is a mere pretence to call them illogical.

That if one sign denotes generally everything denoted by a second, and this second denotes generally everything denoted by a third, then the first denotes generally everything denoted by the third, is not doubted by anybody who distinctly apprehends the meaning of these words. The deduction of the general form of syllogism, therefore, will consist only of an explanation of the *suppositio communis.** Now, what

---

*The word *suppositio* is one of the useful technical terms of the middle ages which was condemned by the purists of the *renaissance* as incorrect. The early logicians made a distinction between *significatio* and *suppositio*. *Significatio* is defined as "rei per vocem secundum placitum representatio."[4] It is a mere affair of lexicography, and depends on a special convention *(secundum placitum)*, and not on a general principle. *Suppositio* belongs, not directly to the *vox*, but to the *vox* as having this or that *significatio*. "Unde significatio prior est suppositione et differunt in hoc, quia significatio est vocis, suppositio vero est termini jam compositi ex voce et significatione." The various *suppositiones* which may belong to one word with one *significatio* are the different senses in which the word may be taken, according to the general principles of the language or of logic. Thus, the word *table* has different *significationes* in the expressions "table of logarithms" and "writing-table"; but the word *man* has one and the same *significatio*, and only different *suppositiones*, in the following sentences: "A man is an animal," "a butcher is a man," "man cooks his food," "man appeared upon the earth at such a date," &c. Some later writers have endeavored to make *"acceptio"* do service for *"suppositio"*; but it seems to

the formal logician means by an expression of the form, "Every M is P," is that anything of which M is predicable is P; thus, if S is M, that S is P. The premise that "Every M is P" may, therefore, be denied; but to admit it, unambiguously, in the sense intended, is to admit that the inference is good that S is P if S is M. He, therefore, who does not deny that S is P—M, S, P, being any terms such that S is M and every M is P—denies nothing that the formal logician maintains in reference to this matter; and he who does deny this, simply is deceived by an ambiguity of language. How we come to make any judgments in the sense of the above "Every M is P," may be understood from the theory of reality put forth in the article in the last number.[5] It was there shown that real things are of a cognitive and therefore significative nature, so that the real is that which signifies something real. Consequently, to predicate anything of anything real is to predicate it of that of which that subject [the real] is itself predicated; for to predicate one thing of another is to state that the former is a sign of the latter.

These considerations show the reason of the validity of the formula,

$$S \text{ is } M; \ M \text{ is } P:$$
$$\therefore S \text{ is } P.$$

They hold good whatever S and P may be, provided that they be such that any middle term between them can be found. That P should be a negative term, therefore, or that S should be a particular term, would not interfere at all with the validity of this formula. Hence, the following formulæ are also valid:

$$S \text{ is } M; \ M \text{ is not } P:$$
$$\therefore S \text{ is not } P.$$

$$\text{Some } S \text{ is } M; \ M \text{ is } P:$$
$$\therefore \text{Some } S \text{ is } P.$$

$$\text{Some } S \text{ is } M; \ M \text{ is not } P:$$
$$\therefore \text{Some } S \text{ is not } P.$$

Moreover, as all that class of inferences which depend upon the introduction of relative terms can be reduced to the general form, they also are shown to be valid. Thus, it is proved to be correct to reason thus:

Every relation of a subject to its predicate is
a relation of the relative "not X'd, except

---

by the X of some," to its correlate, where X
is any relative I please.

Every relation of "man" to "animal" is a
relation of a subject to its predicate.
∴ Every relation of "man" to "animal" is a relation
of the relative "not X'd, except by the X of
some," to its correlate, where X is any
relative I please.

Every relation of the relative "not X'd, except
by the X of some," to its correlate, where X
is any relative I please, is a relation of the
relative "not *headed,* except by the *head* of
some," to its correlate.
∴ Every relation of "man" to "animal" is a relation
of the relative "not headed, except by the
head of some," to its correlate.*

At the same time, as will be seen from this example, the proof of
the validity of these inferences depends upon the assumption of the
truth of certain general statements concerning relatives. These formulæ can all be deduced from the principle, that in a system of signs
in which no sign is taken in two different senses, two signs which differ
only in their manner of representing their object, but which are equivalent in meaning, can always be substituted for one another. Any case
of the falsification of this principle would be a case of the dependence
of the mode of existence of the thing represented upon the mode of this
or that representation of it, which, as has been shown in the article in
the last number, is contrary to the nature of reality.

The next formula of syllogism to be considered is the following:

S is other than P; M is P:
∴ S is other than M.

The meaning of "not" or "other than" seems to have greatly perplexed
the German logicians, and it may be, therefore, that it is used in
different senses. If so, I propose to defend the validity of the above
formula only when *other than* is used in a particular sense. By saying
that one thing or class is other than a second, I mean that any third
whatever is identical with the class which is composed of that third
and of whatever is, at once, the first and second. For example, if I say
that rats are not mice, I mean that any third class as dogs is identical

---

*"If any one will by ordinary syllogism prove that because every man is an animal,
therefore every head of a man is a head of an animal, I shall be ready to—set him another
question."—*De Morgan:* "On the Syllogism No. IV, and on the Logic of Relations."

with dogs and[6] rats-which-are-mice; that is to say, the addition of rats-which-are-mice, to anything, leaves the latter just what it was before. This being all that I mean by S is other than P, I mean absolutely the same thing when I say that S is other than P, that I do when I say that P is other than S; and the same when I say that S is other than M, that I do when I say that M is other than S. Hence the above formula is only another way of writing the following:

M is P; P is not S:
∴ M is not S.

But we have already seen that this is valid.

A very similar formula to the above is the following:

S is M; some S is P:
∴ Some M is P.

By saying that some of a class is of any character, I mean simply that no statement which implies that none of that class is of that character is true. But to say that none of that class is of that character, is, as I take the word "not," to say that nothing of that character is of that class. Consequently, to say that some of A is B, is, as I understand words and in the only sense in which I defend this formula, to say that some B is A. In this way the formula is reduced to the following, which has already been shown to be valid:

Some P is S; S is M:
∴ Some P is M.

The only demonstrative syllogisms which are not included among the above forms are the Theophrastean moods, which are all easily reduced by means of simple conversions.

Let us now consider what can be said against all this, and let us take up the objections which have actually been made to the syllogistic formulæ, beginning with those which are of a general nature and then examining those sophisms which have been pronounced irresolvable by the rules of ordinary logic.

It is a very ancient notion that no proof can be of any value, because it rests on premises which themselves equally require proof, which again must rest on other premises, and so back to infinity. This really does show that nothing can be proved beyond the possibility[7] of a doubt; that no argument could be legitimately used against an absolute sceptic; and that inference is only a transition from one cognition to another, and not the creation of a cognition. But the objection is intended to go much further than this, and to show (as it certainly seems to do) that inference not only cannot produce *infallible* cognition, but that it cannot *produce* cognition at all. It is true, that since some judgment precedes every judgment inferred, either the first premises were not inferred, or there have been no first premises. But it does not follow that because there has been no first in a series, therefore that series has had no beginning in time; for the series may be *continuous*,[8] and may have begun gradually, as was shown in an article in No. 3 of this volume,[9] where this difficulty has already been resolved.

A somewhat similar objection has been made by Locke[10] and others, to the effect that the ordinary demonstrative syllogism is a *petitio principii,* inasmuch as the conclusion is already implicitly stated in the major premise. Take, for example, the syllogism,

> All men are mortal;
> Socrates is a man:
> ∴ Socrates is mortal.

This attempt to prove that Socrates is mortal begs the question, it is said, since if the conclusion is denied by any one, he thereby denies that all men are mortal. But what such considerations really prove is that the syllogism is demonstrative. To call it a *petitio principii* is a mere confusion of language. It is strange that philosophers, who are so suspicious of the words *virtual* and *potential,* should have allowed this "implicit" to pass unchallenged. A *petitio principii* consists in reasoning from the unknown to the unknown. Hence, a logician who is simply engaged in stating what general forms of argument are valid, can, at most, have nothing more to do with the consideration of this fallacy than to note those cases in which from logical principles a premise of a certain form cannot be better known than a conclusion of the corresponding form. But it is plainly beyond the province of the logician, who has only proposed to state what forms of facts involve what others, to inquire whether man can have a knowledge of universal propositions without a knowledge of every particular contained under them, by means of natural insight, divine revelation, induction, or testimony. The only *petitio principii,* therefore, which he can notice is the assumption of the conclusion itself in the premise; and this, no doubt, those who call the syllogism a *petitio principii* believe is done in that formula. But the proposition "All men are mortal" does not in itself involve the statement that Socrates is mortal, but only that "whatever has man truly predicated of it is mortal." In other words, the *conclusion* is not involved in the meaning of the premise, but only the *validity of the syllogism.* So that this objection merely amounts to arguing that the syllogism is not valid, because it is demonstrative.*

---

*Mr. Mill thinks the syllogism is merely a formula for recalling forgotten facts.[11] Whether he means to deny, what all logicians since Kant have held, that the syllogism serves to render confused thoughts distinct, or whether he does not know that this is the usual doctrine, does not appear.

A much more interesting objection is that a syllogism is a purely mechanical process. It proceeds according to a bare rule or formula; and a machine might be constructed which would so transpose the terms of premises. This being so (and it is so), it is argued that this cannot be *thought;* that there is no life in it. Swift has ridiculed the syllogism in the "Voyage to Laputa," by describing a machine for making science:

> By this contrivance, the most ignorant person, at a reasonable charge, and with little bodily labor, might write books in philosophy, poetry, politics, laws, mathematics, and theology, without the least assistance from genius or study.[12]

The idea involved in this objection seems to be that it requires mind to apply any formula or use any machine. If, then, this mind is itself only another formula, it requires another mind behind it to set it into operation, and so on *ad infinitum.* This objection fails in much the same way that the first one which we considered failed. It is as though a man should address a land surveyor as follows:—"You do not make a true representation of the land; you only measure lengths from point to point—that is to say, lines. If you observe angles, it is only to solve triangles and obtain the lengths of their sides. And when you come to make your map, you use a pencil which can only make lines, again. So, you have to do solely with lines. But the land is a surface; and no number of lines, however great, will make any surface, however small. You, therefore, fail entirely to represent the land." The surveyor, I think, would reply, "Sir, you have proved that my lines cannot make up the land, and that, therefore, my map *is not* the land. I never pretended that it was. But that does not prevent it from truly representing the land, as far as it goes. It cannot, indeed, represent every blade of grass; but it does not represent that there is not a blade of grass where there is. To abstract from a circumstance is not to deny it." Suppose the objector were, at this point, to say, "To abstract from a circumstance *is* to deny it. Wherever your map does not represent a blade of grass, it represents there is no blade of grass. Let us take things on their own valuation." Would not the surveyor reply: "This map is my description of the country. Its own valuation can be nothing but what I say, and all the world understands, that I mean by it. Is it very unreasonable that I should demand to be taken as I mean, especially when I succeed in making myself understood?" What the objector's reply to this question would be, I leave it to any one to say who thinks his position well taken. Now this line of objection is parallel to that which is made against the syllogism. It is shown that no number of syllogisms can constitute the sum total of any mental action, however restricted. This may be freely granted, and yet it will not follow that the syllogism does not truly represent the mental action, as far as it purports to represent it at all. There is reason to believe that the action of the mind is, as it were, a continuous movement. Now the doctrine embodied in syllogistic formulæ (so far as it applies to the mind at all) is, that if two successive positions, occupied by the mind in this movement, be taken, they will be found to have certain relations. It is true that no number of successions of positions can make up a continuous movement; and this, I suppose, is what is meant by saying that a syllogism is a dead formula, while thinking is a living process. But the reply is that the syllogism is not intended to represent the mind, as to its life or deadness, but only as to the relation of its different judgments concerning the same thing. And it should be added that the relation between syllogism and thought does not spring from considerations of formal logic, but from those of psychology. All that the formal logician has to say is, that if facts capable of expression in such and such forms of words are true, another fact whose expression is related in a certain way to the expression of these others is also true.

Hegel taught that ordinary reasoning is "one-sided."[13] A part of what he meant was that by such inference a part only of all that is true of an object can be learned, owing to the generality or abstractedness of the predicates inferred. This objection is, therefore, somewhat similar to the last; for the point of it is that no number of syllogisms would give a complete knowledge of the object. This, however, presents a difficulty which the other did not; namely, that if nothing incognizable exists, and all knowledge is by mental action, by mental action everything is cognizable. So that if by syllogism everything is not cognizable, syllogism does not exhaust the modes of mental action. But grant the validity of this argument and it proves too much; for it makes, not the syllogism particularly, but all finite knowledge to be worthless. However much we know, more may come to be found out. Hence, all can never be known. This seems to contradict the fact that nothing is absolutely incognizable; and it would really do so *if our knowledge* were something absolutely limited. For, to say that all can never be known, means that information may increase beyond any assignable point; that is, that an absolute termination of all increase of knowledge is absolutely incognizable, and therefore does not exist. In other words, the proposition merely means that the sum of all that will be known up to any time, however advanced, into the future, has a ratio less than any assignable ratio to all that may be known at a time still more advanced. This does not contradict the fact that everything is cognizable; it only contradicts a proposition, which no one can maintain, that everything will be known at some time some number of years into the future.[14] It may, however, very justly be said that the difficulty still remains, how at every future time, however late, there can be something yet to happen. It is no longer a contradiction, but it is a difficulty; that is to say, *lengths of time* are shown not to afford an adequate conception of futurity in general; and the question arises, in what other way we are to conceive of it. I might indeed, perhaps, fairly drop the question here, and say that the difficulty had become so entirely removed from the syllogism in particular, that the formal logician need not feel himself specially called on to consider it. The solution, however, is very simple. It is that we conceive of the future, as a whole, by considering that this *word,* like any other general term, as "inhabitant of St. Louis," may be taken distributively or collectively. We conceive of the infinite, therefore, not directly or on the side of its infinity, but by means of a consideration concerning words or a second intention.

Another objection to the syllogism is that its "therefore" is merely subjective; that, because a certain conclusion syllogistically follows from a premise, it does not follow that the fact denoted by the conclusion really depends upon the fact denoted by the premise, so that the syllogism does not represent things as they really are. But it has been fully shown that if the facts are as the premises represent, they are also as the conclusion represents. Now this is a purely objective statement: therefore, there is a real connection between the facts stated as premises and those stated as conclusion. It is true that there is often an appearance of reasoning deductively from effects to causes. Thus we may reason as follows:—"There is smoke; there is never smoke without fire: hence, there has been fire." Yet smoke is not the cause of fire, but the effect of it. Indeed, it is evident, that in many cases an event is a demonstrative sign of a certain previous event having occurred. Hence, we can reason deductively from relatively future to relatively past, whereas causation[15] really determines events in the direct order of time. Nevertheless, if we can thus reason against the stream of time, it is because there really are such facts as that "If there is smoke, there has been fire," in which the following event is the antecedent. Indeed, if we consider the manner in which such a proposition became known to us, we shall find that what it really means is that "If we find smoke, we *shall* find evidence on the whole that there has been fire"; and this, if reality consists in the agreement that the whole community would eventually come to, is the very same thing as to say that there really has been fire. In short, the whole present difficulty is resolved instantly by this theory of reality, because it makes all reality something which is constituted by an event indefinitely future.

Another objection, for which I am quite willing to allow a great German philosopher the whole credit, is that sometimes the conclusion is false, although both the premises and the syllogistic form are correct.* Of this he gives the following examples.[16] From the middle term that a wall has been painted blue, it may correctly be concluded that it is blue; but notwithstanding this syllogism it may be green if it has also received a coat of yellow, from which last circumstance by itself it would follow that it is yellow. If from the middle term of the sensuous faculty it be concluded that man is neither good nor bad, since neither can be predicated of the sensuous, the syllogism is correct; but the conclusion is false, since of man in the concrete, spirituality is equally true, and may serve as middle term in an opposite syllogism. From the middle term of the gravitation of the planets, satellites, and comets, towards the sun, it follows correctly that these bodies fall into the sun; but they do not fall into it, because (!) they equally gravitate to their own centres, or, in other words (!!), they are supported by centrifugal force. Now, does Hegel mean to say that these syllogisms satisfy the rules for syllogism given by those who defend syllogism? or does he mean to grant that they do not satisfy *those* rules, but to set up some rules of his own for syllogism which shall insure its yielding false conclusions from true premises? If the latter, he ignores the real issue, which is whether the syllogism as defined by the rules of formal logic is correct, and not whether the syllogism as represented by Hegel is correct. But if he means that the above examples satisfy the usual definition of a true syllogism, he is mistaken. The first, stated in form, is as follows:

> Whatever has been painted blue is blue;
> This wall has been painted blue:
> ∴ This wall is blue.

Now "painted blue" may mean painted with blue paint, or painted so as to be blue. If, in the example, the former were meant, the major premise would be false. As he has stated that it is true, the latter meaning of "painted blue" must be the one intended. Again, "blue" may mean blue at some time, or blue at this time. If the latter be meant, the major premise is plainly false; therefore, the former is meant. But the conclusion is said to contradict the statement that the wall is yellow. If blue were here taken in the more general sense, there would be no such contradiction. Hence, he means in the conclusion that this wall is now blue; that is to say, he reasons thus:

> Whatever has been made blue has been blue;
> This has been made blue:
> ∴ This is blue now.

---

*"So zeight sich jener Schlussatz dadurch als falsch, obgleich für sich dessen Prämissen und ebenso dessen Consequenz ganz richtig sind."—Hegel's *Werke*, vol. v, p. 124.

Now substituting letters for the subjects and predicates, we get the form,

$$M \text{ is } P;$$
$$S \text{ is } M:$$
$$\therefore S \text{ is } Q.$$

This is not a syllogism in the ordinary sense of that term, or in any sense in which anybody maintains that the syllogism is valid.

The second example given by Hegel, when written out in full, is as follows:

Sensuality is neither good nor bad;
Man *has* (not *is*) sensuality:
∴ Man is neither good nor bad.

Or, the same argument may be stated as follows:

The sensuous, *as such*, is neither good nor bad;
Man is sensuous:
∴ Man is neither good nor bad.

When letters are substituted for subject and predicate in either of these arguments, it takes the form,

$$M \text{ is } P;$$
$$S \text{ is } N:$$
$$\therefore S \text{ is } P.$$

This, again, bears but a very slight resemblance to a syllogism.

The third example, when stated at full length, is as follows:

Whatever tends towards the sun, *on the whole*, falls into the sun;
The planets tend toward the sun:
∴ The planets fall into the sun.

This is a fallacy similar to the last.

I wonder that this eminent logician did not add to his list of examples of correct syllogism the following:

It either rains, or it does not rain;
It does not rain:
∴ It rains.

This is fully as deserving of serious consideration as any of those which he has brought forward. The rainy day and the pleasant day are both, in the first place, day. Secondly, each is the negation of a day. It is indifferent which be regarded as the positive. The pleasant is Other to the rainy, and the rainy is in like manner Other to the pleasant. Thus, both are equally Others. Both are Others of each other, or each is Other for itself. So this day being other than rainy, that to which it is Other is itself. But it is Other than itself. Hence, it is itself Rainy.

Some sophisms have, however, been adduced, mostly by the Eleatics and Sophists, which really are extremely difficult to resolve by syllogistic rules; and according to some modern authors this is actually impossible. These sophisms fall into three classes: *1st*, those which relate to continuity; *2d*, those which relate to consequences of supposing things to be other than they are; *3d*, those which relate to propositions which imply their own falsity. Of the first class, the most celebrated are Zeno's arguments concerning motion. One of these is, that if Achilles overtakes a tortoise in any finite time, and the tortoise has the start of him by a distance which may be called *a*, then Achilles has to pass over the sum of distances represented by the polynomial

$$\tfrac{1}{2}a + \tfrac{1}{4}a + \tfrac{1}{8}a + \tfrac{1}{16}a + \tfrac{1}{32}a \ \&c.$$

up to infinity. Every term of this polynomial is finite, and it has an infinite number of terms; consequently, Achilles must in a finite time pass over a distance equal to the sum of an infinite number of finite distances. Now this distance must be infinite, because no finite distance, however small, can be multiplied by an infinite number without giving an infinite distance. So that even if none of these finite distances were larger than the smallest (which is finite since all are finite), the sum of the whole would be infinite. But Achilles cannot pass over an infinite distance in a finite time; therefore, he cannot overtake the tortoise in any time, however great.[17]

The solution of this fallacy is as follows: The conclusion is dependent on the fact[18] that Achilles cannot overtake the tortoise without passing over an infinite number of terms of that series of finite distances. That is, no case of his overtaking the tortoise would be a case of his not passing over a non-finite number of terms; that is (by simple conversion), no case of his not passing over a non-finite number of terms would be a case of his overtaking the tortoise. But if he does not pass over a non-finite number of terms, he either passes over a finite number, or he passes over none; and conversely. Consequently, nothing more has been said than that every case of his passing over only a finite number of terms, or of his not passing over any, is a case of his not overtaking the tortoise. Consequently, nothing more can be concluded than that he passes over a distance greater than the sum of any finite number of the above series of terms. But because a quantity is greater than any quantity of a certain series, it does not follow that it is greater than any quantity.[19]

In fact, the reasoning in this sophism may be exhibited as follows:—We start with the series of numbers,

$$\frac{1}{2}a$$
$$\frac{1}{2}a + \frac{1}{4}a$$
$$\frac{1}{2}a + \frac{1}{4}a + \frac{1}{8}a$$
$$\frac{1}{2}a + \frac{1}{4}a + \frac{1}{8}a + \frac{1}{16}a$$
$$\&c. \quad \&c. \quad \&c.$$

Then, the implied argument is

Any number of this series is less than *a;*
But any number you please is less than the number of
    terms of this series:
Hence, any number you please is less than *a.*

This involves an obvious confusion between the number of terms and the value of the greatest term.

Another argument by Zeno against motion, is that a body fills a space no larger than itself. In that place there is no room for motion. Hence, while in the place where it is, it does not move. But it never is other than in the place where it is. Hence, it never moves. Putting this into form, it will read:

No body in a place no larger than itself is moving;
But every body is a body in a place no larger than itself:
∴ No body is moving.

The error of this consists in the fact that the minor premise is only true in the sense that during a time sufficiently short the space occupied by a body is as little larger than itself as you please. All that can be inferred from this is, that during no time a body will move no distance.

All the arguments of Zeno depend on supposing that a *continuum* has ultimate parts. But a *continuum* is precisely that, every part of which has parts, in the same sense. Hence, he makes out his contradictions only by making a self-contradictory supposition. In ordinary and mathematical language, we allow ourselves to speak of such parts—*points*—and whenever we are led into contradiction thereby, we have simply to express ourselves more accurately to resolve the difficulty.

Suppose a piece of glass to be laid on a sheet of paper so as to cover half of it. Then, every part of the paper is *covered,* or *not covered;* for "not" means merely outside of, or other than. But is the line under the edge of the glass covered or not? It is no more on one side of the edge than it is on the other. Therefore, it is either on both sides, or neither side. It is not on neither side; for if it were it would be *not* on either side, therefore not on the covered side, therefore not covered, therefore on the uncovered side. It is not partly on one side and partly on the other, because it has no width. Hence, it is wholly on both sides, or both covered and not covered.

The solution of this is, that we have supposed a part too narrow to be partly uncovered and partly covered; that is to say, a part which has no parts in a continuous surface, which by definition has no such parts. The reasoning, therefore, simply serves to reduce this supposition to an absurdity.

It may be said that there really is such a thing as a line. If a shadow falls on a surface, there really is a division between the light and the darkness. That is true. But it does not follow that because we attach a definite meaning to the part of a surface being covered, therefore we know what we mean when we say that a line is covered. We may define a covered line as one which separates two surfaces both of which are covered, or as one which separates two surfaces *either* of which is covered. In the former case, the line under the edge is uncovered; in the latter case, it is covered.

In the sophisms thus far considered, the appearance of contradiction depends mostly upon an ambiguity; in those which we are now to consider, two true propositions really do in form conflict with one another. We are apt to think that formal logic forbids this, whereas a familiar argument, the *reductio ad absurdum,* depends on showing that contrary predicates are true of a subject, and *that therefore that subject does not exist.* Many logicians, it is true, make affirmative propositions assert the existence of their subjects.* The objection to this is that it cannot be extended to hypotheticals. The proposition

If *A* then *B*

may conveniently be regarded as equivalent to

Every case of the truth of *A* is a case of the truth of *B*.

But this cannot be done if the latter proposition asserts the existence of its subject; that is, asserts that *A* really happens. If, however, a categorical affirmative be regarded as asserting the existence of its subject, the principle of the *reductio ad absurdum* is that two propositions of the forms,

---

*The usage of ordinary language has no relevancy in the matter.

> If *A* were true, *B* would not be true,

and

> If *A* were true, *B* would be true,

may both be true at once; and that if they are so, *A* is not true. It will be well, perhaps, to illustrate this point. No man of common sense would deliberately upset his inkstand if there were ink in it; that is, if any ink would run out. Hence, by simple conversion,

> If he were deliberately to upset his inkstand,
> no ink would be spilt.

But suppose there is ink in it. Then, it is also true, that

> If he were deliberately to upset his inkstand,
> the ink would be spilt.

These propositions are both true, and the law of contradiction is not violated which asserts only that nothing has contradictory predicates: only, it follows from these propositions that the man will not deliberately overturn his inkstand.

There are two ways in which deceptive sophisms may result from this circumstance. In the first place, contradictory propositions are never both true. Now, as a universal proposition may be true when the subject does not exist, it follows that the contradictory of a universal— that is, a particular—cannot be taken in such a sense as to be true when the subject does not exist. But a particular simply asserts a part of what is asserted in the universal over it; therefore, the universal over it asserts the subject to exist. Consequently, there are two kinds of universals, those which do not assert the subject to exist, and these have no particular propositions under them, and those which do assert that the subject exists, and these strictly speaking have no contradictories. For example, there is no use of such a form of proposition as "Some griffins would be dreadful animals," as particular under the useful form "The griffin would be a dreadful animal"; and the apparent contradictories "All of John Smith's family are ill," and "Some of John Smith's family are not ill," are both false at once if John Smith has no family. Here, though an inference from a universal to the particular under it is always valid, yet a procedure which greatly resembles this would be sophistical if the universal were one of those propositions which does not assert the existence of its subject. The following sophism depends upon this; I call it the True Gorgias:

Gorgias. What say you, Socrates, of black? Is any black, white?
Socrates. No, by Zeus!

Gor. Do you say, then, that no black is white? *Soc.* None at all.

Gor. But is everything either black or non-black? *Soc.* Of course.

Gor. And everything either white or non-white? *Soc.* Yes.

Gor. And everything either rough or smooth? *Soc.* Yes.

Gor. And everything either real or unreal? *Soc.* Oh, bother! yes.

Gor. Do you say, then, that all black is either rough black or smooth black? *Soc.* Yes.

Gor. And that all white is either real white or unreal white? *Soc.* Yes.

Gor. And yet is no black, white? *Soc.* None at all.

Gor. Nor no white, black? *Soc.* By no means.

Gor. What? Is no smooth black, white? *Soc.* No; you cannot prove that, Gorgias.

Gor. Nor no rough black, white? *Soc.* Neither.

Gor. Nor no real white, black? *Soc.* No.

Gor. Nor no unreal white, black? *Soc.* No, I say. No white at all is black.

Gor. What if black is smooth, is it not white? *Soc.* Not in the least.

Gor. And if the last is false, is the first false? *Soc.* It follows.

Gor. If, then, black is white, does it follow, that black is not smooth? *Soc.* It does.

Gor. Black-white is not smooth? *Soc.* What do you mean?

Gor. Can any dead man speak? *Soc.* No, indeed

Gor. And is any speaking man dead? *Soc.* I say, no.

Gor. And is any good king tyrannical? *Soc.* No.

Gor. And is any tyrannical king good? *Soc.* I just said no.

Gor. And you said, too, that no rough black is white, did you not? *Soc.* Yes.

Gor. Then, is any black-white, rough? *Soc.* No.

Gor. And is any unreal black, white? *Soc.* No.

Gor. Then, is any black-white unreal? *Soc.* No.

Gor. No black-white is rough? *Soc.* None.

Gor. All black-white, then, is non-rough? *Soc.* Yes.

Gor. And all black-white, non-unreal? *Soc.* Yes.

Gor. All black-white is then smooth? *Soc.* Yes.

Gor. And all real? *Soc.* Yes.

Gor. Some smooth, then, is black-white? *Soc.* Of course.

Gor. And some real is black-white? *Soc.* So it seems.

Gor. Some black-white smooth is black-white? *Soc.* Yes.

Gor. Some black smooth is black-white? *Soc.* Yes.

Gor. Some black smooth is white. *Soc.* Yes.

Gor. Some black real is black-white? *Soc.* Yes.

Gor. Some black real is white? *Soc.* Yes.

Gor. Some real black is white? *Soc.* Yes.

Gor. And some smooth black is white? *Soc.* Yes.
Gor. Then, some black is white? *Soc.* I think so myself.

The principle of the *reductio ad absurdum* also occasions deceptions in another way, owing to the fact that we have many words, such as *can, may, must,* &c., which imply more or less vaguely an otherwise unexpressed condition, so that these propositions are in fact hypotheticals. Accordingly, if the unexpressed condition is some state of things which does not actually come to pass, the two propositions may appear to be contrary to one another. Thus, the moralist says, "You ought to do this, and you can do it." This "You can do it" is principally hortatory in its force: so far as it is a statement of fact, it means merely, "If you try, you will do it." Now, if the act is an outward one and the act is not performed, the scientific man, in view of the fact that every event in the physical world depends exclusively on physical antecedents, says that in this case the laws of nature prevented the thing from being done, and that therefore, "Even if you had tried, you would not have done it." Yet the reproachful conscience still says you might have done it; that is, that "If you had tried, you would have done it." This is called the paradox of freedom and fate; and it is usually supposed that one of these propositions must be true and the other false. But since, in fact, you have not tried, there is no reason why the supposition that you have tried should not be reduced to an absurdity. In the same way, if you had tried and had performed the action, the conscience might say, "If you had not tried, you would not have done it"; while the understanding would say, "Even if you had not tried, you would have done it." These propositions are perfectly consistent, and only serve to reduce the supposition that you did not try to an absurdity.*

---

*This seems to me to be the main difficulty of freedom and fate. But the question is overlaid with many others. The Necessitarians seem now to maintain less that every physical event is completely determined by physical causes (which seems[20] to me irrefragable), than that every act of will is determined by the strongest motive. This has never been proved. Its advocates seem to think that it follows from universal causation, but why need the cause of an act lie within the consciousness at all? If I act from a reason at all, I act voluntarily; but which of two reasons shall appear strongest to me on a particular occasion may be owing to what I have eaten for dinner. Unless there is a perfect regularity as to what is the strongest motive with me, to say that I act from the strongest motive is mere tautology. If there is no calculating how a man will act except by taking into account external facts, the character of his motives does not determine how he acts. Mill and others have, therefore, not shown that a man always acts from the strongest motive. Hobbes maintained that a man always acts from a reflection upon what will please him most.[21] This is a very crude opinion. Men are not always thinking of themselves.

Self-control seems to be the capacity for rising to an extended view of a practical subject instead of seeing only temporary urgency. This is the only freedom of which man has any reason to be proud; and it is because love of what is good for all on the whole, which is the widest possible consideration, is the essence of Christianity, that it is said that the service of Christ is perfect freedom.

The third class of sophisms consists of the so-called *Insolubilia*. Here is an example of one of them with its resolution:

THIS PROPOSITION IS NOT TRUE.
IS IT TRUE OR NOT?

Suppose it true.
Then,
The proposition is true;
But, that it is not true is the
proposition:
∴ That it is not true is true;
∴ It is not true.
Besides,
It is true.
∴ It is true that it is true,
∴ It is not true that it is not true; .
But, the proposition is that it is
not true,
∴ The proposition is not true.

Suppose it not true.
Then,
It is not true.
∴ It is true that it is not true.
But, the proposition is that it is
not true.
∴ The proposition is true.
Besides,
The proposition is not true.
But that it is not true is the
proposition.
∴ That it is not true, is not true.
∴ That it is true, is true.
∴ It is true.

∴ Whether it is true or not, it is both true and not.
∴ It is both true and not,
which is absurd.

Since the conclusion is false, the reasoning is bad, or the premises are not all true. But the reasoning is a dilemma; either, then, the disjunctive principle that it is either true or not is false, or the reasoning under one or the other branch is bad, or the reasoning is altogether valid. If the principle that it is either true or not is false, it is other than true and other than not true; that is, not true and not not true; that is, not true and true. But this is absurd. Hence, the disjunctive principle is valid. There are two arguments under each horn of the dilemma; both the arguments under one or the other branch must be false. But, in each case, the second argument involves all the premises and forms of inference involved in the first; hence, if the first is false, the second necessarily is so. We may, therefore, confine our attention to the first arguments in the two branches. The forms of argument contained in these are two: first, the simple syllogism in Barbara, and, second, the consequence from the truth of a proposition to the proposition itself. These are both correct. Hence, the whole form of reasoning is correct, and nothing remains to be false but a premise. But since the repetition of an alternative supposition is not a premise, there is, properly speaking, but one premise in the whole. This is that the proposition is the same as that that proposition is not true. This, then, must be false. Hence the proposition signifies either less or more than this. If it does not signify as much as this, it signifies nothing, and hence it is not true, and hence another proposition which says of it what it says of itself is true. But if the proposition in question signifies something more than that it is itself not true, then the premise that

Whatever is said in the proposition is that it is not true,

is not true. And as a proposition is true only if whatever is said in it is true, but is false if anything said in it is false, the first argument on the second side of the dilemma contains a false premise, and the second an undistributed middle. But the first argument on the first side remains good. Hence, if the proposition means more than that it is not true, it is not true, and another proposition which repeats this of it is true. Hence, whether the proposition does or does not mean that it is not true, it is not true, and a proposition which repeats this of it is true.

Since this repeating proposition is true, it has a meaning. Now, a proposition has a meaning if any part of it has a meaning. Hence the original proposition (a part of which repeated has a meaning) has itself a meaning. Hence, it must imply something besides that which it explicitly states. But it has no particular determination to any further implication. Hence, what more it signifies it must signify by virtue of being a proposition at all. That is to say, every proposition must imply something analogous to what this implies. Now, the repetition of this proposition does not contain this implication, for otherwise it could not be true; hence, what every proposition implies must be something concerning itself. What every proposition implies concerning itself must be something which is false of the proposition now under discussion, for the whole falsity of this proposition lies therein, since all that it explicitly lays down is true. It must be something which would not be false if the proposition were true, for in that case some true proposition would be false. Hence, it must be that it is itself true. That is, *every proposition asserts its own truth.*

The proposition in question, therefore, is true in all other respects but its implication of its own truth.*

The difficulty of showing how the law of deductive reasoning is

*This is the principle which was most usually made the basis of the resolution of the *Insolubilia.* See, for example, *Pauli Veneti Sophismata Aurea.* Sophisma 50. The authority of Aristotle is claimed for this mode of solution. *Sophistici Elenchi,* cap. 25. The principal objection which was made to this mode of solution, viz., that the principle that every proposition implies its own truth, cannot be proved, I believe that I have removed. The only arguments against the truth of this principle were based on the imperfect doctrines of *modales* and *obligationes.* Other methods of solution suppose that a part of a proposition cannot denote the whole proposition, or that no intellection is a formal cognition of itself. A solution of this sort will be found in Occam's *Summa Totius Logices,* 3d part of 3d part, cap. 38. Such modern authors as think the solution "very easy" do not understand its difficulties. See Mansel's Aldrich, p. 145.

true depends upon our inability to conceive of its not being true. In the case of probable reasoning the difficulty is of quite another kind; here, where we see precisely what the procedure is, we wonder how such a process can have any validity at all. How magical it is that by examining a part of a class we can know what is true of the whole of the class, and by study of the past can know the future; in short, that we can know what we have not experienced!

Is not this an intellectual intuition! Is it not that besides ordinary experience which is dependent on there being a certain physical connection between our organs and the thing experienced, there is a second avenue of truth dependent only on there being a certain intellectual connection between our previous knowledge and what we learn in that way? Yes, this is true. Man has this faculty, just as opium has a somnific virtue;[22] but some further questions may be asked, nevertheless. How is the existence of this faculty accounted for? In one sense, no doubt, by natural selection. Since it is absolutely essential to the preservation of so delicate an organism as man's, no race which had it not has been able to sustain itself. This accounts for the prevalence of this faculty, provided it was only a possible one. But how can it be possible? What could enable the mind to know physical things which do not physically influence it and which it does not influence? The question cannot be answered by any statement concerning the human mind, for it is equivalent to asking what makes the facts usually to be, as inductive and hypothetic conclusions from true premises represent them to be? Facts of a certain kind are usually true when facts having certain relations to them are true; what is the cause of this? That is the question.

The usual reply is that nature is everywhere regular; as things have been, so they will be; as one part of nature is, so is every other. But this explanation will not do. Nature is not regular. No disorder would be less orderly than the existing arrangement. It is true that the special laws and regularities are innumerable; but nobody thinks of the irregularities, which are infinitely more frequent. Every fact true of any one thing in the universe is related to every fact true of every other. But the immense majority of these relations are fortuitous and irregular. A man in China bought a cow three days and five minutes after a Greenlander had sneezed. Is that abstract circumstance connected with any regularity whatever? And are not such relations infinitely more frequent than those which are regular? But if a very large number of qualities were to be distributed among a very large number of things in almost any way, there would chance to be some few regularities. If, for example, upon a checker-board of an enormous number of squares, painted all sorts of colors, myriads of dice were to be thrown, it could hardly fail to happen, that upon some color, or shade of color, out of so many, some one of the six numbers should not be uppermost on any die. This would be a regularity; for, the universal proposition would be true that upon that color that number is never turned up. But suppose this regularity abolished, then a far more remarkable regularity would be created, namely, that on every color every number is turned up. Either way, therefore, a regularity must occur. Indeed, a little reflection will show that although we have here only variations of color and of the numbers of the dice, many regularities must occur. And the greater the number of objects, the more respects in which they vary, and the greater the number of varieties in each respect, the greater will be the number of regularities. Now, in the universe, all these numbers are infinite. Therefore, however disorderly the chaos, the *number* of regularities must be infinite. The orderliness of the universe, therefore, if it exists, must consist in the large *proportion* of relations which present a regularity to those which are quite irregular. But this proportion in the actual universe is, as we have seen, as small as it can be; and, therefore, the orderliness of the universe is as little as that of any arrangement whatever.

But even if there were such an orderliness in things, it never could be discovered. For it would belong to things either collectively or distributively. If it belonged to things collectively, that is to say, if things formed a system the difficulty would be that a system can only be known by seeing some considerable proportion of the whole. Now we never can know how great a part of the whole of nature we have discovered. If the order were distributive, that is, belonged to all things only by belonging to each thing, the difficulty would be that a character can only be known by comparing something which has it with something which has it not. *Being, quality, relation,* and other universals are not known except as characters of words or other signs, attributed by a figure of speech to things. Thus, in neither case could the order of things be known. But the order of things would not help the validity of our reasoning—that is, would not help us to reason correctly— unless we knew what the order of things required the relation between the known reasoned *from* to the unknown reasoned *to,* to be.

But even if this order both existed and were known, the knowledge would be of no use except as a general principle, from which things could be deduced. It would not explain how knowledge could be increased (in contradistinction to being rendered more distinct), and so it would not explain how it could itself have been acquired.

Finally, if the validity of induction and hypothesis were dependent on a particular constitution of the universe, we could imagine a universe in which these modes of inference should not be valid, just as we can imagine a universe in which there would be no attraction, but things should merely drift about. Accordingly, J. S. Mill, who explains the validity of induction by the uniformity of nature,* maintains that he can imagine a universe without any regularity, so that no probable inference would be valid in it.† In the universe as it is, probable arguments sometimes fail, nor can any definite proportion of cases be stated in which they hold good; all that can be said is that in the long run they prove approximately correct. Can a universe be imagined in which this would not be the case? It must be a universe where probable argument can have some application, in order that it may fail half the time. It must, therefore, be a universe experienced. Of the finite number of propositions true of a finite amount of experience of such a universe, no one would be universal in form, unless the subject of it were an individual. For if there were a plural universal proposition, inferences by analogy from one particular to another would hold good invariably in reference to that subject. So that these arguments might be no better than guesses in reference to other parts of the universe, but they would invariably hold good in a finite proportion of it, and so would on the whole be somewhat better than guesses. There could, also, be no individuals in that universe, for there must be some general class—that is, there must be some things more or less alike—or probable argument would find no premises there; therefore, there must be two mutually exclusive classes, since every class has a residue outside of it; hence, if there were any individual, that individual would be wholly excluded from one or other of these classes. Hence, the universal plural proposition would be true, that no one of a certain class was that individual. Hence, no universal proposition would be true. Accordingly, every combination of characters would occur in such a universe. But this would not be disorder, but the simplest order; it would not be unintelligible, but, on the contrary, everything conceivable would be found in it with equal frequency. The notion, therefore, of a universe in which probable arguments should fail as often as hold true, is absurd. We can suppose it in general terms, but we cannot specify how it should be other than self-contradictory.‡

---

*Logic, Book 3, chap. 3, sec. 1.

†Ibid. Book 3, chap. 21, sec. 1. "I am convinced that any one accustomed to abstraction and analysis, who will fairly exert his faculties for the purpose, will, when his imagination has once learnt to entertain the notion, find no difficulty in conceiving that in some one, for instance, of the many firmaments into which sidereal astronomy divides the universe, events may succeed one another at random, without any fixed law; nor can anything in our experience or mental nature constitute a sufficient, or indeed any, reason for believing that this is nowhere the case.

"Were we to suppose (what it is perfectly possible to imagine) that the present order of the universe were brought to an end, and that a chaos succeeded, in which there was no fixed succession of events, and the past gave no assurance of the future," &c.

‡Boole (Laws of Thought, p. 370) has shown, in a very simple and elegant manner, that an *infinite* number of balls may have characters distributed in such a way, that from the characters of the balls already drawn, we could infer nothing in regard to that of the

Since we cannot conceive of probable inferences as not generally holding good, and since no special supposition will serve to explain their validity, many logicians have sought to base this validity on that of deduction, and that in a variety of ways. The only attempt of this sort, however, which deserves to be noticed is that which seeks to determine the probability of a future event by the theory of probabilities, from the fact that a certain number of similar events have been observed. Whether this can be done or not depends on the meaning assigned to the word *probability*. But if this word is to be taken in such a sense that a form of conclusion which is probable is valid; since the validity of an inference (or its correspondence with facts) consists solely in this, that when such premises are true, such a conclusion is generally true, then probability can mean nothing but the ratio of the frequency of occurrence of a specific event to a general one over it. In this sense of the term, it is plain that the probability of an inductive conclusion cannot be *deduced* from the premises; for from the inductive premises

$$S', S'', S''' \text{ are } M,$$
$$S', S'', S''', \text{ are } P,$$

nothing follows deductively, except that any M, which is S', or S'', or S''' is P; or, less explicitly, that some M is P.

Thus, we seem to be driven to this point. On the one hand, no determination of things, no *fact*, can result in the validity of probable argument; nor, on the other hand, is such argument reducible to that form which holds good, however the facts may be. This seems very much like a reduction to absurdity of the validity of such reasoning; and a paradox of the greatest difficulty is presented for solution.

There can be no doubt of the importance of this problem. According to Kant, the central question of philosophy is "How are synthetical judgments *a priori* possible?"[23] But antecedently to this comes the question how synthetical judgments in general, and still more generally, how synthetical reasoning is possible at all. When the answer to the general problem has been obtained, the particular one will be comparatively simple. This is the lock upon the door of philosophy.

All probable inference, whether induction or hypothesis, is inference from the parts to the whole. It is essentially the same, therefore, as statistical inference. Out of a bag of black and white beans I take a few handfuls, and from this sample I can judge approximately the proportions of black and white in the whole. This is identical with induction. Now we know upon what the validity of this inference

---

characters of the next one. The same is true of some arrangements of a finite number of balls, provided the inference takes place after a fixed number of drawings. But this does not invalidate the reasoning above, although it is an important fact without doubt.

depends. It depends upon the fact that in the long run, any one bean would be taken out as often as any other. For were this not so, the mean of a large number of results of such testings of the contents of the bag would not be precisely the ratio of the numbers of the two colors of beans in the bag. Now we may divide the question of the validity of induction into two parts: 1st, why of all inductions, premises for which occur, the generality should hold good, and 2d, why men are not fated always to light upon the small proportion of worthless inductions. Then, the first of these two questions is readily answered. For since all the members of any class are the same as all that are to be known; and since from any part of those which are to be known an induction is competent to the rest, in the long run any one member of a class will occur as the subject of a premise of a possible induction as often as any other, and, therefore, the validity of induction depends simply upon the fact that the parts make up and constitute the whole. This in its turn depends simply upon there being such a state of things that any general terms are possible. But it has been shown, p. 52, that being at all is being in general. And thus this part of the validity of induction depends merely on there being any reality.

From this it appears that we cannot say that the generality of inductions are true, but only that in the long run they approximate to the truth. This is the truth of the statement, that the universality of an inference from induction is only the analogue of true universality. Hence, also, it cannot be said that we know an inductive conclusion to be true, however loosely we state it; we only know that by accepting inductive conclusions, in the long run our errors balance one another. In fact, insurance companies proceed upon induction;—they do not know what will happen to this or that policy-holder; they only know that they are secure in the long run.

The other question relative to the validity of induction, is why men are not fated always to light upon those inductions which are highly deceptive. The explanation of the former branch of the problem we have seen to be that there is something real. Now, since if there is anything real, then (on account of this reality consisting in the ultimate agreement of all men, and on account of the fact that reasoning from parts to whole, is the only kind of synthetic reasoning which men possess) it follows necessarily that a sufficiently long succession of inferences from parts to whole will lead men to a knowledge of it, so that in that case they cannot be fated on the whole to be thoroughly unlucky in their inductions. This second branch of the problem is in fact equivalent to asking why there is anything real, and thus its solution will carry the solution of the former branch one step further.

The answer to this question may be put into a general and abstract, or a special detailed form. If men were not to be able to learn from induction, it must be because as a general rule, when they had made an induction, the order of things (as they appear in experience), would then undergo a revolution. Just herein would the unreality of such a universe consist; namely, that the order of the universe should depend on how much men should know of it. But this general rule would be capable of being itself discovered by induction; and so it must be a law of such a universe, that when this was discovered it would cease to operate. But this second law would itself be capable of discovery. And so in such a universe there would be nothing which would not sooner or later be known; and it would have an order capable of discovery by a sufficiently long course of reasoning. But this is contrary to the hypothesis, and therefore that hypothesis is absurd. This is the particular answer. But we may also say, in general, that if nothing real exists, then, since every question supposes that something exists—for it maintains its own urgency—it supposes only illusions to exist. But the existence even of an illusion is a reality; for an illusion affects all men, or it does not. In the former case, it is a reality according to our theory of reality; in the latter case, it is independent of the state of mind of any individuals except those whom it happens to affect. So that the answer to the question, Why is anything real? is this: That question means, "supposing anything to exist, why is something real?" The answer is, that that very existence is reality by definition.

All that has here been said, particularly of induction, applies to all inference from parts to whole, and therefore to hypothesis, and so to all probable inference.

Thus, I claim to have shown, in the first place, that it is possible to hold a consistent theory of the validity of the laws of ordinary logic.

But now let us suppose the idealistic theory of reality, which I have in this paper taken for granted to be false. In that case, inductions would not be true unless the world were so constituted that every object should be presented in experience as often as any other; and further, unless we were so constituted that we had no more tendency to make bad inductions than good ones. These facts might be explained by the benevolence of the Creator; but, as has already been argued, they could not explain, but are absolutely refuted by the fact that no state of things can be conceived in which probable arguments should not lead to the truth. This affords a most important argument in favor of that theory of reality, and thus of those denials of certain faculties from which it was deduced, as well as of the general style of philosophizing by which those denials were reached.

Upon our theory of reality and of logic, it can be shown that no inference of any individual can be thoroughly logical without certain determinations of his mind which do not concern any one inference immediately; for we have seen that that mode of inference which alone can teach us anything, or carry us at all beyond what was implied in our premises—in fact, does not give us to know any more than we knew before; only, we know that, by faithfully adhering to that mode of inference, we shall, on the whole, approximate to the truth. Each of us is an insurance company, in short. But, now, suppose that an insurance company, among its risks, should take one exceeding in amount the sum of all the others. Plainly, it would then have no security whatever. Now, has not every single man such a risk? What shall it profit a man if he shall gain the whole world and lose his own soul?[24] If a man has a transcendent personal interest infinitely outweighing all others, then, upon the theory of validity of inference just developed, he is devoid of all security, and can make no valid inference whatever. What follows? That logic rigidly requires, before all else, that no determinate fact, nothing which can happen to a man's self, should be of more consequence to him than everything else. He who would not sacrifice his own soul to save the whole world, is illogical in all his inferences, collectively. So the social principle is rooted intrinsically in logic.

That being the case, it becomes interesting to inquire how it is with men as a matter of fact. There is a psychological theory that man cannot act without a view to his own pleasure.[25] This theory is based on a falsely assumed subjectivism. Upon our principles of the objectivity of knowledge, it could not be based, and if they are correct it is reduced to an absurdity. It seems to me that the usual opinion of the selfishness of man is based in large measure upon this false theory. I do not think that the facts bear out the usual opinion. The immense self-sacrifices which the most wilful men often make, show that wilfulness is a very different thing from selfishness. The care that men have for what is to happen after they are dead, cannot be selfish. And finally and chiefly, the constant use of the word *"we"*—as when we speak of our possessions on the Pacific—our destiny as a republic—in cases in which no personal interests at all are involved, show conclusively that men do not make their personal interests their only ones, and therefore may, at least, subordinate them to the interests of the community.

But just the revelation of the possibility of this complete self-sacrifice in man, and the belief in its saving power, will serve to redeem the logicality of all men. For he who recognizes the logical necessity of complete self-identification of one's own interests with those of the community, and its potential existence in man, even if he has it not himself, will perceive that only the inferences of that man who has it are logical, and so views his own inferences as being valid only so far as they would be accepted by that man. But so far as he has this belief, he becomes identified with that man. And that ideal perfection of knowledge by which we have seen that reality is constituted must thus belong to a community in which this identification is complete.

This would serve as a complete establishment of private logicality, were it not that the assumption that man or the community (which may be wider than man) shall ever arrive at a state of information greater than some definite finite information, is entirely unsupported by reasons. There cannot be a scintilla of evidence to show that at some time all living beings shall not be annihilated at once, and that forever after there shall be throughout the universe any intelligence whatever. Indeed, this very assumption involves itself a transcendent and supreme interest, and therefore from its very nature is unsusceptible of any support from reasons. This infinite hope which we all have (for even the atheist will constantly betray his calm expectation that what is Best will come about) is something so august and momentous, that all reasoning in reference to it is a trifling impertinence. We do not want to know what are the weights of reasons *pro* and *con*—that is, how much *odds* we should wish to receive on such a venture in the long run—because there is no long run in the case; the question is single and supreme, and ALL is at stake upon it. We are in the condition of a man in a life and death struggle; if he have not sufficient strength, it is wholly indifferent to him how he acts, so that the only assumption upon which he can act rationally is the hope of success. So this sentiment is rigidly demanded by logic. If its object were any determinate fact, any private interest, it might conflict with the results of knowledge and so with itself; but when its object is of a nature as wide as the community can turn out to be, it is always a hypothesis uncontradicted by facts and justified by its indispensibleness for making any action rational.

5

Fraser's The Works of George Berkeley

P 60: North American Review *113 (October 1871):449–72. [Also published in W2:462–87 (with Chauncey Wright's criticism and Peirce's response [pp. 487–90]) and in CP 8.7–38.] In what may be the most important of all his reviews, Peirce discusses the realist-nominalist controversy (which he believed to be of fundamental significance for philosophy as well as life) and gives a detailed account of his already slightly modified scholastic realism. Peirce's common-sense account of truth and reality contains important elements of his developing pragmatism.*

The Works of George Berkeley, D.D., formerly Bishop of Cloyne: including many of his Writings hitherto unpublished. With Prefaces, Annotations, his Life and Letters, and an Account of his Philosophy. By Alexander Campbell Fraser, M.A., Professor of Logic and Metaphysics in the University of Edinburgh. In Four Volumes. Oxford: At the Clarendon Press. 8vo. 1871.

This new edition of Berkeley's works is much superior to any of the former ones. It contains some writings not in any of the other editions, and the rest are given with a more carefully edited text. The editor has done his work well. The introductions to the several pieces contain analyses of their contents which will be found of the greatest service to the reader. On the other hand, the explanatory notes which disfigure every page seem to us altogether unnecessary and useless.

Berkeley's metaphysical theories have at first sight an air of paradox and levity very unbecoming to a bishop. He denies the existence of matter, our ability to see distance, and the possibility of forming the simplest general conception; while he admits the existence of Platonic ideas; and argues the whole with a cleverness which every reader admits, but which few are convinced by. His disciples seem to think the present moment a favorable one for obtaining for their philosophy a more patient hearing than it has yet got. It is true that we of this day are sceptical and not given to metaphysics, but so, say they, was the generation which Berkeley addressed, and for which his style was chosen; while it is hoped that the spirit of calm and thorough inquiry which is now, for once, almost the fashion, will save the theory from the perverse misrepresentations which formerly assailed it, and lead to a fair examination of the arguments which, in the minds of his sectators, put the truth of it beyond all doubt. But above all it is anticipated that the Berkeleyan treatment of that question of the validity of human knowledge and of the inductive process of science, which is now so much studied, is such as to command the attention of scientific men to the idealistic system. To us these hopes seem vain. The truth is that the minds from whom the spirit of the age emanates have now no interest in the only problems that metaphysics ever pretended to solve. The abstract acknowledgment of God, Freedom, and Immortality, apart from those other religious beliefs (which cannot possibly rest on metaphysical grounds) which alone may animate this, is now seen to have no practical consequence whatever. The world is getting to think of these creatures of metaphysics, as Aristotle of the Platonic ideas: τερετίσματα γάρ ἐστι, καὶ εἰ ἔστιν, οὐδὲν πρὸς τὸν λόγον ἐστίν.[1] The question of the grounds of the validity of induction has, it is true, excited an interest, and may continue to do so (though the argument is now become too difficult for popular apprehension); but whatever interest it has had has been due to a hope that the solution of it would afford the basis for sure and useful maxims concerning the logic of induction,—a hope which would be destroyed so soon as it were shown that the question was a purely metaphysical one. This is the prevalent feeling, among advanced minds. It may not be just; but it exists. And its existence is an effectual bar (if there were no other) to the general acceptance of Berkeley's system. The few who do now care for metaphysics are not of that bold order of minds who delight to hold a position so unsheltered by the prejudices of common sense as that of the good bishop.

As a matter of history, however, philosophy must always be interesting. It is the best representative of the mental development of each age. It is so even of ours, if we think what really is our philosophy. Metaphysical history is one of the chief branches of history, and ought to be expounded side by side with the history of society, of government, and of war; for in its relations with these we trace the significance of events for the human mind. The history of philosophy in the British Isles is a subject possessing more unity and entirety within itself than has usually been recognized in it. The influence of Descartes was never so great in England as that of traditional conceptions, and we can trace a continuity between modern and mediæval thought there, which is wanting in the history of France, and still more, if possible, in that of Germany.

From very early times, it has been the chief intellectual characteristic of the English to wish to effect everything by the plainest and directest means, without unnecessary contrivance. In war, for example, they rely more than any other people in Europe upon sheer hardihood, and rather despise military science. The main peculiarities of their system of law arise from the fact that every evil has been rectified as it became intolerable, without any thoroughgoing measure. The bill for legalizing marriage with a deceased wife's sister is yearly pressed because it supplies a remedy for an inconvenience actually felt; but nobody has proposed a bill to legalize marriage with a deceased husband's brother. In philosophy, this national tendency appears as a strong preference for the simplest theories, and a resistance to any complication of the theory as long as there is the least possibility that the facts can be explained in the simpler way. And, accordingly, British philosophers have always desired to weed out of philosophy all conceptions which could not be made perfectly definite and easily intelligible, and have shown strong nominalistic tendencies since the time of Edward I, or even earlier.[2] Berkeley is an admirable illustration of this national character, as well as of that strange union of nominalism with Platonism, which has repeatedly appeared in history, and has been such a stumbling-block to the historians of philosophy.

The mediæval metaphysic is so entirely forgotten, and has so close a historic connection with modern English philosophy, and so much bearing upon the truth of Berkeley's doctrine, that we may perhaps be pardoned a few pages on the nature of the celebrated controversy concerning universals. And first let us set down a few dates. It was at the very end of the eleventh century that the dispute concerning nominalism and realism, which had existed in a vague way before, began to attain extraordinary proportions. During the twelfth century it was the matter of most interest to logicians, when William of Champeaux, Abélard, John of Salisbury, Gilbert de la Porrée, and many others, defended as many different opinions. But there was no historic connection between this controversy and those of scholasticism proper, the scholasticism of Aquinas, Scotus, and Ockam. For about the end of the twelfth century a great revolution of thought took place in Europe. What the influences were which produced it requires new historical researches to say. No doubt, it was partly due to the Crusades. But a great awakening of intelligence did take place at that time. It requires, it is true, some examination to distinguish this particular movement from a general awakening which had begun a century earlier, and had been growing stronger ever since. But now there was an accelerated impulse. Commerce was attaining new importance, and was inventing some of her chief conveniences and safeguards. Law, which had hitherto been utterly barbaric, began to be a profession. The civil law was adopted in Europe, the canon law was digested; the common law took some form. The Church, under Innocent III, was assuming the sublime functions of a moderator over kings. And those orders of mendicant friars were established, two of which did so much for the development of the scholastic philosophy. Art felt the spirit of a new age, and there could hardly be a greater change than from the highly ornate round-arched architecture of the twelfth century to the comparatively simple Gothic of the thirteenth. Indeed, if any one wishes to know what a scholastic commentary is like, and what the tone of thought in it is, he has only to contemplate a Gothic cathedral. The first quality of either is a religious devotion, truly heroic. One feels that the men who did these works did really believe in religion as we believe in nothing. We cannot easily understand how Thomas Aquinas can speculate so much on the nature of angels, and whether ten thousand of them could dance on a needle's point. But it was simply because he held them for real. If they are real, why are they not more interesting than the bewildering varieties of insects which naturalists study; or why should the orbits of double stars attract more attention than spiritual intelligences? It will be said that we have no means of knowing anything about them. But that is on a par with censuring the schoolmen for referring questions to the authority of the Bible and of the Church. If they really believed in their religion, as they did, what better could they do? And if they found in these authorities testimony concerning angels, how could they avoid admitting it. Indeed, objections of this sort only make it appear still more clearly how much those were the ages of faith. And if the spirit was not altogether admirable, it is only because faith itself has its faults as a foundation for the intellectual character. The men of that time did fully believe and did think that, for the sake of giving themselves up absolutely to their great task of building or of writing, it was well worth while to resign all the joys of life. Think of the spirit in which Duns Scotus must have worked, who wrote his thirteen volumes in folio, in a style as condensed as the most condensed parts of Aristotle, before the age of thirty-four. Nothing is more striking in either of the great intellectual products of that age, than the complete absence of self-conceit on the part of the artist or philosopher. That anything of value can be added to his sacred and catholic work by its having the smack of individuality about it, is what he has never conceived. His work is not designed to embody *his* ideas, but the universal truth; there will not be one thing in it however minute, for which you will not find that he has his authority; and whatever originality emerges is of that inborn kind which so saturates a man that he cannot himself perceive it. The individual feels his own worthlessness in comparison with his task, and does not dare to introduce his vanity into the doing of it. Then there is no machine-work, no unthinking repetition about the thing. Every part is worked out for itself as a separate problem, no matter how analogous it may be in general to another part. And no matter how small and hidden a detail may be, it has been conscientiously studied, as though it were intended for the eye of God. Allied to this character is a detestation of antithesis or the studied balancing of one thing against another, and of a too geometrical grouping,—a hatred of posing which is as much a moral trait as the others. Finally, there is nothing in which the scholastic philosophy and the Gothic architecture resemble one another more than in the gradually increasing sense of immensity which impresses the mind of the student as he learns to appreciate the real dimensions and cost of each. It is very unfortunate that the thirteenth, fourteenth, and fifteenth centuries should, under the name of Middle Ages, be confounded with others, which they are in every respect as unlike as the Renaissance is from modern times. In the history of logic, the break between the twelfth and thirteenth centuries is so great that only one author of the former age is ever quoted in the latter. If this is to be attributed to the fuller acquaintance with the works of Aristotle, to what, we would ask, is this profounder study itself to be attributed, since it is now known that the knowledge of those works was not imported from the Arabs? The thirteenth century was realistic, but the question concerning universals was not as much agitated as several others. Until about the end of the century, scholasticism was somewhat vague, immature, and unconscious of its own power. Its greatest glory was in the first half of the fourteenth century. Then Duns Scotus,* a Briton (for whether Scotch, Irish, or English is disputed), first stated the realistic position consistently, and developed it with great fulness and applied it to all the different questions which depend upon it. His theory of "formalities" was the subtlest, except perhaps Hegel's logic, ever broached, and he was separated from nominalism only by the division of a hair. It is not therefore surprising that the nominalistic position was soon adopted by several writers, especially by the celebrated William of Ockam, who took the lead of this party by the thoroughgoing and masterly way in which he treated the theory and combined it with a then rather recent but now forgotten addition to the doctrine of logical terms. With Ockam, who died in 1347, scholasticism may be said to have culminated. After him the scholastic philosophy showed a tendency to separate itself from the religious element which alone could dignify it, and sunk first into extreme formalism and fancifulness, and then into the merited contempt of all men; just as the Gothic architecture had a very similar fate, at about the same time, and for much the same reasons.

The current explanations of the realist-nominalist controversy are equally false and unintelligible. They are said to be derived ultimately

---

*Died 1308.

from Bayle's *Dictionary;* at any rate, they are not based on a study of the authors. "Few, very few, for a hundred years past," says Hallam, with truth, "have broken the repose of the immense works of the schoolmen."³ Yet it is perfectly possible so to state the matter that no one shall fail to comprehend what the question was, and how there might be two opinions about it. Are universals real? We have only to stop and consider a moment what was meant by the word *real,* when the whole issue soon becomes apparent. Objects are divided into figments, dreams, etc., on the one hand, and realities on the other. The former are those which exist only inasmuch as you or I or some man imagines them; the latter are those which have an existence independent of your mind or mine or that of any number of persons. The real is that which is not whatever we happen to think it, but is unaffected by what we may think of it. The question, therefore, is whether *man, horse,* and other names of natural classes, correspond with anything which all men, or all horses, really have in common, independent of our thought, or whether these classes are constituted simply by a likeness in the way in which our minds are affected by individual objects which have in themselves no resemblance or relationship whatsoever. Now that this is a real question which different minds will naturally answer in opposite ways, becomes clear when we think that there are two widely separated points of view, from which *reality,* as just defined, may be regarded. Where is the real, the thing independent of how we think it, to be found? There must be such a thing, for we find our opinions constrained; there is something, therefore, which influences our thoughts, and is not created by them. We have, it is true, nothing immediately present to us but thoughts. Those thoughts, however, have been caused by sensations, and those sensations are constrained by something out of the mind. This thing out of the mind, which directly influences sensation, and through sensation thought, because it *is* out of the mind, is independent of how we think it, and is, in short, the real. Here is one view of reality, a very familiar one. And from this point of view it is clear that the nominalistic answer must be given to the question concerning universals. For, while from this standpoint it may be admitted to be true as a rough statement that one man is like another, the exact sense being that the realities external to the mind produce sensations which may be embraced under one conception, yet it can by no means be admitted that the two real men have really anything in common, for to say that they are both men is only to say that the one mental term or thought-sign "man" stands indifferently for either of the sensible objects caused by the two external realities; so that not even the two sensations have in themselves anything in common, and far less is it to be inferred that the external realities have. This conception of reality is so familiar, that it is unnecessary to dwell upon it; but the other, or realist conception, if less familiar, is even more natural and obvious. All human thought and opinion contains an arbitrary, accidental element, dependent on the limitations in circumstances, power, and bent of the individual; an element of error, in short. But human opinion universally tends in the long run to a definite form, which is the truth. Let any human being have enough information and exert enough thought upon any question, and the result will be that he will arrive at a certain definite conclusion, which is the same that any other mind will reach under sufficiently favorable circumstances. Suppose two men, one deaf, the other blind. One hears a man declare he means to kill another, hears the report of the pistol, and hears the victim cry; the other sees the murder done. Their sensations are affected in the highest degree with their individual peculiarities. The first information that their sensations will give them, their first inferences, will be more nearly alike, but still different; the one having, for example, the idea of a man shouting, the other of a man with a threatening aspect; but their final conclusions, the thought the remotest from sense, will be identical and free from the one-sidedness of their idiosyncrasies. There is, then, to every question a true answer, a final conclusion, to which the opinion of every man is constantly gravitating. He may for a time recede from it, but give him more experience and time for consideration, and he will finally approach it. The individual may not live to reach the truth; there is a residuum of error in every individual's opinions. No matter; it remains that there is a definite opinion to which the mind of man is, on the whole and in the long run, tending. On many questions the final agreement is already reached, on all it will be reached if time enough is given. The arbitrary will or other individual peculiarities of a sufficiently large number of minds may postpone the general agreement in that opinion indefinitely; but it cannot affect what the character of that opinion shall be when it is reached. This final opinion, then, is independent, not indeed of thought in general, but of all that is arbitrary and individual in thought; is quite independent of how you, or I, or any number of men think. Everything, therefore, which will be thought to exist in the final opinion is real, and nothing else. What is the POWER of external things, to affect the senses? To say that people sleep after taking opium because it has a soporific *power*,[4] is that to say anything in the world but that people sleep after taking opium because they sleep after taking opium? To assert the existence of a power or potency, is it to assert the existence of anything actual? Or to say that a thing has a potential existence, is it to say that it has an actual existence? In other words, is the present existence of a power anything in the world but a regularity in future events relating to a certain thing regarded as an element which is to be taken account of beforehand, in the conception of that thing? If not, to assert that there are external things which can be known only as exerting a power on our sense, is nothing different from asserting that there is a general *drift* in the history of human thought which will lead it to one general agreement, one catholic consent. And any truth more perfect than this destined conclusion, any reality more absolute than what is thought in it, is a fiction of metaphysics. It is obvious how this way of thinking harmonizes with a belief in an infallible Church, and how much more natural it would be in the Middle Ages than in Protestant or positivist times.

This theory of reality is instantly fatal to the idea of a thing in itself,—a thing existing independent of all relation to the mind's conception of it. Yet it would by no means forbid, but rather encourage us, to regard the appearances of sense as only signs of the realities. Only, the realities which they represent would not be the unknowable cause of sensation, but *noumena,* or intelligible conceptions which are the last products of the mental action which is set in motion by sensation. The matter of sensation is altogether accidental; precisely the same information, practically, being capable of communication through different senses. And the catholic consent which constitutes the truth is by no means to be limited to men in this earthly life or to the human race, but extends to the whole communion of minds to which we belong, including some probably whose senses are very different from ours, so that in that consent no predication of a sensible quality can enter, except as an admission that so certain sorts of senses are affected. This theory is also highly favorable to a belief in external realities. It will, to be sure, deny that there is any reality which is absolutely incognizable in itself, so that it cannot be taken into the mind. But observing that "the external" means simply that which is independent of what phenomenon is immediately present, that is of how we may think or feel; just as "the real" means that which is independent of how we may think or feel *about it;* it must be granted that there are many objects of true science which are external, because there are many objects of thought which, if they are independent of that thinking whereby they are thought (that is, if they are real), are indisputably independent of all *other* thoughts and feelings.

It is plain that this view of reality is inevitably realistic; because general conceptions enter into all judgments, and therefore into true opinions. Consequently a thing in the general is as real as in the concrete. It is perfectly true that all white things have whiteness in them, for that is only saying, in another form of words, that all white things are white; but since it is true that real things possess whiteness, whiteness is real. It is a real which only exists by virtue of an act of thought knowing it, but that thought is not an arbitrary or accidental one dependent on any idiosyncrasies, but one which will hold in the final opinion.

This theory involves a phenomenalism. But it is the phenomenalism of Kant, and not that of Hume. Indeed, what Kant called his

Copernican step[5] was precisely the passage from the nominalistic to the realistic view of reality. It was the essence of his philosophy to regard the real object as determined by the mind. That was nothing else than to consider every conception and intuition which enters necessarily into the experience of an object, and which is not transitory and accidental, as having objective validity. In short, it was to regard the reality as the normal product of mental action, and not as the incognizable cause of it.

This realistic theory is thus a highly practical and common-sense position. Wherever universal agreement prevails, the realist will not be the one to disturb the general belief by idle and fictitious doubts. For according to him it is a consensus or common confession which constitutes reality. What he wants, therefore, is to see questions put to rest. And if a general belief, which is perfectly stable and immovable, can in any way be produced, though it be by the fagot and the rack, to talk of any error in such belief is utterly absurd. The realist will hold that the very same objects which are immediately present in our minds in experience really exist just as they are experienced out of the mind; that is, he will maintain a doctrine of immediate perception. He will not, therefore, sunder existence out of the mind and being in the mind as two wholly improportionable modes. When a thing is in such relation to the individual mind that that mind cognizes it, it is in the mind; and its being so in the mind will not in the least diminish its external existence. For he does not think of the mind as a receptacle, which if a thing is in, it ceases to be out of. To make a distinction between the true conception of a thing and the thing itself is, he will say, only to regard one and the same thing from two different points of view; for the immediate object of thought in a true judgment *is* the reality. The realist will, therefore, believe in the objectivity of all necessary conceptions, space, time, relation, cause, and the like.

No realist or nominalist ever expressed so definitely, perhaps, as is here done, his conception of reality. It is difficult to give a clear notion of an opinion of a past age, without exaggerating its distinctness. But careful examination of the works of the schoolmen will show that the distinction between these two views of the real—one as the fountain of the current of human thought, the other as the unmoving form to which it is flowing—is what really occasions their disagreement on the question concerning universals. The gist of all the nominalist's arguments will be found to relate to a *res extra animam,* while the realist defends his position only by assuming that the immediate object of thought in a true judgment is real. The notion that the controversy between realism and nominalism had anything to do with Platonic ideas is a mere product of the imagination, which the slightest examination of the books would suffice to disprove. But to prove that the statement here given of the essence of these positions is historically true and not a fancy sketch, it will be well to add a brief analysis of the opinions of Scotus and Ockam.

Scotus sees several questions confounded together under the usual *utrum universale est aliquid in rebus.* In the first place, there is the question concerning the Platonic forms. But putting Platonism aside as at least incapable of proof, and as a self-contradictory opinion if the archetypes are supposed to be strictly universal, there is the celebrated dispute among Aristotelians as to whether the universal is really in things or only derives its existence from the mind. Universality is a relation of a predicate to the subjects of which it is predicated. That can exist only in the mind, wherein alone the coupling of subject and predicate takes place. But the word *universal* is also used to denote what are named by such terms as *a man* or *a horse;* these are called universals, because a man is not necessarily this man, nor a horse this horse. In such a sense it is plain universals are real; there really is a man and there really is a horse. The whole difficulty is with the actually indeterminate universal, that which not only is not necessarily *this,* but which, being one single object of thought, is predicable of many things. In regard to this it may be asked, first, is it necessary to its existence that it should be in the mind; and, second, does it exist *in re?* There are two ways in which a thing may be in the mind,— *habitualiter* and *actualiter.* A notion is in the mind *actualiter* when it is actually conceived; it is in the mind *habitualiter* when it can directly produce a conception. It is by virtue of mental association (we moderns should say), that things are in the mind *habitualiter.* In the Aristotelian philosophy, the intellect is regarded as being to the soul what the eye is to the body. The mind *perceives* likenesses and other relations in the objects of sense, and thus just as sense affords sensible images of things, so the intellect affords intelligible images of them. It is as such a *species intelligibilis* that Scotus supposes that a conception exists which is in the mind *habitualiter,* not *actualiter.* This *species* is in the mind, in the sense of being the immediate object of knowledge, but its existence in the mind is independent of *consciousness.* Now that the *actual* cognition of the universal is necessary to its existence, Scotus denies. The subject of science is universal; and if the existence of universal were dependent upon what we happened to be thinking, science would not relate to anything real. On the other hand, he admits that the universal must be in the mind *habitualiter,* so that if a thing be considered as it is independent of its being cognized, there is no universality in it. For there is *in re extra* no one intelligible object attributed to different things. He holds, therefore, that such natures (i.e. sorts of things) as a *man* and a *horse,* which are real, and are not of themselves necessarily *this* man or *this* horse, though they cannot exist *in re* without being some particular man or horse, are in the *species intelligibilis* always represented positively indeterminate, it being the nature of the mind so to represent things. Accordingly any such nature is to be regarded as something which is of itself neither universal nor singular, but is universal in the mind, singular in things out of the mind. If there were nothing in the different men or horses which was not of itself singular, there would be no real unity except the numerical unity of the singulars; which would involve such absurd consequences as that the only real difference would be a numerical difference, and that there would be no real likenesses among things. If, therefore, it is asked whether the universal is in things, the answer is, that the nature which in the mind is universal, and is not in itself singular, exists in things. It is the very same nature which in the mind is universal and *in re* is singular; for if it were not, in knowing anything of a universal we should be knowing nothing of things, but only of our own thoughts, and our opinion would not be converted from true to false by a change in things. This nature is actually indeterminate only so far as it is in the mind. But to say that an object is in the mind is only a metaphorical way of saying that it stands to the intellect in the relation of known to knower. The truth is, therefore, that that real nature which exists *in re*, apart from all action of the intellect, though in itself, apart from its relations, it be singular, yet is actually universal as it exists in relation to the mind. But this universal only differs from the singular in the manner of its being conceived (*formaliter*), but not in the manner of its existence (*realiter*).[6]

Though this is the slightest possible sketch of the realism of Scotus, and leaves a number of important points unnoticed, yet it is sufficient to show the general manner of his thought and how subtle and difficult his doctrine is. That about one and the same nature being in the grade of singularity in existence, and in the grade of universality in the mind, gave rise to an extensive doctrine concerning the various kinds of identity and difference, called the doctrine of the *formalitates;* and this is the point against which Ockam directed his attack.

Ockam's nominalism may be said to be the next stage in English opinion. As Scotus's mind is always running on forms, so Ockam's is on logical terms; and all the subtle distinctions which Scotus effects by his *formalitates,* Ockam explains by implied syncategorematics (or adverbial expressions, such as *per se,* etc.) in terms. Ockam always thinks of a mental conception as a logical term, which, instead of existing on paper, or in the voice, is in the mind, but is of the same general nature, namely, a *sign.* The conception and the word differ in two respects: first, a word is arbitrarily imposed, while a conception is a natural sign; second, a word signifies whatever it signifies only indirectly, through the conception which signifies the same thing directly. Ockam enunciates his nominalism as follows:

It should be known that *singular* may be taken in two senses. In one sense, it signifies that which is one and not many; and in this sense those who hold that the universal is a quality of mind predicable of many, standing however in this predication, not for itself, but for those many (i.e. the nominalists), have to say that every universal is truly and really singular; because as every word, however general we may agree to consider it, is truly and really singular and one in number, because it is one and not many, so every universal is singular. In another sense, the name *singular* is used to denote whatever is one and not many, is a sign of something which is singular in the first sense, and is not fit to be the sign of many. Whence, using the word *universal* for that which is not one in number,—an acceptation many attribute to it,—I say that there is no universal; unless perchance you abuse the word and say that *people* is not one in number and is universal. But that would be puerile. It is to be maintained, therefore, that every universal is one singular thing, and therefore there is no universal except by signification, that is, by its being the sign of many.[7]

The arguments by which he supports this position present nothing of interest.* Against Scotus's doctrine that universals are without the mind in individuals, but are not really distinct from the individuals, but only formally so, he objects that it is impossible there should be any distinction existing out of the mind except between things really distinct. Yet he does not think of denying that an individual consists of matter and form, for these, though inseparable, are really distinct things; though a modern nominalist might ask in what sense things could be said to be distinct independently of any action of the mind, which are so inseparable as matter and form. But as to *relation,* he most emphatically and clearly denies that it exists as anything different from the things related; and this denial he expressly extends to relations of agreement and likeness as well as to those of opposition. While, therefore, he admits the real existence of qualities, he denies that these real qualities are respects in which things agree or differ; but things which agree or differ agree or differ in themselves and in no respect *extra animam.* He allows that things without the mind are similar, but this similarity consists merely in the fact that the mind can abstract one notion from the contemplation of them. A resemblance, therefore, consists solely in the property of the mind by which it naturally imposes one mental sign upon the resembling things. Yet he allows there is something in the things to which this mental sign corresponds.

This is the nominalism of Ockam so far as it can be sketched in a single paragraph, and without entering into the complexities of the Aristotelian psychology nor of the *parva logicalia.* He is not so thor-

---

*The *entia non sunt multiplicanda præter necessitatem* is the argument of Durand de St. Pourçain. But any given piece of popular information about scholasticism may be safely assumed to be wrong.

oughgoing as he might be, yet compared with Durandus and other contemporary nominalists he seems very radical and profound. He is truly the *venerabilis inceptor* of a new way of philosophizing which has now broadened, perhaps deepened also, into English empiricism.

England never forgot these teachings. During that Renaissance period when men could think that human knowledge was to be advanced by the use of Cicero's *Commonplaces,* we naturally see little effect from them; but one of the earliest prominent figures in modern philosophy is a man who carried the nominalistic spirit into everything,—religion, ethics, psychology, and physics, the *plusquam nominalis,* Thomas Hobbes of Malmesbury. His razor cuts off, not merely substantial forms, but every incorporeal substance. As for universals, he not only denies their real existence, but even that there are any universal conceptions except so far as we conceive names. In every part of his logic, names and speech play an extraordinarily important part. Truth and falsity, he says, have no place but among such creatures as use speech, for a true proposition is simply one whose predicate is the name of everything of which the subject is the name. "From hence, also, this may be deduced, that the first truths were arbitrarily made by those that first of all imposed names upon things, or received them from the imposition of others. For it is true (for example), that *man is a living creature,* but it is for this *reason* that it pleased men to impose both those names on the same thing."[8] The difference between true religion and superstition is simply that the state recognizes the former and not the latter.

The nominalistic love of simple theories is seen also in his opinion, that every event is a movement, and that the sensible qualities exist only in sensible beings, and in his doctrine that man is at bottom purely selfish in his actions.

His views concerning matter are worthy of notice, because Berkeley is known to have been a student of Hobbes, as Hobbes confesses himself to have been of Ockam. The following paragraph gives his opinion:—

And as for that matter which is common to all things, and which philosophers, following Aristotle, usually call *materia prima,* that is, *first matter,* it is not a body distinct from all other bodies, nor is it one of them. What then is it? A mere name; yet a name which is not of vain use; for it signifies a conception of body without the consideration of any form or other accident except only magnitude or extension, and aptness to receive form and other accident. So that whensoever we have use of the name *body in general,* if we use that of *materia prima,* we do well. For when a man, not knowing which was first, water or ice, would find out which of the two were the matter of both, he would be fain to suppose some third matter which were neither of these two; so he that would find out what is the matter of all things ought to suppose such as is not the matter of anything that exists. Wherefore *materia prima* is nothing; and therefore they do not attribute to it form or any other accident, besides quantity; whereas all singular things have their forms and accidents certain.

Materia prima therefore is body in general, that is, body considered universally, not as having neither form nor any accident, but in which no form nor any other accident but quantity are at all considered, that is, they are not drawn into argumentation. (p. 118)[9]

The next great name in English philosophy is Locke's. His philosophy is nominalistic, but does not regard things from a logical point of view at all. Nominalism, however, appears in psychology as sensationalism; for nominalism arises from taking that view of reality which regards whatever is in thought as caused by something in sense, and whatever is in sense as caused by something without the mind. But everybody knows that this is the character of Locke's philosophy. He believed that every idea springs from sensation and from his (vaguely explained) reflection.

Berkeley is undoubtedly more the offspring of Locke than of any other philosopher. Yet the influence of Hobbes with him is very evident and great; and Malebranche doubtless contributed to his thought. But he was by nature a radical and a nominalist. His whole philosophy rests upon an extreme nominalism of a sensationalistic type. He sets out with the proposition (supposed to have been already proved by Locke), that all the ideas in our minds are simply reproductions of sensations, external and internal. He maintains, moreover, that sensations can only be thus reproduced in such combinations as might have been given in immediate perception. We can conceive a man without a head, because there is nothing in the nature of sense to prevent our seeing such a thing; but we cannot conceive a sound without any pitch, because the two things are necessarily united in perception. On this principle he denies that we can have any abstract general ideas, that is, that universals can exist in the mind; if I think of a man it must be either of a short or a long or a middle-sized man, because if I see a man he must be one or the other of these. In the first draft of the Introduction of the *Principles of Human Knowledge*, which is now for the first time printed, he even goes so far as to censure Ockam for admitting that we can have general terms in our mind; Ockam's opinion being that we have in our minds conceptions, which are singular themselves, but are *signs* of many things.* But Berkeley probably knew only of

---

*The sole difference between Ockam and Hobbes is that the former admits the universal signs in the mind to be natural, while the latter thinks they only follow instituted language. The consequence of this difference is that, while Ockam regards all truth as depending on the mind's naturally imposing the same sign on two things, Hobbes will have it that the first truths were established by convention. But both would

Ockam from hearsay, and perhaps thought he occupied a position like that of Locke. Locke had a very singular opinion on the subject of general conceptions. He says:—

If we nicely reflect upon them, we shall find that general ideas are fictions, and contrivances of the mind, that carry difficulty with them, and do not so easily offer themselves as we are apt to imagine. For example, does it not require some pains and skill to form the general idea of a triangle (which is none of the most abstract, comprehensive, and difficult); for it must be neither oblique nor rectangle, neither equilateral, equicrural, nor scalenon, but all and none of these at once? In effect, is something imperfect that cannot exist, an idea wherein some parts of several different and inconsistent ideas are put together.[10]

To this Berkeley replies:—

Much is here said of the difficulty that abstract ideas carry with them, and the pains and skill requisite in forming them. And it is on all hands agreed that there is need of great toil and labor of the mind to emancipate our thoughts from particular objects, and raise them to those sublime speculations that are conversant about abstract ideas. From all which the natural consequence should seem to be, that so difficult a thing as the forming of abstract ideas was not necessary to communication, which is so easy and familiar to all sort of men. But we are told, if they seem obvious and easy to grown men, it is only because by constant and familiar use they are made so. Now, I would fain know at what time it is men are employed in surmounting that difficulty. It cannot be when they are grown up, for then it seems they are not conscious of such painstaking; it remains, therefore, to be the business of their childhood. And surely the great and multiplied labor of framing abstract notions will be found a hard task at that tender age. Is it not a hard thing to imagine that a couple of children cannot prate together of their sugar-plums and rattles, and the rest of their little trinkets, till they have first tacked together numberless inconsistencies, and so formed in their minds abstract general ideas, and annexed them to every common name they make use of?[11]

In his private note-book Berkeley has the following:—"*Mem.* To bring the killing blow at the last, e.g. in the matter of abstraction to bring Locke's general triangle in the last."[12]

There was certainly an opportunity for a splendid blow here, and he gave it.

From this nominalism he deduces his idealistic doctrine. And he puts it beyond any doubt that, if this principle be admitted, the exis-

---

doubtless allow that there is something *in re* to which such truths corresponded. But the sense of Berkeley's implication would be that there are no universal thought-signs at all. Whence it would follow that there is no truth and no judgments but propositions spoken or on paper.

tence of matter must be denied. Nothing that we can know or even think can exist without the mind, for we can only think reproductions of sensations, and the *esse* of these is *percipi*. To put it another way, we cannot think of a thing as existing unperceived, for we cannot separate in thought what cannot be separated in perception. It is true, I can think of a tree in a park without anybody by to see it; but I cannot think of it without anybody to imagine it; for I am aware that I am imagining it all the time. Syllogistically: trees, mountains, rivers, and all sensible things are perceived; and anything which is perceived is a sensation; now for a sensation to exist without being perceived is impossible; therefore, for any sensible thing to exist out of perception is impossible. Nor can there be anything out of the mind which *resembles* a sensible object, for the conception of likeness cannot be separated from likeness between ideas, because that is the only likeness which can be given in perception. An idea can be nothing but an idea, and it is absurd to say that anything inaudible can resemble a sound, or that anything invisible can resemble a color. But what exists without the mind can neither be heard nor seen; for we perceive only sensations within the mind. It is said that *Matter* exists without the mind. But what is meant by matter? It is acknowledged to be known only as *supporting* the accidents of bodies; and this word 'supporting' in this connection is a word without meaning. Nor is there any necessity for the hypothesis of external bodies. What we observe is that we have ideas. Were there any use in supposing external things it would be to account for this fact. But grant that bodies exist, and no one can say how they can possibly affect the mind; so that instead of removing a difficulty, the hypothesis only makes a new one.

But though Berkeley thinks we know nothing out of the mind, he by no means holds that all our experience is of a merely phantasmagoric character. It is not all a dream; for there are two things which distinguish experience from imagination: one is the superior vividness of experience; the other and most important is its connected character. Its parts hang together in the most intimate and intricate conjunction, in consequence of which we can infer the future from the past. "These two things it is," says Berkeley, in effect, "which constitute reality. I do not, therefore, deny the reality of common experience, although I deny its externality." Here we seem to have a third new conception of reality, different from either of those which we have insisted are characteristic of the nominalist and realist respectively, or if this is to be identified with either of those, it is with the realist view. Is not this something quite unexpected from so extreme a nominalist? To us, at least, it seems that this conception is indeed required to give an air of common sense to Berkeley's theory, but that it is of a totally different complexion from the rest. It seems to be something imported into his philosophy from without. We shall glance at this point again presently. He goes on to say that ideas are perfectly inert and passive. One idea does not make another and there is no power or agency in it. Hence, as there must be some cause of the succession of ideas, it must be *Spirit.* There is no *idea* of a spirit. But I have a consciousness of the operations of my spirit, what he calls a *notion* of my activity in calling up ideas at pleasure, and so have a relative knowledge of myself as an active being. But there is a succession of ideas not dependent on my will, the ideas of perception. Real things do not depend on my thought, but have an existence distinct from being perceived by me; but the *esse* of everything is *percipi;* therefore, *there must be some other mind wherein they exist.* "As sure, therefore, as the sensible world really exists, so sure do there an infinite omnipotent Spirit who contains and supports it."[13] This puts the keystone into the arch of Berkeleyan idealism, and gives a theory of the relation of the mind to external nature which, compared with the Cartesian Divine Assistance, is very satisfactory. It has been well remarked that, if the Cartesian dualism be admitted, no divine *assistance* can enable things to affect the mind or the mind things, but divine power must do the whole work. Berkeley's philosophy, like so many others, has partly originated in an attempt to escape the inconveniences of the Cartesian dualism. God, who has created our spirits, has the power immediately to raise ideas in them; and out of his wisdom and benevolence, he does this with such regularity that these ideas may serve as signs of one another. Hence, the laws of nature. Berkeley does not explain how our wills act on our bodies, but perhaps he would say that to a certain limited extent we can produce ideas in the mind of God as he does in ours. But a material thing being only an idea, exists only so long as it is in some mind. Should every mind cease to think it for a while, for so long it ceases to exist. Its permanent existence is kept up by its being an idea in the mind of God. Here we see how superficially the just-mentioned theory of reality is laid over the body of his thought. If the reality of a thing consists in its harmony with the body of realities, it is a quite needless extravagance to say that it ceases to exist as soon as it is no longer thought of. For the coherence of an idea with experience in general does not depend at all upon its being actually present to the mind all the time. But it is clear that when Berkeley says that reality consists in the connection of experience, he is simply using the word *reality* in a sense of his own. That *an object's independence of our thought about it* is constituted by its connection with experience in general, he has never conceived. On the contrary, that, according to him, is effected by its being in the mind of God. In the usual sense of the word *reality,* therefore, Berkeley's doctrine is that the reality of sensible things resides only in their archetypes in the divine mind. This is Platonistic, but it is not realistic. On the contrary, since it places reality wholly out of the mind in the cause of sensations, and since it denies reality (in the true sense of the word) to sensible things in so far as they are sensible, it is distinctly nominalistic. Historically there have been prominent examples of an alliance between nominalism and Platonism. Abélard and John of Salisbury, the only two defenders of nominalism of the time of the great controversy whose works remain to us, are both Platonists; and Roscellin, the famous author of the *sententia de flatu vocis*, the first man in the Middle Ages who carried attention to nominalism, is said and believed (all his writings are lost) to have been a follower of Scotus Erigena, the great Platonist of the ninth century. The reason of this odd conjunction of doctrines may perhaps be guessed at. The nominalist, by isolating his reality so entirely from mental influence as he has done, has made it something which the mind cannot conceive; he has created the so often talked of "improportion between the mind and the thing in itself." And it is to overcome the various difficulties to which this gives rise, that he supposes this *noumenon*, which, being totally unknown, the imagination can play about as it pleases, to be the emanation of archetypal ideas. The reality thus receives an intelligible nature again, and the peculiar inconveniences of nominalism are to some degree avoided.[14]

It does not seem to us strange that Berkeley's idealistic writings have not been received with much favor. They contain a great deal of argumentation of doubtful soundness, the dazzling character of which puts us more on our guard against it. They appear to be the productions of a most brilliant, original, powerful, but not thoroughly disciplined mind. He is apt to set out with wildly radical propositions, which he qualifies when they lead him to consequences he is not prepared to accept, without seeing how great the importance of his admissions is. He plainly begins his principles of human knowledge with the assumption that we have nothing in our minds but sensations, external and internal, and reproductions of them in the imagination. This goes far beyond Locke; it can be maintained only by the help of that "mental chemistry" started by Hartley.[15] But soon we find him admitting various *notions* which are not *ideas*, or reproductions of sensations, the most striking of which is the notion of a cause, which he leaves himself no way of accounting for experientially. Again, he lays down the principle that we can have no ideas in which the sensations are reproduced in an order or combination different from what could have occurred in experience; and that therefore we have no abstract conceptions. But he very soon grants that we can consider a triangle, without attending to whether it is equilateral, isosceles, or scalene; and does not reflect that such exclusive attention constitutes a species of abstraction. His want of profound study is also shown in his so wholly mistaking, as he does, the function of the hypothesis of matter. He thinks its only purpose is to account for the production of ideas in our minds, so occupied is he with the Cartesian problem. But the real part that material substance has to play is to account for (or formulate) the constant connection between the accidents. In his theory, this office is performed by the wisdom and benevolence of God in exciting ideas with such regularity that we can know what to expect. This makes the unity of accidents a rational unity, the material theory makes it a unity not of a *directly* intellectual origin. The question is, then, which does experience, which does science decide for? Does it appear that in nature all regularities are directly rational, all causes final causes; or does it appear that regularities extend beyond the requirement of a rational purpose, and are brought about by mechanical causes? Now science, as we all know, is generally hostile to the final causes, the operation of which it would restrict within certain spheres, and it finds decidedly an other than directly intellectual regularity in the universe. Accordingly the claim which Mr. Collyns Simon, Professor Fraser, and Mr. Archer Butler make for Berkeleyanism, that it is especially fit to harmonize with scientific thought, is as far as possible from the truth. The sort of science that his idealism would foster would be one which should consist in saying what each natural production was made for. Berkeley's own remarks about natural philosophy show how little he sympathized with physicists. They should all be read; we have only room to quote a detached sentence or two:—

To endeavor to explain the production of colors or sound by figure, motion, magnitude, and the like, must needs be labor in vain. . . . In the business of gravitation or mutual attraction, because it appears in many instances, some are straightway for pronouncing it *universal;* and that to attract and be attracted by every body is an essential quality inherent in all bodies whatever. . . . There is nothing necessary or essential in the case, but it depends entirely on the will of the Governing Spirit, who causes certain bodies to cleave together or tend towards each other according to various laws, whilst he keeps others at a fixed distance; and to some he gives a quite contrary tendency, to fly asunder just as he sees convenient. . . . First, it is plain philosophers amuse themselves in vain, when they inquire for any natural efficient cause, distinct from *mind* or *spirit.* Secondly, considering the whole creation is the workmanship of a *wise and good Agent,* it should seem to become philosophers to employ their thoughts (contrary to what some hold) about the final causes of things; and I must confess I see no reason why pointing out the various ends to which natural things are adapted, and for which they were originally with unspeakable wisdom contrived, should not be thought one good way of accounting for them, and altogether worthy of a philosopher. (Vol. I, p. 466)[16]

After this how can his disciples say *"that the true logic of physics is the first conclusion from his system!"*[17]

As for that argument which is so much used by Berkeley and others, that such and such a thing cannot exist because we cannot so much as frame the idea of such a thing,—that matter, for example, is impossible because it is an abstract idea, and we have no abstract ideas,—it appears to us to be a mode of reasoning which is to be used with extreme caution. Are the facts such, that if we could have an idea of the thing in question, we should infer its existence, or are they not? If not, no argument is necessary against its existence, until something is found out to make us suspect it exists. But if we ought to infer that it exists, if we only could frame the idea of it, why should we allow our mental incapacity to prevent us from adopting the proposition which logic requires? If such arguments had prevailed in mathematics (and Berkeley was equally strenuous in advocating them there), and if everything about negative quantities, the square root of *minus,* and infinitesimals, had been excluded from the subject on the ground that we can form no idea of such things, the science would have been simplified no doubt, simplified by never advancing to the more difficult matters. A better rule for avoiding the deceits of language is this: Do things fulfil the same function practically? Then let them be signified by the same word. Do they not? Then let them be distinguished. If I have learned a formula in gibberish which in any way jogs my memory so as to enable me in each single case to act as though I had a general idea, what possible utility is there in distinguishing between such a gibberish and formula and an idea? Why use the term *a general idea* in such a sense as to separate things which, for all experiential purposes, are the same?

The great inconsistency of the Berkeleyan theory, which prevents his nominalistic principles from appearing in their true colors, is that he has not treated mind and matter in the same way. All that he has said against the existence of matter might be said against the existence of mind; and the only thing which prevented his seeing that, was the vagueness of the Lockian *reflection,* or faculty of internal perception. It was not until after he had published his systematic exposition of his doctrine, that this objection ever occurred to him. He alludes to it in one of his dialogues, but his answer to it is very lame. Hume seized upon this point, and, developing it, equally denied the existence of mind and matter, maintaining that only appearances exist. Hume's philosophy is nothing but Berkeley's, with this change made in it, and written by a mind of a more sceptical tendency. The innocent bishop generated Hume; and as no one disputes that Hume gave rise to all modern philosophy of every kind, Berkeley ought to have a far more important place in the history of philosophy than has usually been assigned to him. His doctrine was the half-way station, or necessary resting-place between Locke's and Hume's.

Hume's greatness consists in the fact that he was the man who had the courage to carry out his principles to their utmost consequences, without regard to the character of the conclusions he reached. But neither he nor any other one has set forth nominalism in an absolutely thoroughgoing manner; and it is safe to say that no one ever will, unless it be to reduce it to absurdity.

We ought to say one word about Berkeley's theory of vision. It was undoubtedly an extraordinary piece of reasoning, and might have served for the basis of the modern science. Historically it has not had that fortune, because the modern science has been chiefly created in Germany, where Berkeley is little known and greatly misunderstood. We may fairly say that Berkeley taught the English some of the most essential principles of that hypothesis of sight which is now getting to prevail, more than a century before they were known to the rest of the world. This is much; but what is claimed by some of his advocates is astounding. One writer says that Berkeley's theory has been accepted by the leaders of all schools of thought! Professor Fraser admits that it has attracted no attention in Germany, but thinks the German mind too *a priori* to like Berkeley's reasoning.[18] But Helmholtz, who has done more than any other man to bring the empiricist theory into favor, says: "Our knowledge of the phenomena of vision is not so complete as to allow only one theory and exclude every other. It seems to me that the choice which different *savans* make between different theories of vision has thus far been governed more by their metaphysical inclinations than by any constraining power which the facts have had."[19] The best authorities, however, prefer the empiricist hypothesis; the fundamental proposition of which, as it is of Berkeley's, is that the sensations which we have in seeing are signs of the relations of things whose interpretation has to be discovered inductively. In the enumeration of the signs and of their uses, Berkeley shows considerable power in that sort of investigation, though there is naturally no very close resemblance between his and the modern accounts of the matter. There is no modern physiologist who would not think that Berkeley had greatly exaggerated the part that the muscular sense plays in vision.

Berkeley's theory of vision was an important step in the development of the associationalist psychology. He thought all our conceptions of body and of space were simply reproductions in the imagination of sensations of touch (including the muscular sense). This, if it were true, would be a most surprising case of mental chemistry, that is of a sensation being felt and yet so mixed with others that we cannot by an act of simple attention recognize it. Doubtless this theory had its influence in the production of Hartley's system.

Hume's phenomenalism and Hartley's associationalism were put forth almost contemporaneously about 1750. They contain the fundamental positions of the current English "positivism." From 1750 down to 1830—eighty years—nothing of particular importance was added to the nominalistic doctrine. At the beginning of this period Hume was

toning down his earlier radicalism, and Smith's theory of Moral Sentiments appeared. Later came Priestley's materialism, but there was
nothing new in that; and just at the end of the period, Brown's *Lectures
on the Human Mind*. The great body of the philosophy of those eighty
years is of the Scotch common-sense school. It is a weak sort of realistic
reaction, for which there is no adequate explanation within the sphere
of the history of philosophy. It would be curious to inquire whether
anything in the history of society could account for it. In 1829 appeared
James Mill's *Analysis of the Human Mind*, a really great nominalistic
book again. This was followed by Stuart Mill's *Logic* in 1843. Since
then, the school has produced nothing of the first importance; and it
will very likely lose its distinctive character now for a time, by being
merged in an empiricism of a less metaphysical and more working
kind. Already in Stuart Mill the nominalism is less salient than in the
classical writers; though it is quite unmistakable.

Thus we see how large a part of the metaphysical ideas of to-day
have come to us by inheritance from very early times, Berkeley being
one of the intellectual ancestors whose labors did as much as any one's
to enhance the value of the bequest. The realistic philosophy of the last
century has now lost all its popularity, except with the most conservative minds. And science as well as philosophy is nominalistic. The
doctrine of the correlation of forces, the discoveries of Helmholtz, and
the hypotheses of Liebig and of Darwin, have all that character of
explaining familiar phenomena apparently of a peculiar kind by extending the operation of simple mechanical principles, which belongs
to nominalism. Or if the nominalistic character of these doctrines
themselves cannot be detected, it will at least be admitted that they are
observed to carry along with them those daughters of nominalism,—
sensationalism, phenomenalism, individualism, and materialism. That
physical science is necessarily connected with doctrines of a debasing
moral tendency will be believed by few. But if we hold that such an
effect will not be produced by these doctrines on a mind which really
understands them, we are accepting this belief, not on experience,
which is rather against it, but on the strength of our general faith that
what is really true it is good to believe and evil to reject. On the other
hand, it is allowable to suppose that science has no essential affinity
with the philosophical views with which it seems to be every year
more associated. History cannot be held to exclude this supposition;
and science as it exists is certainly much less nominalistic than the
nominalists think it should be. Whewell represents it quite as well as
Mill. Yet a man who enters into the scientific thought of the day and
has not materialistic tendencies, is getting to be an impossibility. So
long as there is a dispute between nominalism and realism, so long as
the position we hold on the question is not determined by any proof
indisputable, but is more or less a matter of inclination, a man as he

gradually comes to feel the profound hostility of the two tendencies will, if he is not less than man, become engaged with one or other and can no more obey both than he can serve God and Mammon. If the two impulses are neutralized within him, the result simply is that he is left without any great intellectual motive. There is, indeed, no reason to suppose the logical question is in its own nature unsusceptible of solution. But that path out of the difficulty lies through the thorniest mazes of a science as dry as mathematics. Now there is a demand for mathematics; it helps to build bridges and drive engines, and therefore it becomes somebody's business to study it severely. But to have a philosophy is a matter of luxury; the only use of that is to make us feel comfortable and easy. It is a study for leisure hours; and we want it supplied in an elegant, an agreeable, an interesting form. The law of natural selection, which is the precise analogue in another realm of the law of supply and demand, has the most immediate effect in fostering the other faculties of the understanding, for the men of mental power succeed in the struggle for life; but the faculty of philosophizing, except in the literary way, is not called for; and therefore a difficult question cannot be expected to reach solution until it takes some practical form. If anybody should have the good luck to find out the solution, nobody else would take the trouble to understand it. But though the question of realism and nominalism has its roots in the technicalities of logic, its branches reach about our life. The question whether the *genus homo* has any existence except as individuals, is the question whether there is anything of any more dignity, worth, and importance than individual happiness, individual aspirations, and individual life. Whether men really have anything in common, so that the *community* is to be considered as an end in itself, and if so, what the relative value of the two factors is, is the most fundamental practical question in regard to every public institution the constitution of which we have it in our power to influence.

6

On a New Class of Observations, Suggested by the Principles of Logic

MS 1104. [First published, as MS 311, in W3:235–37.] Written in the summer of 1877, apparently for presentation, this brief paper recommends the observational study of sensations (as Peirce recommended for all sciences, even mathematics). Opposed to the "ordinary" view that "there are ultimate sensations without any general relations between them," Peirce argues that, although we can never completely capture in general descriptions the differences between different sensations, we can "make an indefinite progress toward such a result." But if that is unconvincing, Peirce goes on to say, perhaps we should try a phenomenological approach. Whether there are pure and completely determinate individual sensations is a question that can be dealt with by observational science; "here then," he concludes, "is a whole world of observation, to which we have been systematically blind, simply because of a wrong metaphysical prejudice."

It is usually admitted that there are two classes of mental representations, Immediate Representations or Sensations and Mediate Representations or Conceptions. The former are completely determinate or individual objects of thought; the latter are partially indeterminate or general objects. Granting that both these classes of objects exist, the question of the principle of Individuation or of the respect in which the individual differs from the general becomes one of extreme difficulty. Duns Scotus after a masterly criticism of all the attempts at answering it, puts forward the theory that the distinction is a peculiar one without any general character, and therefore itself presenting this peculiar aspect of individuality. Occam denies that any general objects of thought exist, which implies that no objects of thought have any resemblances, differences, or relations of any kind.[1] I on the other hand have undertaken to show that just the reverse of this is the case. That no object is individual but that the things the most concrete have still a certain amount of indeterminacy. Take, Phillip of Macedon for example. This object is logically divisible into Phillip drunk and Phillip sober; and so on; and you do not get down to anything completely determinate till you specify an indivisible instant of time, which is an ideal limit not attained in thought or in *re*.

It follows from this doctrine that we have no pure sensations, but only sensational elements of thought. Thus, the difference between *blue* and *red,* since it contains a sensational element, cannot be fully represented by any general description. As the sensational element is in this case very large, the failure of any attempt to describe the difference between *blue* & *red* in general terms is very striking. But, according to my theory of logic, since no pure sensations or individual objects exist, it follows that there must be some relation between *blue* & *red* & some general respect in which they differ, & therefore a step can be made towards a general description of their difference and if that general description is unsatisfactory, as it must be, then another relation must exist between the two colors, & an addition based on it may be made to the general description, & so on *ad infinitum.*

Here, then, are two metaphysical theories; the ordinary one and mine. According to the former, there are ultimate sensations without any general relations between them; according to the latter, although the differences between different sensations can never be completely covered by a general description, yet we may make an indefinite progress toward such a result. Which is true? I have no need to make any special observations to determine that, any more than I would in a question of a Perpetual Motion. I rest upon general principles which are deduced by irrefragable reasoning, from facts so general as to be admitted by all the world. But, for those who cannot understand this reasoning, I point to some facts which are not far to seek.

Different sensations resemble one another. That is sufficiently patent, & there is already a relation between sensations which at once totally & irretrievably overthrows the ordinary theory. Different sensations also differ in intensity. There is another class of relations between them, irreconcileable with their individual character. But it is commonly said that of relations of *kind* between different elementary sensations there are none. What none? When our ordinary language classifies them according to their kinds into colors, sounds, tastes, smells, feelings? This is not commonly noticed, but it is commonly said (I mean by physicists) that there is no *meaning* in the comparison of the intensity of a red and green light. Here I have 74 pieces of different coloured ribbons each one numbered upon which I have made frequent photometric experiments extending over a period of 12 months.[2] Now *I* say that a red and green can be compared in intensity with a considerable degree of accuracy. On another occasion, when the figures are relevant, I will give them. They are not so now, because you can all see that that red is darker than that blue & that that blue is darker than that red. There is an uncertainty in the judgment, a probable error. But that probable error is only another fact, another numerically determinate relation between the two sensations. So with a light & a sound. They can also be compared in intensity. Consider with equal attention the sound of a cannon or the appearance of a sixth magnitude star. Which is most intense? Can there be any doubt. Consider the light of the sun, & the sound of a falling pin. In the laws of these relations of intensity between different sensations there is an immense research, a branch of science. These are not the only relations between sensations but they are the most tangible and the natural starting point.

Here then is a whole world of observation, to which we have been systematically blind, simply because of a wrong metaphysical prejudice. One of the most accomplished men of science in the country went so far as to say to me the other day, that there was no reason to suppose that the sensations of color of one person had *any resemblance* to those of another! Violently as this flies in the face of the principles of inductive reasoning, I was not surprized to hear it said, because as Aristotle says εἴτε φιλοσοφητέον φιλοσοφητέον εἴτε μὴ φιλοσοφητέον φιλοσοφητέον, πάντως δὲ φιλοσοφητέον.[3] Whether we have an antimetaphysical metaphysics or a pro-metaphysical metaphysics, a metaphysics we are sure to have. And the less pains we take with it the more crudely metaphysical it will be.

7

The Fixation of Belief

P 107: Popular Science Monthly *12 (November 1877):1–15.*
[Also published in W3:242–57 (with parts of earlier versions,
MSS 187–189 [pp. 22–28]) and in CP 5.358–87. Peirce intended
to use this paper as essay 8 of his 1893 "Search for a Method,"
as chapter 5 of his 1894 "How to Reason" (MS 407), and as
the first essay in his 1909/10 "Essays on the Reasoning of
Science" (MS 334). Substantive changes in these two are re-
corded in the Notes; for the handwritten sections in MS 407
and the changes taken from an offprint that is no longer
extant, see the CP.] This is the first of a series of six papers,
collectively titled "Illustrations of the Logic of Science"; at
least one more paper was projected, and they were once listed
as a forthcoming book in Appleton's International Scientific
Series. The objective of the "Illustrations" is "to describe the
method of scientific investigation," and they contain, as
Peirce later recalled, "the earliest formulation of a method of
logical analysis that [I] had had the habit of alluding to as
[my] 'pragmatism,' " or "the tiny seed that under the culture
of richer minds, grew into the goodly tree of that same appel-
lation that already begins to afford a comfortable and whole-
some lodge for many a soul." In the first paper, he develops
his thesis that thought is a form of inquiry, and belief the
cessation of doubt, and he emphasizes the self-corrective na-
ture of the scientific method. He further discusses four methods
of fixing belief (those of tenacity and of authority, the a
priori *method, and the method of science) and argues that*
only the fourth, which alone appeals to an "external perma-
nency," can lead to success in the long run.

I

Few persons care to study logic, because everybody conceives himself to be proficient enough in the art of reasoning already. But I
observe that this satisfaction is limited to one's own ratiocination, and
does not extend to that of other men.

We come to the full possession of our power of drawing inferences the last of all our faculties, for it is not so much a natural gift as a long and difficult art. The history of its practice would make a grand subject for a book. The mediæval schoolmen, following the Romans, made logic the earliest of a boy's studies after grammar, as being very easy. So it was, as they understood it. Its fundamental principle, according to them, was, that all knowledge rests on either authority or reason; but that whatever is deduced by reason depends ultimately on a premise derived from authority. Accordingly, as soon as a boy was perfect in the syllogistic procedure, his intellectual kit of tools was held to be complete.

To Roger Bacon, that remarkable mind who in the middle of the thirteenth century was almost a scientific man, the schoolmen's conception of reasoning appeared only an obstacle to truth. He saw that experience alone teaches anything—a proposition which to us seems easy to understand, because a distinct conception of experience has been handed down to us from former generations; which to him also seemed perfectly clear, because its difficulties had not yet unfolded themselves. Of all kinds of experience, the best, he thought, was interior illumination, which teaches many things about Nature which the external senses could never discover, such as the transubstantiation of bread.[1]

Four centuries later, the more celebrated Bacon, in the first book of his *Novum Organum,* gave his clear account of experience as something which must be open to verification and reëxamination. But, superior as Lord Bacon's conception is to earlier notions, a modern reader who is not in awe of his grandiloquence is chiefly struck by the inadequacy of his view of scientific procedure. That we have only to make some crude experiments, to draw up briefs of the results in certain blank forms, to go through these by rule, checking off everything disproved and setting down the alternatives, and that thus in a few years physical science would be finished up—what an idea! "He wrote on science like a Lord Chancellor," indeed.[2]

The early scientists, Copernicus, Tycho Brahe, Kepler, Galileo, and Gilbert,[3] had methods more like those of their modern brethren. Kepler undertook to draw a curve through the places of Mars;* and[4] his greatest service to science was in impressing on men's minds that this was the thing to be done if they wished to improve astronomy; that they were not to content themselves with inquiring whether one system of epicycles was better than another, but that they were to sit down to the figures and find out what the curve, in truth, was. He accomplished this by his incomparable energy and courage, blundering along in the most inconceivable way (to us),[5] from one irrational

---

*Not quite so, but as nearly so as can be told in a few words.

hypothesis to another, until, after trying twenty-two of these, he fell, by the mere exhaustion of his invention, upon the orbit which a mind well furnished with the weapons of modern logic would have tried almost at the outset.

In the same way, every work of science great enough to be remembered for a few generations affords some exemplification of the defective state of the art of reasoning of the time when it was written; and each[6] chief step in science has been a lesson in logic. It was so when Lavoisier and his contemporaries took up the study of chemistry. The old chemist's maxim had been, "*Lege, lege, lege, labora, ora, et relege.*"[7] Lavoisier's method was not to read and pray, not to dream that some long and complicated chemical process would have a certain effect, to put it into practice with dull patience, after its inevitable failure to dream that with some modification it would have another result, and to end by publishing the last dream as a fact: his way was to carry his mind into his laboratory, and to make of his alembics and cucurbits instruments[8] of thought, giving a new conception of reasoning, as something which was to be done with one's eyes open, by manipulating real things instead of words and fancies.

The Darwinian controversy is, in large part, a question of logic. Mr. Darwin proposed to apply the statistical method to biology. The same thing had been done in a widely different branch of science, the theory of gases.[9] Though unable to say what the movements of any particular molecule of a gas would be on a certain hypothesis regarding the constitution of this class of bodies, Clausius and Maxwell were yet able,[10] by the application of the doctrine of probabilities, to predict that in the long run such and such a proportion of the molecules would, under given circumstances, acquire such and such velocities; that there would take place, every second, such and such a number[11] of collisions, etc.; and from these propositions were able to deduce certain properties of gases, especially in regard to their heat-relations. In like manner, Darwin, while unable to say what the operation of variation and natural selection in any individual case will be, demonstrates that in the long run they will adapt animals to their circumstances. Whether or not existing animal forms are due to such action, or what position the theory ought to take, forms the subject of a discussion in which questions of fact and questions of logic are curiously interlaced.

II

The object of reasoning is to find out, from the consideration of what we already know, something else which we do not know. Consequently, reasoning is good if it be such as to give a true conclusion from true premises, and not otherwise. Thus, the question of its validity is purely one of fact and not of thinking. A being the premises and B the conclusion,[12] the question is, whether these facts are really so related that if A is B is. If so, the inference is valid; if not, not. It is not in the least the question whether, when the premises are accepted by the mind, we feel an impulse to accept the conclusion also. It is true that we do generally reason correctly by nature. But that is an accident; the true conclusion would remain true if we had no impulse to accept it; and the false one would remain false, though we could not resist the tendency to believe in it.

We are, doubtless, in the main logical animals, but we are not perfectly so. Most of us, for example, are naturally more sanguine and hopeful than logic would justify. We seem to be so constituted that in the absence of any facts to go upon we are happy and self-satisfied; so that the effect of experience is continually to contract our hopes and aspirations. Yet a lifetime of the application of this corrective does not usually eradicate our sanguine disposition. Where hope is unchecked by any experience, it is likely that our optimism is extravagant. Logicality in regard to practical matters[13] is the most useful quality an animal can possess, and might, therefore, result from the action of natural selection; but outside of these it is probably of more advantage to the animal to have his mind filled with pleasing and encouraging visions, independently of their truth; and thus, upon unpractical subjects, natural selection might occasion a fallacious tendency of thought.

That which determines us, from given premises, to draw one inference rather than another, is some habit of mind, whether it be constitutional or acquired. The habit is good or otherwise, according as it produces true conclusions from true premises or not; and an inference is regarded as valid or not, without reference to the truth or falsity of its conclusion specially, but according as the habit which determines it is such as to produce true conclusions in general or not. The particular habit of mind which governs this or that inference may be formulated in a proposition whose truth depends on the validity of the inferences which the habit determines; and such a formula is called a *guiding principle* of inference. Suppose, for example, that we observe that a rotating disk of copper quickly comes to rest when placed between the poles of a magnet, and we infer that this will happen with every disk of copper. The guiding principle is, that what is true of one piece of copper is true of another. Such a guiding principle with regard to copper would be much safer than with regard to many other substances—brass, for example.

A book might be written to signalize all the most important of these guiding principles of reasoning. It would probably be, we must confess, of no service to a person whose thought is directed wholly to practical subjects, and whose activity moves along thoroughly-beaten paths. The problems which present themselves to such a mind are matters of routine which he has learned once for all to handle in learning his business. But let a man venture into an unfamiliar field, or where his results are not continually checked by experience, and all history shows that the most masculine intellect will ofttimes lose his orientation and waste his efforts in directions which bring him no nearer to his goal, or even carry him entirely astray. He is like a ship in the open sea, with no one on board who understands the rules of navigation. And in such a case some general study of the guiding principles of reasoning would be sure to be found useful.

The subject could hardly be treated, however, without being first limited; since almost any fact may serve as a guiding principle. But it so happens that there exists a division among facts, such that in one class are all those which are absolutely essential as guiding principles, while in the others are all which have any other interest as objects of research. This division is between those which are necessarily taken for granted in asking whether a certain conclusion follows[14] from certain premises, and those which are not implied in that question. A moment's thought will show that a variety of facts are already assumed when the logical question is first asked. It is implied, for instance, that there are such states of mind as doubt and belief—that a passage from one to the other is possible, the object of thought remaining the same, and that this transition is subject to some rules which all minds are alike bound by. As these are facts which we must already know before we can have any clear conception of reasoning at all, it cannot be supposed to be any longer of much interest to inquire into their truth or falsity. On the other hand, it is easy to believe that those rules of reasoning which are deduced from the very idea of the process are the ones which are the most essential; and, indeed, that so long as it conforms to these it will, at least, not lead to false conclusions from true premises. In point of fact, the importance of what may be deduced from the assumptions involved in the logical question turns out to be greater than might be supposed, and this for reasons which it is difficult to exhibit at the outset. The only one which I shall here mention is, that conceptions which are really products of logical reflection, without being readily seen to be so, mingle with our ordinary thoughts, and are frequently the causes of great confusion. This is the case, for example, with the conception of quality. A quality as such is never an object of observation. We can see that a thing is blue or green, but the quality of being blue and the quality of being green are not things which we see; they are products of logical reflection. The truth is, that common-sense, or thought as it first emerges above the level of the narrowly practical, is deeply imbued with that bad logical quality to which the epithet *metaphysical* is commonly applied; and nothing can clear it up but a severe course of logic.

III

We generally know when we wish to ask a question and when we wish to pronounce a judgment, for there is a dissimilarity between the sensation of doubting and that of believing.

But this is not all which distinguishes doubt from belief. There is a practical difference. Our beliefs guide our desires and shape our actions. The Assassins, or followers of the Old Man of the Mountain,[15] used to rush into death at his least command, because they believed that obedience to him would insure everlasting felicity. Had they doubted this, they would not have acted as they did. So it is with every belief, according to its degree. The feeling of believing is a more or less sure indication of there being established in our nature some habit which will determine our actions. Doubt never has such an effect.

Nor must we overlook a third point of difference. Doubt is an uneasy and dissatisfied state from which we struggle to free ourselves and pass into the state of belief; while the latter is a calm and satisfactory state which we do not wish to avoid, or to change to a belief in anything else.* On the contrary, we cling tenaciously, not merely to believing, but to believing just what we do believe.

Thus, both doubt and belief have positive effects upon us, though very different ones. Belief does not make us act at once, but puts us into such a condition that we shall behave in a certain way, when the occasion arises. Doubt has not the least effect of this sort, but stimulates us to action[16] until it is destroyed. This reminds us of the irritation of a nerve and the reflex action produced thereby; while for the analogue of belief, in the nervous system, we must look to what are called nervous associations—for example, to that habit of the nerves in consequence of which the smell of a peach will make the mouth water.

IV

The irritation of doubt causes a struggle to attain a state of belief. I shall term this struggle *inquiry*, though it must be admitted that this is sometimes not a very apt designation.

The irritation of doubt is the only immediate motive for the struggle to attain belief. It is certainly best for us that our beliefs should be such as may truly guide our actions so as to satisfy our desires; and this reflection will make us reject any belief which does not seem to have been so formed as to insure this result. But it will only do so by creating a doubt in the place of that belief. With the doubt, therefore, the struggle begins, and with the cessation of doubt it ends. Hence, the

*I am not speaking of secondary effects occasionally produced by the interference of other impulses.[17]

sole object of inquiry is the settlement of opinion. We may fancy that this is not enough for us, and that we seek, not merely an opinion, but a true opinion. But put this fancy to the test, and it proves groundless; for as soon as a firm belief is reached we are entirely satisfied, whether the belief be true or false. And it is clear that nothing out of the sphere of our knowledge can be our object, for nothing which does not affect the mind can be the motive for a mental effort. The most that can be maintained is, that we seek for a belief that we shall *think* to be true. But we think each one of our beliefs to be true, and, indeed, it is mere tautology to say so.

That the settlement of opinion is the sole end of inquiry is a very important proposition. It sweeps away, at once, various vague and erroneous conceptions of proof. A few of these may be noticed here.

1. Some philosophers have imagined that to start an inquiry it was only necessary to utter a question or set it down upon paper, and have even recommended us to begin our studies with questioning everything! But the mere putting of a proposition into the interrogative form does not stimulate the mind to any struggle after belief. There must be a real and living doubt, and without this all discussion is idle.

2. It is a very common idea that a demonstration must rest on some ultimate and absolutely indubitable propositions. These, according to one school, are first principles of a general nature; according to another, are first sensations. But, in point of fact, an inquiry, to have that completely satisfactory result called demonstration, has only to start with propositions perfectly free from all actual doubt. If the premises are not in fact doubted at all, they cannot be more satisfactory than they are.

3. Some people seem to love to argue a point after all the world is fully convinced of it. But no further advance can be made. When doubt ceases, mental action on the subject comes to an end; and, if it did go on, it would be without a purpose.

V

If the settlement of opinion is the sole object of inquiry, and if belief is of the nature of a habit, why should we not attain the desired end, by taking any answer to a question which we may fancy, and[18] constantly reiterating it to ourselves, dwelling on all which may conduce to that belief, and learning to turn with contempt and hatred from anything which might disturb it? This simple and direct method is really pursued by many men. I remember once being entreated not to read a certain newspaper lest it might change my opinion upon free-trade. "Lest I might be entrapped by its fallacies and misstatements," was the form of expression. "You are not," my friend said, "a special student of political economy. You might, therefore, easily be deceived by fallacious arguments upon the subject. You might, then, if you read this paper, be led to believe in protection. But you admit that free-trade is the true doctrine; and you do not wish to believe what is not true." I have often known this system to be deliberately adopted. Still oftener, the instinctive dislike of an undecided state of mind, exaggerated into a vague dread of doubt, makes men cling spasmodically to the views they already take. The man feels that, if he only holds to his belief without wavering, it will be entirely satisfactory. Nor can it be denied that a steady and immovable faith yields great peace of mind. It may, indeed, give rise to inconveniences, as if a man should resolutely continue to believe that fire would not burn him, or that he would be eternally damned if he received his *ingesta* otherwise than through a stomach-pump. But then the man who adopts this method will not allow that its inconveniences are greater than its advantages. He will say, "I hold steadfastly to the truth, and the truth is always wholesome." And in many cases it may very well be that the pleasure he derives from his calm faith overbalances any inconveniences resulting from its deceptive character. Thus, if it be true that death is annihilation, then the man who believes that he will certainly go straight to heaven when he dies, provided he have fulfilled certain simple observances in this life, has a cheap pleasure which will not be followed by the least disappointment. A similar consideration seems to have weight with many persons in religious topics, for we frequently hear it said, "Oh, I could not believe so-and-so, because I should be wretched if I did." When an ostrich buries its head in the sand as danger approaches, it very likely takes the happiest course. It hides the danger, and then calmly says there is no danger; and, if it feels perfectly sure there is none, why should it raise its head to see? A man may go through life, systematically keeping out of view all that might cause a change in his opinions, and if he only succeeds—basing his method, as he does, on two fundamental psychological laws—I do not see what can be said against his doing so. It would be an egotistical impertinence to object that his procedure is irrational, for that only amounts to saying that his method of settling belief is not ours. He does not propose to himself to be rational, and, indeed, will often talk with scorn of man's weak and illusive reason. So let him think as he pleases.

But this method of fixing belief, which may be called the method of tenacity, will be unable to hold its ground in practice. The social impulse is against it. The man who adopts it will find that other men think differently from him, and it will be apt to occur to him, in some saner moment, that their opinions are quite as good as his own, and this will shake his confidence in his belief. This conception, that another man's thought or sentiment may be equivalent to one's own, is a distinctly new step, and a highly important one. It arises from an impulse too strong in man to be suppressed, without danger of destroying the human species. Unless we make ourselves hermits, we shall necessarily influence each other's opinions; so that the problem becomes how to fix belief, not in the individual merely, but in the community.

Let the will of the state act, then, instead of that of the individual. Let an institution be created which shall have for its object to keep correct doctrines before the attention of the people, to reiterate them perpetually, and to teach them to the young; having at the same time power to prevent contrary doctrines from being taught, advocated, or expressed. Let all possible causes of a change of mind be removed from men's apprehensions. Let them be kept ignorant, lest they should learn of some reason to think otherwise than they do. Let their passions be enlisted, so that they may regard private and unusual opinions with hatred and horror. Then, let all men who reject the established belief be terrified into silence. Let the people turn out and tar-and-feather such men, or let inquisitions be made into the manner of thinking of suspected persons, and, when they are found guilty of forbidden beliefs, let them be subjected to some signal punishment. When complete agreement could not otherwise be reached, a general massacre of all who have not thought in a certain way has proved a very effective means of settling opinion in a country. If the power to do this be wanting, let a list of opinions be drawn up, to which no man of the least independence of thought can assent, and let the faithful be required to accept all these propositions, in order to segregate them as radically as possible from the influence of the rest of the world.

This method has, from the earliest times, been one of the chief means of upholding correct theological and political doctrines, and of preserving their universal or catholic character. In Rome, especially, it has been practised from the days of Numa Pompilius to those of Pius Nonus.[19] This is the most perfect example in history; but wherever there is a priesthood—and no religion has been without one—this method has been more or less made use of. Wherever there is an aristocracy, or a guild, or any association of a class of men whose interests depend or are supposed to depend on certain propositions, there will be inevitably found some traces of this natural product of social feeling. Cruelties always accompany this system; and when it is consistently carried out, they become atrocities of the most horrible kind in the eyes of any rational man. Nor should this occasion surprise, for the officer of a society does not feel justified in surrendering the interests of that society for the sake of mercy, as he might his own private interests. It is natural, therefore, that sympathy and fellowship should thus produce a most ruthless power.

In judging this method of fixing belief, which may be called the method of authority, we must, in the first place, allow its immeasurable mental and moral superiority to the method of tenacity. Its success is proportionately greater; and, in fact, it has over and over again worked the most majestic results. The mere structures of stone which it has caused to be put together—in Siam, for example, in Egypt, and in Europe—have many of them a sublimity hardly more than rivaled by the greatest works of Nature. And, except the geological epochs, there are no periods of time so vast as those which are measured by some of these organized faiths. If we scrutinize the matter closely, we shall find that there has not been one of their creeds which has remained always the same; yet the change is so slow as to be imperceptible during one person's life, so that individual belief remains sensibly fixed. For the mass of mankind, then, there is perhaps no better method than this. If it is their highest impulse to be intellectual slaves, then slaves they ought to remain.

But no institution can undertake to regulate opinions upon every subject. Only the most important ones can be attended to, and on the rest men's minds must be left to the action of natural causes. This imperfection will be no source of weakness so long as men are in such a state of culture that one opinion does not influence another—that is, so long as they cannot put two and two together. But in the most priestridden states some individuals will be found who are raised above that condition. These men possess a wider sort of social feeling; they see that men in other countries and in other ages have held to very different doctrines from those which they themselves have been brought up to believe; and they cannot help seeing that it is the mere accident of their having been taught as they have, and of their having been surrounded with the manners and associations they have, that has caused them to believe as they do and not far differently. And their candor cannot resist the reflection that there is no reason to rate their own views at a higher value than those of other nations and other centuries; and this gives rise to doubts in their minds.

They will further perceive that such doubts as these must exist in their minds with reference to every belief which seems to be determined by the caprice either of themselves or of those who originated the popular opinions. The willful adherence to a belief, and the arbitrary forcing of it upon others, must, therefore, both be given up, and a new method of settling opinions must be adopted, which shall not only produce an impulse to believe, but shall also decide what proposition it is which is to be believed. Let the action of natural preferences be unimpeded, then, and under their influence let men, conversing together and regarding matters in different lights, gradually develop beliefs in harmony with natural causes. This method resembles that by which conceptions of art have been brought to maturity. The most perfect example of it is to be found in the history of metaphysical philosophy. Systems of this sort have not usually rested upon any observed facts, at least not in any great degree. They have been chiefly adopted because their fundamental propositions seemed "agreeable to reason." This is an apt expression; it does not mean that which agrees with experience, but that which we find ourselves inclined to believe. Plato, for example, finds it agreeable to reason that the distances of the celestial spheres from one another should be proportional to the different lengths of strings which produce harmonious chords.[20] Many philosophers have been led to their main conclusions by considerations like this; but this is the lowest and least developed form which the method takes, for it is clear that another man might find Kepler's theory, that the celestial spheres are proportional to the inscribed and circumscribed spheres of the different regular solids, more agreeable to *his* reason. But the shock of opinions will soon lead men to rest on preferences of a far more universal nature. Take, for example, the doctrine that man only acts selfishly—that is, from the consideration that acting in one way will afford him more pleasure than acting in another.[21] This rests on no fact in the world, but it has had a wide acceptance as being the only reasonable theory.

This method is far more intellectual and respectable from the point of view of reason than either of the others which we have noticed.[22] But its failure has been the most manifest. It makes of inquiry something similar to the development of taste; but taste, unfortunately, is always more or less a matter of fashion, and accordingly metaphysicians have never come to any fixed agreement, but the pendulum has swung backward and forward between a more material and a more spiritual philosophy, from the earliest times to the latest. And so from this, which has been called the *a priori* method, we are driven, in Lord Bacon's phrase, to a true induction.[23] We have examined into this *a priori* method as something which promised to deliver our opinions from their accidental and capricious element. But development, while it is a process which eliminates the effect of some casual circumstances, only magnifies that of others. This method, therefore, does not differ in a very essential way from that of authority. The government may not have lifted its finger to influence my convictions; I may have been left outwardly quite free to choose, we will say, between monogamy and polygamy, and, appealing to my conscience only, I may have concluded that the latter practice is in itself licentious. But when I come to see that the chief obstacle to the spread of Christianity among a people of as high culture as the Hindoos has been a conviction of the immorality of our way of treating women, I cannot help seeing that, though governments do not interfere, sentiments in their development will be very greatly determined by accidental causes. Now, there are some people, among whom I must suppose that my reader is to be found, who, when they see that any belief of theirs is determined by any circumstance extraneous to the facts, will from that moment not merely admit in words that that belief is doubtful, but will experience a real doubt of it, so that it ceases to be a belief.[24]

To satisfy our doubts, therefore, it is necessary that a method should be found by which our beliefs may be caused by nothing human, but by some external permanency—by something upon which our thinking has no effect. Some mystics imagine that they have such a method in a private inspiration from on high. But that is only a form of the method of tenacity, in which the conception of truth as something public is not yet developed. Our external permanency would not be external, in our sense, if it was restricted in its influence to one individual. It must be something which affects, or might affect, every man. And, though these affections are necessarily as various as are individual conditions, yet the method must be such that the ultimate conclusion of every man shall be the same. Such is the method of science. Its fundamental hypothesis, restated in more familiar language, is this: There are real things, whose characters are entirely independent of our opinions about them; those realities affect our senses according to regular laws, and, though our sensations are as different as our relations to the objects, yet, by taking advantage of the laws of perception, we can ascertain by reasoning how things really are, and any man, if he have sufficient experience and reason enough about it, will be led to the one true conclusion. The new conception here involved is that of reality. It may be asked how I know that there are any realities. If this hypothesis is the sole support of my method of inquiry, my method of inquiry must not be used to support my hypothesis. The reply is this: 1. If investigation cannot be regarded as proving that there are real things, it at least does not lead to a contrary conclusion; but the method and the conception on which it is based remain ever in harmony. No doubts of the method, therefore, necessarily arise from its practice, as is the case with all the others. 2. The feeling which gives rise to any method of fixing belief is a dissatisfaction at two repugnant propositions. But here already is a vague concession that there is some *one* thing to which a proposition should conform. Nobody, therefore, can really doubt that there are realities, or,[25] if he did, doubt would not be a source of dissatisfaction. The hypothesis, therefore, is one which every mind admits. So that the social impulse does not cause me to doubt it. 3. Everybody uses[26] the scientific method about a great many things, and only ceases to use it when he does not know how to apply it. 4. Experience of the method has not led me[27] to doubt it, but, on the contrary, scientific investigation has had the most wonderful triumphs in the way of settling opinion. These afford the explanation of my not doubting the method or the hypothesis which it supposes; and not having any doubt, nor believing that anybody else whom I could influence has, it would be the merest babble for me to say more about it. If there be anybody with a living doubt upon the subject, let him consider it.

To describe the method of scientific investigation is the object of this series of papers. At present I have only room to notice some points of contrast between it and other methods of fixing belief.

This is the only one of the four methods which presents any distinction of a right and a wrong way. If I adopt the method of tenacity and shut myself out from all influences, whatever I think necessary to doing this is necessary according to that method. So with the method of authority: the state may try to put down heresy by means which, from a scientific point of view, seem very ill-calculated to accomplish its purposes; but the only test *on that method* is what the state thinks, so that it cannot pursue the method wrongly. So with the *a priori* method. The very essence of it is to think as one is inclined to think. All metaphysicians will be sure to do that, however they may be inclined to judge each other to be perversely wrong. The Hegelian system recognizes every natural tendency of thought as logical, although it be certain to be abolished by counter-tendencies. Hegel thinks there is a regular system in the succession of these tendencies, in consequence of which, after drifting one way and the other for a long time, opinion will at last go right. And it is true that metaphysicians get the right ideas at last; Hegel's system of Nature represents tolerably the science of that[28] day; and one may be sure that whatever scientific investigation has put out of doubt will presently receive *a priori* demonstration on the part of the metaphysicians. But with the scientific method the case is different. I may start with known and observed facts to proceed to the unknown; and yet the rules which I follow in doing so may not be such as investigation would approve. The test of whether I am truly following the method is not an immediate appeal to my feelings and purposes, but, on the contrary, itself involves the application of the method. Hence it is that bad reasoning as well as good reasoning is possible; and this fact is the foundation of the practical side of logic.

It is not to be supposed that the first three methods of settling opinion present no advantage whatever over the scientific method.[29] On the contrary, each has some peculiar convenience of its own. The *a priori* method is distinguished for its comfortable conclusions. It is the nature of the process to adopt whatever belief we are inclined to, and there are certain flatteries to the vanity of man which we all believe by nature, until we are awakened from our pleasing dream by some rough facts. The method of authority will always govern the mass of mankind; and those who wield the various forms of organized force in the state will never be convinced that dangerous reasoning ought not to be suppressed in some way. If liberty of speech is to be untrammeled from the grosser forms of constraint, then uniformity of opinion will be secured by a moral terrorism to which the respectability of society will give its thorough approval. Following the method of authority is the path of peace. Certain non-conformities are permitted; certain others (considered unsafe) are forbidden. These are different in different countries and in different ages; but, wherever you are, let it be known that you seriously hold a tabooed belief, and you may be perfectly sure of being treated with a cruelty less brutal but more refined than hunting you like a wolf. Thus, the greatest intellectual benefactors of mankind have never dared, and dare not now, to utter the whole of their thought; and thus a shade of *prima facie* doubt is cast upon every proposition which is considered essential to the security of society. Singularly enough, the persecution does not all come from without; but a man torments himself and is oftentimes most distressed at finding himself believing propositions which he has been brought up to regard with aversion. The peaceful and sympathetic man will, therefore, find it hard to resist the temptation to submit his opinions to authority. But most of all I admire the method of tenacity for its strength, simplicity, and directness. Men who pursue it are distinguished for their decision of character, which becomes very easy with such a mental rule. They do not waste time in trying to make up their minds what they want, but, fastening like lightning upon whatever alternative comes first, they hold to it to the end, whatever happens, without an instant's irresolution. This is one of the splendid qualities which generally accompany brilliant, unlasting success. It is impossible not to envy the man who can dismiss reason, although we know how it must turn out at last.

Such are the advantages which the other methods of settling opinion have over scientific investigation. A man should consider well of them; and then he should consider that, after all, he wishes his opinions to coincide with the fact, and that there is no reason why the results of these three methods should do so. To bring about this effect is the prerogative of the method of science. Upon such considerations he has to make his choice—a choice which is far more than the adoption of any intellectual opinion, which is one of the ruling decisions of his life, to which, when once made, he is bound to adhere. The force of habit will sometimes cause a man to hold on to old beliefs, after he is in a condition to see that they have no sound basis. But reflection upon the state of the case will overcome these habits, and he ought to allow reflection its full weight. People sometimes shrink from doing this, having an idea that beliefs are wholesome which they cannot help feeling rest on nothing. But let such persons suppose an analogous though different case from their own. Let them ask themselves what they would say to a reformed Mussulman who should hesitate to give up his old notions in regard to the relations of the sexes; or to a reformed Catholic who should still shrink from reading the Bible. Would they not say that these persons ought to consider the matter fully, and clearly understand the new doctrine, and then ought to embrace it, in its entirety? But, above all, let it be considered that what is more wholesome than any particular belief is integrity of belief, and that to avoid looking into the support of any belief from a fear that it may turn out rotten is quite as immoral as it is disadvantageous. The person who confesses that there is such a thing as truth, which is distinguished from falsehood simply by this, that if acted on it will carry us to the point we aim at and not astray, and then, though convinced of this, dares not know the truth and seeks to avoid it, is in a sorry state of mind indeed.

Yes, the other methods do have their merits: a clear logical conscience does cost something—just as any virtue, just as all that we cherish, costs us dear. But we should not desire it to be otherwise. The genius of a man's logical method should be loved and reverenced as his bride, whom he has chosen from all the world. He need not contemn the others; on the contrary, he may honor them deeply, and in doing so he only honors her the more. But she is the one that he has chosen, and he knows that he was right in making that choice. And having made it, he will work and fight for her, and will not complain that there are blows to take, hoping that there may be as many and as hard to give, and will strive to be the worthy knight and champion of her from the blaze of whose splendors he draws his inspiration and his courage.

8

How to Make Our Ideas Clear

P 119: Popular Science Monthly *12 (January 1878):286–302. [Also published in W3:257–76 and in CP 5.388–410. Peirce intended to use this paper as essay 9 of his 1893 "Search for a Method" and as chapter 16 of his 1894 "How to Reason" (MS 422); the changes in MS 422 are recorded in the Notes.]* *Written between 13 and 24 September 1877, while Peirce was sailing to Plymouth, England, this paper criticizes Descartes' doctrine of the clearness of ideas and goes on to develop Peirce's own theory, according to which there are three levels or grades of clearness. The theory of meaning associated with the third grade of clearness is represented in the pragmatic maxim (and is sometimes thought of as an operationalist theory). Peirce ends the paper by applying the pragmatic maxim in his examination of the meaning of several conceptions, including 'realism'. (He later thought that his early pragmatism was too nominalistic.)*

I

Whoever has looked into a modern treatise on logic of the common sort, will doubtless remember the two distinctions between *clear* and *obscure* conceptions, and between *distinct* and *confused* conceptions. They have lain in the books now for nigh two centuries, unimproved and unmodified, and are generally reckoned by logicians as among the gems of their doctrine.

A clear idea is defined as one which is so apprehended that it will be recognized wherever it is met with, and so that no other will be mistaken for it. If it fails of this clearness, it is said to be obscure.

This is rather a neat bit of philosophical terminology; yet, since it is clearness that they were defining, I wish the logicians had made their definition a little more plain. Never to fail to recognize an idea, and under no circumstances to mistake another for it, let it come in how recondite a form it may, would indeed imply such prodigious force and clearness of intellect as is seldom met with in this world. On the other hand, merely to have such an acquaintance with the idea as to have become familiar with it, and to have lost all hesitancy in recognizing it in ordinary cases, hardly seems to deserve the name of clearness of apprehension, since after all it only amounts to a subjective feeling of mastery which may be entirely mistaken. I take it, however, that when the logicians speak of "clearness," they mean nothing more than such a familiarity with an idea, since they regard the quality as but a small merit, which needs to be supplemented by another, which they call *distinctness*.

A distinct idea is defined as one which contains nothing which is not clear. This is technical language; by the *contents* of an idea logicians understand whatever is contained in its definition. So that an idea is *distinctly* apprehended, according to them, when we can give a precise definition of it, in abstract terms. Here the professional logicians leave the subject; and I would not have troubled the reader with what they have to say, if it were not such a striking example of how they have been slumbering through ages of intellectual activity, listlessly disregarding the enginery of modern thought, and never dreaming of applying its lessons to the improvement of logic. It is easy to show that the doctrine that familiar use and abstract distinctness make the perfection of apprehension has its only true place in philosophies which have long been extinct; and it is now time to formulate the method of attaining to a more perfect clearness of thought, such as we see and admire in the thinkers of our own time.

When Descartes set about the reconstruction of philosophy, his first step was to (theoretically) permit skepticism and to discard the practice of the schoolmen of looking to authority as the ultimate source of truth. That done, he sought a more natural fountain of true principles, and professed to find it in the human mind; thus passing, in the directest way, from the method of authority to that of apriority, as described in my first paper. Self-consciousness was to furnish us with our fundamental truths, and to decide what was agreeable to reason. But since, evidently, not all ideas are true, he was led to note, as the first condition of infallibility, that they must be clear. The distinction between an idea *seeming* clear and really being so, never occurred to him. Trusting to introspection, as he did, even for a knowledge of external things, why should he question its testimony in respect to the contents of our own minds? But then, I suppose, seeing men, who seemed to be quite clear and positive, holding opposite opinions upon fundamental principles, he was further led to say that clearness of ideas is not sufficient, but that they need also to be distinct, i.e., to have nothing unclear about them. What he probably meant by this (for he did not explain himself with precision) was, that they must sustain the test of dialectical examination; that they must not only seem clear at the outset, but that discussion must never be able to bring to light points of obscurity connected with them.

Such was the distinction of Descartes, and one sees that it was precisely on the level of his philosophy.[1] It was somewhat developed by Leibnitz. This great and singular genius was as remarkable for what he failed to see as for what he saw. That a piece of mechanism could not do work perpetually without being fed with power in some form, was a thing perfectly apparent to him; yet he did not understand that the machinery of the mind can only transform knowledge, but never originate it, unless it be fed with facts of observation. He thus missed the most essential point of the Cartesian philosophy, which is, that to accept propositions which seem perfectly evident to us is a thing which, whether it be logical or illogical, we cannot help doing.[2] Instead of regarding the matter in this way, he sought to reduce the first principles of science to formulas which cannot be denied without self-contradiction, and was apparently unaware of the great difference between his position and that of Descartes. So he reverted to the old formalities of logic, and, above all, abstract definitions played a great part in his philosophy. It was quite natural, therefore, that on observing that the method of Descartes labored under the difficulty that we may seem to ourselves to have clear apprehensions of ideas which in truth are very hazy, no better remedy occurred to him than to require an abstract definition of every important term. Accordingly, in adopting the distinction of *clear* and *distinct* notions,[3] he described the latter quality as the clear apprehension of everything contained in the definition; and the books have ever since copied his words. There is no danger that his chimerical scheme will ever again be over-valued. Nothing new can ever be learned by analyzing definitions. Nevertheless, our existing beliefs can be set in order by this process, and order is an essential element of intellectual economy, as of every other. It may be acknowledged, therefore, that the books are right in making familiarity with a notion the first step toward clearness of apprehension, and the defining of it the second. But in omitting all mention of any higher perspicuity of thought, they simply mirror a philosophy which was exploded a hundred years ago. That much-admired "ornament of logic"—the doctrine of clearness and distinctness—may be pretty enough, but it is high time to relegate to our cabinet of curiosities the antique *bijou*, and to wear about us something better adapted to modern uses.

The very first lesson that we have a right to demand that logic shall teach us is, how to make our ideas clear; and a most important one it is, depreciated only by minds who stand in need of it. To know what we think, to be masters of our own meaning, will make a solid foundation for great and weighty thought. It is most easily learned by those whose ideas are meagre and restricted; and far happier they than such as wallow helplessly in a rich mud of conceptions. A nation, it is true, may, in the course of generations, overcome the disadvantage of an excessive wealth of language and its natural concomitant, a vast, un-fathomable deep of ideas. We may see it in history, slowly perfecting its literary forms, sloughing at length its metaphysics, and, by virtue of the untirable patience which is often a compensation, attaining great excellence in every branch of mental acquirement. The page of history is not yet unrolled which is to tell us whether such a people will or will not in the long-run prevail over one whose ideas (like the words of their language) are few, but which possesses a wonderful mastery over those which it has. For an individual, however, there can be no question that a few clear ideas are worth more than many confused ones. A young man would hardly be persuaded to sacrifice the greater part of his thoughts to save the rest; and the muddled head is the least apt to see the necessity of such a sacrifice. Him we can usually only commiserate, as a person with a congenital defect. Time will help him, but intellectual maturity with regard to clearness comes rather late, an unfortunate arrangement of Nature, inasmuch as clear-ness is of less use to a man settled in life, whose errors have in great measure had their effect, than it would be to one whose path lies before him. It is terrible to see how a single unclear idea, a single formula without meaning, lurking in a young man's head, will sometimes act like an obstruction of inert matter in an artery, hindering the nutrition of the brain, and condemning its victim to pine away in the fullness of his intellectual vigor and in the midst of intellectual plenty. Many a man has cherished for years as his hobby some vague shadow of an idea, too meaningless to be positively false; he has, nevertheless, pas-sionately loved it, has made it his companion by day and by night, and has given to it his strength and his life, leaving all other occupations for its sake, and in short has lived with it and for it, until it has become, as it were, flesh of his flesh and bone of his bone; and then he has waked up some bright morning to find it gone, clean vanished away like the beautiful Melusina of the fable,[4] and the essence of his life gone with it. I have myself known such a man; and who can tell how many histories of circle-squarers, metaphysicians, astrologers, and what not, may not be told in the old German story?

II

The principles set forth in the first of these papers[5] lead, at once, to a method of reaching a clearness of thought of a far higher grade than the "distinctness" of the logicians. We have there found that the action of thought is excited by the irritation of doubt, and ceases when belief is attained; so that the production of belief is the sole function of thought. All these words, however, are too strong for my purpose. It is as if I had described the phenomena as they appear under a mental microscope. Doubt and Belief, as the words are commonly employed, relate to religious or other grave discussions. But here I use them to designate the starting of any question, no matter how small or how great, and the resolution of it. If, for instance, in a horse-car, I pull out my purse and find a five-cent nickel and five coppers, I decide, while my hand is going to the purse, in which way I will pay my fare. To call such a question Doubt, and my decision Belief, is certainly to use words very disproportionate to the occasion. To speak of such a doubt as causing an irritation which needs to be appeased, suggests a temper which is uncomfortable to the verge of insanity. Yet, looking at the matter minutely, it must be admitted that, if there is the least hesitation as to whether I shall pay the five coppers or the nickel (as there will be sure to be, unless I act from some previously contracted habit in the matter), though irritation is too strong a word, yet I am excited to such small mental activity as may be necessary to deciding how I shall act. Most frequently doubts arise from some indecision, however momentary, in our action. Sometimes it is not so. I have, for example, to wait in a railway-station, and to pass the time I read the advertisements on the walls, I compare the advantages of different trains and different routes which I never expect to take, merely fancying myself to be in a state of hesitancy, because I am bored with having nothing to trouble me. Feigned hesitancy, whether feigned for mere amusement or with a lofty purpose, plays a great part in the production of scientific inquiry. However the doubt may originate, it stimulates the mind to an activity which may be slight or energetic, calm or turbulent. Images pass rapidly through consciousness, one incessantly melting into another, until at last, when all is over—it may be in a fraction of a second, in an hour, or after long years—we find ourselves decided as to how we should act under such circumstances as those which occasioned our hesitation. In other words, we have attained belief.

In this process we observe two sorts of elements of consciousness, the distinction between which may best be made clear by means of an illustration. In a piece of music there are the separate notes, and there is the air. A single tone may be prolonged for an hour or a day, and it exists as perfectly in each second of that time as in the whole taken together; so that, as long as it is sounding, it might be present to a sense from which everything in the past was as completely absent as the future itself. But it is different with the air, the performance of which occupies a certain time, during the portions of which only portions of it are played. It consists in an orderliness in the succession of sounds which strike the ear at different times; and to perceive it there must be some continuity of consciousness which makes the events of a lapse of time present to us. We certainly only perceive the air by hearing the separate notes; yet we cannot be said to directly hear it, for we hear only what is present at the instant, and an orderliness of succession cannot exist in an instant. These two sorts of objects, what we are *immediately* conscious of and what we are *mediately* conscious of, are found in all consciousness. Some elements (the sensations) are completely present at every instant so long as they last, while others (like thought) are actions having beginning, middle, and end, and consist in a congruence in the succession of sensations which flow through the mind. They cannot be immediately present to us, but must cover some portion of the past or future. Thought is a thread of melody running through the succession of our sensations.

We may add that just as a piece of music may be written in parts, each part having its own air, so various systems of relationship of succession subsist together between the same sensations. These different systems are distinguished by having different motives, ideas, or functions. Thought is only one such system, for its sole motive, idea, and function, is to produce belief, and whatever does not concern that purpose belongs to some other system of relations. The action of thinking may incidentally have other results; it may serve to amuse us, for example, and among *dilettanti* it is not rare to find those who have so perverted thought to the purposes of pleasure that it seems to vex them to think that the questions upon which they delight to exercise it may ever get finally settled; and a positive discovery which takes a favorite subject out of the arena of literary debate is met with ill-concealed dislike. This disposition is the very debauchery of thought. But the soul and meaning of thought, abstracted from the other elements which accompany it, though it may be voluntarily thwarted, can never be made to direct itself toward anything but the production of belief. Thought in action has for its only possible motive the attainment of thought at rest; and whatever does not refer to belief is no part of the thought itself.

And what, then, is belief? It is the demi-cadence which closes a musical phrase in the symphony of our intellectual life. We have seen that it has just three properties: First, it is something that we are aware of; second, it appeases the irritation of doubt; and, third, it involves the establishment in our nature of a rule of action, or, say for short, a *habit*. As it appeases the irritation of doubt, which is the motive for thinking, thought relaxes, and comes to rest for a moment when belief is reached. But, since belief is a rule for action, the application of which involves further doubt and further thought, at the same time that it is a stopping-place, it is also a new starting-place for thought. That is why I have permitted myself to call it thought at rest, although thought is essentially an action. The *final* upshot of thinking is the exercise of volition, and of this thought no longer forms a part; but belief is only a stadium of mental action, an effect upon our nature due to thought, which will influence future thinking.

The essence of belief is the establishment of a habit, and different beliefs are distinguished by the different modes of action to which they give rise. If beliefs do not differ in this respect, if they appease the same doubt by producing the same rule of action, then no mere differences in the manner of consciousness of them can make them different beliefs, any more than playing a tune in different keys is playing different tunes. Imaginary distinctions are often drawn between beliefs which differ only in their mode of expression;—the wrangling which ensues is real enough, however. To believe that any objects are arranged as in Fig. 1, and to believe that they are arranged[6] in Fig. 2, are one and the same belief; yet it is conceivable that a man should assert one proposition and deny the other. Such false distinctions do as much harm as the confusion of beliefs really different, and are among the pitfalls of which we ought constantly to beware, especially when we are upon metaphysical ground. One singular deception of this sort, which often occurs, is to mistake the sensation produced by our own unclearness of thought for a character of the object we are thinking. Instead of perceiving that the obscurity is purely subjective, we fancy that we contemplate a quality of the object which is essentially mysterious; and if our conception be afterward presented to us in a clear form we do not recognize it as the same, owing to the absence of the feeling of unintelligibility. So long as this deception lasts, it obviously puts an impassable barrier in the way of perspicuous thinking; so that it equally interests the opponents of rational thought to perpetuate it, and its adherents to guard against it.

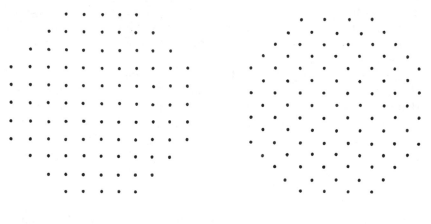

Fig. 1.   Fig. 2.

Another such deception is to mistake a mere difference in the grammatical construction of two words for a distinction between the ideas they express. In this pedantic age, when the general mob of writers attend so much more to words than to things, this error is common enough. When I just said that thought is an *action*, and that it consists in a *relation*, although a person performs an action but not a relation, which can only be the result of an action, yet there was no inconsistency in what I said, but only a grammatical vagueness.

From all these sophisms we shall be perfectly safe so long as we reflect that the whole function of thought is to produce habits of action; and that whatever there is connected with a thought, but irrelevant to its purpose, is an accretion to it, but no part of it. If there be a unity among our sensations which has no reference to how we shall act on a given occasion, as when we listen to a piece of music, why we do not call that thinking. To develop its meaning, we have, therefore, simply to determine what habits it produces, for what a thing means is simply what habits it involves. Now, the identity of a habit depends on how it might lead us to act, not merely under such circumstances as are likely to arise, but under such as might possibly occur, no matter how improbable they may be.[7] What the habit is depends on *when* and *how* it causes us to act. As for the *when*, every stimulus to action is derived from perception; as for the *how*, every purpose of action is to produce some sensible result. Thus, we come down to what is tangible and practical,[8] as the root of every real distinction of thought, no matter how subtle it may be; and there is no distinction of meaning so fine as to consist in anything but a possible difference of practice.

To see what this principle leads to, consider in the light of it such a doctrine as that of transubstantiation. The Protestant churches generally hold that the elements of the sacrament are flesh and blood only in a tropical sense; they nourish our souls as meat and the juice of it would our bodies. But the Catholics maintain that they are literally just that; although they possess all the sensible qualities of wafer-cakes and diluted wine. But we can have no conception of wine except what may enter into a belief, either—

1. That this, that, or the other, is wine; or,
2. That wine possesses certain properties.

Such beliefs are nothing but self-notifications that we should, upon occasion, act in regard to such things as we believe to be wine according to the qualities which we believe wine to possess. The occasion of such action would be some sensible perception, the motive of it to produce some sensible result. Thus our action has exclusive reference to what affects the senses, our habit has the same bearing as our action, our belief the same as our habit, our conception the same as our belief; and we can consequently mean nothing by wine but what has certain effects, direct or indirect, upon our senses; and to talk of something as having all the sensible characters of wine, yet being in reality blood, is senseless jargon. Now, it is not my object to pursue the theological question; and having used it as a logical example I drop it, without caring to anticipate the theologian's reply. I only desire to point out how impossible it is that we should have an idea in our minds which relates to anything but conceived sensible effects of things. Our idea of anything *is* our idea of its sensible effects; and if we fancy that we have any other we deceive ourselves, and mistake a mere sensation accompanying the thought for a part of the thought itself. It is absurd to say that thought has any meaning unrelated to its only function. It is foolish for Catholics and Protestants to fancy themselves in disagreement about the elements of the sacrament, if they agree in regard to all their sensible effects, here or[9] hereafter.

It appears, then, that the rule for attaining the third grade of clearness of apprehension is as follows: Consider what effects, which might conceivably have practical bearings, we conceive the object of our conception to have. Then, our conception of these effects is the whole of our conception of the object.[10]

III

Let us illustrate this rule by some examples;[11] and, to begin with the simplest one possible, let us ask what we mean by calling a thing *hard*. Evidently that it will not be scratched by many other substances. The whole conception of this quality, as of every other, lies in its conceived effects. There is absolutely no difference between a hard thing and a soft thing so long as they are not brought to the test. Suppose, then, that a diamond could be crystallized in the midst of a cushion of soft cotton, and should remain there until it was finally burned up. Would it be false to say that that diamond was soft? This seems a foolish question, and would be so, in fact, except in the realm of logic. There such questions are often of the greatest utility as serving to bring logical principles into sharper relief than real discussions ever could. In studying logic we must not put them aside with hasty answers, but must consider them with attentive care, in order to make out the principles involved. We may, in the present case, modify our question, and ask what prevents us from saying that all hard bodies remain perfectly soft until they are touched, when their hardness increases with the pressure until they are scratched. Reflection will show that the reply is this: there would be no *falsity* in such modes of speech. They would involve a modification of our present usage of speech with regard to the words hard and soft, but not of their meanings. For they represent no fact to be different from what it is; only they involve arrangements of facts which would be exceedingly maladroit. This leads us to remark that the question of what would occur under circumstances which do not actually arise is not a question of fact, but only of the most perspicuous arrangement of them. For example, the question of free-will and fate in its simplest form, stripped of verbiage, is something like this: I have done something of which I am ashamed; could I, by an effort of the will, have resisted the temptation, and done otherwise? The philosophical reply is, that this is not a question of fact, but only of the arrangement of facts. Arranging them so as to exhibit what is particularly pertinent to my question—namely, that I ought to blame myself for having done wrong—it is perfectly true to say that, if I had willed to do otherwise than I did, I should have done otherwise. On the other hand, arranging the facts so as to exhibit another important consideration, it is equally true that, when a temptation has once been allowed to work, it will, if it has a certain force, produce its effect, let me struggle how I may. There is no objection to a contradiction in what would result from a false supposition. The *reductio ad absurdum* consists in showing that contradictory results would follow from a hypothesis which is consequently judged to be false. Many questions are involved in the free-will discussion, and I am far from desiring to say that both sides are equally right. On the contrary, I am of opinion that one side denies important facts, and that the other does not. But what I do say is, that the above single question was the origin of the whole doubt; that, had it not been for this question, the controversy would never have arisen; and that this question is perfectly solved in the manner which I have indicated.

Let us next seek a clear idea of Weight. This is another very easy case. To say that a body is heavy means simply that, in the absence of opposing force, it will fall. This (neglecting certain specifications of how it will fall, etc., which exist in the mind of the physicist who uses the word) is evidently the whole conception of weight. It is a fair question whether some particular facts may not *account* for gravity; but what we mean by the force itself is completely involved in its effects.

This leads us to undertake an account of the idea of Force in general. This is the great conception which, developed in the early part of the seventeenth century from the rude idea of a cause, and constantly improved upon since, has shown us how to explain all the changes of motion which bodies experience, and how to think about all physical phenomena; which has given birth to modern science, and changed the face of the globe; and which, aside from its more special uses, has played a principal part in directing the course of modern thought, and in furthering modern social development. It is, therefore, worth some pains to comprehend it. According to our rule, we must begin by asking what is the immediate use of thinking about force; and the answer is, that we thus account for changes of motion. If bodies were left to themselves, without the intervention of forces, every motion would continue unchanged both in velocity and in direction.

Furthermore, change of motion never takes place abruptly; if its direction is changed, it is always through a curve without angles; if its velocity alters, it is by degrees. The gradual changes which are constantly taking place are conceived by geometers to be compounded together according to the rules of the parallelogram of forces. If the reader does not already know what this is, he will find it, I hope, to his advantage to endeavor to follow the following explanation; but if mathematics are insupportable to him, pray let him skip three paragraphs rather than that we should part company here.

A *path* is a line whose beginning and end are distinguished. Two paths are considered to be equivalent, which, beginning at the same point, lead to the same point. Thus the two paths, *ABCDE* and *AFGHE*, are equivalent. Paths which do *not* begin at the same point are considered to be equivalent, provided that, on moving either of them without turning it, but keeping it always parallel to its original position, when its beginning coincides with that of the other path, the ends also coincide. Paths are considered as geometrically added together, when one begins where the other ends; thus the path *AE* is conceived to be a sum of *AB*, *BC*, *CD*, and *DE*. In the parallelogram of Fig. 4 the diagonal *AC* is the sum of *AB* and *BC*; or, since *AD* is geometrically equivalent to *BC*, *AC* is the geometrical sum of *AB* and *AD*.

All this is purely conventional. It simply amounts to this: that we choose to call paths having the relations I have described equal or

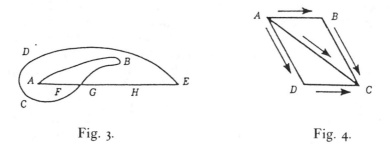

Fig. 3.   Fig. 4.

added. But, though it is a convention, it is a convention with a good reason. The rule for geometrical addition may be applied not only to paths, but to any other things which can be represented by paths. Now, as a path is determined by the varying direction and distance of the point which moves over it from the starting-point, it follows that anything which from its beginning to its end is determined by a varying direction and a varying magnitude is capable of being represented by a line. Accordingly, *velocities* may be represented by lines, for they have only directions and rates. The same thing is true of *accelerations,* or changes of velocities. This is evident enough in the case of velocities; and it becomes evident for accelerations if we consider

that precisely what velocities are to positions—namely, states of
change of them—that accelerations are to velocities.

The so-called "parallelogram of forces" is simply a rule for com-
pounding accelerations. The rule is, to represent the accelerations by
paths, and then to geometrically add the paths. The geometers, however, not only use the "parallelogram of forces" to compound different
accelerations, but also to resolve one acceleration into a sum of several.
Let *AB* (Fig. 5) be the path which represents a certain acceleration—
say, such a change in the motion of a body that at the end of one second
the body will, under the influence of that change, be in a position
different from what it would have had if its motion had continued

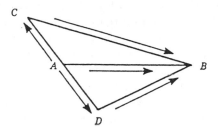

Fig. 5.

unchanged such that a path equivalent to *AB* would lead from the
latter position to the former. This acceleration may be considered as
the sum of the accelerations represented by *AC* and *CB*. It may also
be considered as the sum of the very different accelerations represented by *AD* and *DB*, where *AD* is almost the opposite of *AC*. And
it is clear that there is an immense variety of ways in which *AB* might
be resolved into the sum of two accelerations.

After this tedious explanation, which I hope, in view of the extraordinary interest of the conception of force, may not have exhausted the
reader's patience, we are prepared at last to state the grand fact which
this conception embodies. This fact is that if the actual changes of
motion which the different particles of bodies experience are each
resolved in its appropriate way, each component acceleration is precisely such as is prescribed by a certain law of Nature, according to
which bodies in the relative positions which the bodies in question
actually have at the moment,* always receive certain accelerations,
which, being compounded by geometrical addition, give the acceleration which the body actually experiences.

This is the only fact which the idea of force represents, and who-

---

*Possibly the velocities also have to be taken into account.

ever will take the trouble clearly to apprehend what this fact is, perfectly comprehends what force is. Whether we ought to say that a force *is* an acceleration, or that it *causes* an acceleration, is a mere question of propriety of language, which has no more to do with our real meaning than the difference between the French idiom *"Il fait froid"* and its English equivalent *"It is cold."* Yet it is surprising to see how this simple affair has muddled men's minds. In how many profound treatises is not force spoken of as a "mysterious entity," which seems to be only a way of confessing that the author despairs of ever getting a clear notion of what the word means! In a recent admired work on "Analytic Mechanics" it is stated that we understand precisely the effect of force, but what force itself is we do not understand![12] This is simply a self-contradiction. The idea which the word force excites in our minds has no other function than to affect our actions, and these actions can have no reference to force otherwise than through its effects. Consequently, if we know what the effects of force are, we are acquainted with every fact which is implied in saying that a force exists, and there is nothing more to know. The truth is, there is some vague notion afloat that a question may mean something which the mind cannot conceive; and when some hair-splitting philosophers have been confronted with the absurdity of such a view, they have invented an empty distinction between positive and negative conceptions, in the attempt to give their non-idea a form not obviously nonsensical. The nullity of it is sufficiently plain from the considerations given a few pages back; and, apart from those considerations, the quibbling character of the distinction must have struck every mind accustomed to real thinking.

IV

Let us now approach the subject of logic, and consider a conception which particularly concerns it, that of *reality*. [13] Taking clearness in the sense of familiarity, no idea could be clearer than this. Every child uses it with perfect confidence, never dreaming that he does not understand it. As for clearness in its second grade, however, it would probably puzzle most men, even among those of a reflective turn of mind, to give an abstract definition of the real. Yet such a definition may perhaps be reached by considering the points of difference between reality and its opposite, fiction. A figment is a product of somebody's imagination; it has such characters as his thought impresses upon it. That whose characters are independent of how you or I think is an external reality. There are, however, phenomena within our own minds, dependent upon our thought, which are at the same time real in the sense that we really think them. But though their characters depend on how we think, they do not depend on what we think those characters to be. Thus, a dream has a real existence as a mental phenomenon, if somebody has really dreamt it; that he dreamt so and so, does not depend on what anybody thinks was dreamt, but is completely independent of all opinion on the subject. On the other hand, considering, not the fact of dreaming, but the thing dreamt, it retains its peculiarities by virtue of no other fact than that it was dreamt to possess them. Thus we may define the real as that whose characters are independent of what anybody may think them to be.

But, however satisfactory such a definition may be found, it would be a great mistake to suppose that it makes the idea of reality perfectly clear. Here, then, let us apply our rules. According to them, reality, like every other quality, consists in the peculiar sensible effects which things partaking of it produce. The only effect which real things have is to cause belief, for all the sensations which they excite emerge into consciousness in the form of beliefs. The question therefore is, how is true belief (or belief in the real) distinguished from false belief (or belief in fiction). Now, as we have seen in the former paper, the ideas of truth and falsehood, in their full development, appertain exclusively to the scientific[14] method of settling opinion. A person who arbitrarily chooses the propositions which he will adopt can use the word truth only to emphasize the expression of his determination to hold on to his choice. Of course, the method of tenacity never prevailed exclusively; reason is too natural to men for that. But in the literature of the dark ages we find some fine examples of it. When Scotus Erigena is commenting upon a poetical passage in which hellebore is spoken of as having caused the death of Socrates, he does not hesitate to inform the inquiring reader that Helleborus and Socrates were two eminent Greek philosophers, and that the latter having been overcome in argument by the former took the matter to heart and died of it![15] What sort of an idea of truth could a man have who could adopt and teach, without the qualification of a perhaps, an opinion taken so entirely at random? The real spirit of Socrates, who I hope would have been delighted to have been "overcome in argument," because he would have learned something by it, is in curious contrast with the naïve idea of the glossist, for whom[16] discussion would seem to have been simply a struggle. When philosophy began to awake from its long slumber, and before theology completely dominated it, the practice seems to have been for each professor to seize upon any philosophical position he found unoccupied and which seemed a strong one, to intrench himself in it, and to sally forth from time to time to give battle to the others. Thus, even the scanty records we possess of those disputes enable us to make out a dozen or more opinions held by different teachers at one time concerning the question of nominalism and realism. Read the opening part of the "Historia Calamitatum" of Abelard,[17] who was certainly as philosophical as any of his contemporaries, and see the spirit of combat which it breathes. For him, the truth is simply his particular stronghold. When the method of authority prevailed, the truth meant little more than the Catholic faith. All the efforts of the scholastic doctors are directed toward harmonizing their faith in Aristotle and their faith in the Church, and one may search their ponderous folios through without finding an argument which goes any further. It is noticeable that where different faiths flourish side by side, renegades are looked upon with contempt even by the party whose belief they adopt; so completely has the idea of loyalty replaced that of truth-seeking. Since the time of Descartes, the defect in the conception of truth has been less apparent. Still, it will sometimes strike a scientific man that the philosophers have been less intent on finding out what the facts are, than on inquiring what belief is most in harmony with their system. It is hard to convince a follower of the *a priori* method by adducing facts; but show him that an opinion he is defending is inconsistent with what he has laid down elsewhere, and he will be very apt to retract it. These minds do not seem to believe that disputation is ever to cease; they seem to think that the opinion which is natural for one man is not so for another, and that belief will, consequently, never be settled. In contenting themselves with fixing their own opinions by a method which would lead another man to a different result, they betray their feeble hold of the conception of what truth is.

On the other hand, all the followers of science are fully persuaded that the processes of investigation, if only pushed far enough, will give one certain solution to every question to which they can be applied.[18] One man may investigate the velocity of light by studying the transits of Venus and the aberration of the stars; another by the oppositions of Mars and the eclipses of Jupiter's satellites; a third by the method of Fizeau; a fourth by that of Foucault; a fifth by the motions of the curves of Lissajous; a sixth, a seventh, an eighth, and a ninth, may follow the different methods of comparing the measures of statical and dynamical electricity. They may at first obtain different results, but, as each perfects his method and his processes, the results will move[19] steadily together toward a destined centre. So with all scientific research. Different minds may set out with the most antagonistic views, but the progress of investigation carries them by a force outside of themselves to one and the same conclusion. This activity of thought by which we are carried, not where we wish, but to a foreordained goal, is like the operation of destiny. No modification of the point of view taken, no selection of other facts for study, no natural bent of mind even, can enable a man to escape the predestinate opinion. This great law[20] is embodied in the conception of truth and reality. The opinion which is fated* to be ultimately agreed to by all who investigate, is what we mean by the truth, and the object represented in this opinion is the real. That is the way I would explain reality.

But it may be said that this view is directly opposed to the abstract definition which we have given of reality, inasmuch as it makes the characters of the real to depend on what is ultimately thought about them. But the answer to this is that, on the one hand, reality is independent, not necessarily of thought in general, but only of what you or I or any finite number of men may think about it; and that, on the other hand, though the object of the final opinion depends on what that opinion is, yet what that opinion is does not depend on what you or I or any man thinks. Our perversity and that of others may indefinitely postpone the settlement of opinion; it might even conceivably cause an arbitrary proposition to be universally accepted as long as the human race should last. Yet even that would not change the nature of the belief, which alone could be the result of investigation carried sufficiently far; and if, after the extinction of our race, another should arise with faculties and disposition for investigation, that true opinion must be the one which they would ultimately come to. "Truth crushed to earth shall rise again,"[21] and the opinion which would finally result from investigation does not depend on how anybody may actually think. But the reality of that which is real does depend on the real fact that investigation is destined to lead, at last, if continued long enough, to a belief in it.

But I may be asked what I have to say to all the minute facts of history, forgotten never to be recovered, to the lost books of the ancients, to the buried secrets.

> Full many a gem of purest ray serene
>   The dark, unfathomed caves of ocean bear;
> Full many a flower is born to blush unseen,
>   And waste its sweetness on the desert air.[22]

Do these things not really exist because they are hopelessly beyond the reach of our knowledge? And then, after the universe is dead (according to the prediction of some scientists), and all life has ceased forever, will not the shock of atoms continue though there will be no mind to know it? To this I reply that, though in no possible state of knowledge can any number be great enough to express the relation between the

---

*Fate means merely that which is sure to come true, and can nohow be avoided. It is a superstition to suppose that a certain sort of events are ever fated, and it is another to suppose that the word fate can never be freed from its superstitious taint. We are all fated to die.

amount of what rests unknown to the amount of the known, yet it is unphilosophical to suppose that, with regard to any given question (which has any clear meaning), investigation would not bring forth a solution of it, if it were carried far enough. Who would have said, a few years ago, that we could ever know of what substances stars are made whose light may have been longer in reaching us than the human race has existed? Who can be sure of what we shall not know in a few hundred years? Who can guess what would be the result of[23] continuing the pursuit of science for ten thousand years, with the activity of the last hundred? And if it were to go on for a million, or a billion, or any number of years you please, how is it possible to say that there is any question which might not ultimately be solved?

But it may be objected, "Why make so much of these remote considerations, especially when it is your principle that only practical distinctions have a meaning?" Well, I must confess that it makes very little difference whether we say that a stone on the bottom of the ocean, in complete darkness, is brilliant or not—that is to say, that it *probably* makes no difference, remembering always that that stone *may* be fished up to-morrow. But that there are gems at the bottom of the sea, flowers in the untraveled desert, etc., are propositions which, like that about a diamond being hard when it is not pressed, concern much more the arrangement of our language than they do the meaning of our ideas.

It seems to me, however, that we have, by the application of our rule, reached so clear an apprehension of what we mean by reality, and of the fact which the idea rests on, that we should not, perhaps, be making a pretension so presumptuous as it would be singular, if we were to offer a metaphysical theory of existence for universal acceptance among those who employ the scientific method of fixing belief. However, as metaphysics is a subject much more curious than useful, the knowledge of which, like that of a sunken reef, serves chiefly to enable us to keep clear of it, I will not trouble the reader with any more Ontology at this moment. I have already been led much further into that path than I should have desired; and I have given the reader such a dose of mathematics, psychology, and all that is most abstruse, that I fear he may already have left me, and that what I am now writing is for the compositor and proof-reader exclusively. I trusted to the importance of the subject. There is no royal road to logic, and really valuable ideas can only be had at the price of close attention. But I know that in the matter of ideas the public prefer the cheap and nasty; and in my next paper I am going to return to the easily intelligible, and not wander from it again. The reader who has been at the pains of wading through this month's paper, shall be rewarded in the next one by seeing how beautifully what has been developed in this tedious way can be applied to the ascertainment of the rules of scientific reasoning.

We have, hitherto, not crossed the threshold of scientific logic. It is certainly important to know how to make our ideas clear, but they may be ever so clear without being true. How to make them so, we have next to study. How to give birth to those vital and procreative ideas which multiply into a thousand forms and diffuse themselves everywhere, advancing civilization and making the dignity of man, is an art not yet reduced to rules, but of the secret of which the history of science affords some hints.

9

The Doctrine of Chances

P 120: Popular Science Monthly *12 (March 1878):604–15.
[Also published in W3:276–89 and in CP 2.645–60. Although
the third and fourth "Illustrations" were intended as one
paper, the* PSM *editors published it in two parts in two
successive months. In 1893, Peirce retyped the third paper to
serve as essay 10 of "Search for a Method" and chapter 18 of
"How to Reason" (MS 424) and, in 1910, he wrote several
"Notes to C.S.P.'s Third Paper in the Pop. Sci. Monthly. 1878,
March" (in MSS 703 and 704); some of the changes in the
typescript and one of the notes of 1910 are recorded in the
Notes.] In an early discussion of what will later become his
synechism, Peirce argues that the assumption of continuity
provides a powerful engine for logic, and he develops his
theory of probabilities as the science of logic quantitatively
treated (or as general logic). To be logical, Peirce says, men
must not be selfish, for logic requires the identification of one's
interests with those of an unlimited community. (Peirce also
discusses the probability of a non-repeatable event in a case
that Hilary Putnam has named "Peirce's Puzzle.")*

I

It is a common observation that a science first begins to be exact
when it is quantitatively treated. What are called the exact sciences are
no others than the mathematical ones. Chemists reasoned vaguely
until Lavoisier showed them how to apply the balance to the verification of their theories, when chemistry leaped suddenly into the position of the most perfect of the classificatory sciences. It has thus
become so precise and certain that we usually think of it along with
optics, thermotics, and electrics. But these are studies of general laws,
while chemistry considers merely the relations and classification of
certain objects; and belongs, in reality, in the same category as systematic botany and zoölogy. Compare it with these last, however, and the
advantage that it derives from its quantitative treatment is very evident.[1]

The rudest numerical scales, such as that by which the mineralogists distinguish the different degrees of hardness, are found useful. The mere counting of pistils and stamens sufficed to bring botany out of total chaos into some kind of form. It is not, however, so much from *counting* as from *measuring*, not so much from the conception of number as from that of continuous quantity, that the advantage of mathematical treatment comes. Number, after all, only serves to pin us down to a precision in our thoughts which, however beneficial, can seldom lead to lofty conceptions, and frequently descends to pettiness. Of those two faculties of which Bacon speaks,[2] that which marks differences and that which notes resemblances, the employment of number can only aid the lesser one; and the excessive use of it must tend to narrow the powers of the mind. But the conception of continuous quantity has a great office to fulfill, independently of any attempt at precision. Far from tending to the exaggeration of differences, it is the direct instrument of the finest generalizations. When a naturalist wishes to study a species, he collects a considerable number of specimens more or less similar. In contemplating them, he observes certain ones which are more or less alike in some particular respect. They all have, for instance, a certain S-shaped marking. He observes that they are not *precisely* alike, in this respect; the S has not precisely the same shape, but the differences are such as to lead him to believe that forms could be found intermediate between any two of those he possesses. He, now, finds other forms apparently quite dissimilar—say a marking in the form of a C—and the question is, whether he can find intermediate ones which will connect these latter with the others. This he often succeeds in doing in cases where it would at first be thought impossible; whereas, he sometimes finds those which differ, at first glance, much less, to be separated in Nature by the non-occurrence of intermediaries. In this way, he builds up from the study of Nature a new general conception of the character in question. He obtains, for example, an idea of a leaf which includes every part of the flower, and an idea of a vertebra which includes the skull. I surely need not say much to show what a logical engine there is here. It is the essence of the method of the naturalist. How he applies it first to one character, and then to another, and finally obtains a notion of a species of animals, the differences between whose members, however great, are confined within limits, is a matter which does not here concern us. The whole method of classification must be considered later; but, at present, I only desire to point out that it is by taking advantage of the idea of continuity, or the passage from one form to another by insensible degrees, that the naturalist builds his conceptions. Now, the naturalists are the great builders of conceptions; there is no other branch of science where so much of this work is done as in theirs; and we must, in great measure, take them for our teachers in this important part of logic. And it will be found everywhere that the idea of continuity is a powerful aid to the formation of true and fruitful conceptions. By means of it, the greatest differences are broken down and resolved into differences of degree, and the incessant application of it is of the greatest value in broadening our conceptions. I propose to make a great use of this idea in the present series of papers; and the particular series of important fallacies, which, arising from a neglect of it, have desolated philosophy, must further on be closely studied. At present, I simply call the reader's attention to the utility of this conception.

In studies of numbers, the idea of continuity is so indispensable, that it is perpetually introduced even where there is no continuity in fact, as where we say that there are in the United States 10.7 inhabitants per square mile, or that in New York 14.72 persons live in the average house.* Another example is that law of the distribution of errors which Quételet, Galton,[3] and others, have applied with so much success to the study of biological and social matters. This application of continuity to cases where it does not really exist illustrates, also, another point which will hereafter demand a separate study, namely, the great utility which fictions sometimes have in science.

II

The theory of probabilities is simply the science of logic quantitatively treated. There are two conceivable certainties with reference to any hypothesis, the certainty of its truth and the certainty of its falsity. The numbers *one* and *zero* are appropriated, in this calculus, to marking these extremes of knowledge; while fractions having values intermediate between them indicate, as we may vaguely say, the degrees in which the evidence leans toward one or the other. The general problem of probabilities is, from a given state of facts, to determine the numerical probability of a possible fact. This is the same as to inquire how much the given facts are worth, considered as evidence to prove the possible fact. Thus the problem of probabilities is simply the general problem of logic.

Probability is a continuous quantity, so that great advantages may be expected from this mode of studying logic. Some writers have gone so far as to maintain that, by means of the calculus of chances, every solid inference may be represented by legitimate arithmetical operations upon the numbers given in the premises. If this be, indeed, true,

---

*This mode of thought is so familiarly associated with all exact numerical consideration, that the phrase appropriate to it is imitated by shallow writers in order to produce the appearance of exactitude where none exists. Certain newspapers which affect a learned tone talk of "the average man," when they simply mean *most men*, and have no idea of striking an average.

the great problem of logic, how it is that the observation of one fact can give us knowledge of another independent fact, is reduced to a mere question of arithmetic. It seems proper to examine this pretension before undertaking any more recondite solution of the paradox.

But, unfortunately, writers on probabilities are not agreed in regard to this result. This branch of mathematics is the only one, I believe, in which good writers frequently get results entirely erroneous. In elementary geometry the reasoning is frequently fallacious, but erroneous conclusions are avoided; but it may be doubted if there is a single extensive treatise on probabilities in existence which does not contain solutions absolutely indefensible. This is partly owing to the want of any regular method of procedure; for the subject involves too many subtilties to make it easy to put its problems into equations without such an aid. But, beyond this, the fundamental principles of its calculus are more or less in dispute. In regard to that class of questions to which it is chiefly applied for practical purposes, there is comparatively little doubt; but in regard to others to which it has been sought to extend it, opinion is somewhat unsettled.

This last class of difficulties can only be entirely overcome by making the idea of probability perfectly clear in our minds in the way set forth in our last paper.[4]

III

To get a clear idea of what we mean by probability, we have to consider what real and sensible difference there is between one degree of probability and another.

The character of probability belongs primarily, without doubt, to certain inferences. Locke explains it as follows: After remarking that the mathematician positively knows that the sum of the three angles of a triangle is equal to two right angles because he apprehends the geometrical proof, he thus continues:

But another man who never took the pains to observe the demonstration, hearing a mathematician, a man of credit, affirm the three angles of a triangle to be equal to two right ones, *assents* to it; i.e., receives it for true. In which case the foundation of his assent is the probability of the thing, the proof being such as, for the most part, carries truth with it; the man on whose testimony he receives it not being wont to affirm anything contrary to, or besides his knowledge, especially in matters of this kind.[5]

The celebrated *Essay concerning Humane Understanding* contains many passages which, like this one, make the first steps in profound analyses which are not further developed. It was shown in the first of these papers[6] that the validity of an inference does not depend on any tendency of the mind to accept it, however strong such tendency may be; but consists in the real fact that, when premises like those of the argument in question are true, conclusions related to them like that of this argument are also true. It was remarked that in a logical mind an argument is always conceived as a member of a *genus* of arguments all constructed in the same way, and such that, when their premises are real facts, their conclusions are so also. If the argument is demonstrative, then this is always so; if it is only probable, then it is for the most part so. As Locke says, the probable argument is *"such as* for the most part carries truth with it."[7]

According to this, that real and sensible difference between one degree of probability and another, in which the meaning of the distinction lies, is that in the frequent employment of two different modes of inference, one will carry truth with it oftener than the other. It is evident that this is the only difference there is in the existing fact. Having certain premises, a man draws a certain conclusion, and as far as this inference alone is concerned the only possible practical question is whether that conclusion is true or not, and between existence and non-existence there is no middle term. "Being only is and nothing is altogether not," said Parmenides;[8] and this is in strict accordance with the analysis of the conception of reality given in the last paper.[9] For we found that the distinction of reality and fiction depends on the supposition that sufficient investigation would cause one opinion to be universally received and all others to be rejected. That presupposition involved in the very conceptions of reality and figment involves a complete sundering of the two. It is the heaven-and-hell idea in the domain of thought. But, in the long run, there is a real fact which corresponds to the idea of probability, and it is that a given mode of inference sometimes proves successful and sometimes not, and that in a ratio ultimately fixed. As we go on drawing inference after inference of the given kind, during the first ten or hundred cases the ratio of successes may be expected to show considerable fluctuations; but when we come into the thousands and millions, these fluctuations become less and less; and if we continue long enough, the ratio will approximate toward a fixed limit. We may therefore define the probability of a mode of argument as the proportion of cases in which it carries truth with it.

The inference from the premise, A, to the conclusion, B, depends, as we have seen, on the guiding principle, that if a fact of the class A is true, a fact of the class B is true. The probability consists of the fraction whose numerator is the number of times in which both A and B are true, and whose denominator is the total number of times in which A is true, whether B is so or not. Instead of speaking of this as the probability of the inference, there is not the slightest objection to calling it the probability that, if A happens, B happens. But to speak of the probability of the event B, without naming the condition, really has no meaning at all. It is true that when it is perfectly obvious what condition is meant, the ellipsis may be permitted. But we should avoid contracting the habit of using language in this way (universal as the habit is), because it gives rise to a vague way of thinking, as if the action of causation might either determine an event to happen or determine it not to happen, or leave it more or less free to happen or not, so as to give rise to an *inherent* chance in regard to its occurrence. It is quite clear to me that some of the worst and most persistent errors in the use of the doctrine of chances have arisen from this vicious mode of expression.*

IV

But there remains an important point to be cleared up. According to what has been said, the idea of probability essentially belongs to a kind of inference which is repeated indefinitely. An individual inference must be either true or false, and can show no effect of probability; and, therefore, in reference to a single case considered in itself, probability can have no meaning. Yet if a man had to choose between drawing a card from a pack containing twenty-five red cards and a black one, or from a pack containing twenty-five black cards and a red one, and if the drawing of a red card were destined to transport him to eternal felicity, and that of a black one to consign him to everlasting woe, it would be folly to deny that he ought to prefer the pack containing the larger proportion of red cards, although, from the nature of the risk, it could not be repeated. It is not easy to reconcile this with our analysis of the conception of chance. But suppose he should choose the red pack, and should draw the wrong card, what consolation would he have? He might say that he had acted in accordance with reason, but that would only show that his reason was absolutely worthless. And if he should choose the right card, how could he regard it as anything but a happy accident? He could not say that if he had drawn from the other pack, he might have drawn the wrong one, because an hypothetical proposition such as, "if A, then B," means nothing with reference to a single case. Truth consists in the existence of a real fact corresponding to the true proposition. Corresponding to the proposition, "if A, then B," there may be the fact that *whenever* such an event as A happens such an event as B happens. But in the case supposed, which has no parallel as far as this man is concerned, there would be no real

*The conception of probability here set forth is substantially that first developed by Mr. Venn, in his *Logic of Chance*. Of course, a vague apprehension of the idea had always existed, but the problem was to make it perfectly clear, and to him belongs the credit of first doing this.[10]

fact whose existence could give any truth to the statement that, if he had drawn from the other pack, he might have drawn a black card. Indeed, since the validity of an inference consists in the truth of the hypothetical proposition that *if* the premises be true the conclusion will also be true, and since the only real fact which can correspond to such a proposition is that whenever the antecedent is true the consequent is so also, it follows that there can be no sense in reasoning in an isolated case, at all.

These considerations appear, at first sight, to dispose of the difficulty mentioned. Yet the case of the other side is not yet exhausted. Although probability will probably manifest its effect in, say, a thousand risks, by a certain proportion between the numbers of successes and failures, yet this, as we have seen, is only to say that it certainly will, at length, do so. Now the number of risks, the number of probable inferences, which a man draws in his whole life, is a finite one, and he cannot be absolutely *certain* that the mean result will accord with the probabilities at all. Taking all his risks collectively, then, it cannot be certain that they will not fail, and his case does not differ, except in degree, from the one last supposed. It is an indubitable result of the theory of probabilities that every gambler, if he continues long enough, must ultimately be ruined. Suppose he tries the martingale, which some believe infallible, and which is, as I am informed, disallowed in the gambling-houses. In this method of playing, he first bets say $1; if he loses it he bets $2; if he loses that he bets $4; if he loses that he bets $8; if he then gains he has lost $1 + 2 + 4 = 7$, and he has gained $1 more; and no matter how many bets he loses, the first one he gains will make him $1 richer than he was in the beginning. In that way, he will probably gain at first; but, at last, the time will come when the run of luck is so against him that he will not have money enough to double, and must therefore let his bet go. This will *probably* happen before he has won as much as he had in the first place, so that this run against him will leave him poorer than he began; some time or other it will be sure to happen. It is true that there is always a possibility of his winning any sum the bank can pay, and we thus come upon a celebrated paradox that, though he is certain to be ruined, the value of his expectation calculated according to the usual rules (which omit this consideration) is large. But, whether a gambler plays in this way or any other, the same thing is true, namely, that if he plays long enough he will be sure some time to have such a run against him as to exhaust his entire fortune. The same thing is true of an insurance company. Let the directors take the utmost pains to be independent of great conflagrations and pestilences, their actuaries can tell them that, according to the doctrine of chances, the time must come, at last, when their losses will bring them to a stop. They may tide over such a crisis by extraordinary means, but then they will start again in a weakened state, and the same thing will happen again all the sooner. An actuary might be inclined to deny this, because he knows that the expectation of his company is large, or perhaps (neglecting the interest upon money) is infinite. But calculations of expectations leave out of account the circumstance now under consideration, which reverses the whole thing. However, I must not be understood as saying that insurance is on this account unsound, more than other kinds of business. All human affairs rest upon probabilities, and the same thing is true everywhere. If man were immortal he could be perfectly sure of seeing the day when everything in which he had trusted should betray his trust, and, in short, of coming eventually to hopeless misery. He would break down, at last, as every great fortune, as every dynasty, as every civilization does. In place of this we have death.

But what, without death, would happen to every man, with death must happen to some man. At the same time, death makes the number of our risks, of our inferences, finite, and so makes their mean result uncertain. The very idea of probability and of reasoning rests on the assumption that this number is indefinitely great. We are thus landed in the same difficulty as before, and I can see but one solution of it. It seems to me that we are driven to this, that logicality inexorably requires that our interests shall *not* be limited. They must not stop at our own fate, but must embrace the whole community. This community, again, must not be limited, but must extend to all races of beings with whom we can come into immediate or mediate intellectual relation. It must reach, however vaguely, beyond this geological epoch, beyond all bounds. He who would not sacrifice his own soul to save the whole world, is, as it seems to me, illogical in all his inferences, collectively. Logic is rooted in the social principle.

To be logical men should not be selfish; and, in point of fact, they are not so selfish as they are thought. The willful prosecution of one's desires is a different thing from selfishness. The miser is not selfish; his money does him no good, and he cares for what shall become of it after his death. We are constantly speaking of *our* possessions on the Pacific, and of *our* destiny as a republic, where no personal interests are involved, in a way which shows that we have wider ones. We discuss with anxiety the possible exhaustion of coal in some hundreds of years, or the cooling-off of the sun in some millions, and show in the most popular of all religious tenets that we can conceive the possibility of a man's descending into hell for the salvation of his fellows.

Now, it is not necessary for logicality that a man should himself be capable of the heroism of self-sacrifice. It is sufficient that he should recognize the possibility of it, should perceive that only that man's inferences who has it are really logical, and should consequently regard his own as being only so far valid as they would be accepted by the hero. So far as he thus refers his inferences to that standard, he becomes identified with such a mind.

This makes logicality attainable enough. Sometimes we can personally attain to heroism. The soldier who runs to scale a wall knows that he will probably be shot, but that is not all he cares for. He also knows that if all the regiment, with whom in feeling he identifies himself, rush forward at once, the fort will be taken. In other cases we can only imitate the virtue. The man whom we have supposed as having to draw from the two packs, who if he is not a logician will draw from the red pack from mere habit, will see, if he is logician enough, that he cannot be logical so long as he is concerned only with his own fate, but that that man who should care equally for what was to happen in all possible cases of the sort could act logically, and would draw from the pack with the most red cards, and thus, though incapable himself of such sublimity, our logician would imitate the effect of that man's courage in order to share his logicality.

But all this requires a conceived identification of one's interests with those of an unlimited community. Now, there exist no reasons, and a later discussion will show that there can be no reasons, for thinking that the human race, or any intellectual race, will exist forever. On the other hand, there can be no reason against it;* and, fortunately, as the whole requirement is that we should have certain sentiments, there is nothing in the facts to forbid our having a *hope*, or calm and cheerful wish, that the community may last beyond any assignable date.

It may seem strange that I should put forward three sentiments, namely, interest in an indefinite community, recognition of the possibility of this interest being made supreme, and hope in the unlimited continuance of intellectual activity, as indispensable requirements of logic. Yet, when we consider that logic depends on a mere struggle to escape doubt, which, as it terminates in action, must begin in emotion, and that, furthermore, the only cause of our planting ourselves on reason is that other methods of escaping doubt fail on account of the social impulse, why should we wonder to find social sentiment presupposed in reasoning? As for the other two sentiments which I find necessary, they are so only as supports and accessories of that. It interests me to notice that these three sentiments seem to be pretty much the same as that famous trio of Charity, Faith, and Hope, which, in the estimation of St. Paul, are the finest and greatest of spiritual gifts.[11] Neither Old nor New Testament is a text-book of the logic of

---

*I do not here admit an absolutely unknowable. Evidence could show us what would probably be the case after any given lapse of time; and though a subsequent time might be assigned which that evidence might not cover, yet further evidence would cover it.

science, but the latter is certainly the highest existing authority in regard to the dispositions of heart which a man ought to have.

V

Such average statistical numbers as the number of inhabitants per square mile, the average number of deaths per week, the number of convictions per indictment, or, generally speaking, the number of x's per y, where the x's are a class of things some or all of which are connected with another class of things, their y's, I term *relative numbers*. Of the two classes of things to which a relative number refers, that one of which it is a number may be called its *relate*, and that one *per* which the numeration is made may be called its *correlate*.

Probability is a kind of relative number; namely, it is the ratio of the number of arguments of a certain genus which carry truth with them to the total number of arguments of that genus, and the rules for the calculation of probabilities are very easily derived from this consideration. They may all be given here, since they are extremely simple, and it is sometimes convenient to know something of the elementary rules of calculation of chances.

RULE I. *Direct Calculation.*—To calculate, directly, any relative number, say for instance the number of passengers in the average trip of a street-car, we must proceed as follows·

Count the number of passengers for each trip; add all these numbers, and divide by the number of trips. There are cases in which this rule may be simplified. Suppose we wish to know the number of inhabitants to a dwelling in New York. The same person cannot inhabit two dwellings. If he divide his time between two dwellings he ought to be counted a half-inhabitant of each. In this case we have only to divide the total number of the inhabitants of New York by the number of their dwellings, without the necessity of counting separately those which inhabit each one. A similar proceeding will apply wherever each individual relate belongs to one individual correlate exclusively. If we want the number of x's per y, and no x belongs to more than one y, we have only to divide the whole number of x's of y's by the number of y's. Such a method would, of course, fail if applied to finding the average number of street-car passengers per trip. We could not divide the total number of travelers by the number of trips, since many of them would have made many passages.

To find the probability that from a given class of premises, A, a given class of conclusions, B, follow, it is simply necessary to ascertain what proportion of the times in which premises of that class are true, the appropriate conclusions are also true. In other words, it is the number of cases of the occurrence of both the events A and B, divided by the total number of cases of the occurrence of the event A.

RULE II. *Addition of Relative Numbers.*—Given two relative numbers having the same correlate, say the number of x's per y, and the number of z's per y; it is required to find the number of x's and z's together per y. If there is nothing which is at once an x and a z to the same y, the sum of the two given numbers would give the required number. Suppose, for example, that we had given the average number of friends that men have, and the average number of enemies, the sum of these two is the average number of persons interested in a man. On the other hand, it plainly would not do to add the average number of persons having constitutional diseases to the average number over military age, and to the average number exempted by each special cause from military service, in order to get the average number exempt in any way, since many are exempt in two or more ways at once.

This rule applies directly to probabilities. Given the probability that two different and mutually exclusive events will happen under the same supposed set of circumstances. Given, for instance, the probability that if A then B, and also the probability that if A then C, then the sum of these two probabilities is the probability that if A then either B or C, so long as there is no event which belongs at once to the two classes B and C.

RULE III. *Multiplication of Relative Numbers.*—Suppose that we have given the relative number of x's per y; also the relative number of z's per x of y; or, to take a concrete example, suppose that we have given, first, the average number of children in families living in New York; and, second, the average number of teeth in the head of a New York child—then the product of these two numbers would give the average number of children's teeth in a New York family. But this mode of reckoning will only apply in general under two restrictions. In the first place, it would not be true if the same child could belong to different families, for in that case those children who belonged to several different families might have an exceptionally large or small number of teeth, which would affect the average number of children's teeth in a family more than it would affect the average number of teeth in a child's head. In the second place, the rule would not be true if different children could share the same teeth, the average number of children's teeth being in that case evidently something different from the average number of teeth belonging to a child.

In order to apply this rule to probabilities, we must proceed as follows: Suppose that we have given the probability that the conclusion B follows from the premise A, B and A representing as usual certain classes of propositions. Suppose that we also knew the probability of an inference in which B should be the premise, and a proposition of a third kind, C, the conclusion. Here, then, we have the materials for the application of this rule. We have, first, the relative number of B's per A. We next should have the relative number of C's per B following from A. But the classes of propositions being so selected that the probability of C following from any B in general is just the same as the probability of C's following from one of those B's which is deducible from an A, the two probabilities may be multiplied together, in order to give the probability of C following from A. The same restrictions exist as before. It might happen that the probability that B follows from A was affected by certain propositions of the class B following from several different propositions of the class A. But, practically speaking, all these restrictions are of very little consequence, and it is usually recognized as a principle universally true that the probability that, if A is true, B is, multiplied by the probability that, if B is true, C is, gives the probability that, if A is true, C is.

There is a rule supplementary to this, of which great use is made. It is not universally valid, and the greatest caution has to be exercised in making use of it—a double care, first, never to use it when it will involve serious error; and, second, never to fail to take advantage of it in cases in which it can be employed. This rule depends upon the fact that in very many cases the probability that C is true if B is, is substantially the same as the probability that C is true if A is. Suppose, for example, we have the average number of males among the children born in New York; suppose that we also have the average number of children born in the winter months among those born in New York. Now, we may assume without doubt, at least as a closely approximate proposition (and no very nice calculation would be in place in regard to probabilities), that the proportion of males among all the children born in New York is the same as the proportion of males born in summer in New York, and, therefore, if the names of all the children born during a year were put into an urn, we might multiply the probability that any name drawn would be the name of a male child by the probability that it would be the name of a child born in summer, in order to obtain the probability that it would be the name of a male child born in summer. The questions of probability, in the treatises upon the subject, have usually been such as relate to balls drawn from urns, and games of cards, and so on, in which the question of the *independence* of events, as it is called—that is to say, the question of whether the probability of C, under the hypothesis B, is the same as its probability under the hypothesis A, has been very simple; but, in the application of probabilities to the ordinary questions of life, it is often an exceedingly nice question whether two events may be considered as independent with sufficient accuracy or not. In all calculations about cards it is assumed that the cards are thoroughly shuffled, which makes one deal quite independent of another. In point of fact the cards seldom are, in practice, shuffled sufficiently to make this true; thus, in a game of whist, in which the cards have fallen in suits of four of the same suit, and are so gathered up, they will lie more or less in sets of four of the same suit, and this will be true even after they are shuffled. At least some traces of this arrangement will remain, in consequence of which the number of "short suits," as they are called—that is to say, the number of hands in which the cards are very unequally divided in regard to suits—is smaller than the calculation would make it to be; so that, when there is a misdeal, where the cards, being thrown about the table, get very thoroughly shuffled, it is a common saying that in the hands next dealt out there are generally short suits. A few years ago a friend of mine, who plays whist a great deal, was so good as to count the number of spades dealt to him in 165 hands, in which the cards had been, if anything, shuffled better than usual. According to calculation, there should have been 85 of these hands in which my friend held either three or four spades, but in point of fact there were 94, showing the influence of imperfect shuffling.

According to the view here taken, these are the only fundamental rules for the calculation of chances. An additional one, derived from a different conception of probability, is given in some treatises, which if it be sound might be made the basis of a theory of reasoning. Being, as I believe it is, absolutely absurd, the consideration of it serves to bring us to the true theory; and it is for the sake of this discussion, which must be postponed to the next number, that I have brought the doctrine of chances to the reader's attention at this early stage of our studies of the logic of science.

10

The Probability of Induction

P 121: Popular Science Monthly *12 (April 1878):705–18. [Also published in W3:290–305 and in CP 2.669–93.]* In this paper, Peirce continues to develop his theory of probability and gives rules for calculating the probability of multiple events. He compares the conceptualistic view (which refers probabilities to events) with the materialistic view (which makes probability the ratio of the frequency of favorable cases to all cases) and differentiates chance from probability. He argues for the frequency view (which he held until nearly the turn of the century) and then connects his views on probability with the nature of inductive (or synthetic) reasoning and the problem of induction, for which he considers the need for an appeal to possible worlds.

I

We have found that every argument derives its force from the general truth of the class of inferences to which it belongs; and that probability is the proportion of arguments carrying truth with them among those of any *genus.* This is most conveniently expressed in the nomenclature of the mediæval logicians. They called the fact expressed by a premise an *antecedent,* and that which follows from it its *consequent;* while the leading principle, that every (or almost every) such antecedent is followed by such a consequent, they termed the *consequence.* Using this language, we may say that probability belongs exclusively to *consequences,* and the probability of any consequence is the number of times in which antecedent and consequent both occur divided by the number of all the times in which the antecedent occurs. From this definition are deduced the following rules for the addition and multiplication of probabilities:

Rule for the Addition of Probabilities.—Given the separate probabilities of two consequences having the same antecedent and incompatible consequents. Then the sum of these two numbers is the probability of the consequence, that from the same antecedent one or other of those consequents follows.

Rule for the Multiplication of Probabilities.—Given the separate probabilities of the two consequences, "If A then B," and "If both A and B, then C." Then the product of these two numbers is the probability of the consequence, "If A, then both B and C."

Special Rule for the Multiplication of Independent Probabilities.—Given the separate probabilities of two consequences having the same antecedents, "If A, then B," and "If A, then C." Suppose that these consequences are such that the probability of the second is equal to the probability of the consequence, "If both A and B, then C." Then the product of the two given numbers is equal to the probability of the consequence, "If A, then both B and C."

To show the working of these rules we may examine the probabilities in regard to throwing dice. What is the probability of throwing a six with one die? The antecedent here is the event of throwing a die; the consequent, its turning up a six. As the die has six sides, all of which are turned up with equal frequency, the probability of turning up any one is $\frac{1}{6}$. Suppose two dice are thrown, what is the probability of throwing sixes? The probability of either coming up six is obviously the same when both are thrown as when one is thrown—namely, $\frac{1}{6}$. The probability that either will come up six when the other does is also the same as that of its coming up six whether the other does or not. The probabilities are, therefore, independent; and, by our rule, the probability that both events will happen together is the product of their several probabilities, or $\frac{1}{6} \times \frac{1}{6}$. What is the probability of throwing deuce-ace? The probability that the first die will turn up ace and the second deuce is the same as the probability that both will turn up sixes—namely, $\frac{1}{36}$; the probability that the *second* will turn up ace and the *first* deuce is likewise $\frac{1}{36}$; these two events—first, ace; second, deuce; and, second, ace; first, deuce—are incompatible. Hence the rule for addition holds, and the probability that either will come up ace and the other deuce is $\frac{1}{36} + \frac{1}{36}$, or $\frac{1}{18}$.

In this way all problems about dice, etc., may be solved. When the number of dice thrown is supposed very large, mathematics (which may be defined as the art of making groups to facilitate numeration) comes to our aid with certain devices to reduce the difficulties.

II

The conception of probability as a matter of *fact*, i.e., as the proportion of times in which an occurrence of one kind is accompanied by an occurrence of another kind, is termed by Mr. Venn the materialistic view of the subject.[1] But probability has often been regarded as being simply the degree of belief which ought to attach to a proposition; and this mode of explaining the idea is termed by Venn the conceptualistic view. Most writers have mixed the two conceptions together. They, first, define the probability of an event as the reason we have to believe that it has taken place, which is conceptualistic; but shortly after they state that it is the ratio of the number of cases favorable to the event to the total number of cases favorable or contrary, and all equally possible. Except that this introduces the thoroughly unclear idea of cases equally possible in place of cases equally frequent, this is a tolerable statement of the materialistic view. The pure conceptualistic theory has been best expounded by Mr. De Morgan in his *Formal Logic: or, the Calculus of Inference, Necessary and Probable.*

The great difference between the two analyses is, that the conceptualists refer probability to an event, while the materialists make it the ratio of frequency of events of a *species* to those of a *genus* over that *species,* thus *giving it two terms instead of one.* The opposition may be made to appear as follows:

Suppose that we have two rules of inference, such that, of all the questions to the solution of which both can be applied, the first yields correct answers to $\frac{81}{100}$, and incorrect answers to the remaining $\frac{19}{100}$; while the second yields correct answers to $\frac{93}{100}$, and incorrect answers to the remaining $\frac{7}{100}$. Suppose, further, that the two rules are entirely independent as to their truth, so that the second answers correctly $\frac{93}{100}$ of the questions which the first answers correctly, and also $\frac{93}{100}$ of the questions which the first answers incorrectly, and answers incorrectly the remaining $\frac{7}{100}$ of the questions which the first answers correctly, and also the remaining $\frac{7}{100}$ of the questions which the first answers incorrectly. Then, of all the questions to the solution of which both rules can be applied—

both answer correctly . . . . $\frac{93}{100}$ of $\frac{81}{100}$, or $\frac{93 \times 81}{100 \times 100}$;

the second answers correctly and the first incorrectly . . . . $\frac{93}{100}$ of $\frac{19}{100}$, or $\frac{93 \times 19}{100 \times 100}$;

the second answers incorrectly and the first correctly . . . . $\frac{7}{100}$ of $\frac{81}{100}$, or $\frac{7 \times 81}{100 \times 100}$;

and both answer correctly . . . . $\frac{7}{100}$ of $\frac{19}{100}$, or $\frac{7 \times 19}{100 \times 100}$.

Suppose, now, that, in reference to any question, both give the same answer. Then (the questions being always such as are to be answered by *yes* or *no*), those in reference to which their answers agree are the same as those which both answer correctly together with those which both answer falsely, or $\frac{93 \times 81}{100 \times 100} + \frac{7 \times 19}{100 \times 100}$ of all. The proportion of those which both answer correctly out of those their answers to which agree is, therefore—

$$\frac{\dfrac{93 \times 81}{100 \times 100}}{\dfrac{93 \times 81}{100 \times 100} + \dfrac{7 \times 19}{100 \times 100}} \quad \text{or} \quad \frac{93 \times 81}{(93 \times 81) + (7 \times 19)}.$$

This is, therefore, the probability that, if both modes of inference yield the same result, that result is correct. We may here conveniently make use of another mode of expression. *Probability* is the ratio of the favorable cases to all the cases. Instead of expressing our result in terms of this ratio, we may make use of another—the ratio of favorable to unfavorable cases. This last ratio may be called the *chance* of an event. Then the chance of a true answer by the first mode of inference is $\frac{81}{19}$ and by the second is $\frac{93}{7}$; and the chance of a correct answer from both, when they agree, is—

$$\frac{81 \times 93}{19 \times 7} \quad \text{or} \quad \frac{81}{19} \times \frac{93}{7},$$

or the product of the chances of each singly yielding a true answer.

It will be seen that a chance is a quantity which may have any magnitude, however great. An event in whose favor there is an even chance, or $\frac{1}{1}$, has a probability of $\frac{1}{2}$. An argument having an even chance can do nothing toward reënforcing others, since according to the rule its combination with another would only multiply the chance of the latter by 1.

Probability and chance undoubtedly belong primarily to consequences, and are relative to premises; but we may, nevertheless, speak of the chance of an event absolutely, meaning by that the chance of the combination of all arguments in reference to it which exist for us in the given state of our knowledge. Taken in this sense it is incontestable that the chance of an event has an intimate connection with the degree of our belief in it. Belief is certainly something more than a mere feeling; yet there is a feeling of believing, and this feeling does and ought to vary with the chance of the thing believed, as deduced from all the arguments. Any quantity which varies with the chance might, therefore, it would seem, serve as a thermometer for the proper intensity of belief. Among all such quantities there is one which is peculiarly appropriate. When there is a very great chance, the feeling of belief ought to be very intense. Absolute certainty, or an infinite chance, can never be attained by mortals, and this may be represented appropriately by an infinite belief. As the chance diminishes the feeling of believing should diminish, until an even chance is reached, where it should completely vanish and not incline either toward or away from the proposition. When the chance becomes less, then a contrary belief should spring up and should increase in intensity as the chance diminishes, and as the chance almost vanishes (which it can never quite do) the contrary belief should tend toward an infinite intensity. Now, there is one quantity which, more simply than any other, fulfills these conditions; it is the *logarithm* of the chance. But there is another consideration which must, if admitted, fix us to this choice for our thermometer. It is that our belief ought to be proportional to the weight of evidence, in this sense, that two arguments which are entirely independent, neither weakening nor strengthening each other, ought, when they concur, to produce a belief equal to the sum of the intensities of belief which either would produce separately. Now, we have seen that the chances of independent concurrent arguments are to be multiplied together to get the chance of their combination, and therefore the quantities which best express the intensities of belief should be such that they are to be *added* when the *chances* are multiplied in order to produce the quantity which corresponds to the combined chance. Now, the logarithm is the only quantity which fulfills this condition. There is a general law of sensibility, called Fechner's psycho-physical law.[2] It is that the intensity of any sensation is proportional to the logarithm of the external force which produces it. It is entirely in harmony with this law that the feeling of belief should be as the logarithm of the chance, this latter being the expression of the state of facts which produces the belief.

The rule for the combination of independent concurrent arguments takes a very simple form when expressed in terms of the intensity of belief, measured in the proposed way. It is this: Take the sum of all the feelings of belief which would be produced separately by all the arguments *pro*, subtract from that the similar sum for arguments *con*, and the remainder is the feeling of belief which we ought to have on the whole. This is a proceeding which men often resort to, under the name of *balancing reasons*.

These considerations constitute an argument in favor of the conceptualistic view. The kernel of it is that the conjoint probability of all the arguments in our possession, with reference to any fact, must be intimately connected with the just degree of our belief in that fact; and this point is supplemented by various others showing the consistency of the theory with itself and with the rest of our knowledge.

But probability, to have any value at all, must express a fact. It is, therefore, a thing to be inferred upon evidence. Let us, then, consider for a moment the formation of a belief of probability. Suppose we have a large bag of beans from which one has been secretly taken at random and hidden under a thimble. We are now to form a probable judgment of the color of that bean, by drawing others singly from the bag and looking at them, each one to be thrown back, and the whole well mixed up after each drawing. Suppose the first drawing is white and the next black. We conclude that there is not an immense preponderance of either color, and that there is something like an even chance that the bean under the thimble is black. But this judgment may be altered by the next few drawings. When we have drawn ten times, if 4, 5, or 6, are white, we have more confidence that the chance is even. When we have drawn a thousand times, if about half have been white, we have great confidence in this result. We now feel pretty sure that, if we were to make a large number of bets upon the color of single beans drawn from the bag, we could approximately insure ourselves in the long run by betting each time upon the white, a confidence which would be entirely wanting if, instead of sampling the bag by 1,000 drawings, we had done so by only two. Now, as the whole utility of probability is to insure us in the long run, and as that assurance depends, not merely on the value of the chance, but also on the accuracy of the evaluation, it follows that we ought not to have the same feeling of belief in reference to all events of which the chance is even. In short, to express the proper state of our belief, not *one* number but *two* are requisite, the first depending on the inferred probability, the second on the amount of knowledge on which that probability is based.* It is true that when our knowledge is very precise, when we have made many drawings from the bag, or, as in most of the examples in the books, when the total contents of the bag are absolutely known, the number which expresses the uncertainty of the assumed probability and its liability to be changed by further experience may become insignificant, or utterly vanish. But, when our knowledge is very slight, this number may be even more important than the probability itself; and when we have no knowledge at all this completely overwhelms the other, so that there is no sense in saying that the chance of the totally unknown event is even (for what expresses absolutely no fact has absolutely no meaning), and what ought to be said is that the chance is entirely indefinite. We thus perceive that the conceptualistic view, though answering well enough in some cases, is quite inadequate.

Suppose that the first bean which we drew from our bag were black. That would constitute an argument, no matter how slender, that the bean under the thimble was also black. If the second bean were also to turn out black, that would be a second independent argument reën-forcing the first. If the whole of the first twenty beans drawn should prove black, our confidence that the hidden bean was black would justly attain considerable strength. But suppose the twenty-first bean were to be white and that we were to go on drawing until we found that we had drawn 1,010 black beans and 990 white ones. We should conclude that our first twenty beans being black was simply an extraordinary accident, and that in fact the proportion of white beans to black was sensibly equal, and that it was an even chance that the

*Strictly we should need an infinite series of numbers each depending on the probable error of the last.

hidden bean was black. Yet according to the rule of *balancing reasons*, since all the drawings of black beans are so many independent arguments in favor of the one under the thimble being black, and all the white drawings so many against it, an excess of twenty black beans ought to produce the same degree of belief that the hidden bean was black, whatever the total number drawn.

In the conceptualistic view of probability, complete ignorance, where the judgment ought not to swerve either toward or away from the hypothesis, is represented by the probability $\frac{1}{2}$.*

But let us suppose that we are totally ignorant what colored hair the inhabitants of Saturn have. Let us, then, take a color-chart in which all possible colors are shown shading into one another by imperceptible degrees. In such a chart the relative areas occupied by different classes of colors are perfectly arbitrary. Let us inclose such an area with a closed line, and ask what is the chance on conceptualistic principles that the color of the hair of the inhabitants of Saturn falls within that area? The answer cannot be indeterminate because we must be in some state of belief; and, indeed, conceptualistic writers do not admit indeterminate probabilities. As there is no certainty in the matter, the answer lies between *zero* and *unity*. As no numerical value is afforded by the data, the number must be determined by the nature of the scale of probability itself, and not by calculation from the data. The answer can, therefore, only be one-half, since the judgment should neither favor nor oppose the hypothesis. What is true of this area is true of any other one; and it will equally be true of a third area which embraces the other two. But the probability for each of the smaller areas being one-half, that for the larger should be at least unity, which is absurd.

III

All our reasonings are of two kinds: 1. *Explicative, analytic,* or *deductive;* 2. *Amplificative, synthetic,* or (loosely speaking) *inductive.* In explicative reasoning, certain facts are first laid down in the premises. These facts are, in every case, an inexhaustible multitude, but they may often be summed up in one simple proposition by means of some regularity which runs through them all. Thus, take the proposition that Socrates was a man; this implies (to go no further) that during every fraction of a second of his whole life (or, if you please, during the greater part of them) he was a man. He did not at one instant appear as a tree and at another as a dog; he did not flow into water, or appear in two places at once; you could not put your finger through him as if he were an optical image, etc. Now, the facts being thus laid down, some order

---

*"Perfect indecision, belief inclining neither way, an even chance."
—De Morgan [*Formal Logic* (1847)], p. 182.

among some of them, not particularly made use of for the purpose of stating them, may perhaps be discovered; and this will enable us to throw part or all of them into a new statement, the possibility of which might have escaped attention. Such a statement will be the conclusion of an analytic inference. Of this sort are all mathematical demonstrations. But synthetic reasoning is of another kind. In this case the facts summed up in the conclusion are not among those stated in the premises. They are different facts, as when one sees that the tide rises m times and concludes that it will rise the next time. These are the only inferences which increase our real knowledge, however useful the others may be.

In any problem in probabilities, we have given the relative frequency of certain events, and we perceive that in these facts the relative frequency of another event is given in a hidden way. This being stated makes the solution. This is therefore mere explicative reasoning, and is evidently entirely inadequate to the representation of synthetic reasoning, which goes out beyond the facts given in the premises. There is, therefore, a manifest impossibility in so tracing out any probability for a synthetic conclusion.

Most treatises on probability contain a very different doctrine. They state, for example, that if one of the ancient denizens of the shores of the Mediterranean, who had never heard of tides, had gone to the bay of Biscay, and had there seen the tide rise, say m times, he could know that there was a probability equal to

$$\frac{m + 1}{m + 2}$$

that it would rise the next time. In a well-known work by Quételet, much stress is laid on this, and it is made the foundation of a theory of inductive reasoning.[3]

But this solution betrays its origin if we apply it to the case in which the man has never seen the tide rise at all; that is, if we put $m = 0$. In this case, the probability that it will rise the next time comes out $\frac{1}{2}$, or, in other words, the solution involves the conceptualistic principle that there is an even chance of a totally unknown event. The manner in which it has been reached has been by considering a number of urns all containing the same number of balls, part white and part black. One urn contains all white balls, another, one black and the rest white, a third, two black and the rest white, and so on, one urn for each proportion, until an urn is reached containing only black balls. But the only possible reason for drawing any analogy between such an arrangement and that of Nature is the principle that alternatives of which we know nothing must be considered as equally probable. But this principle, is absurd. There is an indefinite variety of ways of enumerating the different possibilities, which, on the application of this principle, would give different results. If there be any way of enumerating the possibilities so as to make them all equal, it is not that from which this solution is derived, but is the following: Suppose we had an immense granary filled with black and white balls well mixed up; and suppose each urn were filled by taking a fixed number of balls from this granary quite at random. The relative number of white balls in the granary might be anything, say one in three. Then in one-third of the urns the first ball would be white, and in two-thirds black. In one-third of those urns of which the first ball was white, and also in one-third of those in which the first ball was black, the second ball would be white. In this way, we should have a distribution like that shown in the following table, where *w* stands for a white ball and *b* for a black one. The reader can, if he chooses, verify the table for himself.

wwww.

wwwb.	*wwbw.*	*wbww.*	*bwww.*		
wwwb.	*wwbw.*	*wbww.*	*bwww.*		

wwbb.	*wbwb.*	*bwwb.*	*wbbw.*	*bwbw.*	*bbww.*
wwbb.	*wbwb.*	*bwwb.*	*wbbw.*	*bwbw.*	*bbww.*
wwbb.	*wbwb.*	*bwwb.*	*wbbw.*	*bwbw.*	*bbww.*
wwbb.	*wbwb.*	*bwwb.*	*wbbw.*	*bwbw.*	*bbww.*

wbbb.	*bwbb.*	*bbwb.*	*bbbw*
wbbb.	*bwbb.*	*bbwb.*	*bbbw.*
wbbb.	*bwbb.*	*bbwb.*	*bbbw.*
wbbb.	*bwbb.*	*bbwb.*	*bbbw.*
wbbb.	*bwbb.*	*bbwb.*	*bbbw.*
wbbb.	*bwbb.*	*bbwb.*	*bbbw.*
wbbb.	*bwbb.*	*bbwb.*	*bbbw.*
wbbb.	*bwbb.*	*bbwb.*	*bbbw.*

bbbb.
bbbb.
bbbb.
bbbb.
bbbb.
bbbb.
bbbb.
bbbb.
bbbb.
bbbb.
bbbb.
bbbb.
bbbb.
bbbb.
bbbb.
bbbb.

In the second group, where there is one b, there are two sets just alike; in the third there are 4, in the fourth 8, and in the fifth 16, doubling every time. This is because we have supposed twice as many black balls in the granary as white ones; had we supposed 10 times as many, instead of

$$1, 2, 4, 8, 16$$

sets we should have had

$$1, 10, 100, 1000, 10000$$

sets; on the other hand, had the numbers of black and white balls in the granary been even, there would have been but one set in each group. Now suppose two balls were drawn from one of these urns and were found to be both white, what would be the probability of the next one being white? If the two drawn out were the first two put into the urns, and the next to be drawn out were the third put in, then the probability of this third being white would be the same whatever the colors of the first two, for it has been supposed that just the same proportion of urns has the third ball white among those which have the first two *white-white, white-black, black-white,* and *black-black.* Thus, in this case, the chance of the third ball being white would be the same whatever the first two were. But, by inspecting the table, the reader can see that in each group all orders of the balls occur with equal frequency, so that it makes no difference whether they are drawn out in the order they were put in or not. Hence the colors of the balls already drawn have no influence on the probability of any other being white or black.

Now, if there be any way of enumerating the possibilities of Nature so as to make them equally probable, it is clearly one which should make one arrangement or combination of the elements of Nature as probable as another, that is, a distribution like that we have supposed, and it, therefore, appears that the assumption that any such thing can be done, leads simply to the conclusion that reasoning from past to future experience is absolutely worthless. In fact, the moment that you assume that the chances in favor of that of which we are totally ignorant are even, the problem about the tides does not differ, in any arithmetical particular, from the case in which a penny (known to be equally likely to come up heads and tails) should turn up heads m times successively. In short, it would be to assume that Nature is a pure chaos, or chance combination of independent elements, in which reasoning from one fact to another would be impossible; and since, as we shall hereafter see, there is no judgment of pure observation without reasoning, it would be to suppose all human cognition illusory and no real knowledge possible. It would be to suppose that if we have found the order of Nature more or less regular in the past, this has been by a pure run of luck which we may expect is now at an end. Now, it may be we have no scintilla of proof to the contrary, but reason is unnecessary in reference to that belief which is of all the most settled, which nobody doubts or can doubt, and which he who should deny would stultify himself in so doing.

The relative probability of this or that arrangement of Nature is something which we should have a right to talk about if universes were as plenty as blackberries, if we could put a quantity of them in a bag, shake them well up, draw out a sample, and examine them to see what proportion of them had one arrangement and what proportion another. But, even in that case, a higher universe would contain us, in regard to whose arrangements the conception of probability could have no applicability.

IV

We have examined the problem proposed by the conceptualists, which, translated into clear language, is this: Given a synthetic conclusion; required to know out of all possible states of things how many will accord, to any assigned extent, with this conclusion; and we have found that it is only an absurd attempt to reduce synthetic to analytic reason, and that no definite solution is possible.

But there is another problem in connection with this subject. It is this: Given a certain state of things, required to know what proportion of all synthetic inferences relating to it will be true within a given degree of approximation. Now, there is no difficulty about this problem (except for its mathematical complication); it has been much studied, and the answer is perfectly well known. And is not this, after all, what we want to know much rather than the other? Why should we want to know the probability that the fact will accord with our conclusion? That implies that we are interested in all possible worlds, and not merely the one in which we find ourselves placed. Why is it not much more to the purpose to know the probability that our conclusion will accord with the fact? One of these questions is the first above stated and the other the second, and I ask the reader whether, if people, instead of using the word probability without any clear apprehension of their own meaning, had always spoken of relative frequency, they could have failed to see that what they wanted was not to follow along the synthetic procedure with an analytic one, in order to find the probability of the conclusion; but, on the contrary, to begin with the fact at which the synthetic inference aims, and follow back to the facts it uses for premises in order to see the probability of their being such as will yield the truth.

As we cannot have an urn with an infinite number of balls to represent the inexhaustibleness of Nature, let us suppose one with a finite number, each ball being thrown back into the urn after being drawn out, so that there is no exhaustion of them. Suppose one ball out of three is white and the rest black, and that four balls are drawn. Then the table on page 163 represents the relative frequency of the different ways in which these balls might be drawn. It will be seen that if we should judge by these four balls of the proportion in the urn, 32 times out of 81 we should find it $\frac{1}{4}$, and 24 times out of 81 we should find it $\frac{1}{2}$, the truth being $\frac{1}{3}$. To extend this table to high numbers would be great labor, but the mathematicians have found some ingenious ways of reckoning what the numbers would be. It is found that, if the true proportion of white balls is p, and s balls are drawn, then the error of the proportion obtained by the induction will be—

half the time within	$0.477\sqrt{\dfrac{2p\,(1-p)}{s}}$
9 times out of 10 within	$1.163\sqrt{\dfrac{2p\,(1-p)}{s}}$
99 times out of 100 within	$1.821\sqrt{\dfrac{2p\,(1-p)}{s}}$
999 times out of 1,000 within	$2.328\sqrt{\dfrac{2p\,(1-p)}{s}}$
9,999 times out of 10,000 within	$2.751\sqrt{\dfrac{2p\,(1-p)}{s}}$
9,999,999,999 times out of 10,000,000,000 within	$4.77\sqrt{\dfrac{2p\,(1-p)}{s}}$

The use of this may be illustrated by an example. By the census of 1870, it appears that the proportion of males among native white children under one year old was 0.5082, while among colored children of the same age the proportion was only 0.4977. The difference between these is 0.0105, or about one in a 100. Can this be attributed to chance, or would the difference always exist among a great number of white and colored children under like circumstances? Here p may be taken at $\frac{1}{2}$; hence $2p(1-p)$ is also $\frac{1}{2}$. The number of white children counted was near 1,000,000; hence the fraction whose square-root is to be taken is about $\frac{1}{2000000}$. The root is about $\frac{1}{1400}$, and this multiplied by 0.477 gives about 0.0003 as the probable error in the ratio of males among the whites as obtained from the induction. The number of black children was about 150,000, which gives 0.0008 for the probable error. We see that the actual discrepancy is ten times the sum of these, and such a result would happen, according to our table, only once out of 10,000,-000,000 censuses, in the long run.

It may be remarked that when the real value of the probability sought inductively is either very large or very small, the reasoning is more secure. Thus, suppose there were in reality one white ball in 100 in a certain urn, and we were to judge of the number by 100 drawings.

The probability of drawing no white ball would be $\frac{366}{1000}$; that of drawing one white ball would be $\frac{370}{1000}$; that of drawing two would be $\frac{185}{1000}$; that of drawing three would be $\frac{61}{1000}$; that of drawing four would be $\frac{15}{1000}$; that of drawing five would be only $\frac{3}{1000}$, etc. Thus we should be tolerably certain of not being in error by more than one ball in 100.

It appears, then, that in one sense we can, and in another we cannot, determine the probability of synthetic inference. When I reason in this way:

Ninety-nine Cretans in a hundred are liars;

But Epimenides is a Cretan;

Therefore, Epimenides is a liar:—

I know that reasoning similar to that would carry truth 99 times in 100. But when I reason in the opposite direction:

Minos, Sarpedon, Rhadamanthus, Deucalion, and Epimenides, are all the Cretans I can think of;

But these were all atrocious liars,

Therefore, pretty much all Cretans must have been liars; I do not in the least know how often such reasoning would carry me right. On the other hand, what I do know is that some definite proportion of Cretans must have been liars, and that this proportion can be probably approximated to by an induction from five or six instances. Even in the worst case for the probability of such an inference, that in which about half the Cretans are liars, the ratio so obtained would probably not be in error by more than $\frac{1}{6}$. So much I know; but, then, in the present case the inference is that pretty much all Cretans are liars, and whether there may not be a special improbability in that I do not know.

V

Late in the last century, Immanuel Kant asked the question, "How are synthetical judgments *a priori* possible?"[4] By synthetical judgments he meant such as assert positive fact and are not mere affairs of arrangement; in short, judgments of the kind which synthetical reasoning produces, and which analytic reasoning cannot yield. By *a priori* judgments he meant such as that all outward objects are in space, every event has a cause, etc., propositions which according to him can never be inferred from experience. Not so much by his answer to this question as by the mere asking of it, the current philosophy of that time was shattered and destroyed, and a new epoch in its history was begun. But before asking *that* question he ought to have asked the more general one, "How are any synthetical judgments at all possible?" How is it that a man can observe one fact and straightway pronounce judgment concerning another different fact not involved in the first? Such reasoning, as we have seen, has, at least in the usual sense of the phrase, no definite probability; how, then, can it add to our knowledge? This is a strange paradox; the Abbé Gratry says it is a miracle, and that every true induction is an immediate inspiration from on high.* I respect this explanation far more than many a pedantic attempt to solve the question by some juggle with probabilities, with the forms of syllogism, or what not. I respect it because it shows an appreciation of the depth of the problem, because it assigns an adequate cause, and because it is intimately connected—as the true account should be—with a general philosophy of the universe. At the same time, I do not accept this explanation, because an explanation should tell *how* a thing is done, and to assert a perpetual miracle seems to be an abandonment of all hope of doing that, without sufficient justification.

It will be interesting to see how the answer which Kant gave to his question about synthetical judgments *a priori* will appear if extended to the question of synthetical judgments in general. That answer is, that synthetical judgments *a priori* are possible because whatever is universally true is involved in the conditions of experience. Let us apply this to a general synthetical reasoning. I take from a bag a handful of beans; they are all purple, and I infer that all the beans in the bag are purple. How can I do that? Why, upon the principle that whatever is universally true of my experience (which is here the appearance of these different beans) is involved in the condition of experience. The condition of this special experience is that all these beans were taken from that bag. According to Kant's principle, then, whatever is found true of all the beans drawn from the bag must find its explanation in some peculiarity of the contents of the bag. This is a satisfactory statement of the principle of induction.

When we draw a deductive or analytic conclusion, our rule of inference is that facts of a certain general character are either invariably or in a certain proportion of cases accompanied by facts of another general character. Then our premise being a fact of the former class, we infer with certainty or with the appropriate degree of probability the existence of a fact of the second class. But the rule for synthetic inference is of a different kind. When we sample a bag of beans we do not in the least assume that the fact of some beans being purple involves the necessity or even the probability of other beans being so. On the contrary, the conceptualistic method of treating probabilities, which really amounts simply to the deductive treatment of them, when rightly carried out leads to the result that a synthetic inference has just an even chance in its favor, or in other words is

---

*Logique. The same is true, according to him, of every performance of a differentiation, but not of integration. He does not tell us whether it is the supernatural assistance which makes the former process so much the easier.[5]

absolutely worthless. The color of one bean is entirely independent of that of another. But synthetic inference is founded upon a classification of facts, not according to their characters, but according to the manner of obtaining them. Its rule is, that a number of facts obtained in a given way will in general more or less resemble other facts obtained in the same way; or, *experiences whose conditions are the same will have the same general characters.*

In the former case, we know that premises precisely similar in form to those of the given ones will yield true conclusions, just once in a calculable number of times. In the latter case, we only know that premises obtained under circumstances similar to the given ones (though perhaps themselves very different) will yield true conclusions, at least once in a calculable number of times. We may express this by saying that in the case of analytic inference we know the probability of our conclusion (if the premises are true), but in the case of synthetic inferences we only know the degree of trustworthiness of our proceeding. As all knowledge comes from synthetic inference, we must equally infer that all human certainty consists merely in our knowing that the processes by which our knowledge has been derived are such as must generally have led to true conclusions.

Though a synthetic inference cannot by any means be reduced to deduction, yet that the rule of induction will hold good in the long run may be deduced from the principle that reality is only the object of the final opinion to which sufficient investigation would lead. That belief gradually tends to fix itself under the influence of inquiry is, indeed, one of the facts with which logic sets out.

11

The Order of Nature

P 122: Popular Science Monthly *13 (June 1878):203–17. [Also published in W3:306–22 and in CP 6.395–427.] In the fifth "Illustrations" paper, Peirce argues against Mill's view that the uniformity of nature is the sole warrant for induction and for the theory set out in the preceding paper: that induction should be explained by the doctrine of probabilities (which, as he points out, should pose no problem for religion). He also proclaims, as he did throughout his life, that "the mind of man is strongly adapted to the comprehension of the world," a capacity explained as the result of natural selection and as being fundamental for success in abductive reasoning (or hypothesis). Finally, he turns to some of the cosmological questions that open the line of inquiry that will eventually result in his guess at the riddle of the universe.*

I

Any proposition whatever concerning the order of Nature must touch more or less upon religion. In our day, belief, even in these matters, depends more and more upon the observation of facts. If a remarkable and universal orderliness be found in the universe, there must be some cause for this regularity, and science has to consider what hypotheses might account for the phenomenon. One way of accounting for it, certainly, would be to suppose that the world is ordered by a superior power. But if there is nothing in the universal subjection of phenomena to laws, nor in the character of those laws themselves (as being benevolent, beautiful, economical, etc.), which goes to prove the existence of a governor of the universe, it is hardly to be anticipated that any other sort of evidence will be found to weigh very much with minds emancipated from the tyranny of tradition.

Nevertheless, it cannot truly be said that even an absolutely negative decision of that question could altogether destroy religion, inasmuch as there are faiths in which, however much they differ from our own, we recognize those essential characters which make them worthy to be called religions, and which, nevertheless, do not postulate an actually existing Deity. That one, for instance, which has had the most numerous and by no means the least intelligent following of any on earth, teaches that the Divinity in his highest perfection is wrapped away from the world in a state of profound and eternal sleep, which really does not differ from non-existence, whether it be called by that name or not. No candid mind who has followed the writings of M. Vacherot can well deny that his religion is as earnest as can be.[1] He worships the Perfect, the Supreme Ideal; but he conceives that the very notion of the Ideal is repugnant to its real existence. In fact, M. Vacherot finds it agreeable to his reason to assert that non-existence is an essential character of the perfect, just as St. Anselm and Descartes found it agreeable to theirs to assert the extreme opposite. I confess that there is one respect in which either of these positions seems to me more congruous with the religious attitude than that of a theology which stands upon evidences; for as soon as the Deity presents himself to either Anselm or Vacherot, and manifests his glorious attributes, whether it be in a vision of the night or day, either of them recognizes his adorable God, and sinks upon his knees at once; whereas the theologian of evidences will first demand that the divine apparition shall identify himself, and only after having scrutinized his credentials and weighed the probabilities of his being found among the totality of existences, will he finally render his circumspect homage, thinking that no characters can be adorable but those which belong to a real thing.

If we could find out any general characteristic of the universe, any mannerism in the ways of Nature, any law everywhere applicable and universally valid, such a discovery would be of such singular assistance to us in all our future reasoning, that it would deserve a place almost at the head of the principles of logic. On the other hand, if it can be shown that there is nothing of the sort to find out, but that every discoverable regularity is of limited range, this again will be of logical importance. What sort of a conception we ought to have of the universe, how to think of the *ensemble* of things, is a fundamental problem in the theory of reasoning.

II

It is the legitimate endeavor of scientific men now, as it was twenty-three hundred years ago, to account for the formation of the solar system and of the cluster of stars which forms the galaxy, by the fortuitous concourse of atoms. The greatest expounder of this theory, when asked how he could write an immense book on the system of the world without one mention of its author, replied, very logically, "Je n'avais pas besoin de cette hypothèse-là."[2] But, in truth, there is nothing atheistical in the theory, any more than there was in this answer. Matter is supposed to be composed of molecules which obey the laws of mechanics and exert certain attractions upon one another; and it is to these regularities (which there is no attempt to account for) that general arrangement of the solar system would be due, and not to hazard.

If any one has ever maintained that the universe is a pure throw of the dice, the theologians have abundantly refuted him. "How often," says Archbishop Tillotson, "might a man, after he had jumbled a set of letters in a bag, fling them out upon the ground before they would fall into an exact poem, yea, or so much as make a good discourse in prose! And may not a little book be as easily made by chance as this great volume of the world?"[3] The chance world here shown to be so different from that in which we live would be one in which there were no laws, the characters of different things being entirely independent; so that, should a sample of any kind of objects ever show a prevalent character, it could only be by accident, and no general proposition could ever be established. Whatever further conclusions we may come to in regard to the order of the universe, thus much may be regarded as solidly established, that the world is not a mere chance-medley.

But whether the world makes an exact poem or not, is another question. When we look up at the heavens at night, we readily perceive that the stars are not simply splashed on to the celestial vault; but there does not seem to be any precise system in their arrangement either. It will be worth our while, then, to inquire into the degree of orderliness in the universe; and, to begin, let us ask whether the world we live in is any more orderly than a purely chance-world would be.

Any uniformity, or law of Nature, may be stated in the form, "Every A is B"; as, every ray of light is a non-curved line, every body is accelerated toward the earth's centre, etc. This is the same as to say, "There does not exist any A which is not B"; there is no curved ray; there is no body not accelerated toward the earth; so that the uniformity consists in the non-occurrence in Nature of a certain combination of characters (in this case, the combination of being A with being non-B).* And, conversely, every case of the non-occurence of a combination of characters would constitute a uniformity in Nature. Thus, suppose the quality A is never found in combination with the quality

---

*For the present purpose, the negative of a character is to be considered as much a character as the positive, for a uniformity may either be affirmative or negative. I do not say that no distinction can be drawn between positive and negative uniformities.

C: for example, suppose the quality of idiocy is never found in combination with that of having a well-developed brain. Then nothing of the sort A is of the sort C, or everything of the sort A is of the sort non-C (or say, every idiot has an ill-developed brain), which, being something universally true of the A's, is a uniformity in the world. Thus we see that, in a world where there were no uniformities, no logically possible combination of characters would be excluded, but every combination would exist in some object. But two objects not identical must differ in some of their characters, though it be only in the character of being in such-and-such a place. Hence, precisely the same combination of characters could not be found in two different objects; and, consequently, in a chance-world every combination involving either the positive or negative of every character would belong to just one thing. Thus, if there were but five simple characters in such a world,* we might denote them by A, B, C, D, E, and their negatives by a, b, c, d, e; and then, as there would be 2^5 or 32 different combinations of these characters, completely determinate in reference to each of them, that world would have just 32 objects in it, their characters being as in the following table:

TABLE I

ABCDE	AbCDE	aBCDE	abCDE
ABCDe	AbCDe	aBCDe	abCDe
ABCdE	AbCdE	aBCdE	abCdE
ABCde	AbCde	aBCde	abCde
ABcDE	AbcDE	aBcDE	abcDE
ABcDe	AbcDe	aBcDe	abcDe
ABcdE	AbcdE	aBcdE	abcdE
ABcde	Abcde	aBcde	abcde

For example, if the five primary characters were *hard, sweet, fragrant, green, bright,* there would be one object which reunited all these qualities, one which was hard, sweet, fragrant, and green, but not bright; one which was hard, sweet, fragrant, and bright, but not green; one which was hard, sweet, and fragrant, but neither green nor bright; and so on through all the combinations.

This is what a thoroughly chance-world would be like, and certainly nothing could be imagined more systematic. When a quantity of letters are poured out of a bag, the appearance of disorder is due to the circumstance that the phenomena are only partly fortuitous. The

---

*There being 5 simple characters, with their negatives, they could be compounded in various ways so as to make 241 characters in all, without counting the characters *existence* and *non-existence*, which make up 243 or 3^5.

laws of space are supposed, in that case, to be rigidly preserved, and there is also a certain amount of regularity in the formation of the letters. The result is that some elements are orderly and some are disorderly, which is precisely what we observe in the actual world. Tillotson, in the passage of which a part has been quoted, goes on to ask, "How long might 20,000 blind men, which should be sent out from the several remote parts of England, wander up and down before they would all meet upon Salisbury Plains, and fall into rank and file in the exact order of an army? And yet this is much more easy to be imagined than how the innumerable blind parts of matter should rendezvous themselves into a world."[4] This is very true, but in the actual world the *blind men* are, as far as we can see, *not* drawn up in any particular order at all. And, in short, while a certain amount of order exists in the world, it would seem that the world is not so orderly as it might be, and, for instance, not so much so as a world of pure chance would be.

But we can never get to the bottom of this question until we take account of a highly-important logical principle* which I now proceed to enounce. This principle is that any plurality or lot of objects whatever have some character in common (no matter how insignificant) which is peculiar to them and not shared by anything else. The word "character" here is taken in such a sense as to include negative characters, such as incivility, inequality, etc., as well as their positives, civility, equality, etc. To prove the theorem, I will show what character any two things, A and B, have in common, not shared by anything else. The things, A and B, are each distinguished from all other things by the possession of certain characters which may be named A-ness and B-ness. Corresponding to these positive characters, are the negative characters un-A-ness, which is possessed by everything except A, and un-B-ness, which is possessed by everything except B. These two characters are united in everything except A and B; and this union of the characters un-A-ness and un-B-ness makes a compound character which may be termed A-B-lessness. This is not possessed by either A or B, but it is possessed by everything else. This character, like every other, has its corresponding negative un-A-B-lessness, and this last is the character possessed by both A and B, and by nothing else. It is obvious that what has thus been shown true of two things is, *mutatis mutandis,* true of any number of things. Q.E.D.

In any world whatever, then, there must be a character peculiar to each possible group of objects. If, as a matter of nomenclature, characters peculiar to the same group be regarded as only different aspects

---

*This principle was, I believe, first stated by Mr. De Morgan [*Formal Logic,* p. 39].

of the same character, then we may say that there will be precisely one character for each possible group of objects. Thus, suppose a world to contain five things, α, β, γ, δ, ϵ. Then it will have a separate character for each of the 31 groups (with *non-existence* making up 32 or 2^5) shown in the following table:

TABLE II

	$\alpha\beta$	$\alpha\beta\gamma$	$\alpha\beta\gamma\delta$	$\alpha\beta\gamma\delta\epsilon$
α	$\alpha\gamma$	$\alpha\beta\delta$	$\alpha\beta\gamma\epsilon$	
β	$\alpha\delta$	$\alpha\beta\epsilon$	$\alpha\beta\delta\epsilon$	
γ	$\alpha\epsilon$	$\alpha\gamma\delta$	$\alpha\gamma\delta\epsilon$	
δ	$\beta\gamma$	$\alpha\gamma\epsilon$	$\beta\gamma\delta\epsilon$	
ϵ	$\beta\delta$	$\alpha\delta\epsilon$		
	$\beta\epsilon$	$\beta\gamma\delta$		
	$\gamma\delta$	$\beta\gamma\epsilon$		
	$\gamma\epsilon$	$\beta\delta\epsilon$		
	$\delta\epsilon$	$\gamma\delta\epsilon$		

This shows that a contradiction is involved in the very idea of a chance-world, for in a world of 32 things, instead of there being only 3^5 or 243 characters, as we have seen that the notion of a chance-world requires, there would, in fact, be no less than 2^{32}, or 4,294,967,296 characters, which would not be all independent, but would have all possible relations with one another.

We further see that so long as we regard characters abstractly, without regard to their relative importance, etc., there is no possibility of a more or less degree of orderliness in the world, the whole system of relationship between the different characters being given by mere logic; that is, being implied in those facts which are tacitly admitted as soon as we admit that there is any such thing as reasoning.

In order to descend from this abstract point of view, it is requisite to consider the characters of things as relative to the perceptions and active powers of living beings. Instead, then, of attempting to imagine a world in which there should be no uniformities, let us suppose one in which none of the uniformities should have reference to characters interesting or important to us. In the first place, there would be nothing to puzzle us in such a world. The small number of qualities which would directly meet the senses would be the ones which would afford the key to everything which could possibly interest us. The whole universe would have such an air of system and perfect regularity that there would be nothing to ask. In the next place, no action of ours, and no event of Nature, would have important consequences in such a world. We should be perfectly free from all responsibility, and there would be nothing to do but to enjoy or suffer whatever happened to come along. Thus there would be nothing to stimulate or develop either the mind or the will, and we consequently should neither act nor think. We should have no memory, because that depends on a law of our organization. Even if we had any senses, we should be situated toward such a world precisely as inanimate objects are toward the present one, provided we suppose that these objects have an absolutely transitory and instantaneous consciousness without memory—a supposition which is a mere mode of speech, for that would be no consciousness at all. We may, therefore, say that a world of chance is simply our actual world viewed from the standpoint of an animal at the very vanishing-point of intelligence. The actual world is almost a chance-medley to the mind of a polyp. The interest which the uniformities of Nature have for an animal measures his place in the scale of intelligence.

Thus, nothing can be made out from the orderliness of Nature in regard to the existence of a God, unless it be maintained that the existence of a finite mind proves the existence of an infinite one.

III

In the last of these papers[5] we examined the nature of inductive or synthetic reasoning. We found it to be a process of sampling. A number of specimens of a class are taken, not by selection within that class, but at random. These specimens will agree in a great number of respects. If, now, it were likely that a second lot would agree with the first in the majority of these respects, we might base on this consideration an inference in regard to any one of these characters. But such an inference would neither be of the nature of induction, nor would it (except in special cases) be valid, because the vast majority of points of agreement in the first sample drawn would generally be entirely accidental, as well as insignificant. To illustrate this, I take the ages at death of the first five poets given in Wheeler's *Biographical Dictionary.* They are:

> Aagard, 48.
> Abeille, 70.
> Abulola, 84.
> Abunowas, 48.
> Accords, 45.

These five ages have the following characters in common:

1. The difference of the two digits composing the number, divided by three, leaves a remainder of *one.*

2. The first digit raised to the power indicated by the second, and divided by three, leaves a remainder of *one.*

3. The sum of the prime factors of each age, including one, is divisible by three.

It is easy to see that the number of accidental agreements of this sort would be quite endless. But suppose that, instead of considering a character because of its prevalence in the sample, we designate a character before taking the sample, selecting it for its importance, obviousness, or other point of interest. Then two considerable samples drawn at random are extremely likely to agree approximately in regard to the proportion of occurrences of a character so chosen. *The inference that a previously designated character has nearly the same frequency of occurrence in the whole of a class that it has in a sample drawn at random out of that class is induction.* If the character be not previously designated, then a sample in which it is found to be prevalent can only serve to suggest that it *may be* prevalent in the whole class. We may consider this surmise as an inference if we please—an inference of possibility; but a second sample must be drawn to test the question of whether the character actually is prevalent. Instead of designating beforehand a single character in reference to which we will examine a sample, we may designate two, and use the same sample to determine the relative frequencies of both. This will be making two inductive inferences at once; and, of course, we are less certain that both will yield correct conclusions than we should be that either separately would do so. What is true of two characters is true of any limited number. Now, the number of characters which have any considerable interest for us in reference to any class of objects is more moderate than might be supposed. As we shall be sure to examine any sample with reference to these characters, they may be regarded not exactly as predesignated, but as predetermined (which amounts to the same thing); and we may infer that the sample represents the class in all these respects if we please, remembering only that this is not so secure an inference as if the particular quality to be looked for had been fixed upon beforehand.

The demonstration of this theory of induction rests upon principles and follows methods which are accepted by all those who display in other matters the particular knowledge and force of mind which qualify them to judge of this. The theory itself, however, quite unaccountably seems never to have occurred to any of the writers who have undertaken to explain synthetic reasoning. The most widely-spread opinion in the matter is one which was much promoted by Mr. John Stuart Mill—namely, that induction depends for its validity upon the uniformity of Nature—that is, on the principle that what happens once will, under a sufficient degree of similarity of circumstances, happen again as often as the same circumstances recur.[6] The application is this: The fact that different things belong to the same class constitutes the similarity of circumstances, and the induction is good, provided this similarity is "sufficient." What happens once is, that a number of these things are found to have a certain character; what may be expected, then, to happen again as often as the circumstances recur consists in this, that all things belonging to the same class should have the same character.

This analysis of induction has, I venture to think, various imperfections, to some of which it may be useful to call attention. In the first place, when I put my hand in a bag and draw out a handful of beans, and, finding three-quarters of them black, infer that about three-quarters of all in the bag are black, my inference is obviously of the same kind as if I had found any larger proportion, or the whole, of the sample black, and had assumed that it represented in that respect the rest of the contents of the bag. But the analysis in question hardly seems adapted to the explanation of this *proportionate* induction, where the conclusion, instead of being that a certain event uniformly happens under certain circumstances, is precisely that it does not uniformly occur, but only happens in a certain proportion of cases. It is true that the whole sample may be regarded as a single object, and the inference may be brought under the formula proposed by considering the conclusion to be that any similar sample will show a similar proportion among its constituents. But this is to treat the induction as if it rested on a single instance, which gives a very false idea of its probability.

In the second place, if the uniformity of Nature were the sole warrant of induction, we should have no right to draw one in regard to a character whose constancy we knew nothing about. Accordingly, Mr. Mill says that, though none but white swans were known to Europeans for thousands of years, yet the inference that all swans were white was "not a good induction," because it was not known that color was a usual generic character (it, in fact, not being so by any means).[7] But it is mathematically demonstrable that an inductive inference may have as high a degree of probability as you please independent of any antecedent knowledge of the constancy of the character inferred. Before it was known that color is not usually a character of *genera*, there was certainly a considerable probability that all swans were white. But the further study of the *genera* of animals led to the induction of their non-uniformity in regard to color. A deductive application of this general proposition would have gone far to overcome the probability of the universal whiteness of swans before the black species was discovered. When we do know anything in regard to the general constancy or inconstancy of a character, the application of that general knowledge to the particular class to which any induction relates, though it serves to increase or diminish the force of the induction, is, like every application of general knowledge to particular cases, deductive in its nature and not inductive.

In the third place, to say that inductions are true because similar events happen in similar circumstances—or, what is the same thing, because objects similar in some respects are likely to be similar in others—is to overlook those conditions which really are essential to the validity of inductions. When we take all the characters into account, any pair of objects resemble one another in just as many particulars as any other pair. If we limit ourselves to such characters as have for us any importance, interest, or obviousness, then a synthetic conclusion may be drawn, but only on condition that the specimens by which we judge have been taken at random from the class in regard to which we are to form a judgment, and not selected as belonging to any sub-class. The induction only has its full force when the character concerned has been designated before examining the sample. These are the essentials of induction, and they are not recognized in attributing the validity of induction to the uniformity of Nature. The explanation of induction by the doctrine of probabilities, given in the last of these papers,[8] is not a mere metaphysical formula, but is one from which all the rules of synthetic reasoning can be deduced systematically and with mathematical cogency. But the account of the matter by a principle of Nature, even if it were in other respects satisfactory, presents the fatal disadvantage of leaving us quite as much afloat as before in regard to the proper method of induction. It does not surprise me, therefore, that those who adopt this theory have given erroneous rules for the conduct of reasoning, nor that the greater number of examples put forward by Mr. Mill in his first edition, as models of what inductions should be, proved in the light of further scientific progress so particularly unfortunate that they had to be replaced by others in later editions. One would have supposed that Mr. Mill might have based an induction on *this* circumstance, especially as it is his avowed principle that, if the conclusion of an induction turns out false, it cannot have been a good induction. Nevertheless, neither he nor any of his scholars seem to have been led to suspect, in the least, the perfect solidity of the framework which he devised for securely supporting the mind in its passage from the known to the unknown, although at its first trial it did not answer quite so well as had been expected.

IV

When we have drawn any statistical induction—such, for instance, as that one-half of all births are of male children—it is always possible to discover, by investigation sufficiently prolonged, a class of which the same predicate may be affirmed universally; to find out, for instance, *what sort of* births are of male children. The truth of this principle follows immediately from the theorem that there is a character peculiar to every possible group of objects. The form in which the principle is usually stated is, that *every event must have a cause.*

But, though there exists a cause for every event, and that of a kind which is capable of being discovered, yet if there be nothing to guide us to the discovery; if we have to hunt among all the events in the world without any scent; if, for instance, the sex of a child might equally be supposed to depend on the configuration of the planets, on what was going on at the antipodes, or on anything else—then the discovery would have no chance of ever getting made.

That we ever do discover the precise causes of things, that any induction whatever is absolutely without exception, is what we have no right to assume. On the contrary, it is an easy corollary, from the theorem just referred to, that every empirical rule has an exception. But there are certain of our inductions which present an approach to universality so extraordinary that, even if we are to suppose that they are not strictly universal truths, we cannot possibly think that they have been reached merely by accident. The most remarkable laws of this kind are those of *time* and *space.* With reference to space, Bishop Berkeley first showed, in a very conclusive manner, that it was not a thing *seen,* but a thing *inferred.* [9] Berkeley chiefly insists on the impossibility of directly seeing the third dimension of space, since the retina of the eye is a surface. But, in point of fact, the retina is not even a surface; it is a conglomeration of nerve-needles directed toward the light and having only their extreme points sensitive, these points lying at considerable distances from one another compared with their areas. Now, of these points, certainly the excitation of no one singly can produce the perception of a surface, and consequently not the aggregate of all the sensations can amount to this. But certain relations subsist between the excitations of different nerve-points, and these constitute the premises upon which the hypothesis of space is founded, and from which it is inferred. That space is not immediately perceived is now universally admitted; and a mediate cognition is what is called an inference, and is subject to the criticism of logic. But what are we to say to the fact of every chicken as soon as it is hatched solving a problem whose data are of a complexity sufficient to try the greatest mathematical powers? It would be insane to deny that the tendency to light upon the conception of space is inborn in the mind of the chicken and of every animal. The same thing is equally true of time. That time is not directly perceived is evident, since no lapse of time is present, and we only perceive what is present. That, not having the idea of time, we should ever be able to perceive the flow in our sensations without some particular aptitude for it, will probably also be admitted. The idea of force—at least, in its rudiments—is another conception so early arrived at, and found in animals so low in the scale of intelligence, that it must be supposed innate. But the innateness of an idea admits of degree, for it consists in the tendency of that idea to present itself to the mind. Some ideas, like that of space, do so present themselves irresistibly at the very dawn of intelligence, and take possession of the mind on small provocation, while of other conceptions we are prepossessed, indeed, but not so strongly, down a scale which is greatly extended. The tendency to personify every thing, and to attribute human characters to it, may be said to be innate; but it is a tendency which is very soon overcome by civilized man in regard to the greater part of the objects about him. Take such a conception as that of gravitation varying inversely as the square of the distance. It is a very simple law. But to say that it is simple is merely to say that it is one which the mind is particularly adapted to apprehend with facility. Suppose the idea of a quantity multiplied into another had been no more easy to the mind than that of a quantity raised to the power indicated by itself—should we ever have discovered the law of the solar system?

It seems incontestable, therefore, that the mind of man is strongly adapted to the comprehension of the world; at least, so far as this goes, that certain conceptions, highly important for such a comprehension, naturally arise in his mind; and, without such a tendency, the mind could never have had any development at all.

How are we to explain this adaptation? The great utility and indispensableness of the conceptions of time, space, and force, even to the lowest intelligence, are such as to suggest that they are the results of natural selection. Without something like geometrical, kinetical, and mechanical conceptions, no animal could seize his food or do anything which might be necessary for the preservation of the species. He might, it is true, be provided with an instinct which would generally have the same effect; that is to say, he might have conceptions different from those of time, space, and force, but which coincided with them in regard to the ordinary cases of the animal's experience. But, as that animal would have an immense advantage in the struggle for life whose mechanical conceptions did not break down in a novel situation (such as development must bring about), there would be a constant selection in favor of more and more correct ideas of these matters. Thus would be attained the knowledge of that fundamental law upon which all science rolls; namely, that forces depend upon relations of time, space, and mass. When this idea was once sufficiently clear, it would require no more than a comprehensible degree of genius to discover the exact nature of these relations. Such an hypothesis naturally suggests itself, but it must be admitted that it does not seem sufficient to account for the extraordinary accuracy with which these conceptions apply to the phenomena of Nature, and it is probable that there is some secret here which remains to be discovered.

V

Some important questions of logic depend upon whether we are to consider the material universe as of limited extent and finite age, or quite boundless in space and in time. In the former case, it is conceivable that a general plan or design embracing the whole universe should be discovered, and it would be proper to be on the alert for some traces of such a unity. In the latter case, since the proportion of the world of which we can have any experience is less than the smallest assignable fraction, it follows that we never could discover any *pattern* in the universe except a repeating one; any design embracing the whole would be beyond our powers to discern, and beyond the united powers of all intellects during all time. Now, what is absolutely incapable of being known is, as we have seen in a former paper, not real at all. An absolutely incognizable existence is a nonsensical phrase. If, therefore, the universe is infinite, the attempt to find in it any design embracing it as a whole is futile, and involves a false way of looking at the subject. If the universe never had any beginning, and if in space world stretches beyond world without limit, there is no *whole* of material things, and consequently no general character to the universe, and no need or possibility of any governor for it. But if there was a time before which absolutely no matter existed, if there are certain absolute bounds to the region of things outside of which there is a mere void, then we naturally seek for an explanation of it, and, since we cannot look for it among material things, the hypothesis of a great disembodied animal, the creator and governor of the world, is natural enough.

The actual state of the evidence as to the limitation of the universe is as follows: As to time, we find on our earth a constant progress of development since the planet was a red-hot ball; the solar system seems to have resulted from the condensation of a nebula, and the process appears to be still going on. We sometimes see stars (presumably with systems of worlds) destroyed and apparently resolved back into the nebulous condition, but we have no evidence of any existence of the world previous to the nebulous stage from which it seems to have been evolved. All this rather favors the idea of a beginning than otherwise. As for limits in space, we cannot be sure that we see anything outside of the system of the milky-way. Minds of theological predilections have therefore no need of distorting the facts to reconcile them with their views.

But the only scientific presumption is, that the unknown parts of space and time are like the known parts, occupied; that, as we see cycles of life and death in all development which we can trace out to the end, the same holds good in regard to solar systems; that as enormous distances lie between the different planets of our solar system, relatively to their diameters, and as still more enormous distances lie between our system relatively to its diameter and other systems, so it may be supposed that other galactic clusters exist so remote from ours as not to be recognized as such with certainty. I do not say that these are strong inductions; I only say that they are the presumptions which, in our ignorance of the facts, should be preferred to hypotheses which involve conceptions of things and occurrences totally different in their character from any of which we have had any experience, such as disembodied spirits, the creation of matter, infringements of the laws of mechanics, etc.

The universe ought to be presumed too vast to have any character. When it is claimed that the arrangements of Nature are benevolent, or just, or wise, or of any other peculiar kind, we ought to be prejudiced against such opinions, as being the offspring of an ill-founded notion of the finitude of the world. And examination has hitherto shown that such beneficences, justice, etc., are of a most limited kind— limited in degree and limited in range.

In like manner, if any one claims to have discovered a plan in the structure of organized beings, or a scheme in their classification, or a regular arrangement among natural objects, or a system of proportionality in the human form, or an order of development, or a correspondence between conjunctions of the planets and human events, or a significance in numbers, or a key to dreams, the first thing we have to ask is whether such relations are susceptible of explanation on mechanical principles, and if not they should be looked upon with disfavor as having already a strong presumption against them; and examination has generally exploded all such theories.

There are minds to whom every prejudice, every presumption, seems unfair. It is easy to say what minds these are. They are those who never have known what it is to draw a well-grounded induction, and who imagine that other people's knowledge is as nebulous as their own. That all science rolls upon presumption (not of a formal but of a real kind) is no argument with them, because they cannot imagine that there is anything solid in human knowledge. These are the people who waste their time and money upon perpetual motions and other such rubbish.

But there are better minds who take up mystical theories (by which I mean all those which have no possibility of being mechanically explained). These are persons who are strongly prejudiced in favor of such theories. We all have natural tendencies to believe in such things; our education often strengthens this tendency; and the result is, that to many minds nothing seems so antecedently probable as a theory of this kind. Such persons find evidence enough in favor of their views, and in the absence of any recognized logic of induction they cannot be driven from their belief.

But to the mind of a physicist there ought to be a strong presumption against every mystical theory; and therefore it seems to me that those scientific men who have sought to make out that science was not hostile to theology have not been so clear-sighted as their opponents.

It would be extravagant to say that science can at present disprove religion; but it does seem to me that the spirit of science is hostile to any religion except such a one as that of M. Vacherot. Our appointed teachers inform us that Buddhism is a miserable and atheistical faith, shorn of the most glorious and needful attributes of a religion; that its priests can be of no use to agriculture by praying for rain, nor to war by commanding the sun to stand still. We also hear the remonstrances of those who warn us that to shake the general belief in the living God would be to shake the general morals, public and private. This, too, must be admitted; such a revolution of thought could no more be accomplished without waste and desolation than a plantation of trees could be transferred to new ground, however wholesome in itself, without all of them languishing for a time, and many of them dying. Nor is it, by-the-way, a thing to be presumed that a man would have taken part in a movement having a possible atheistical issue without having taken serious and adequate counsel in regard to that responsibility. But, let the consequences of such a belief be as dire as they may, one thing is certain: that the state of the facts, whatever it may be, will surely get found out, and no human prudence can long arrest the triumphal car of truth—no, not if the discovery were such as to drive every individual of our race to suicide!

But it would be folly to suppose that any metaphysical theory in regard to the mode of being of the perfect is to destroy that aspiration toward the perfect which constitutes the essence of religion. It is true that, if the priests of any particular form of religion succeed in making it generally believed that religion cannot exist without the acceptance of certain formulas, or if they succeed in so interweaving certain dogmas with the popular religion that the people can see no essential analogy between a religion which accepts these points of faith and one which rejects them, the result may very well be to render those who cannot believe these things irreligious. Nor can we ever hope that any body of priests should consider themselves more teachers of religion in general than of the particular system of theology advocated by their own party. But no man need be excluded from participation in the common feelings, nor from so much of the public expression of them as is open to all the laity, by the unphilosophical narrowness of those who guard the mysteries of worship. Am I to be prevented from joining in that common joy at the revelation of enlightened principles of religion, which we celebrate at Easter and Christmas, because I think that certain scientific, logical, and metaphysical ideas which have been mixed up with these principles are untenable? No; to do so would be to estimate those errors as of more consequence than the truth—an opinion which few would admit. People who do not believe what are really the fundamental principles of Christianity are rare to find, and all but these few ought to feel at home in the churches.

12

Deduction, Induction, and Hypothesis

P 123: Popular Science Monthly *13 (August 1878):470–82. [Also published in W3:323–38 and in CP 2.619–44.]* Peirce concludes his six "Illustrations" with a discussion of the three kinds of reasoning (deduction, induction, hypothesis) based on the general form of syllogistic argument composed of rule, case, and result. With examples from the history of science, he demonstrates that hypothesis is different from induction proper in that "hypothesis supposes something of a different kind from what we have directly observed, and frequently something which it would be impossible for us to observe directly," while induction only "infers the existence of phenomena such as we have observed in cases which are similar."*

I

The chief business of the logician is to classify arguments; for all testing clearly depends on classification. The classes of the logicians are defined by certain typical forms called syllogisms. For example, the syllogism called *Barbara* is as follows:

> S is M; M is P:
> Hence, S is P.

Or, to put words for letters—

> Enoch and Elijah were men; all men die:
> Hence, Enoch and Elijah must have died.

The "is P" of the logicians stands for any verb, active or neuter. It is capable of strict proof (with which, however, I will not trouble the reader) that all arguments whatever can be put into this form;[1] but only under the condition that the *is* shall mean "*is* for the purposes of the argument" or "*is* represented by." Thus, an induction will appear in this form something like this:

These beans are two-thirds white;
But, the beans in this bag are (represented by) these beans;
∴ The beans in the bag are two-thirds white.

But, because all inference may be reduced in some way to *Barbara*, it does not follow that this is the most appropriate form in which to represent every kind of inference. On the contrary, to show the distinctive characters of different sorts of inference, they must clearly be exhibited in different forms peculiar to each. *Barbara* particularly typifies deductive reasoning; and so long as the *is* is taken literally, no inductive reasoning can be put into this form. *Barbara* is, in fact, nothing but the application of a rule. The so-called major premise lays down this rule; as, for example, *All men are mortal.* The other or minor premise states a case under the rule; as, *Enoch was a man.* The conclusion applies the rule to the case and states the result: *Enoch is mortal.* All deduction is of this character; it is merely the application of general rules to particular cases. Sometimes this is not very evident, as in the following:

All quadrangles are figures,
But no triangle is a quadrangle;
Therefore, some figures are not triangles.

But here the reasoning is really this:

Rule.—Every quadrangle is other than a triangle.
Case.—Some figures are quadrangles.
Result.—Some figures are not triangles.

Inductive or synthetic reasoning, being something more than the mere application of a general rule to a particular case, can never be reduced to this form.

If, from a bag of beans of which we know that $\frac{2}{3}$ are white, we take one at random, it is a deductive inference that this bean is probably white, the probability being $\frac{2}{3}$. We have, in effect, the following syllogism:

Rule.—The beans in this bag are $\frac{2}{3}$ white.
Case.—This bean has been drawn in such a way that in the long run the relative number of white beans so drawn would be equal to the relative number in the bag.
Result.—This bean has been drawn in such a way that in the long run it would turn out white $\frac{2}{3}$ of the time.

If instead of drawing one bean we draw a handful at random and conclude that about $\frac{2}{3}$ of the handful are probably white, the reasoning is of the same sort. If, however, not knowing what proportion of white beans there are in the bag, we draw a handful at random and, finding $\frac{2}{3}$ of the beans in the handful white, conclude that about $\frac{2}{3}$ of those in the bag are white, we are rowing up the current of deductive sequence, and are concluding a rule from the observation of a result in a certain case. This is particularly clear when all the handful turn out one color. The induction then is:

> These beans were in this bag. ——————————
> These beans are white. ——————————
> ∴ All the beans in the bag were white. ——————————

Which is but an inversion of the deductive syllogism.

> *Rule.*—All the beans in the bag were white. ——————
> *Case.*—These beans were in the bag. ——————————
> *Result.*—These beans are white. ——————————

So that induction is the inference of the *rule* from the *case* and *result*.

But this is not the only way of inverting a deductive syllogism so as to produce a synthetic inference. Suppose I enter a room and there find a number of bags, containing different kinds of beans. On the table there is a handful of white beans; and, after some searching, I find one of the bags contains white beans only. I at once infer as a probability, or as a fair guess, that this handful was taken out of that bag. This sort of inference is called *making an hypothesis*. It is the inference of a *case* from a *rule* and *result*. We have, then—

DEDUCTION

> *Rule.*—All the beans from this bag are white.
> *Case.*—These beans are from this bag.
> ∴ *Result.*—These beans are white.

INDUCTION

> *Case.*—These beans are from this bag.
> *Result.*—These beans are white.
> ∴ *Rule.*—All the beans from this bag are white.

HYPOTHESIS

> *Rule.*—All the beans from this bag are white.
> *Result.*—These beans are white.
> ∴ *Case.*—These beans are from this bag.

We, accordingly, classify all inference as follows:

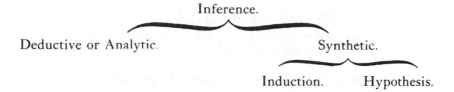

Inference.

Deductive or Analytic.   Synthetic.

Induction.   Hypothesis.

Induction is where we generalize from a number of cases of which something is true, and infer that the same thing is true of a whole class. Or, where we find a certain thing to be true of a certain proportion of cases and infer that it is true of the same proportion of the whole class. Hypothesis is where we find some very curious circumstance, which would be explained by the supposition that it was a case of a certain general rule, and thereupon adopt that supposition. Or, where we find that in certain respects two objects have a strong resemblance, and infer that they resemble one another strongly in other respects.

I once landed at a seaport in a Turkish province;[2] and, as I was walking up to the house which I was to visit, I met a man upon horseback, surrounded by four horsemen holding a canopy over his head. As the governor of the province was the only personage I could think of who would be so greatly honored, I inferred that this was he. This was an hypothesis.

Fossils are found; say, remains like those of fishes, but far in the interior of the country. To explain the phenomenon, we suppose the sea once washed over this land. This is another hypothesis.

Numberless documents and monuments refer to a conqueror called Napoleon Bonaparte. Though we have not seen the man, yet we cannot explain what we have seen, namely, all these documents and monuments, without supposing that he really existed. Hypothesis again.

As a general rule, hypothesis is a weak kind of argument. It often inclines our judgment so slightly toward its conclusion that we cannot say that we believe the latter to be true; we only surmise that it may be so. But there is no difference except one of degree between such an inference and that by which we are led to believe that we remember the occurrences of yesterday from our feeling as if we did so.

II

Besides the way just pointed out of inverting a deductive syllogism to produce an induction or hypothesis, there is another. If from the truth of a certain premise the truth of a certain conclusion would necessarily follow, then from the falsity of the conclusion the falsity of the premise would follow. Thus, take the following syllogism in *Barbara:*

>*Rule.*—All men are mortal.
>*Case.*—Enoch and Elijah were men.
>∴ *Result.*—Enoch and Elijah were mortal.

Now, a person who denies this result may admit the rule, and, in that case, he must deny the case. Thus:

>*Denial of Result.*—Enoch and Elijah were not mortal.
>*Rule.*—All men are mortal.
>∴ *Denial of Case.*—Enoch and Elijah were not men.

This kind of syllogism is called *Baroco,* which is the typical mood of the second figure. On the other hand, the person who denies the result may admit the case, and in that case he must deny the rule. Thus:

>*Denial of the Result.*—Enoch and Elijah were not mortal.
>*Case.*—Enoch and Elijah were men.
>∴ *Denial of the Rule.*—Some men are not mortal.

This kind of syllogism is called *Bocardo,* which is the typical mood of the third figure.

Baroco and *Bocardo* are, of course, deductive syllogisms; but of a very peculiar kind. They are called by logicians indirect moods, because they need some transformation to appear as the application of a rule to a particular case. But if, instead of setting out as we have here done with a necessary deduction in *Barbara,* we take a probable deduction of similar form, the indirect moods which we shall obtain will be—

>Corresponding to *Baroco,* an hypothesis;
>and, Corresponding to *Bocardo,* an induction.

For example, let us begin with this probable deduction in *Barbara:*

>*Rule.*—Most of the beans in this bag are white.
>*Case.*—This handful of beans are from this bag.
>∴ *Result.*—Probably, most of this handful of beans are white.

Now, deny the result, but accept the rule:

>*Denial of Result.*—Few beans of this handful are white.
>*Rule.*—Most beans in this bag are white.
>∴ *Denial of Case.*—Probably, these beans were taken from
>   another bag.

This is an hypothetical inference. Next, deny the result, but accept the case:

> *Denial of Result.*—Few beans of this handful are white.
> *Case.*—These beans came from this bag.
> ∴ *Denial of Rule.*—Probably, few beans in the bag are white.

This is an induction.

The relation thus exhibited between synthetic and deductive reasoning is not without its importance. When we adopt a certain hypothesis, it is not alone because it will explain the observed facts, but also because the contrary hypothesis would probably lead to results contrary to those observed. So, when we make an induction, it is drawn not only because it explains the distribution of characters in the sample, but also because a different rule would probably have led to the sample being other than it is.

But the advantage of this way of considering the subject might easily be overrated. An induction is really the inference of a rule, and to consider it as the denial of a rule is an artificial conception, only admissible because, when statistical or proportional propositions are considered as rules, the denial of a rule is itself a rule. So, an hypothesis is really a subsumption of a case under a class and not the denial of it, except for this, that to deny a subsumption under one class is to admit a subsumption under another.

Bocardo may be considered as an induction, so timid as to lose its amplificative character entirely. Enoch and Elijah are specimens of a certain kind of men. All that kind of men are shown by these instances to be immortal. But instead of boldly concluding that all very pious men, or all men favorites of the Almighty, etc., are immortal, we refrain from specifying the description of men, and rest in the merely explicative inference that *some* men are immortal. So *Baroco* might be considered as a very timid hypothesis. Enoch and Elijah are not mortal. Now, we might boldly suppose them to be gods or something of that sort, but instead of that we limit ourselves to the inference that they are of *some* nature different from that of man.

But, after all, there is an immense difference between the relation of *Baroco* and *Bocardo* to *Barbara* and that of Induction and Hypothesis to Deduction. *Baroco* and *Bocardo* are based upon the fact that if the truth of a conclusion necessarily follows from the truth of a premise, then the falsity of the premise follows from the falsity of the conclusion. This is always true. It is different when the inference is only probable. It by no means follows that, because the truth of a certain premise would render the truth of a conclusion probable, therefore the falsity of the conclusion renders the falsity of the premise probable. At least, this is only true, as we have seen in a former paper, when the word probable is used in one sense in the antecedent and in another in the consequent.

III

A certain anonymous writing is upon a torn piece of paper. It is suspected that the author is a certain person. His desk, to which only he has had access, is searched, and in it is a found a piece of paper, the torn edge of which exactly fits, in all its irregularities, that of the paper in question. It is a fair hypothetic inference that the suspected man was actually the author. The ground of this inference evidently is that two torn pieces of paper are extremely unlikely to fit together by accident. Therefore, of a great number of inferences of this sort, but a very small proportion would be deceptive. The analogy of hypothesis with induction is so strong that some logicians have confounded them. Hypothesis has been called an induction of characters. A number of characters belonging to a certain class are found in a certain object; whence it is inferred that all the characters of that class belong to the object in question. This certainly involves the same principle as induction; yet in a modified form. In the first place, characters are not susceptible of simple enumeration like objects; in the next place, characters run in categories. When we make an hypothesis like that about the piece of paper, we only examine a single line of characters, or perhaps two or three, and we take no specimen at all of others. If the hypothesis were nothing but an induction, all that we should be justified in concluding, in the example above, would be that the two pieces of paper which matched in such irregularities as have been examined would be found to match in other, say slighter, irregularities. The inference from the shape of the paper to its ownership is precisely what distinguishes hypothesis from induction, and makes it a bolder and more perilous step.

The same warnings that have been given against imagining that induction rests upon the uniformity of Nature might be repeated in regard to hypothesis. Here, as there, such a theory not only utterly fails to account for the validity of the inference, but it also gives rise to methods of conducting it which are absolutely vicious. There are, no doubt, certain uniformities in Nature, the knowledge of which will fortify an hypothesis very much. For example, we suppose that iron, titanium, and other metals exist in the sun, because we find in the solar spectrum many lines coincident in position with those which these metals would produce; and this hypothesis is greatly strengthened by our knowledge of the remarkable distinctiveness of the particular line of characters observed. But such a fortification of hypothesis is of a deductive kind, and hypothesis may still be probable when such reënforcement is wanting.

There is no greater nor more frequent mistake in practical logic than to suppose that things which resemble one another strongly in some respects are any the more likely for that to be alike in others. That this is absolutely false, admits of rigid demonstration; but, inasmuch as the reasoning is somewhat severe and complicated (requiring, like all such reasoning, the use of A, B, C, etc., to set it forth), the reader would probably find it distasteful, and I omit it. An example, however, may illustrate the proposition: The comparative mythologists occupy themselves with finding points of resemblance between solar phenomena and the careers of the heroes of all sorts of traditional stories; and upon the basis of such resemblances they infer that these heroes are impersonations of the sun. If there be anything more in their reasonings, it has never been made clear to me. An ingenious logician, to show how futile all that is, wrote a little book, in which he pretended to prove, in the same manner, that Napoleon Bonaparte is only an impersonation of the sun. It was really wonderful to see how many points of resemblance he made out. The truth is, that any two things resemble one another just as strongly as any two others, if recondite resemblances are admitted. But, in order that the process of making an hypothesis should lead to a probable result, the following rules must be followed:

1. The hypothesis should be distinctly put as a question, before making the observations which are to test its truth. In other words, we must try to see what the result of predictions from the hypothesis will be.

2. The respect in regard to which the resemblances are noted must be taken at random. We must not take a particular kind of predictions for which the hypothesis is known to be good.

3. The failures as well as the successes of the predictions must be honestly noted. The whole proceeding must be fair and unbiased.

Some persons fancy that bias and counter-bias are favorable to the extraction of truth—that hot and partisan debate is the way to investigate. This is the theory of our atrocious legal procedure. But Logic puts its heel upon this suggestion. It irrefragably demonstrates that knowledge can only be furthered by the real desire for it, and that the methods of obstinacy, of authority, and every mode of trying to reach a foregone conclusion, are absolutely of no value. These things are proved. The reader is at liberty to think so or not as long as the proof is not set forth, or as long as he refrains from examining it. Just so, he can preserve, if he likes, his freedom of opinion in regard to the propositions of geometry; only, in that case, if he takes a fancy to read Euclid, he will do well to skip whatever he finds with A, B, C, etc., for, if he reads attentively that disagreeable matter, the freedom of his opinion about geometry may unhappily be lost forever.

How many people there are who are incapable of putting to their own consciences this question, "Do I want to know how the fact stands, or not?"

The rules which have thus far been laid down for induction and hypothesis are such as are absolutely essential. There are many other maxims expressing particular contrivances for making synthetic inferences strong, which are extremely valuable and should not be neglected. Such are, for example, Mr. Mill's four methods.³ Nevertheless, in the total neglect of these, inductions and hypotheses may and sometimes do attain the greatest force.

IV

Classifications in all cases perfectly satisfactory hardly exist. Even in regard to the great distinction between explicative and ampliative inferences, examples could be found which seem to lie upon the border between the two classes, and to partake in some respects of the characters of either. The same thing is true of the distinction between induction and hypothesis. In the main, it is broad and decided. By induction, we conclude that facts, similar to observed facts, are true in cases not examined. By hypothesis, we conclude the existence of a fact quite different from anything observed, from which, according to known laws, something observed would necessarily result. The former, is reasoning from particulars to the general law; the latter, from effect to cause. The former classifies, the latter explains. It is only in some special cases that there can be more than a momentary doubt to which category a given inference belongs. One exception is where we observe, not facts similar under similar circumstances, but facts different under different circumstances—the difference of the former having, however, a definite relation to the difference of the latter. Such inferences, which are really inductions, sometimes present nevertheless some indubitable resemblances to hypotheses.

Knowing that water expands by heat, we make a number of observations of the volume of a constant mass of water at different temperatures. The scrutiny of a few of these suggests a form of algebraical formula which will approximately express the relation of the volume to the temperature. It may be, for instance, that v being the relative volume, and t the temperature, the few observations examined indicate a relation of the form—

$$v = 1 + at + bt^2 + ct^3.$$

Upon examining observations at other temperatures taken at random, this idea is confirmed; and we draw the inductive conclusion that all observations within the limits of temperature from which we have drawn our observations could equally be so satisfied. Having once ascertained that such a formula is possible, it is a mere affair of arithmetic to find the values of *a, b,* and *c,* which will make the formula satisfy the observations best. This is what physicists call an *empirical formula,* because it rests upon mere induction, and is not explained by any hypothesis.

Such formulæ, though very useful as means of describing in general terms the results of observations, do not take any high rank among scientific discoveries. The induction which they embody, that expansion by heat (or whatever other phenomenon is referred to) takes place in a perfectly gradual manner without sudden leaps or innumerable fluctuations, although really important, attracts no attention, because it is what we naturally anticipate. But the defects of such expressions are very serious. In the first place, as long as the observations are subject to error, as all observations are, the formula cannot be expected to satisfy the observations exactly. But the discrepancies cannot be due solely to the errors of the observations, but must be partly owing to the error of the formula which has been deduced from erroneous observations. Moreover, we have no right to suppose that the real facts, if they could be had free from error, could be expressed by such a formula at all. They might, perhaps, be expressed by a similar formula with an infinite number of terms; but of what use would that be to us, since it would require an infinite number of coefficients to be written down? When one quantity varies with another, if the corresponding values are exactly known, it is a mere matter of mathematical ingenuity to find some way of expressing their relation in a simple manner. If one quantity is of one kind—say, a specific gravity—and the other of another kind—say, a temperature—we do not desire to find an expression for their relation which is wholly free from numerical constants, since if it were free from them when, say, specific gravity as compared with water, and temperature as expressed by the centigrade thermometer, were in question, numbers would have to be introduced when the scales of measurement were changed. We may, however, and do desire to find formulas expressing the relations of physical phenomena which shall contain no more arbitrary numbers than changes in the scales of measurement might require.

When a formula of this kind is discovered, it is no longer called an empirical formula, but a law of Nature; and is sooner or later made the basis of an hypothesis which is to explain it. These simple formulæ are not usually, if ever, exactly true, but they are none the less important for that; and the great triumph of the hypothesis comes when it explains not only the formula, but also the deviations from the formula. In the current language of the physicists, an hypothesis of this importance is called a theory, while the term hypothesis is restricted to suggestions which have little evidence in their favor. There is some justice in the contempt which clings to the word hypothesis. To think that we can strike out of our own minds a true preconception of how

Nature acts, is a vain fancy. As Lord Bacon well says: "The subtlety of Nature far exceeds the subtlety of sense and intellect: so that these fine meditations, and speculations, and reasonings of men are a sort of insanity, only there is no one at hand to remark it."[4] The successful theories are not pure guesses, but are guided by reasons.

The kinetical theory of gases is a good example of this. This theory is intended to explain certain simple formulæ, the chief of which is called the law of Boyle.[5] It is, that if air or any other gas be placed in a cylinder with a piston, and if its volume be measured under the pressure of the atmosphere, say fifteen pounds on the square inch, and if then another fifteen pounds per square inch be placed on the piston, the gas will be compressed to one-half its bulk, and in similar inverse ratio for other pressures. The hypothesis which has been adopted to account for this law is that the molecules of a gas are small, solid particles at great distances from each other (relatively to their dimensions), and moving with great velocity, without sensible attractions or repulsions, until they happen to approach one another very closely. Admit this, and it follows that when a gas is under pressure what prevents it from collapsing is not the incompressibility of the separate molecules, which are under no pressure at all, since they do not touch, but the pounding of the molecules against the piston. The more the piston falls, and the more the gas is compressed, the nearer together the molecules will be; the greater number there will be at any moment within a given distance of the piston, the shorter the distance which any one will go before its course is changed by the influence of another, the greater number of new courses of each in a given time, and the oftener each, within a given distance of the piston, will strike it. This explains Boyle's law. The law is not exact; but the hypothesis does not lead us to it exactly. For, in the first place, if the molecules are large, they will strike each other oftener when their mean distances are diminished, and will consequently strike the piston oftener, and will produce more pressure upon it. On the other hand, if the molecules have an attraction for one another, they will remain for a sensible time within one another's influence, and consequently they will not strike the wall so often as they otherwise would, and the pressure will be less increased by compression.

When the kinetical theory of gases was first proposed by Daniel Bernoulli, in 1738,[6] it rested only on the law of Boyle, and was therefore pure hypothesis. It was accordingly quite naturally and deservedly neglected. But, at present, the theory presents quite another aspect; for, not to speak of the considerable number of observed facts of different kinds with which it has been brought into relation, it is supported by the mechanical theory of heat. That bringing together bodies which attract one another, or separating bodies which repel one another, when sensible motion is not produced nor destroyed, is always accompanied by the evolution of heat, is little more than an induction. Now, it has been shown by experiment that, when a gas is allowed to expand without doing work, a very small amount of heat disappears. This proves that the particles of the gas attract one another slightly, and but very slightly. It follows that, when a gas is under pressure, what prevents it from collapsing is not any repulsion between the particles, since there is none. Now, there are only two modes of force known to us, force of position or attractions and repulsions, and force of motion. Since, therefore, it is not the force of position which gives a gas its expansive force, it must be the force of motion. In this point of view, the kinetical theory of gases appears as a deduction from the mechanical theory of heat. It is to be observed, however, that it supposes the same law of mechanics (that there are only those two modes of force) which holds in regard to bodies such as we can see and examine, to hold also for what are very different, the molecules of bodies. Such a supposition has but a slender support from induction. Our belief in it is greatly strengthened by its connection with the law of Boyle, and it is, therefore, to be considered as an hypothetical inference. Yet it must be admitted that the kinetical theory of gases would deserve little credence if it had not been connected with the principles of mechanics.

The great difference between induction and hypothesis is, that the former infers the existence of phenomena such as we have observed in cases which are similar, while hypothesis supposes something of a different kind from what we have directly observed, and frequently something which it would be impossible for us to observe directly. Accordingly, when we stretch an induction quite beyond the limits of our observation, the inference partakes of the nature of hypothesis. It would be absurd to say that we have no inductive warrant for a generalization extending a little beyond the limits of experience, and there is no line to be drawn beyond which we cannot push our inference; only it becomes weaker the further it is pushed. Yet, if an induction be pushed very far, we cannot give it much credence unless we find that such an extension explains some fact which we can and do observe. Here, then, we have a kind of mixture of induction and hypothesis supporting one another; and of this kind are most of the theories of physics.

V

That synthetic inferences may be divided into induction and hypothesis in the manner here proposed,* admits of no question. The

---

*This division was first made in a course of lectures by the author before the Lowell Institute, Boston, in 1866, and was printed in the *Proceedings of the American Academy of Arts and Sciences,* for April 9, 1867.[7]

utility and value of the distinction are to be tested by their applications.

Induction is, plainly, a much stronger kind of inference than hypothesis; and this is the first reason for distinguishing between them. Hypotheses are sometimes regarded as provisional resorts, which in the progress of science are to be replaced by inductions. But this is a false view of the subject. Hypothetic reasoning infers very frequently a fact not capable of direct observation. It is an hypothesis that Napoleon Bonaparte once existed. How is that hypothesis ever to be replaced by an induction? It may be said that from the premise that such facts as we have observed are as they would be if Napoleon existed, we are to infer by induction that *all* facts that are hereafter to be observed will be of the same character. There is no doubt that every hypothetic inference may be distorted into the appearance of an induction in this way. But the essence of an induction is that it infers from one set of facts another set of similar facts, whereas hypothesis infers from facts of one kind to facts of another. Now, the facts which serve as grounds for our belief in the historic reality of Napoleon are not by any means necessarily the only kind of facts which are explained by his existence. It may be that, at the time of his career, events were being recorded in some way not now dreamed of, that some ingenious creature on a neighboring planet was photographing the earth, and that these pictures on a sufficiently large scale may some time come into our possession, or that some mirror upon a distant star will, when the light reaches it, reflect the whole story back to earth. Never mind how improbable these suppositions are; everything which happens is infinitely unprobable. I am not saying that *these* things are likely to occur, but that *some* effect of Napoleon's existence which now seems impossible is certain nevertheless to be brought about. The hypothesis asserts that such facts, when they do occur, will be of a nature to confirm, and not to refute, the existence of the man. We have, in the impossibility of inductively inferring hypothetical conclusions, a second reason for distinguishing between the two kinds of inference.

A third merit of the distinction is, that it is associated with an important psychological or rather physiological difference in the mode of apprehending facts. Induction infers a rule. Now, the belief of a rule is a habit. That a habit is a rule active in us, is evident. That every belief is of the nature of a habit, in so far as it is of a general character, has been shown in the earlier papers of this series. Induction, therefore, is the logical formula which expresses the physiological process of formation of a habit. Hypothesis substitutes, for a complicated tangle of predicates attached to one subject, a single conception. Now, there is a peculiar sensation belonging to the act of thinking that each of these predicates inheres in the subject. In hypothetic inference this complicated feeling so produced is replaced by a single feeling of greater intensity, that belonging to the act of thinking the hypothetic conclusion. Now, when our nervous system is excited in a complicated way, there being a relation between the elements of the excitation, the result is a single harmonious disturbance which I call an emotion. Thus, the various sounds made by the instruments of an orchestra strike upon the ear, and the result is a peculiar musical emotion, quite distinct from the sounds themselves. This emotion is essentially the same thing as an hypothetic inference, and every hypothetic inference involves the formation of such an emotion. We may say, therefore, that hypothesis produces the *sensuous* element of thought, and induction the *habitual* element. As for deduction, which adds nothing to the premises, but only out of the various facts represented in the premises selects one and brings the attention down to it, this may be considered as the logical formula for paying attention, which is the *volitional* element of thought, and corresponds to nervous discharge in the sphere of physiology.

Another merit of the distinction between induction and hypothesis is, that it leads to a very natural classification of the sciences and of the minds which prosecute them. What must separate different kinds of scientific men more than anything else are the differences of their *techniques*. We cannot expect men who work with books chiefly to have much in common with men whose lives are passed in laboratories. But, after differences of this kind, the next most important are differences in the modes of reasoning. Of the natural sciences, we have, first, the classificatory sciences, which are purely inductive—systematic botany and zoölogy, mineralogy, and chemistry. Then, we have the sciences of theory, as above explained—astronomy, pure physics, etc. Then, we have sciences of hypothesis—geology, biology, etc.

There are many other advantages of the distinction in question which I shall leave the reader to find out by experience. If he will only take the custom of considering whether a given inference belongs to one or other of the two forms of synthetic inference given on page 188, I can promise him that he will find his advantage in it, in various ways.

13

[from] On the Algebra of Logic (1880)

P 167: American Journal of Mathematics *3 (1880):15–57.
[Also published in W4:163–73 (with two earlier versions of
part of the first chapter, MSS 350 and 354 [pp. 38–46], and
a fragmentary continuation of the whole article, which ends
with "to be continued," in MS 371 [pp. 210–11]) and in CP
3.154–81. (Three further attempts at a continuation are in
W5:107–15.)]* This article holds a place of some importance in
the history of formal logic and mathematics. In what is
published here from the first chapter, Peirce discusses the relationship between thinking and cerebration (or logic and physiology), formulates the theory for his logic of the copula em-
ploying statements of inclusion rather than Boolean
equations, and places some of his important epistemological
conceptions into the context of formal logic. (Item 16 represents the subsequent stage of his development of this part
of the algebra of logic and should be read in conjuction with
item 13.)*

Chapter I.—Syllogistic.

§1. Derivation of Logic.

In order to gain a clear understanding of the origin of the various
signs used in logical algebra and the reasons of the fundamental formulæ, we ought to begin by considering how logic itself arises.

Thinking, as cerebration, is no doubt subject to the general laws of
nervous action.

When a group of nerves are stimulated, the ganglions with which
the group is most intimately connected on the whole are thrown into
an active state, which in turn usually occasions movements of the
body. The stimulation continuing, the irritation spreads from ganglion to ganglion (usually increasing meantime). Soon, too, the parts
first excited begin to show fatigue; and thus for a double reason the

bodily activity is of a changing kind. When the stimulus is withdrawn, the excitement quickly subsides.

It results from these facts that when a nerve is affected, the reflex action, if it is not at first of the sort to remove the irritation, will change its character again and again until the irritation is removed; and then the action will cease.

Now, all vital processes tend to become easier on repetition.[1] Along whatever path a nervous discharge has once taken place, in that path a new discharge is the more likely to take place.

Accordingly, when an irritation of the nerves is repeated, all the various actions which have taken place on previous similar occasions are the more likely to take place now, and those are most likely to take place which have most frequently taken place on those previous occasions. Now, the various actions which did not remove the irritation may have previously sometimes been performed and sometimes not; but the action which removes the irritation must have always been performed, because the action must have every time continued until it was performed. Hence, a strong habit of responding to the given irritation in this particular way must quickly be established.

A habit so acquired may be transmitted by inheritance.

One of the most important of our habits is that one by virtue of which certain classes of stimuli throw us at first, at least, into a purely cerebral activity.

Very often it is not an outward sensation but only a fancy which starts the train of thought. In other words, the irritation instead of being peripheral is visceral. In such a case the activity has for the most part the same character; an inward action removes the inward excitation. A fancied conjuncture leads us to fancy an appropriate line of action. It is found that such events, though no external action takes place, strongly contribute to the formation of habits of really acting in the fancied way when the fancied occasion really arises.

A cerebral habit of the highest kind, which will determine what we do in fancy as well as what we do in action, is called a *belief*. The representation to ourselves that we have a specified habit of this kind is called a *judgment*. A belief-habit in its development begins by being vague, special, and meagre; it becomes more precise, general, and full, without limit. The process of this development, so far as it takes place in the imagination, is called *thought*. A judgment is formed; and under the influence of a belief-habit this gives rise to a new judgment, indicating an addition to belief. Such a process is called an *inference*; the antecedent judgment is called the *premise*; the consequent judgment, the *conclusion*; the habit of thought, which determined the passage from the one to the other (when formulated as a proposition), the *leading principle*.

At the same time that this process of inference, or the spontaneous development of belief, is continually going on within us, fresh peripheral excitations are also continually creating new belief-habits. Thus, belief is partly determined by old beliefs and partly by new experience. Is there any law about the mode of the peripheral excitations? The logician maintains that there is, namely, that they are all adapted to an end, that of carrying belief, in the long run, toward certain predestinate conclusions which are the same for all men. This is the faith of the logician. This is the matter of fact, upon which all maxims of reasoning repose. In virtue of this fact, what is to be believed at last is independent of what has been believed hitherto, and therefore has the character of *reality*. Hence, if a given habit, considered as determining an inference, is of such a sort as to tend toward the final result, it is correct; otherwise not. Thus, inferences become divisible into the valid and the invalid; and thus logic takes its reason of existence.

§2. Syllogism and Dialogism.

The general type of inference is

$$P$$
$$\therefore C,$$

where $\therefore$ is the sign of illation.

The passage from the premise (or set of premises) P to the conclusion C takes place according to a habit or rule active within us. All the inferences which that habit would determine when once the proper premises were admitted, form a class. The habit is logically good provided it would never (or in the case of a probable inference, seldom) lead from a true premise to a false conclusion; otherwise it is logically bad. That is, every possible case of the operation of a good habit would either be one in which the premise was false or one in which the conclusion would be true; whereas, if a habit of inference is bad, there is a possible case in which the premise would be true, while the conclusion was false. When we speak of a *possible* case, we conceive that from the general description of cases we have struck out all those kinds which we know how to describe in general terms but which we know never will occur; those that then remain, embracing all whose non-occurrence we are not certain of, together with all those whose non-occurrence we cannot explain on any general principle, are called possible.

A habit of inference may be formulated in a proposition which shall state that every proposition *c*, related in a given general way to any true proposition *p*, is true. Such a proposition is called the *leading principle* of the class of inferences whose validity it implies. When the inference is first drawn, the leading principle is not present to the mind, but the habit it formulates is active in such a way that, upon contemplating the believed premise, by a sort of perception the conclusion is judged to be true.* Afterwards, when the inference is subjected to logical criticism, we make a new inference, of which one premise is that leading principle of the former inference, according to which propositions related to one another in a certain way are fit to be premise and conclusion of a valid inference, while another premise is a fact of observation, namely, that the given relation does subsist between the premise and conclusion of the inference under criticism; whence it is concluded that the inference was valid.

Logic supposes inferences not only to be drawn, but also to be subjected to criticism; and therefore we not only require the form $P \therefore C$ to express an argument, but also a form, $P_i \prec C_i$, to express the truth of its leading principle. Here P_i denotes any one of the class of premises, and C_i the corresponding conclusion. The symbol $\prec$ is the copula, and signifies primarily that every state of things in which a proposition of the class P_i is true is a state of things in which the corresponding propositions of the class C_i are true. But logic also supposes some inferences to be invalid, and must have a form for denying the leading premise. This we shall write $P_i \overline{\prec} C_i$, *a dash over any symbol signifying in our notation the negative of that symbol.†*

Thus, the form $P_i \prec C_i$ implies
either, 1, that it is impossible that a premise of the class P_i should be true,
or, 2, that every state of things in which P_i is true is a state of things in which the corresponding C_i is true.

The form $P_i \overline{\prec} C_i$ implies
both, 1, that a premise of the class P_i is possible,
and, 2, that among the possible cases of the truth of a P_i there is one in which the corresponding C_i is not true.

This acceptation of the copula differs from that of other systems of syllogistic in a manner which will be explained below in treating of the negative.

In the form of inference $P \therefore C$ the leading principle is not expressed; and the inference might be justified on several separate principles. One of these, however, $P_i \prec C_i$, is the formulation of the habit which, in point of fact, has governed the inferences. This principle contains all that is necessary besides the premise P to justify the conclusion. (It will generally assert more than is necessary.) We may, therefore, construct a new argument which shall have for its premises the two propositions P and $P_i \prec C_i$ taken together, and for its conclu-

---

*Though the leading principle itself is not present to the mind, we are generally conscious of inferring on some general principle.

†This dash was used by Boole [*Laws of Thought*, p. 119], but not over other than class-signs.

sion, C. This argument, no doubt, has, like every other, its leading principle, because the inference is governed by some habit; but yet the substance of the leading principle must already be contained implicitly in the premises, because the proposition $P_i \prec C_i$ contains by hypothesis all that is requisite to justify the inference of C from P. Such a leading principle, which contains no fact not implied or observable in the premises, is termed a *logical* principle, and the argument it governs is termed a *complete*, in contradistinction to an *incomplete*, argument, or *enthymeme*.

The above will be made clear by an example. Let us begin with the enthymeme,

> Enoch was a man,
> ∴ Enoch died.

The leading principle of this is, "All men die." Stating it, we get the complete argument,

> All men die,
> Enoch was a man;
> ∴ Enoch was to die.

The leading principle of this is *nota notae est nota rei ipsius.*[2] Stating this as a premise, we have the argument,

> *Nota notae est nota rei ipsius,*
> Mortality is a mark of humanity, which is a mark of Enoch;
> ∴ Mortality is a mark of Enoch.

But this very same principle of the *nota notae* is again active in the drawing of this last inference, so that the last state of the argument is no more complete than the last but one.

There is another way of rendering an argument complete, namely, instead of adding the leading principle $P_i \prec C_i$ conjunctively to the premise P, to form a new argument, we might add its denial disjunctively to the conclusion; thus,

> P
> ∴ Either C or $P_i \precneq C_i$.

A logical principle is said to be an *empty* or merely formal proposition, because it can add nothing to the premises of the argument it governs, although it is relevant; so that it implies no fact except such as is presupposed in all discourse, as we have seen in §1 that certain facts are implied. We may here distinguish between *logical* and *extralogical* validity; the former being that of a *complete*, the latter that of an *incomplete* argument. The term *logical leading principle* we may take to mean the principle which must be supposed true in order to sustain the logical validity of any argument. Such a principle states that among all the states of things which can be supposed without conflict with logical principles, those in which the premise of the argument would be true would also be cases of the truth of the conclusion. Nothing more than this would be relevant to the *logical leading principle*, which is, therefore, perfectly determinate and not vague, as we have seen an extralogical leading principle to be.

A complete argument, with only one premise, is called an *immediate* inference. *Example:* All crows are black birds; therefore, all crows are birds. If from the premise of such an argument everything redundant is omitted, the state of things expressed in the premise is the same as the state of things expressed in the conclusion, and only the form of expression is changed. Now, the logician does not undertake to enumerate all the ways of expressing facts: he supposes the facts to be already expressed in certain standard or canonical forms. But the equivalence between different ones of his own standard forms is of the highest importance to him, and thus certain immediate inferences play the great part in formal logic. Some of these will not be reciprocal inferences or logical equations, but the most important of them will have that character.

If one fact has such a relation to a different one that, if the former be true, the latter is necessarily or probably true, this relation constitutes a determinate fact; and therefore, since the leading principle of a complete argument involves no matter of fact (beyond those employed in all discourse), it follows that every complete and *material* (in opposition to a merely *formal*) argument must have at least two premises.

From the doctrine of the leading principle it appears that if we have a valid and complete argument from more than one premise, we may suppress all premises but one and still have a valid but incomplete argument. This argument is justified by the suppressed premises; hence, from these premises alone we may infer that the conclusion would follow from the remaining premises. In this way, then, the original argument

$$P \, Q \, R \, S \, T$$
$$\therefore C$$

is broken up into two, namely, 1st,

$$P \, Q \, R \, S$$
$$\therefore T \prec C$$

and, 2nd,

$$T \prec C$$
$$T$$
$$\therefore C.$$

By repeating this process, any argument may be broken up into arguments of two premises each. A complete argument having two premises is called a *syllogism*.*

An argument may also be broken up in a different way by substituting for the second constituent above, the form

$$T \prec C$$
$$\therefore \text{Either C or not T.}$$

In this way, any argument may be resolved into arguments, each of which has one premise and two alternative conclusions. Such an argument, when complete, may be called a *dialogism*.

§3. Forms of Propositions.

In place of the two expressions $A \prec B$ and $B \prec A$ taken together we may write $A = B$;† in place of the two expressions $A \prec B$ and $B \overline{\prec} A$ taken together we may write $A < B$ or $B > A$; and in place of the two expressions $A \overline{\prec} B$ and $B \overline{\prec} A$ taken together we may write $A \not\prec B$.

De Morgan, in the remarkable memoir with which he opened his

---

*The general doctrine of this section is contained in my paper, "On the Classification of Arguments," 1867. [W2:23–48.]

†There is a difference of opinion among logicians as to whether $\prec$ or $=$ is the simpler relation. But in my paper on the "Logic of Relatives,"[3] I have strictly demonstrated that the preference must be given to $\prec$ in this respect. The term *simpler* has an exact meaning in logic; it means that whose logical depth is smaller; that is, if one conception implies another, but not the reverse, then the latter is said to be the simpler. Now to say that $A = B$ implies that $A \prec B$, but not conversely. *Ergo*, etc. It is to no purpose to reply that $A \prec B$ implies $A = (A$ that is $B)$; it would be equally relevant to say that $A \prec B$ implies $A = A$. Consider an analogous case. Logical sequence is a simpler conception than causal sequence, because every causal sequence is a logical sequence but not every logical sequence is a causal sequence; and it is no reply to this to say that a logical sequence between two facts implies a causal sequence between some two facts whether the same or different. The idea that $=$ is a very simple relation is probably due to the fact that the discovery of such a relation teaches us that instead of two objects we have only one, so that it simplifies our conception of the universe. On this account the existence of such a relation is an important fact to learn; in fact, it has the sum of the importances of the two facts of which it is compounded. It frequently happens that it is more convenient to treat the propositions $A \prec B$ and $B \prec A$ together in their form $A = B$; but it also frequently happens that it is more convenient to treat them separately. Even in geometry we can see that to say that two figures A and B are equal is to say that when they are properly put together A will cover B and B will cover A; and it is generally necessary to examine these facts separately. So, in comparing the numbers of two lots of objects, we set them over against one another, each to each, and observe that for every one of the lot A there is one of the lot B, and for every one of the lot B there is one of the lot A.

In logic, our great object is to analyze all the operations of reason and reduce them to their ultimate elements; and to make a calculus of reasoning is a subsidiary object. Accordingly, it is more philosophical to use the copula $\prec$, apart from all considerations of convenience. Besides, this copula is intimately related to our natural logical and metaphysical ideas; and it is one of the chief purposes of logic to show what validity those ideas have. Moreover, it will be seen further on that the more analytical copula does in point of fact give rise to the easiest method of solving problems of logic.

discussion of the syllogism (1846, p. 380), has pointed out that we often carry on reasoning under an implied restriction as to what we shall consider as possible, which restriction, applying to the whole of what is said, need not be expressed.[4] The total of all that we consider possible is called the *universe* of discourse, and may be very limited. One mode of limiting our universe is by considering only what actually occurs, so that everything which does not occur is regarded as impossible.

The forms A $\prec$ B, or A implies B, and A $\overline{\prec}$ B, or A does not imply B, embrace both hypothetical and categorical propositions. Thus, to say that all men are mortal is the same as to say that if any man possesses any character whatever then a mortal possesses that character. To say, 'if A, then B' is obviously the same as to say that from A, B follows, logically or extralogically. By thus identifying the relation expressed by the copula with that of illation, we identify the proposition with the inference, and the term with the proposition. This identification, by means of which all that is found true of term, proposition, or inference is at once known to be true of all three, is a most important engine of reasoning, which we have gained by beginning with a consideration of the genesis of logic.*

Of the two forms A $\prec$ B and A $\overline{\prec}$ B, no doubt the former is the more primitive, in the sense that it is involved in the idea of reasoning, while the latter is only required in the criticism of reasoning. The two kinds of proposition are essentially different, and every attempt to reduce the latter to a special case of the former must fail. Boole attempts to express 'some men are not mortal', in the form 'whatever men have a certain unknown character *v* are not mortal'.[5] But the propositions are not identical, for the latter does not imply that some men have that character *v*; and, accordingly, from Boole's proposition we may legitimately infer that 'whatever mortals have the unknown character *v* are not men'; yet we cannot reason from 'some men are not mortal' to 'some mortals are not men'.† On the other hand, we can rise to a more general form under which A $\prec$ B and A $\overline{\prec}$ B are both included. For this purpose we write A $\overline{\prec}$ B in the form Ă $\prec$ B̄, where Ă is *some*-A and B̄ is *not*-B. This more general form is equivocal in so far as it is left undetermined whether the proposition would be true if the subject were impossible. When the subject is general this is the case, but when the subject is particular (i.e., is subject to the modifica-

---

*In consequence of the identification in question, in S $\prec$ P, I speak of S indifferently as *subject, antecedent,* or *premise,* and of P as *predicate, consequent,* or *conclusion.*

†Equally unsuccessful is Mr. Jevons's attempt to overcome the difficulty by omitting particular propositions, "because we can always substitute for it [*some*] more definite expressions if we like." The same reason might be alleged for neglecting the consideration of *not.* But in fact the form A $\overline{\prec}$ B is required to enable us to simply deny A $\prec$ B.[6]

tion *some*) it is not. The general form supposes merely inclusion of the subject under the predicate. The short curved mark over the letter in the subject shows that some part of the term denoted by that letter is the subject, and that that is asserted to be in possible existence.

The modification of the subject by the curved mark and of the predicate by the straight mark gives the old set of propositional forms, viz.:

A. $a \prec b$ Every *a* is *b*.   Universal affirmative.

E. $a \prec \bar{b}$ No   *a* is *b*.   Universal negative.

I. $\breve{a} \prec b$ Some *a* is *b*.   Particular affirmative.

O. $\breve{a} \prec \bar{b}$ Some *a* is not *b*.   Particular negative.

There is, however, a difference between the senses in which these propositions are here taken and those which are traditional; namely, it is usually understood that affirmative propositions imply the existence of their subjects, while negative ones do not. Accordingly, it is said that there is an immediate inference from A to I and from E to O. But in the sense assumed in this paper, universal propositions do not, while particular propositions do, imply the existence of their subjects. The following figure illustrates the precise sense here assigned to the four forms A, E, I, O.

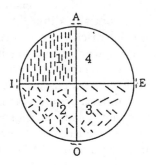

In the quadrant marked 1 there are lines which are all vertical; in the quadrant marked 2 some lines are vertical and some not; in quadrant 3 there are lines none of which are vertical; and in quadrant 4 there are no lines. Now, taking *line* as subject and *vertical* as predicate,

A is true of quadrants 1 and 4 and false of 2 and 3.
E is true of quadrants 3 and 4 and false of 1 and 2.
I is true of quadrants 1 and 2 and false of 3 and 4.
O is true of quadrants 2 and 3 and false of 1 and 4.

Hence, A and O precisely deny each other, and so do E and I. But any other pair of propositions may be either both true or both false or one true while the other is false.

De Morgan ("On the Syllogism," No. I, 1846, p. 381) has enlarged the system of propositional forms by applying the sign of negation which first appears in $A \preceq B$ to the subject and predicate. He thus gets

$A \prec B$.	Every A is B.	A is species of B.
$A \preceq B$.	Some A is not B.	A is exient of B.
$A \prec \bar{B}$.	No A is B.	A is external of B.
$A \preceq \bar{B}$.	Some A is B.	A is partient of B.
$\bar{A} \prec B$.	Everything is either A or B.	A is complement of B.
$\bar{A} \preceq B$.	There is something besides A and B.	A is coinadequate of B.
$\bar{A} \prec \bar{B}$.	A includes all B.	A is genus of B.
$\bar{A} \preceq \bar{B}$.	A does not include all B.	A is deficient of B.

De Morgan's table of the relations of these propositions must be modified to conform to the meanings here attached to $\prec$ and to $\preceq$.

We might confine ourselves to the two propositional forms $S \prec P$ and $S \preceq P$. If we once go beyond this and adopt the form $S \prec \bar{P}$, we must, for the sake of completeness, adopt the whole of De Morgan's system. But this system, as we shall see in the next section, is itself incomplete, and requires to complete it the admission of particularity in the predicate. This has already been attempted by Hamilton, with an incompetence which ought to be extraordinary.[7] I shall allude to this matter further on, but I shall not attempt to say how many forms of propositions there would be in the completed system.*[8]

---

*In this connection see De Morgan, "On the Syllogism, No. V," 1863.

14

Introductory Lecture on the Study of Logic

P 225: Johns Hopkins University Circulars *2:19 (Novem-*
ber 1882):11–12. [Also published in W4:378–82, in CP 7.59–76,
and in HPPLS 940–44.] In this "Outline of the Remarks
made by Prof. C. S. Peirce, at the beginning of his Course,
September, 1882," Peirce reflects on the achievements of Dar-
win (who had died in April) and attributes them mainly to
Darwin's method. In describing the lecture to his eldest
brother, James Mills, in a 4 October 1882 letter, Peirce said:
"I spoke of our time as the age of method and said that the
highest honors could no longer be paid to the mere scientific
specialist but to those who adapted the methods of one science
to the uses of another. That a liberal education so far as it
regards the intellect means logic, *considered as the method of*
methods,—the via ad principia methodorum. That the stu-
dent ought to feel from the beginning to the end of his course,
that in whatever lecture room he is, it is logic *he is studying."*
Peirce is now defining his task as applying the methods of
logic, especially induction and hypothesis, to philosophy and
science. [1]

It might be supposed that logic taught that much was to be accomplished by mere rumination, though every one knows that experiment,
observation, comparison, active scrutiny of facts, is what is wanted,
and that mere *thinking* will accomplish nothing even in mathematics.
Logic had certainly been defined as the "art of thinking," and as the
"science of the normative laws of thought."[2] But those are not true
definitions. *"Dyalectica,"* says the logical text-book of the middle ages,
"est ars artium et scientia scientiarum, ad omnium aliarum scientiarum me-
thodorum principia viam habens,"[3] and although the logic of our day must
naturally be utterly different from that of the Plantagenet epoch, yet
this general conception that it is the *art of devising methods of research,—*
the *method of methods,—*is the true and worthy idea of the science. Logic
will not undertake to inform you what kind of experiments you ought

to make in order best to determine the acceleration of gravity, or the value of the Ohm;[4] but it will tell you how to proceed to form a plan of experimentation.

It is impossible to maintain that the superiority of the science of the moderns over that of the ancients is due to anything but a better *logic*. No one can think that the Greeks were inferior to any modern people whatever in natural aptitude for science. We may grant that their opportunities for research were less; and it may be said that ancient astronomy could make no progress beyond the Ptolemaic system until sufficient time had elapsed to prove the insufficiency of Ptolemy's tables. The ancients could have no dynamics so long as no important dynamical problem had presented itself; they could have no theory of heat without the steam-engine, etc. Of course, these causes had their influence, and of course they were not the main reason of the defects of the ancient civilization. Ten years' astronomical observations with instruments such as the ancients could have constructed would have sufficed to overthrow the old astronomy. The great mechanical discoveries of Galileo were made with no apparatus to speak of. If, in any direction whatever, the ancients had once commenced research by right methods, opportunities for new advances would have been brought along in the train of those that went before. But read the logical treatise of Philodemus;[5] see how he strenuously argues that inductive reasoning is not utterly without value, and you see where the fault lay. When such an elementary point as that needed serious argumentation it is clear that the conception of scientific method was almost entirely wanting.

Modern methods have created modern science; and this century, and especially the last twenty-five years, have done more to create new methods than any former equal period. We live in the very age of methods. Even mathematics and astronomy have put on new faces. Chemistry and physics are on completely new tracks. Linguistic, history, mythology, sociology, biology, are all getting studied in new ways. Jurisprudence and law have begun to feel the impulse, and must in the future be more and more rapidly influenced by it.

This is the age of methods; and the university which is to be the exponent of the living condition of the human mind, must be the university of methods.

Now I grant you that to say that this is the age of the development of new methods of research is so far from saying that it is the age of the theory of methods, that it is almost to say the reverse. Unfortunately practice generally precedes theory, and it is the usual fate of mankind to get things done in some boggling way first, and find out afterward how they could have been done much more easily and perfectly. And it must be confessed that we students of the science of modern methods are as yet but a voice crying in the wilderness, and saying prepare ye the way for this lord of the sciences which is to come.[6]

Yet even now we can do a little more than that. The theory of any act in no wise aids the doing of it, so long as what is to be done is of a narrow description, so that it can be governed by the unconscious part of our organism. For such purposes, rules of thumb or no rules at all are the best. You cannot play billiards by analytical mechanics nor keep shop by political economy. But when new paths have to be struck out, a spinal cord is not enough; a brain is needed, and that brain an organ of mind, and that mind perfected by a liberal education. And a liberal education—so far as its relation to the understanding goes—means *logic*. That is indispensible to it, and no other one thing is.

I do not need to be told that science consists of specialties. I know all that, for I belong to the guild of science, have learned one of its trades and am saturated with its current notions. But in my judgment there are scientific men, all whose training has only served to belittle them, and I do not see that a mere scientific specialist stands intellectually much higher than an artisan. I am quite sure that a young man who spends his time exclusively in the laboratory of physics or chemistry or biology, is in danger of profiting but little more from his work than if he were an apprentice in a machine shop.

The scientific specialists—pendulum swingers and the like—are doing a great and useful work; each one very little, but altogether something vast. But the higher places in science in the coming years are for those who succeed in adapting the methods of one science to the investigation of another. That is what the greatest progress of the passing generation has consisted in. Darwin adapted to biology the methods of Malthus and the economists;[7] Maxwell adapted to the theory of gases the methods of the doctrine of chances, and to electricity the methods of hydrodynamics. Wundt adapts to psychology the methods of physiology; Galton adapts to the same study the methods of the theory of errors; Morgan adapted to history a method from biology; Cournot adapted to political economy the calculus of variations. The philologists[8] have adapted to their science the methods of the decipherers of dispatches. The astronomers have learned the methods of chemistry; radiant heat is investigated with an ear trumpet; the mental temperament is read off on a vernier.[9]

Now although a man needs not the theory of a method in order to apply it as it has been applied already, yet in order to adapt to his own science the method of another with which he is less familiar, and to properly modify it so as to suit it to its new use, an acquaintance with the principles upon which it depends will be of the greatest benefit. For that sort of work a man needs to be more than a mere specialist; he needs such a general training of his mind, and such knowledge as shall show him how to make his powers most effective in a new direction. That knowledge is logic.

In short, if my view is the true one, a young man wants a physical education and an aesthetic education, an education in the ways of the world and a moral education, and with all these logic has nothing in particular to do; but so far as he wants an intellectual education, it is precisely logic that he wants; and whether he be in one lecture-room or another, his ultimate purpose is to improve his logical power and his knowledge of methods. To this great end a young man's attention ought to be directed when he first comes to the university; he ought to keep it steadily in view during the whole period of his studies; and finally, he will do well to review his whole work in the light which an education in logic throws upon it.

I should be the very first to insist that logic can never be learned from logic-books or logic lectures. The material of positive science must form its basis and its vehicle. Only relatively little could be done by the lecturer on method even were he master of the whole circle of the sciences. Nevertheless, I do think that I can impart to you something of real utility, and that the theory of method will shed much light on all your other studies.

The impression is rife that success in logic requires a mathematical head. But this is not true. The habit of looking at questions in a mathematical way is, I must say, of great advantage, and thus a turn for mathematics is of more or less service in any science, physical or moral. But no brilliant talent for mathematics is at all necessary for the study of logic.

The course which I am to give this year begins with some necessary preliminaries upon the theory of cognition.[10] For it is requisite to form a clear idea at the outset of what knowledge consists of, and to consider a little what are the operations of the mind by which it is produced. But I abridge this part of the course as much as possible, partly because it will be treated by other instructors, and partly because I desire to push on to my main subject, the method of science.

I next take up syllogism, the lowest and most rudimentary of all forms of reasoning, but very fundamental because it is rudimentary. I treat this after the general style of De Morgan, with references to the old traditional doctrine. Next comes the logical algebra of Boole, a subject in itself extremely easy, but very useful both from a theoretical point of view and also as giving a method of solving certain rather frequently occurring and puzzling problems. From this subject, I am naturally led to the consideration of relative terms. The logic of relatives, so far as it has been investigated, is clear and easy, and at the same time it furnishes the key to many of the difficulties of logic, and has already served as the instrument of some discoveries in mathematics.[11]

An easy application of this branch of logic is to the doctrine of breadth and depth or the relations between objects and characters. I next introduce the conception of number, and after showing how to treat certain statistical problems, I take up the doctrine of chances. A very simple and elegant mathematical method of treating equations of finite differences puts the student into possession of a powerful instrument for the solution of all problems of probability that do not import difficulties extraneous to the theory of probability itself.

We thus arrive at the study of that kind of probable inference that is really distinctive; that is to say, Induction in its broadest sense—Scientific Reasoning.[12] The general theory of the subject is carefully worked out with the aid of real examples in great variety, and rules for the performance of the operation are given. These rules have not been picked up by hazard, nor are they merely such as experience recommends; they are deduced methodically from the general theory.

Finally, it is desirable to illustrate a long concatenation of scientific inferences. For this purpose we take up Kepler's great work, *De Motibus Stellae Martis,* the greatest piece of inductive reasoning ever produced.[13] Owing to the admirable and exceptional manner in which the work is written, it is possible to follow Kepler's whole course of investigation from beginning to end, and to show the application of all the maxims of induction already laid down.

In order to illustrate the method of reasoning about a subject of a more metaphysical kind, I shall then take up the scientific theories of the constitution of matter.

Last of all, I shall give a few lectures to show what are the lessons that a study of scientific procedure teaches with reference to philosophical questions, such as the conception of causation and the like.

15

Design and Chance

MS 875. [First published, as MS 494, in W4:544–54.] Written in December 1883/January 1884, this fragmentary manuscript was used for a lecture entitled "Design and Chance," given before the Johns Hopkins University Metaphysical Club on 17 January 1884. Despite its brevity and incompleteness, it represents a major advance in Peirce's progress toward his guess at the riddle of the universe, and it marks the beginning of his evolutionary explanation of the laws of nature (and his architectonic metaphysics detailed in items 21–25). By the hypotheses of absolute chance, habit-taking, and universal evolution, Peirce extends the postulate that "everything is explicable . . . in a general way."

The epoch of intellectual history at which the world is now arrived finds thought still strongly under the influence imparted to it in 1859 by Darwin's great work.[1] But a new element has crept in, not introduced by any great book, yet already showing itself in different directions, and destined as it seems to me to play a considerable part in the coming years,—I mean the tendency to question the exact truth of axioms. It appears to me that the development of this general idea in the various realms of mathematics, positive science, and philosophy is, in the immediate future, likely to teach us more than any other general conception. It has already done important work in geometry, in which our own Professor Story has an honorable share.[2] In physics we see its influence in the investigations of Crookes and Zöllner[3] into the phenomena of spiritualism & supernaturalism, in regard to which the attitude of scientific men must now be essentially different from what it was 25 years ago. For my part, I cannot withhold my approval of the proceedings of the society for the prosecution of psychical research, which is engaged in the careful examination of all kinds of phenomena which suggest the possibility of the relation between body and soul being different from what ordinary experience leads us to conceive it.[4] I do not mean to say, and that society does not say, that any facts have yet been established sufficient to call for a modification of existing conceptions; but I do say that enough evidence has been collected to make a careful & serious examination of the matter no waste of time; and that the bias that formerly existed and was rightly entertained in favor of the dicta of common sense upon this subject, is sensibly weakened and rightly weakened by its having been proved that the axioms of geometry are mere empirical laws whose perfect exactitude we have no reason whatever to feel confident of.

The scientific world will not be disturbed because all the weak-minded persons whose mental equilibrium was shaken by spiritualism during the period when it was in fashion will now turn round and say, we investigated these things long ago and always told you you were wrong not to investigate them,—and now we are glad you see your error. The scientific world was entirely right before, when it declined to waste time in absurd inquiries; and it is quite consistent in saying,—as I think it is about to say,—that the pretended facts seem now to deserve examination. More than that, as a general maxim in scientific method, I maintain that at one stage of inquiry it is quite right to insist strongly on the exactitude of established laws, to question which would only lead to confusion, while at a later stage it is proper to question the exactitude of those same laws when we are in possession of a guiding idea which shows us in what manner they may possibly be corrected.

I may illustrate this point by something which comes within the experience of every man. Every man at some time *mislays* something; I for my part, I am ashamed to confess, am rather apt to do so. I entirely forget what I did with the object and am obliged to hunt it up. Now at the beginning of my hunt, I am guided by the knowledge that I have of my own habits; I look for the object where the ordinary rule of my action would have led me to place it, and I rightly decline to spend my time in looking where I almost know I should never have left it. But at a later stage of my search when the likely places are exhausted I begin to look in the unlikely ones, and in doing so I am equally in the right.

In a somewhat similar way, when we first begin to question an axiom, we do not say that it is likely to be inexact;—far from it. We only say that the question whether it is exact or not has come to have a claim to consideration greater than it had had in a former state of science.

What I propose to do tonight is, following the lead of those mathematicians who question whether the sum of the three angles of a triangle is exactly equal to two right angles, to call in question the perfect accuracy of the fundamental axiom of logic.

This axiom is that *real things exist* or in other words, what comes to the same thing, that every intelligible question whatever is susceptible in its own nature of receiving a definitive and satisfactory answer, if it be sufficiently investigated by observation and reasoning. This is the way I should put it; different logicians would state the axiom differently. Mill, for instance, throws it into the form: *Nature is uniform.*[5] I am not now concerned with inquiring how it ought to be stated. It is the axiom itself whatever be the proper form of it which I wish to call into doubt.

Let me be quite understood. As far as all ordinary and practical questions go I insist upon this axiom as much as ever,—as much as anybody can do. I should think that any man who proposed to *go* on any other principle as a maxim of reasoning would be as *insane* as Gauss, Lobachewsky, Riemann or Helmholtz would hold that geodesist to be, who should think that he could detect any departure from the accepted laws of geometry, in any triangle measured on this earth. It is worth while to notice how much it means to question the exactitude of an axiom. There are 25 stars whose parallaxes have been determined by unexceptionable methods. According to ordinary geometry, this parallax should slightly exceed *zero.* According to the non-Euclidean geometry, it might be either more or less than zero, and the value the nearest possible to zero should be proportional to the area of the triangle. Now of the 25 stars, there is but one for which the parallax comes out negative. It is α Cygni of which there is but one determination and the probable error is more than half the value of the negative parallax. There are however several whose parallax is less than 0."1, among them Groombridge 1830, one of the best determined of all. We may therefore conclude that for a star so far distant that the area of the triangle is over a thousand millions of millions of millions of square miles the error of the ordinary Geometry is a quantity less than $\frac{1}{500}$ of the smallest speck that can be seen on the broad horizon, and the extinction of the human race is to be expected sooner than the applicability of the non-Euclidean geometry to any geodesic triangle. It is a doubt comparable to this which I propose in regard to the axiom of logic.

In order to explain what I mean, let us take one of the most familiar, although not one of the most scientifically accurate statements of the axiom viz.: that *every event has a cause.* I question whether this is exactly true. Bodies obey sensibly the laws of mechanics; but may it not be that if our means of measurement were inconceivably nicer, or if we were to wait inconceivable ages for an exception, exceptions irreducible in their own nature to any law would be found? In short, may it not be that *chance,* in the Aristotelian sense, mere absence of cause, has to be admitted as having some slight place in the universe.

Is this a mere idle doubt? Are there any considerations which lead to such a supposition and can any use be made of it if it be granted?

In the first place for the motive of the doubt. If we are to admit that every event has a cause, we are bound by every maxim of consistency to grant that every fact has an explanation, a reason. When we detect a motion among bodies, the demand for a cause is held to be just. Suppose then we find that cause to be that the bodies repel one another inversely as the fifth power of the distance, according to Maxwell's theory about molecules. Now that force is itself not an event; but are we, merely because it is not an event, but is a different kind of fact, not entitled to ask *why* molecules should repel one another inversely as the fifth power of the distance, with the confidence that some reason for it there must be? Gravitation seems less strange in its law, which is that of an emanation. In the case of heat we have energy radiated from the sun; but the energy of gravity does not follow the law of radiation. The singular analogy, therefore, between the acceleration of gravitation and the energy of heat demands an explanation. There has been an attempt to explain gravitation by the impact of particles, but the law of impact is as unreasonable as that of gravity or more so.

Among the things that demand explanation, then, are the laws of physics; and not this law or that law only but every single law. Why are the three laws of mechanics as they are and not otherwise? What is the cause of the restriction of extended bodies to three dimensions?

And then the general fact that there are laws, how is that to be explained?

The general idea of evolution governs science more and more; and every system of philosophy since Kant, however idealistic or however materialistic has strongly felt its influence. Evolution is the postulate of logic, itself; for what is an *explanation* but the adoption of a simpler supposition to account for a complex state of things.

Every theory of evolution that I have seen is more or less special. It is true that in order to be scientifically grounded a theory must be special; but nevertheless evolutionist science and evolutionist philosophy are more closely connected in logic than scientists //commonly suppose/are apt to think// them to be. Upon this subject, I refer to the remarks of Clifford's concerning very general conclusions *à propos* of Spontaneous Generation.[6] A most important premise, playing a great part in the establishment of the Nebular Hypothesis or the Theory of Natural Selection, is that things must on the whole have proceeded from the Homogeneous to the Heterogeneous.

Now the theories of evolution that have hitherto been set forth, at least to the very limited extent, I am sorry to confess it, with which I am familiar with them, while they do go to make it probable that organisms and worlds have taken their origin from a state of things indefinitely homogeneous, all suppose essentially the same basis of physical law to have been operative in every age of the universe.

But I maintain that the postulate that things shall be explicable extends itself to *laws* as well as to states of things. We want a theory of the evolution of physical law. We ought to suppose that as we go back into the indefinite past not merely special laws but *law* itself is found to be less and less determinate. And how can that be if causation was always as rigidly necessary as it is now?

But let me state the point in all its generality. That very postulate of logic whose rigid accuracy I call in question, itself demands that every determinate fact shall have an explanation, and there is no reason in making any exception. Now among the determinate facts which ought thus to be explained is the very fact supposed in this postulate. This must also be explained, must be among the things which have been somehow brought about. How then can it be absolutely, rigidly & immoveably true?

So much for the motive of the doubt. Now for the question to what useful result will this hypothesis lead? It is not my purpose to offer any determinate explanation of a single one of the laws of nature. All that I can do is to suggest that they may perhaps be explicable by means of hypotheses having a certain general [. . .]

It has always seemed to me singular that when we put the question to an evolutionist, Spencerian, Darwinian, or whatever school he may belong to, what are the agencies which have brought about evolution, he mentions various determinate facts and laws, but among the agencies at work he never once mentions *Chance*. Yet it appears to me that chance is the one essential agency upon which the whole process depends. About the nature of the ordinary phenomena of chance there can be no dispute whatever. A certain antecedent, for example that I throw a die from a box, determines the general character of a consequent, namely that a number is turned up, but does not specifically determine the character of the consequent, that is what number that is to be; but that is determined by other causes which cannot be taken into account. I suppose that on excessively rare sporadic occasions a law of nature is violated in some infinitesimal degree; that may be called *absolute chance*; but ordinary chance is merely relative to the causes that are taken into account.

The laws of the two kinds of chance are in the main the same. Speaking first of ordinary and relative chance, a man with an indefinite number of silver dollars who sits down to a perfectly fair game and bets one dollar on every throw of the dice will go on losing and winning in about equal measure. Speaking of absolute chance, the same thing will happen, for if not there would *ipso facto* be a definite tendency toward winning or losing. The only difference between the two cases is this, that the hypothesis of absolute chance is part and parcel of the hypothesis that everything is explicable, not absolutely, rigidly without the smallest inexactitude or sporadic exception, for that is a self-contradictory supposition but yet explicable in a general way. Explicability has no determinate & absolute limit. Everything being explicable, everything has been brought about; and consequently everything is subject to change and subject to chance. Now everything that can happen by chance, sometime or other will happen by chance. Chance will sometime bring about a change in every condition; or, at least, this is as near a correct statement of the matter as can readily be drawn up, for quite correct it certainly is not.

Now I propose to prove that the operation of chance will always present this phenomenon when the objects operated upon are very manifold.

A million players sit down to play a fair game. Each bets one dollar each time which he has an even chance of winning or losing. Let each player be provided at the outset with a pile of a million silver dollars. Now it is a curious & apparently paradoxical result that although everything is supposed to happen by pure chance yet we know very closely how those million players will stand at the end of a million bets. About 10 will have lost $2000 or more, no one over $3000; and half of them after playing day and night for nearly a fortnight at the rate of one bet a second will stand within $300 of where they started.

But now we will suppose that the dice used by the players become worn down in the course of time. Chance changes everything & chance will change that. And we will suppose that they are worn down in such a way that every time a man wins, he has a slightly better chance of winning on subsequent trials. This will make little difference in the first million bets, but its ultimate effect would be to separate the players into two classes those who had gained and those who had lost with few or none who had neither gained nor lost and these classes would separate themselves more and more, faster and faster.

If on the other hand the wearing down of the dice were to have the opposite effect and were to tend to make him lose who had heretofore gained and *vice versa,* the tendency would be to prevent the separation of rich and poor. But chance will act in various ways. At one time it will have one effect at another time another.

If these effects were to be alternated after billions of trials, the effect would be to make numbers of distinct classes of players.

It would be easy if I had time to state the solutions to a number of similar problems in probabilities.

Suffice it to say that as everything is subject to change everything will change after a time by chance, and among these changeable circumstances will be the effects of changes on the probability of further change. And from this it follows that chance must act to move things in the long run from a state of homogeneity to a state of heterogeneity.

These are unlikely states of things. It is unlikely that a player should go on winning money billions of times and never be poorer than he began. But this is the effect of chance. Nor can you prevent it by killing the player whom you see taking such a course. You deprive chance of one means but it supplies another in the person of another player and the ultimate result is unaffected.

The operation of chance, therefore, does show a definite tendency to bring about unlikely events by varying means under varying circumstances.

I have no time to give more than a slight inkling of the consequences upon science and philosophy of attention to this principle.

You have all heard of the dissipation of energy. It is found that in all transformations of energy a part is converted into heat and heat is always tending to equalize its temperature. The consequence is that the energy of the universe is tending by virtue of its necessary laws toward a death of the universe in which there shall be no force but heat and the temperature everywhere the same. This is a truly astounding result, and the most materialistic the most anti-teleological conceivable.

We may say that we know enough of the forces at work in the universe to know that there is none that can counteract this tendency away from every definite end but death.

But although no force can counteract this tendency, chance may and will have the opposite influence. Force is in the long run dissipative; chance is in the long run concentrative. The dissipation of energy by the regular laws of nature is by those very laws accompanied by circumstances more and more favorable to its reconcentration by chance. There must therefore be a point at which the two tendencies are balanced and that is no doubt the actual condition of the whole universe at the present time.

Certain laws of nature, the laws of Boyle and Charles,[7] the second law of thermodynamics, and some others are known to be results of chance,—statistical facts so to say. Molecules are so inconceivably numerous, their encounters so inconceivably frequent, that chance with them is omnipotent. I cannot help believing that more of the molecular laws—the principles of chemistry for example—will be found to involve the same element, especially as almost all these laws present the peculiarity of not being rigidly exact.

Now when we take into account that feature of chance which I have been bringing to your notice we find that this agent, although it can only work upon the basis of some law or uniformity, or more or less definite ratio towards a uniformity, has the property of being able to produce uniformities far more strict than those from which it works.

It is therefore possible to suppose that not only the laws of chemistry but the other known laws of matter are statistical results. Thomson supposes matter to consist of eddies in fluid. If a fluid is composed again of molecules its laws will be mainly due to chance. Now I will suppose that all known laws are due to chance and repose upon others far less rigid themselves due to chance and so on in an infinite regress, the further we go back the more indefinite being the nature of the laws, and in this way we see the possibility of an indefinite approximation toward a complete explanation of nature.

Chance is indeterminacy, is freedom. But the action of freedom issues in the strictest rule of law.

[Design and Chance (A)]

Epicurus makes the Gods consist of atoms but their superiority is due to the finer material of which they are composed. Thus, divineness comes from a special cause & does not originate by chance from elements not containing it.

Darwin's view is nearer to mine. Indeed, my opinion is only Darwinism analyzed, generalized, and brought into the realm of Ontology. But Darwin holds the development of Animals and Plants to be due to certain special characters, Reproduction, Spontaneous Variation, Heredity, etc.

Herbert Spencer and many other evolutionists hold that the operation of chance is an important factor in the development of self-consciousness. But they all admit other primordial elements, the conservation of energy and the like, to be necessary factors. Whereas my principle is that [. . .][8] holds a place in Nature independent of every accident of matter.

Before I can prove my proposition I must first show what it means. I must analyze the conception of *Design* or *Intelligence* and find what it consists in.

In the first place, then, to eliminate the element of *feeling* as being either no essential element of intelligence or at least only a subsidiary one. The internal sense, reflection, which makes us aware of what we think, is, in truth, the main thing which distinguishes us from the brutes. It is by this means that we control our thoughts, and conquer impulses which we do not approve. But because it happens to be thus valuable to us, because it happens to be the instrument by which we make ourselves rational, it does not follow that it is essential to rationality. What is essential is that all our cognitions should be gathered into a unity and that our actions should proceed from the entirety of our knowledge. Because our thought is only imperfectly brought to unity, it requires effort to collect it, and it requires a watchful eye to be directed to the imperfections of this unity. But were we so happily constituted that we should always without reflection completely assimilate everything we learned, so as to take due account of it in every act, we might well be spared the trouble of reflecting; and we should be only the more rational if we could thus behave with intelligence by the first intention of the mind, without reflection,—and knowing no more of what was going on in our minds than a healthy man does of what is going on in his stomach.

I have several times shown to my classes how some of the main laws of cerebration and particularly the formation of habits could be accounted for by the principles of probability, and I have shown by experiment how a certain regularity of arrangement can be impressed upon a pack of cards by imitating the action of habit.

The main element of habit is the tendency to repeat any action which has been performed before. It is a phenomenon at least coëxtensive with life, and it may cover a still wider real realm. Imagine a large number of systems in some of which there is a decided tendency toward doing again what has once been done, in others a tendency against doing what has once been done, in others elements having one tendency and elements having the other. Let us consider the effects of chance upon these different systems. To fix our ideas suppose players playing with dice, some of their dice are worn down in such a way that the act of losing tends to make them lose again, others in such a way that the act of losing tends to make them win. The latter will win or lose much more slowly, yet after a sufficient length of time they will be in danger of being ruined and if the game is quite even, they will eventually be ruined and destroyed. Those whose dice are so worn as to reproduce the same effects, will be divided into two parts, one of which will quickly be destroyed, the other made stronger and stronger. For every kind of an organism, system, form, or compound, there is an absolute limit to a weakening process. It ends in destruction; there is no limit to strength. The result is that chance in its action tends to destroy the weak & increase the average strength of the objects remaining. Systems or compounds which have bad habits are quickly destroyed, those which have no habits follow the same course; only those which have good habits tend to survive.

May not the laws of physics be habits gradually acquired by systems. Why, for instance, do the heavenly bodies tend to attract one another? Because in the long run bodies that repel or do not attract will get thrown out of the region of space leaving only the mutually attracting bodies. Why do they attract inversely as the square of the distance? This may be only their average law of attraction; we see how a comet throws away its repulsive material as it approaches the sun. But in the long run, matter that attracts inversely to a higher power of the distance tends perhaps to aggregate itself together, so that the masses of planets which have long been separate tend to attract in this manner.

16

[from] On the Algebra of Logic: A Contribution to the Philosophy of Notation

P 296: American Journal of Mathematics *7 (1885):180–202. [Also published in W5:162–90 (with several related manuscripts, MSS 506–508 and 538–539 [pp. 107–16 and 191–220]) and in CP 3.359–403.] This paper, which Peirce first presented (at least in part) at the 14–17 October 1884 meeting of the National Academy of Sciences in Newport, RI, consists of four parts, and it is recognized as a substantial contribution to modern logic and to the philosophy of logic and the theory of notation. In the first part published here, Peirce considers the different kinds of signs required for a fully adequate logic notation, and he concludes that it is necessary to have* tokens *(conventional or general signs, usually called* symbols*),* indexes *(demonstrative signs), and* icons *(signs of resemblance). This is the first published appearance of the icon-index-symbol trichotomy and Peirce's first application of his theory of signs to his algebraic logic.*

I.—THREE KINDS OF SIGNS.

Any character or proposition either concerns one subject, two subjects, or a plurality of subjects. For example, one particle has mass, two particles attract one another, a particle revolves about the line joining two others. A fact concerning two subjects is a dual character or relation; but a relation which is a mere combination of two independent facts concerning the two subjects may be called *degenerate*, just as two lines are called a degenerate conic. In like manner a plural character or conjoint relation is to be called degenerate if it is a mere compound of dual characters.

A sign is in a conjoint relation to the thing denoted and to the mind. If this triple relation is not of a degenerate species, the sign is related to its object only in consequence of a mental association, and depends upon a habit. Such signs are always abstract and general, because habits are general rules to which the organism has become subjected. They are, for the most part, conventional or arbitrary. They include all general words, the main body of speech, and any mode of conveying a judgment. For the sake of brevity I will call them *tokens*. [1]

But if the triple relation between the sign, its object, and the mind, is degenerate, then of the three pairs

sign	object
sign	mind
object	mind

two at least are in dual relations which constitute the triple relation. One of the connected pairs must consist of the sign and its object, for if the sign were not related to its object except by the mind thinking of them separately, it would not fulfil the function of a sign at all. Supposing, then, the relation of the sign to its object does not lie in a mental association, there must be a direct dual relation of the sign to its object independent of the mind using the sign. In the second of the three cases just spoken of, this dual relation is not degenerate, and the sign signifies its object solely by virtue of being really connected with it. Of this nature are all natural signs and physical symptoms. I call such a sign an *index*, a pointing finger being the type of the class.

The index asserts nothing; it only says "There!" It takes hold of our eyes, as it were, and forcibly directs them to a particular object, and there it stops. Demonstrative and relative pronouns are nearly pure indices, because they denote things without describing them; so are the letters on a geometrical diagram, and the subscript numbers which in algebra distinguish one value from another without saying what those values are.

The third case is where the dual relation between the sign and its object is degenerate and consists in a mere resemblance between them. I call a sign which stands for something merely because it resembles it, an *icon*. Icons are so completely substituted for their objects as hardly to be distinguished from them. Such are the diagrams of geometry. A diagram, indeed, so far as it has a general signification, is not a pure icon; but in the middle part of our reasonings we forget that abstractness in great measure, and the diagram is for us the very thing. So in contemplating a painting, there is a moment when we lose the consciousness that it is not the thing, the distinction of the real and the copy disappears, and it is for the moment a pure dream,—not any particular existence, and yet not general. At that moment we are contemplating an *icon*.

I have taken pains to make my distinction* of icons, indices, and

---

*See *Proceedings of the American Academy of Arts and Sciences*, Vol. VII, p. 294, May 14, 1867. [Item 1 above, p. 7.]

tokens clear, in order to enunciate this proposition: in a perfect system of logical notation signs of these several kinds must all be employed. Without tokens there would be no generality in the statements, for they are the only general signs; and generality is essential to reasoning. Take, for example, the circles by which Euler represents the relations of terms. They well fulfil the function of icons, but their want of generality and their incompetence to express propositions must have been felt by everybody who has used them. Mr. Venn has, therefore, been led to add shading to them; and this shading is a conventional sign of the nature of a token.[2] In algebra, the letters, both quantitative and functional, are of this nature. But tokens alone do not state what is the subject of discourse; and this can, in fact, not be described in general terms; it can only be indicated. The actual world cannot be distinguished from a world of imagination by any description. Hence the need of pronouns and indices, and the more complicated the subject the greater the need of them. The introduction of indices into the algebra of logic is the greatest merit of Mr. Mitchell's system.[*] He writes F_1 to mean that the proposition F is true of every object in the universe, and F_u to mean that the same is true of some object. This distinction can only be made in some such way as this. Indices are also required to show in what manner other signs are connected together. With these two kinds of signs alone any proposition can be expressed; but it cannot be reasoned upon, for reasoning consists in the observation that where certain relations subsist certain others are found, and it accordingly requires the exhibition of the relations reasoned with in an icon. It has long been a puzzle how it could be that, on the one hand, mathematics is purely deductive in its nature, and draws its conclusions apodictically, while on the other hand, it presents as rich and apparently unending a series of surprising discoveries as any observational science. Various have been the attempts to solve the paradox by breaking down one or other of these assertions, but without success. The truth, however, appears to be that all deductive reasoning, even simple syllogism, involves an element of observation; namely, deduction consists in constructing an icon or diagram the relations of whose parts shall present a complete analogy with those of the parts of the object of reasoning, of experimenting upon this image in the imagination, and of observing the result so as to discover unnoticed and hidden relations among the parts. For instance, take the syllogistic formula,

$$\text{All } M \text{ is } P$$
$$S \text{ is } M$$
$$\therefore \ S \text{ is } P.$$

Studies in Logic. By Members of the Johns Hopkins University. Boston: Little, Brown, & Co., 1883. ["On a New Algebra of Logic," pp. 72–106.]

This is really a diagram of the relations of *S*, *M*, and *P*. The fact that the middle term occurs in the two premises is actually exhibited, and this must be done or the notation will be of no value. As for algebra, the very idea of the art is that it presents formulae which can be manipulated, and that by observing the effects of such manipulation we find properties not to be otherwise discerned. In such manipulation, we are guided by previous discoveries which are embodied in general formulae. These are patterns which we have the right to imitate in our procedure, and are the *icons par excellence* of algebra. The letters of applied algebra are usually tokens, but the *x*, *y*, *z*, etc. of a general formula, such as

$$(x + y)z = xz + yz,$$

are blanks to be filled up with tokens, they are indices of tokens. Such a formula might, it is true, be replaced by an abstractly stated rule (say that multiplication is distributive); but no application could be made of such an abstract statement without translating it into a sensible image.

In this paper, I purpose to develope an algebra adequate to the treatment of all problems of deductive logic, showing as I proceed what kinds of signs have necessarily to be employed at each stage of the development. I shall thus attain three objects. The first is the extension of the power of logical algebra over the whole of its proper realm. The second is the illustration of principles which underlie all algebraic notation. The third is the enumeration of the essentially different kinds of necessary inference; for when the notation which suffices for exhibiting one inference is found inadequate for explaining another, it is clear that the latter involves an inferential element not present to the former. Accordingly, the procedure contemplated should result in a list of categories of reasoning, the interest of which is not dependent upon the algebraic way of considering the subject. I shall not be able to perfect the algebra sufficiently to give facile methods of reaching logical conclusions: I can only give a method by which any legitimate conclusion may be reached and any fallacious one avoided. But I cannot doubt that others, if they will take up the subject, will succeed in giving the notation a form in which it will be highly useful in mathematical work. I even hope that what I have done may prove a first step toward the resolution of one of the main problems of logic, that of producing a method for the discovery of methods in mathematics.

17

An American Plato: Review of *Royce's* Religious Aspect of Philosophy

MS 1369. [Published, as MS 541, in W5:221–34 and in CP 8.39–54 (without the opening paragraph).] Written for the Popular Science Monthly *in the summer of 1885 (but rejected by the editor, E. L. Youmans), this lengthy review is, according to Peirce's 28 October 1885 letter to William James, "something really very good." After praising Royce for his style of reasoning, which is like Plato's, Peirce criticizes his idealism as being too much like Hegel's, whose "capital error . . . which permeates his whole system . . . is that he almost altogether ignores the Outward Clash." Peirce repeats the thesis of item 16, that three kinds of signs are indispensable in all reasoning, and emphasizes that indexes are necessary to refer to individuals: "One such index must enter into every proposition, its function being to designate the subject of discourse." (According to Max Fisch, items 16 and 17 mark an important stage in Peirce's passage from a one-category to a two-category realism.)*

When I meet with an opinion held by sane and instructed men, which is so radically different from my own that it seems strange and incomprehensible to me how men can believe such a thing, I for my part (and I suppose others have the same curiosity) am always tempted to examine the grounds of that opinion with a good deal of care, and am not satisfied until I have either become a convert to it or at least can fully understand and feel how it is that others hold to it. Such an opinion the scientific man finds in Hegelianism; not so much in its conclusions, which relate for the most part to matters upon which science does not touch, as in the extraordinary modes of reasoning by which it professes to reach those conclusions. But, as every one knows, the system of Hegel is very difficult to understand. A real mastership of it is what neither Hegel himself nor any of his followers or critics has possessed. It contains many distinct elements; and the study of logic has not yet been carried far enough to estimate precisely the value of all of them.

Dr. Royce has produced a work which will form a good introduction to Hegel. His language and his thought are equally lucid and within the capacity of ordinary minds; his style is animated and readable, and in passages rises without effort to true philosophical eloquence. His method is a dialectic one; that is to say, it proceeds by the criticism of opinions, first, destructively to absolute scepticism, and then finds hidden in that scepticism itself the highest truth. It differs, however, very decidedly from the dialectic of Hegel; and in its simplicity and general tone reminds us rather of the reasoning of Plato.

But before we examine the method, let us glance at the philosophical upshot of the book. This is, that the reality of whatever really exists consists in the real thing being thought by God.[1] Ordinary people think that things exist by the *will* of God; and if thought be taken in so wide a sense as to include volition, they have no difficulty in admitting the proposition which Dr. Royce has borrowed from Hegel and Schelling.[2] But ordinary people say that not merely the real but all that can possibly enter into the mind of man must be within the thought of God in some sense; so that it must be some particular kind of divine thought which constitutes reality; and that particular kind of thought must be distinguished by a volitional element. In short, ordinary people make, at once, the very same criticism that the profoundest students of philosophy have made, namely, that the Hegelian school overlooks the importance of the will as an element of thought.

A certain writer has suggested that reality, the fact that there is such a thing as a true answer to a question, consists in this: that human inquiries,—human reasoning and observation,—tend toward the settlement of disputes and ultimate agreement in definite conclusions which are independent of the particular stand-points from which the different inquirers may have set out; so that the real is that which any man would believe in, and be ready to act upon, if his investigations were to be pushed sufficiently far.[3] Upon the luckless putter-forth of this opinion Dr. Royce is extremely severe. He will not even name him (perhaps to spare the family), but refers to him by various satirical nick-names, especially as *"Thrasymachus,"*—a foolish character introduced into the *Republic* and another dialogue of Plato for the purpose of showing how vastly such an ignorant pretender to philosophy is inferior to Socrates (that is, to Plato himself) in every quality of mind and heart, and especially in good manners.[4] But I must with shame confess that if I understand what the opinion of this poor, Royceforsaken Thrasymachus is, I coincide with it exactly. I ask any man, Suppose you could be miraculously assured that a certain answer to any question that interests you would be the one in which, were your life and mental vigor to be indefinitely prolonged, you must eventually rest, would you not cease all inquiries at once, and be content with that answer now, as being the very thing you had been striving after? This question Dr. Royce answers explicitly in the negative. "No barely possible judge," he says, "who *would* see the error, *if* he were there, will do for us."[5] Yet if I were to represent Dr. Royce as preferring to believe for a little while that which a certain Being—no matter who— imagines, rather than to come at once to the belief to which investiga- tion is destined at last to carry him, I should probably be doing him injustice; because I suppose he would say that the thing which God imagines, and the opinion to which investigation would ultimately lead him, in point of fact coincide. If, however, these two things coincide, I fail to understand why he should be so cruel to the childish Thrasymachus; since after all there is no real difference between them, but only a formal one,—each maintaining as a theorem that which the other adopts as a definition. As was just remarked, the Hegelian school do not sufficiently take into account the volitional element of cogni- tion. Dr. Royce admits in words that belief is what a man will act from;[6] but he does not seem to have taken the truth of this proposition home to him, or else he would see that the whole end of inquiry is the settlement of belief;[7] so that a man shall not war against himself, nor undo tomorrow that which he begins to do today. Dr. Royce's main argument in support of his own opinion, to the confusion of Thrasymachus, is drawn from the existence of error. Namely, the subject of an erroneous proposition could not be identified with the subject of the corresponding true proposition, except by being com- pletely known, and in that knowledge no error would be possible. The truth must, therefore, be present to the actual consciousness of a living being. This is an argument drawn from Formal Logic, for formal logic it is which inquires how different propositions are made to refer to the same subject, and the like. German metaphysics has, since Kant, drawn its best arguments from formal logic; and it is quite right in doing so, for the conceptions which are proved to be indispensible in formal logic, must have been already rooted in the nature of the mind when reasoning first began, and are, so far, *à priori*. But one would surely have supposed that when the German philosophers[8] were thus drawing their arguments from formal logic, they would have post- poned their venturesome flights into the thin air of theology and the vacuum of pure reason, until they had carefully tried the strength of every part of that logical machine on which they were to depend. Instead of that, they have left the great work of creating a true system of formal logic to English authors, who, while they have done most excellent work, have (with the insignificant exception of the present writer) been quite indifferent to the transcendental bearings of their results. Kant gives a half dozen only of his brief pages to the development of the system of logic upon which his whole philosophy rests;[9] and though many valuable treatises on the science have appeared in Germany, there is hardly one of them which is not more or less marred by some arrant absurdity, acknowledged to be so by all the others; Grassmann[10] and Schroeder alone pursuing the one method which will yield positive results properly secured against error. We must not, therefore, wonder that Dr. Royce's argument from formal logic overlooks one of the most important discoveries that have lately resulted from the study of that exact branch of philosophy. He seems to think that the real subject of a proposition can be denoted by a general term of the proposition; that is, that precisely what it is that you are talking about can be distinguished from other things by giving a general description of it. Kant already showed, in a celebrated passage of his cataclysmic work,[11] that this is not so; and recent studies in formal logic* have put it in a clearer light. We now find that, besides general terms, two other kinds of signs are perfectly indispensible in all reasoning. One of these kinds is the *index*, which like a pointing finger, exercises a real physiological *force* over the attention, like the power of a mesmerizer, and directs it to a particular object of sense. One such index at least must enter into every proposition, its function being to designate the subject of discourse. Now observe that Dr. Royce does not merely say that there are no means by which an erroneous proposition can be produced; what he says is that the conception of an erroneous proposition (without an actual including consciousness) is absurd. If the subject of discourse had to be distinguished from other things, if at all, by a general term, that is, by its peculiar characters, it would be quite true that its complete segregation would require a full knowledge of its characters and would preclude ignorance. But the index, which in point of fact alone can designate the subject of a proposition, designates it without implying any characters at all. A blinding flash of lightning forces my attention and directs it to a certain moment of time with an emphatic "Now!" Directly following it, I may judge that there will be a terrific peal of thunder, and if it does not come I acknowledge an error. One instant of time is, in itself, exactly like any other instant, one point of space like any other point; nevertheless dates and positions can be approximately distinguished. And how are they so distinguished? By *intuition* says Kant;[13] perhaps

*Mitchell in *Studies in Logic. By Members of the Johns Hopkins University*, and Peirce in *The American Journal of Mathematics*, vol. vii [item 16 above].[12]

not in so many words; but it is because of this property that he distinguishes Space and Time from the general conceptions of the understanding and sets them off by themselves under the head of intuition. But I should prefer to say that it is by volitional acts that dates and positions are distinguished. The element of feeling is so prominent in sensations, that we do not observe that something like Will enters into them, too. You may quarrel with the word *volition* if you like; I wish I had a more general one at my hand.[14] But what I mean is that that strong, clear, and voluntary consciousness in which we act upon our muscles is nothing more than the most marked variety of a kind of consciousness which enters into many other phenomena of our life, a consciousness of duality or dual consciousness. Feeling is simple consciousness, the consciousness that can be contained within an instant of time, the consciousness of the excitation of nerve-cells; it has no parts and no unity. What I call volition is the consciousness of the discharge of nerve-cells, either into the muscles, etc., or into other nerve-cells; it does not involve the sense of time (i.e. not of a continuum) but it does involve the sense of action and reaction, resistance, externality, otherness, pair-edness. It is the sense that something has hit me or that I am hitting something; it might be called the sense of collision or clash. It has an outward and an inward variety, corresponding to Kant's outer and inner sense,[15] to will and self-control, to nerve-action and inhibition, to the two logical types *A:B* and *A:A*. The capital error of Hegel which permeates his whole system in every part of it is that he almost altogether ignores the Outward Clash.* Besides the lower consciousness of feeling and the higher consciousness of nutrition, this direct consciousness of hitting and of getting hit enters into all cognition and serves to make it mean something real. It is formal logic which teaches us this; not that of a Whately or a Jevons, but formal logic in its new development, drawing nutriment from physiology and from history without leaving the solid ground of logical forms.

An objection different from that of Dr. Royce might be raised. Namely it might be asked *how* two different men can know they are speaking of the same thing. Suppose, for instance, one man should say a flash of lightning was followed by thunder and another should deny it. How would they know they meant the same flash? The answer is that they would compare notes somewhat as follows. One would say, "I mean that very brilliant flash which was preceded by three slighter flashes, you know." The second man would recognize the mark, and

---

*"We must be in contact with our subject-matter," says he in one place, "whether it be by means of our external senses, *or, what is better*, by our profounder mind and our innermost self-consciousness."[16]

thus by a probable and approximate inference they would conclude they meant the same flash.

Dr. Royce in describing the opinion of Thrasymachus has selected the expression "a *barely* possible judge."[17] Is there not an ambiguity in this mode of speech which is unfair to Thrasymachus? The final opinion which would be sure to result from sufficient investigation may possibly, in reference to a given question, never be actually attained, owing to a final extinction of intellectual life or for some other reason.[18] In that sense, this final judgment is not *certain* but only possible. But when Dr. Royce says "bare possibility is blank nothingness,"[19] he would seem to be speaking of mere logical possibility, and not a possibility which differs but by a hair's-breadth from entire certainty. Let us consider what probability there is that a given question, say one capable of being answered by *yes* or *no*, will never get answered. Let us reason upon this matter by inductive logic. Dr. Royce and his school, I am well aware, consider inductive reasoning to be radically vicious; so that we unhappily cannot carry them along with us. [They often deny this, by the way, and say they rest entirely on experience. This is because they so overlook the Outward Clash, that they do not know what experience is. They are like Roger Bacon, who after stating in eloquent terms that all knowledge comes from experience, goes on to mention spiritual illumination from on high as one of the most valuable kinds of experiences.][20] But they will not succeed in exploding the method of modern science; and there is no reason why those who believe in induction at all, should not be willing to apply it to the subject now in hand. In the first place, then, upon innumerable questions, we have already reached the final opinion. How do we know that? Do we fancy ourselves infallible? Not at all; but throwing off as probably erroneous a thousandth or even a hundredth of all the beliefs established beyond present doubt, there must remain a vast multitude in which the final opinion has been reached. Every directory, guidebook, dictionary, history, and work of science is crammed with such facts. In the history of science, it has sometimes occurred that a really wise man has said concerning one question or another that there was reason to believe it never would be answered. The proportion of these which have in point of fact been conclusively settled very soon after the prediction has been surprizingly large. Our experience in this direction warrants us in saying with the highest degree of empirical confidence that questions that are either practical or could conceivably become so are susceptible of receiving final solutions provided the existence of the human race be indefinitely prolonged and the particular question excite sufficient interest. As for questions which have no conceivable practical bearings, as the question whether force is an entity, they mean nothing, and may be answered as we like, without error. We may take it as certain that the human race will ultimately be extirpated; because there is a certain chance of it every year, and in an indefinitely long time the chance of survival compounds itself nearer and nearer to zero. But, on the other hand, we may take it as certain that other intellectual races exist on other planets,—if not of our solar system, then of others; and also that innumerable new intellectual races have yet to be developed; so that on the whole, it may be regarded as most certain that intellectual life in the universe will never finally cease. The problem whether a given question will ever get answered or not is not so simple; the number of questions asked is constantly increasing, and the capacity for answering them is also on the increase. If the rate of the latter increase is greater than that of the former[21] the probability is unity that any given question will be answered; otherwise the probability is *zero*. Considerations too long to be explained here lead me to think that the former state of things is the actual one. In that case, there is but an infinitesimal proportion of questions which do not get answered, although the multitude of unanswered questions is forever on the increase. It plainly is not fair to call a judgment which is certain to be made a "barely possible" one. But I will admit (if the reader thinks the admission has any meaning, and is not an empty proposition) that some finite number of questions, we can never know which ones, will escape getting answered forever. Nor must I forget that I have not given the reader my proof that out of the questions asked at any time the proportion that will never be answered is infinitesimal; so that he may be in doubt upon this point. That is not a thing to be regretted; for scepticism about the reality of things,— provided it be genuine and sincere, and not a sham,—is a healthful and growing stage of mental development.[22] Let us suppose, then, for the sake of argument, that some questions eventually get settled, and that some others, indistinguishable from the former by any marks, never do. In that case, I should say that the conception of reality was rather a faulty one, for while there is a real so far as a question that will get settled goes, there is none for a question that will never be settled; for an unknowable reality is nonsense. The non-idealistic reader will start at this last assertion; but consider the matter from a practical point of view. You say that real things are manifested by their effects. True; for example, if the timbers of my house are inwardly rotting, it will some day fall down, and thus there will be a practical effect for me, whether I know the beams be rotten or not. Well, but if all the effects consistently point to the theory that the beams are rotting, it will come to be admitted at last that they are so; and if nothing is ever settled about the matter, it will be because the phenomena do not consistently point to any theory; and in that case there is a want of that "uniformity of nature" (to use a popular but very loose expression) which constitutes reality, and makes it differ from a dream.[23] In that way, if we think that some questions are never going to get settled, we ought to admit that our conception of nature as absolutely real is only partially correct. Still, we shall have to be governed by it practically; because there is nothing to distinguish the unanswerable questions from the answerable ones, so that investigation will have to proceed as if all were answerable. In ordinary life, no matter how much we believe in questions ultimately getting answered, we shall always put aside an innumerable throng of them as beyond our powers. We shall not in our day seek to know whether the centre of the sun is distant from that of the earth by an odd or an even number of miles on the average; we shall act as if neither man nor God could ever ascertain it. There is, however, an economy of thought, in assuming that it is an answerable question. From this practical and economical point of view, it really makes no difference whether or not all questions are actually answered, by man or by God, so long as we are satisfied that investigation has a universal tendency toward the settlement of opinion; and this I conceive to be the position of Thrasymachus.

If there be any advantage to religion in supposing God to be omniscient, this sort of scepticism about reality can do no practical harm. We can still suppose that He knows all that there is of reality to be known. On the theory of Dr. Royce, the real existence of God would consist in his imagining or positing Himself; it would thus be, according to him, of the same nature as the reality of anything else. For my part, I hold another theory, which I intend to take an early opportunity of putting into print. I think that the existence of God, as well as we can conceive of it, consists in this, that a tendency toward ends is so necessary a constituent of the universe that the mere action of chance upon innumerable atoms has an inevitable teleological result. One of the ends so brought about is the development of intelligence and of knowledge; and therefore I should say that God's omniscience, humanly conceived, consists in the fact that knowledge in its development leaves no question unanswered. The scepticism just spoken of would admit this omniscience as a regulative but not a speculative conception. I believe that even that view is more religiously fruitful than the opinion of Dr. Royce.

Let us now turn to the examination of Dr. Royce's peculiar method of reasoning; for that is always the most important element in every system of philosophy. His work is divided into a brief introduction and two books, the first entitled "The search for a moral ideal"; the second "The search for a religious truth." These titles seem to me to point, at the outset, to a fault of method. The pursuit of a conscience, if one hasn't one already, or of a religion, which is the subjective basis of conscience, seems to me an aimless and hypochondriac pursuit. If a man finds himself under no sense of obligation, let him congratulate himself. For such a man to hanker after a bondage to conscience, is as if a man with a good digestion should cast about for a regimen of food. A conscience, too, is not a theorem or a piece of information which may be acquired by reading a book; it must be bred in a man from infancy or it will be a poor imitation of the genuine article. If a man has a conscience, it may be an article of faith with him that he should reflect upon that conscience, and thus it may receive a further development. But it never will do him the least good to get up a make-believe scepticism and pretend to himself not to believe what he really does believe. In point of fact, every man born and reared in a christian community, however little he may believe the dogmas of the Church, does find himself believing with the strongest conviction in the moral code of christendom. He has a horror of murder and incest, a disapproval of lying, etc., which he cannot escape from. The modern dialectician (if he will pardon a touch of exaggeration) would have such a man say to himself, Now I am going to be sceptical, but only provisionally so, in order to return to my faith with renewed conviction! But the whole history of thought shows that men cannot doubt at pleasure or merely because they find they have no positive reason for the belief they already hold. Reasons concern the man who is coming to believe, not the man who believes already. It has often been remarked that metaphysics is an imitation of mathematics; and it may be added that the philosophic doubt is an imitation of the absurd proceedure of elementary geometry, which begins by giving worthless demonstrations of propositions nobody ever questions. When Hegel tells me that thought has three stages, that of naïve acceptance, that of reaction and criticism, and that of rational conviction;[24] in a general sense, I agree to it. And a down-right living scepticism, without *arrière-pensée*, may be beneficial. It is not perhaps easy to see why an imaginary scepticism might not sometimes serve the same purpose; but experience shows that in questions of magnitude men haven't imagination enough to put themselves in the true doubter's shoes. But be that as it may, the idea that the mere reaction of assent and doubt, the mere play of thought, the heat-lightning of the brain, is going to settle anything in this real world to which we appertain,—such an idea only shows again how the Hegelians overlook the facts of volitional action & reaction in the development of thought. I find myself in a world of forces which act upon me, and it is they and not the logical transformations of my thought which determine what I shall ultimately believe.

Dr. Royce seems to hold that at least in the philosophy of morals and religion a mere contemplation of our own crude beliefs will lead us to absolute scepticism and that then a mere contemplation of our own absolute scepticism will lead us back to rational conviction. Neither I nor the readers of the *Popular Science Monthly* can possibly believe that, in advance. But let us see how the method will work when applied to the discussion of ethics.

The moral stand-point from which every man with a christian training sets out, even if he be a dogmatic atheist, is pretty nearly the same. He has a horror of certain crimes and a disapproval of certain lesser sins. He is also more or less touched with the spirit of christian love, which he believes should be his beacon, and which in point of fact, by its power in his heart, shall and will govern him in all questions of disputed morals. More or less, in all of us, this sentiment replaces and abolishes conscience; like Huckleberry Finn, we act from christian charity without caring very much whether conscience approves of the act or not.

This is the state of mind of the ordinary man or woman who will open Dr. Royce's book. And now Dr. Royce proposes that this person shall ask himself the question what validity or truth is there in the distinction of right and wrong. To me, it plainly appears that such a person, if he have a clear head, will at once reply, right and wrong are nothing to me except so far as they are connected with certain rules of living by which I am enabled to satisfy a real impulse which works in my heart; and this impulse is the love of my neighbor elevated into a love of an ideal and divine humanity which I identify with the providence that governs the world. But Dr. Royce says that different people will answer the question in different ways; some will take the position of the "moral realist" and say that moral distinctions are founded on some matter of fact (say a decree from Sinai), while others will take the position of the "moral idealist" and say that these distinctions are founded on an inward sentiment,—an ideal.[25] Two such persons come into collision; they find by mutual criticism that both positions are unsatisfactory; external fact can only determine what *is*, not what *ought* to be; while inward sentiment cannot be a resting-place, because it is only individual caprice and has no authority for another man. From this criticism the only outcome is ethical scepticism.

This is a fair specimen of Dr. Royce's logical method, which is a mere apotheosis of the dilemma, as the great instrument of thought. As compared with syllogistic method of the middle ages (which survives in certain quarters, yet) it is certainly wonderfully superior; but as compared with the mathematical reasoning upon which modern science is built, it is inefficacious and restricted.

In the particular case in hand, it appears to me that the ordinary christian does not find himself caught in Dr. Royce's dilemma at all. He is a moral idealist; yet far from being shaken by the spectacle of different men having different passions, he feels that every man may come to the same passion which animates him by a mere enlargement of his horizon, and that his is the only sentiment in which all others may be reconciled. For altruism is but a developed egoism; that same sensitiveness which in its lowest state is selfishness, first transforms itself into *esprit de corps* or collective selfishness; then, passing from feeling for others collectively to feeling for them individually, it becomes philanthropy, pity, sympathy tossed hither and thither rudderless on the ocean of human misery; finally, steadying itself by the conception of an ideal humanity and a divine providence, it passes into christian charity, which gathers up all selfishnesses and all pities and is ready to give each its due measure.

The author having stated the above argument with admirable clearness, fills a hundred pages with a perhaps not altogether necessary, though a charmingly written and highly interesting elaboration and illustration of it. He here passes in review a goodly number of the ethical theories which have been proposed at different times. After the Sophists, Plato, Aristotle, and the Stoics, he criticizes what he conceives to be the ethics of Jesus.[26] Every christian will tell him that he makes the mistake of viewing that as a *theory* or speculation which is really a spiritual *experience;*—another example of his neglect of the volitional element. For instance, he asks, "If I feel not the love of God, how prove to me that I ought to feel it?"[27] The answer to that need not be pointed out.

In what he says about Herbert Spencer, he seems to forget that Mr. Spencer is not addressing a body of moral sceptics but readers animated by the sentiments which, in our day, animate every man who reads at all.[28]

At last he takes up the thread of his argument as follows. The conflict between moral realism and idealism can only lead to moral scepticism. Now what is this scepticism? It is the contemplation of two opposing aims. Here he adduces the testimony of modern psychologists to show that we cannot think of willing without actually willing.[29] (But for all that, I fancy I notice a difference sometimes in cold weather between thinking of willing to take my morning dash of cold water and actually willing to take it.) Scepticism, then, shares at once these opposing aims, or strives to share them. It has thus itself an aim, namely, to reconcile opposing aims. So absolute moral scepticism is self-destructive. "Possibly this result may be somewhat unexpected," says our author.[30] Not at all unexpected to one who does not believe in the dialectical method. You started with a hypochondriac hankering after an aim; and now you have acquired it. *Eurekas!* Well, what is it, this aim which you have at last got? Why, to have an aim! But that is nothing but the old nonsensical longing with which you set out. Like Kant's dove,[31] you have been winging a vacuum, without remarking that you never advanced an inch. I do not misrepresent the author. "For behold," he says, "made practical, brought down from its lonesome height, my Ideal very simply means the Will to direct my acts *towards* the attainment of universal Harmony."[32] But this, I must insist, was obviously implied in the original fantastic desire to have an aim. When I say that this is a fantastic desire, I do not of course mean to deny that there may be such an operation as the *choice of an aim*, if by that aim be meant a secondary or derived one; but I do say that it is absurd to speak of choosing an original and ultimate aim. That is something which if you haven't it, you have nothing to do but wait till the grace of God confers it on you. I should think, however, that were it once admitted to be a rational performance to go a-hunting for an ultimate aim or end, the first preliminary would be to recognize the axiom that such an end must have unity, after which the hunt might begin. But Royce, calling this axiom the "ideal of ideals," as it certainly is, in a sense, exclaims "Here I have the aim I wanted, and the hunt is over."[33] If one might be permitted to enliven a dry subject with a little folly, I should say that it reminded me of the surveyor Phoenix, who after purchasing 365 solar compasses and a vast amount of other paraphernalia, in order to ascertain the distance between San Francisco and the Mission of Dolores, stepped into a grocery and inquired how far it was, and returned "much pleased at so easily acquiring so much valuable information."[34] If Dr. Royce merely means that it can be shown that a man who fancies he has no moral ideal really has one, I heartily grant it; and I will further admit that dialectic is the proper instrument to show this. But then a very lowly kind of dialectic will do; and a rather more definite ideal may be pointed out.

The rest of Book I is occupied, as it seems to me, with illicitly slipping some content into an empty formula. Much of this part of the book is splendidly said. But other passages seem to me to preach, in a way quite uncalled for by the premises, an ethics of the evil eye. "It is well that we should feel . . . joy whenever pride has a fall. . . . In all such ways . . . we must show *no mercy*." "When the hedonist gives us his picture of a peaceful society, where, in the midst of good humor, his ideal, the happiness of everybody concerned, is steadfastly pursued, we find ourselves disappointed and contemptuous. . . . Who cares whether that wretched set . . . think themselves happy or not?" "The appearance of anybody who pretends to be content with himself must be the signal not for admiration at the sight of his success, but for a good deal of contempt." etc.[35] Some of the students to whom this ethics is taught at Harvard may upon reflection think that christian charity is not so much lower a frame of mind after all.

In Book II Dr. Royce undertakes by the same dialectic proceedure to establish the existence of a God. [S]pace does not permit me to enter into a criticism of the second book; nor is it necessary, for it consists only of an application of the same method to a subject to which dialectics is far less suited. Besides, to the reader who has had the kindness and the resolution to follow me to this point I can say, "You are the man to enjoy Dr. Royce's own book, which I can promise you you shall find, in comparison with harsh and crabbed matter you have been reading here, to be 'as musical as is Apollo's lute.' "[36]

18

One, Two, Three:
Kantian Categories

MS 897. [First published, as MS 572, in W5:292–94; see also MSS 545, 546, 548, 573, 575, 578, and 582.] Sometime in 1885, it occurred to Peirce that he may have found the key to the secret of the universe, and he wrote to William James on 20 October: "I have something very vast now. . . . It is . . . an attempt to explain the laws of nature, to show their general characteristics and to trace them to their origin & predict new laws by the laws of the laws of nature." He then made his famous 'guess': "three elements are active in the world, first, chance; second, law; and third, habit-taking. Such is our guess of the secret of the sphynx." It remained for him to work the details and consequences of this grand hypothesis into a full-fledged theory. The present paper, written in the summer of 1886 for a book to be entitled "One, Two, Three," is one of several attempts to organize the principal claims needed to support his guess (and is an early version of the first chapter of item 19).

This is the day for doubting axioms. With mathematicians, the question is settled; there is no reason to believe that the geometrical axioms are exactly true. Metaphysics is an imitation of geometry, and with the geometrical axioms the metaphysical axioms must go too.

We have no reason to think that the sum of the three angles of a triangle is exactly equal to two right-angles. All that we can say is that the excess or defect is proportional to the area of the triangle, and that it is excessively minute even for the most enormous triangles of astronomy. The sum of the three angles of a triangle of unit size is a physical constant nearly equal to 180 degrees; but its exact value is unknown to us.

Since we have no reason to think that this constant is exactly equal to 180 degrees, and there is an infinite multitude of other values that it can equally well have, the odds are at present infinity to one against its being exactly 180 degrees, so that that hypothesis ought to be entirely dismissed from our minds.

It is difficult for us to believe that any physical constant, any finite quantity in nature, is primordial. It may be so, but we cannot help at least asking how it came to have the precise value that it has. Especially do we feel the need of an explanation when the quantity in question comes very near to unity, zero, or any other remarkable number. For then it is suggested that there must have been some cause tending to change the value of the constant and to bring it nearer and nearer to the number that it nearly equals. In such a case, therefore, we have a positive reason for thinking that the quantity is not primordial.

Thus the principles of logic require us to think that space did not always have its present simple construction, but that this has been brought about by some gradual process. This is not quite a correct statement, however, because space, as an individual receptacle of things, is a fiction. Were it otherwise, absolute position and absolute velocity in space would mean something, which we have no reason to think that they do. What is true is that there are certain general laws of position, but not that there is a receptacle which accounts for those laws. This is a fiction of geometry.

The same reasoning applies to the axiom that every thing that happens is completely determined by exact laws. We have no reason to think that the accordance of phenomena with formulae is absolutely exact. Whenever we attempt to verify the accordance of fact with law, we find discrepancies which we rightly enough attribute to errors of observation. But we cannot be sure that there are not similar, though much smaller, aberrations in the events themselves. Since we have no reason to think that the mean aberration of phenomena from law is equal to zero, it is infinitely more probable that it is not. We must therefore suppose an element of absolute chance, sporting, spontaneity, originality, freedom, in nature.[1] We must further suppose that this element in the ages of the past was indefinitely more prominent than now, and that the present almost exact conformity of nature to law is something that has been gradually brought about. We have to suppose that in looking back into the indefinite past we are looking back towards times when the element of law played an indefinitely small part in the universe.

If the universe is thus progressing from a state of all but pure chance to a state of all but complete determination by law, we must suppose that there is an original, elemental, tendency of things to acquire determinate properties, to take habits. This is the Third or mediating element between chance, which brings forth First and original events, and law which produces sequences or Seconds. Now the tendency to take habits is something essentially finite in amount, an infinitely strong tendency of this sort [unlike an absolute conformity to law] is inconceivable and self-contradictory. Consequently this tendency must itself have been gradually evolved; and it would evidently tend to strengthen itself.[2]

Here then is a rational physical hypothesis, which is calculated to account, or all but account for everything in the universe except pure originality itself. The next step in order would be to attempt to verify this hypothesis by seeing how far it would account for and explain the observed characteristics of the laws of nature. But I postpone that to another chapter[3] in order now to sketch the remainder of the theory of which this hypothesis is but a part.

19

A Guess at the Riddle

MS 909. [First published in CP 1.354 (the opening outline), 1.1–2 (the next two paragraphs), 1.355–68 (chapter 1), 1.373 (chapter 3), 1.374–75 and 379–83 (chapter 4; missing are the final sentence of the second paragraph, the third paragraph, and the first half of the fourth paragraph), and 1.385–416 (chapters 5, 6, and 7). An earlier opening page has the title "Notes for a Book, to be entitled 'A Guess at the Riddle,' with a Vignette of the Sphynx below the Title."] Although chapters 2, 8, and 9 are missing (and probably were never written) and chapter 3 is a mere outline, "A Guess at the Riddle" is perhaps Peirce's greatest and most original contribution to speculative philosophy, and it marks his deliberate turn to architectonic thought. His three categories, which he speculates are isomorphic with the three elements that are active in the universe (chance, law, and habit-taking), serve as the structure for organizing the branches of philosophy and science, and it is clear that he anticipated a complete reorganization of human knowledge around his triad of universal conceptions; for as he wrote, on a variant opening page, "this book, if ever written, as it soon will be if I am in a situation to do it, will be one of the births of time." Although, unfortunately, Peirce never was in such a situation, it is fortunate that many of his major ideas in the "Guess" would soon appear in the papers of the Monist *Metaphysical Series (items 21–25).*

Chapter 1. One, Two, Three. Already written.[1]
Chapter 2. The triad in reasoning. Not touched.[2] It is to be made as follows. 1. Three kinds of signs; as best shown in my last paper in the *Am. Jour. Math.*[3] 2. Term, proposition, and argument, mentioned in my paper on a new list of categories.[4] 3. Three kinds of argument, deduction, induction, hypothesis, as shown in my paper in *Studies in Logic.*[5] Also three figures of syllogism, as shown there and in my paper on the classification of arguments.[6] 4. Three kinds of terms, absolute, relative, and conjugative, as shown in my first paper on Logic of Relatives.[7] There are various other triads which may be alluded to. The dual

divisions of logic result from a false way of looking at things absolutely. Thus, besides affirmative and negative, there are really probable enunciations, which are intermediate. So besides universal and particular there are all sorts of propositions of numerical quantity. For example, the particular proposition Some A is B, means At least one A is B. But we can also say At least 2 A's are B's. Also, All the A's but one are B's, etc. etc. ad infinitum. We pass from dual quantity, or a system of quantity such as that of Boolian algebra, where there are only two values, to plural quantity.

Chapter 3. The triad in metaphysics. This chapter one of the best, is to treat of the theory of cognition.

Chapter 4. The triad in psychology. The greater part is written.

Chapter 5. The triad in physiology. The greater part is written.

Chapter 6. The triad in biology. This is to show the true nature of the Darwinian hypothesis.

Chapter 7. The triad in physics. The germinal chapter. 1. The necessity of a natural history of the laws of nature, so that we may get some notion of what to expect. 2. The logical postulate for explanation forbids the assumption of any absolute. That is, it calls for the introduction of thirdness. 3. Metaphysics is an imitation of geometry; and mathematicians having declared against axioms, the metaphysical axioms are destined to fall too. 4. Absolute chance. 5. The universality of the principle of habit. 6. The whole theory stated. 7. Consequences.

Chapter 8. The triad in sociology or shall I say pneumatology. That the consciousness is a sort of public spirit among the nerve-cells. Man as a community of cells; compound animals and composite plants; society; nature. Feeling implied in firstness.

Chapter 9. The triad in theology. Faith requires to be materialists without flinching.[8]

To erect a philosophical edifice that shall outlast the vicissitudes of time, my care must be, not so much to set each brick with nicest accuracy, as to lay the foundations deep and massive. Aristotle built upon a few deliberately chosen concepts—such as matter and form, act and power—very broad, and in their outlines vague and rough, but solid, unshakable, and not easily undermined; and thence it has come to pass that Aristotelianism is babbled in every nursery, that "English Common Sense," for example, is thoroughly peripatetic, and that ordinary men live so completely within the house of the Stagyrite that whatever they see out of the windows appears to them incomprehensible and metaphysical. Long it has been only too manifest that, fondly habituated though we be to it, the old structure will not do for modern needs; and accordingly, under Descartes, Hobbes, Kant, and others, repairs, alterations, and partial demolitions have been carried on for the last three centuries. One system, also, stands upon its own ground; I mean the new Schelling-Hegel mansion, lately run up in the German taste, but with such oversights in its construction that, although brand new, it is already pronounced uninhabitable. The undertaking which this volume inaugurates is to make a philosophy like that of Aristotle, that is to say, to outline a theory so comprehensive that, for a long time to come, the entire work of human reason, in philosophy of every school and kind, in mathematics, in psychology, in physical science, in history, in sociology, and in whatever other department there may be, shall appear as the filling up of its details. The first step toward this is to find simple concepts applicable to every subject.

But before all else, let me make the acquaintance of my reader, and express my sincere esteem for him and the deep pleasure it is to me to address one so wise and so patient. I know his character pretty well, for both the subject and the style of this book ensure his being one out of millions. He will comprehend that it has not been written for the purpose of confirming him in his preconceived opinions, and he would not take the trouble to read it if it had. He is prepared to meet with propositions that he is inclined at first to dissent from; and he looks to being convinced that some of them are true, after all. He will reflect, too, that the thinking and writing of this book has taken, I won't say how long, quite certainly more than a quarter of an hour, and consequently fundamental objections of so obvious a nature that they must strike everyone instantaneously will have occurred to the author, although the replies to them may not be of that kind whose full force can be instantly apprehended.

Chapter I. Trichotomy

Perhaps I might begin by noticing how different numbers have found their champions. Two was extolled by Peter Ramus, Four by Pythagoras, Five by Sir Thomas Browne, and so on. For my part, I am a determined foe of no innocent number; I respect and esteem them all their several ways; but I am forced to confess to a leaning to the number three in philosophy. In fact, I make so much use of three-fold divisions in my speculations, that it seems best to commence by making a slight preliminary study of the conceptions upon which all such divisions must rest. I mean no more than the ideas of First, Second, Third,—ideas so broad that they may be looked upon rather as moods or tones of thought, than as definite notions, but which have great significance for all that. Viewed as numerals, to be applied to what objects we like, they are indeed thin skeletons of thought, if not mere words. If we only wanted to make enumerations, it would be out of place to ask for the significations of the numbers we should have to use;

but then the distinctions of philosophy are supposed to attempt something far more than that; they are intended to go down to the very essence of things, and if we are to make one single three-fold philosophical distinction, it behooves us to ask beforehand what are the kinds of objects that are first, second, and third, not as being so counted, but in their own true characters. That there are such ideas of the really First, Second, and Third, we shall presently find reason to admit.

The First is that whose being is simply in itself, not referring to anything nor lying behind anything. The Second is that which is what it is by force of something to which it is second. The Third is that which is what it is owing to things between which it mediates and which it brings into relation to each other.

The idea of the absolutely First must be entirely separated from all conception of or reference to anything else; for what involves a second is itself a second to that second. The First must therefore be present and immediate, so as not to be second to a representation. It must be fresh and new, for if old it is second to its former state. It must be initiative, original, spontaneous, and free; otherwise it is second to a determining cause. It is also something vivid and conscious; so only it avoids being the object of some sensation. It precedes all synthesis and all differentiation: it has no unity and no parts. It cannot be articulately thought: assert it, and it has already lost its characteristic innocence; for assertion always implies a denial of something else. Stop to think of it, and it has flown! What the world was to Adam on the day he opened his eyes to it, before he had drawn any distinctions, or had become conscious of his own existence,—that is first, present, immediate, fresh, new, initiative, original, spontaneous, free, vivid, conscious, and evanescent. Only, remember that every description of it must be false to it.

Just as the first is not absolutely first if thought along with a second, so likewise to think the Second in its perfection we must banish every third. The Second is therefore the absolute last. But we need not, and must not, banish the idea of the first from the second; on the contrary, the Second is precisely that which cannot be without the first. It meets us in such facts as Another, Relation, Compulsion, Effect, Dependence, Independence, Negation, Occurrence, Reality, Result. A thing cannot be other, negative, or independent, without a first to or of which it shall be other, negative, or independent. Still, this is not a very deep kind of secondness; for the first might in these cases be destroyed yet leave the real character of the second absolutely unchanged. When the second suffers some change from the action of the first, and is dependent upon it, the secondness is more genuine. But the dependence must not go so far that the second is a mere accident or incident of the first; otherwise the secondness again degenerates. The genuine second suffers and yet resists, like dead matter, whose existence consists in its inertia. Note, too, that for the Second to have the Finality that we have seen belongs to it, it must be determined by the first immoveably, and thenceforth be fixed; so that unalterable fixity becomes one of its attributes. We find secondness in occurrence, because an occurrence is something whose existence consists in our knocking up against it. A hard fact is of the same sort; that is to say, it is something which is there, and which I cannot think away, but am forced to acknowledge as an object or second beside myself, the subject or number one, and which forms material for the exercise of my will.

The idea of second must be reckoned as an easy one to comprehend. That of first is so tender that you cannot touch it without spoiling it; but that of second is eminently hard and tangible. It is very familiar, too; it is forced upon us daily: it is the main lesson of life. In youth, the world is fresh and we seem free; but limitation, conflict, constraint, and secondness generally, make up the teaching of experience. With what firstness

> The scarfed bark puts from her native bay;

with what secondness

> doth she return,
> With overweathered ribs and ragged sails.[9]

But familiar as the notion is, and compelled as we are to acknowledge it at every turn, still we never can realize it; we never can be immediately conscious of finiteness, or of anything but a divine freedom that in its own original firstness knows no bounds.

First and Second, Agent and Patient, Yes and No, are categories which enable us roughly to describe the facts of experience, and they satisfy the mind for a very long time. But at last they are found inadequate, and the Third is the conception which is then called for. The Third is that which bridges over the chasm between the absolute first and last, and brings them into relationship. We are told that every science has its Qualitative and its Quantitative stage; now its qualitative stage is when dual distinctions,—whether a given subject has a given predicate or not,—suffice; the quantitative stage comes when, no longer content with such rough distinctions, we require to insert a possible half-way between every two possible conditions of the subject in regard to its possession of the quality indicated by the predicate. Ancient mechanics recognized forces as causes which produced motions as their immediate effects, looking no further than the essentially dual relation of cause and effect. That was why it could make no progress with dynamics. The work of Galileo and his successors lay in showing that forces are accelerations by which a state of velocity is gradually brought about. The words cause and effect still linger, but the old conceptions have been dropped from mechanical philosophy; for the fact now known is that in certain relative positions bodies undergo certain accelerations. Now an acceleration, instead of being like a velocity a relation between two successive positions, is a relation between three; so that the new doctrine has consisted in the suitable introduction of the conception of Threeness. On this idea, the whole of modern physics is built. The superiority of modern geometry, too, has certainly been due to nothing so much as to the bridging over of the innumerable distinct cases with which the ancient science was encumbered; and we may go so far as to say that all the great steps in the method of science in every department have consisted in bringing into relation cases previously discrete.[10]

We can easily recognize the man whose thought is mainly in the dual stage by his unmeasured use of language. In former days, when he was natural, everything with him was unmitigated, absolute, ineffable, utter, matchless, supreme, unqualified, root and branch; but now that it is the fashion to be depreciatory, he is just as plainly marked by the ridiculous inadequacy of his expressions. The principle of contradiction is a shibboleth for such minds; to disprove a proposition they will always try to prove there lurks a contradiction in it, notwithstanding that it may be as clear and comprehensible as the day. Remark for your amusement the grand unconcern with which mathematics, since the invention of the calculus, has pursued its way, caring no more for the peppering of contradiction-mongers than an ironclad for an American fort.

We have seen that it is the immediate consciousness that is preeminently first, the external dead thing that is preeminently second. In like manner, it is evidently the representation mediating between these two that is preeminently third. Other examples, however, should not be neglected. The first is agent, the second patient, the third is the action by which the former influences the latter. Between the beginning as first, and the end as last, comes the process which leads from first to last.

According to the mathematicians, when we measure along a line, were our yardstick replaced by a yard marked off on an infinitely long rigid bar, then in all the shiftings of it which we make for the purpose of applying it to successive portions of the line to be measured, two points on that bar would remain fixed and unmoved. To that pair of points, the mathematicians accord the title of the absolute; they are the points that are at an infinite distance one way and the other as measured by that yard. These points are either really distinct, coincident, or imaginary (in which case there is but a finite distance completely round the line), according to the relation of the mode of measurement to the nature of the line upon which the measurement is made. These two points are the absolute first and the absolute last or second, while every measurable point on the line is of the nature of a third. We have seen that the conception of the absolute first eludes every attempt to grasp it; and so in another sense does that of the absolute second; but there is no absolute third, for the third is of its own nature relative, and this is what we are always thinking, even when we aim at the first or second. The starting-point of the universe, God the Creator, is the Absolute First; the terminus of the universe, God completely revealed, is the Absolute Second; every state of the universe at a measurable point of time is the third. If you think the measurable is all there is, and deny it any definite tendency whence or whither, then you are considering the pair of points that makes the absolute to be imaginary and are an Epicurean. If you hold that there is a definite drift to the course of nature as a whole, but yet believe its absolute end is nothing but the nirvana from which it set out, you make the two points of the absolute to be coincident, and are a pessimist. But if your creed is that the whole universe is approaching in the infinitely distant future a state having a general character different from that toward which we look back in the infinitely distant past, you make the absolute to consist in two distinct real points and are an evolutionist.*

This is one of the matters concerning which a man can only learn from his own reflections, but I believe that if my suggestions are followed out, the reader will grant that One, Two, Three, are more than mere count-words like "eeny, meeny, mony, mi," but carry vast, though vague ideas.

But it will be asked, why stop at three? Why not go on to find a // new conception in / distinct idea for // Four, Five, and so on indefinitely? The reason is that while it is impossible to form a genuine three by any modification of the pair, without introducing something of a different nature from the unit and the pair, four, five, and every higher number can be formed by mere complications of threes. To make this clear, I will first show it in an example. The fact that A presents B with a gift C, is a triple relation, and as such cannot possibly be resolved into any combination of dual relations. Indeed, the very

---

*The last view is essentially that of Christian theology, too. The theologians hold the physical universe to be finite, but considering that universe which they will admit to have existed from all time, it would appear to be in a different condition in the end from what it was in the beginning, the whole spiritual creation having been accomplished, and abiding.

idea of a combination involves that of thirdness, for a combination is something which is what it is owing to the parts which it brings into mutual relationship. But we may waive that consideration, and still we cannot build up the fact that A presents C to B by any aggregate of dual relations between A and B, B and C, and C and A. A may enrich B, B may receive C, and A may part with C, and yet A need not necessarily give C to B. For that, it would be necessary that these three dual relations should not only coexist, but be welded into one fact. Thus, we see that a triad cannot be analyzed into dyads. But now I will show by an example that a four can be analyzed into threes. Take the quadruple fact that A sells C to B for the price D. This is a compound of two facts: 1st, that A makes with C a certain transaction, which we may name E; and 2nd, that this transaction E is a sale of B for the price D. Each of these two facts is a triple fact, and their combination makes up as genuine a quadruple fact as can be found. The explanation of this striking difference is not far to seek. A dual relative term, such as "lover" or "servant," is a sort of blank form, where there are two places left blank. I mean that in building a sentence round lover, as the principal word of the predicate, we are at liberty to make anything we see fit the subject, and then, besides that, anything we please the object of the action of loving. But a triple relative term such as "giver" has two correlates, and is thus a blank form with three places left blank. Consequently, we can take two of these triple relatives and fill up one blank place in each with the same letter, X, which has only the force of a pronoun or identifying index, and then the two taken together will form a whole having four blank places; and from that we can go on in a similar way to any higher number. But when we attempt to imitate this proceeding with dual relatives, and combine two of them by means of an X, we find we only have two blank places in the combination, just as we had in either of the relatives taken by itself. A road with only three-way forkings may have any number of termini, but no number of straight roads put end on end will give more than two termini. Thus any number, however large, can be built out of triads; and consequently no idea can be involved in such a number, radically different from the idea of three. I do not mean to deny that the higher numbers may present interesting special configurations from which notions may be derived of more or less general applicability; but these cannot rise to the height of philosophical categories so fundamental as those that have been considered.

The argument of this book has been developed in the mind of the author, substantially as it is presented, as a following out of these three conceptions, in a sort of game of "follow my leader" from one field of thought into another. Their importance was originally brought home to me in the study of logic, where they play so remarkable a part that I was led to look for them in psychology. Finding them there again,

I could not help asking myself whether they did not enter into the physiology of the nervous system. By drawing a little on hypothesis, I succeeded in detecting them there; and then the question naturally came how they would appear in the theory of protoplasm in general. Here I seemed to break into an interesting avenue of reflections giving instructive aperçus both into the nature of protoplasm and into the conceptions themselves; though it was not till later that I mapped out my thoughts on the subject as they are presented in Chapter V.[11] I had no difficulty in following the lead into the domain of natural selection; and once arrived at that point, I was irresistibly carried on to speculations concerning physics. One bold saltus landed me in a garden of fruitful and beautiful suggestions, the exploration of which long prevented my looking further.[12] As soon, however, as I was induced to look further, and to examine the application of the three ideas to the deepest problems of the soul, nature, and God, I saw at once that they must carry me far into the heart of those primeval mysteries. That is the way the book has grown in my mind: it is also the order in which I have written it; and only this first chapter is more or less an afterthought, since at an earlier stage of my studies I should have looked upon the matter here set down as too vague to have any value. I should have discerned in it too strong a resemblance to many a crack-brained book that I had laughed over. A deeper study has taught me that even out of the mouths of babes and sucklings strength may be brought forth, and that weak metaphysical trash has sometimes contained the germs of conceptions capable of growing up into important and positive doctrines.

Thus, the whole book being nothing but a continual exemplification of the triad of ideas, we need linger no longer upon this preliminary exposition of them. There is, however, one feature of them upon which it is quite indispensible to dwell. It is that there are two distinct grades of secondness and three grades of thirdness. There is a close analogy to this in geometry. Conic sections are either the curves usually so called, or they are pairs of straight lines. A pair of straight lines is called a degenerate conic. So plane cubic curves are either the genuine curves of the third order, or they are conics paired with straight lines, or they consist of three straight lines; so that there are two orders of degenerate cubics. Nearly in this same way, besides genuine secondness, there is a degenerate sort which does not exist as such, but is only so conceived. The medieval logicians (following a hint of Aristotle) distinguished between real relations and relations of reason. A real relation subsists in virtue of a fact which would be totally impossible were either of the related objects destroyed; while a relation of reason subsists in virtue of two facts, one only of which would disappear on the annihilation of either of the relates. Such are all resemblances: for any two objects in nature resemble each other, and indeed in themselves just as much as any other two; it is only with reference to our senses and needs that one resemblance counts for more than another. Rumford and Franklin resembled one another by virtue of being both Americans;[13] but either would have been just as much an American if the other had never lived. On the other hand, the fact that Cain killed Abel cannot be stated as a mere aggregate of two facts one concerning Cain and the other concerning Abel. Resemblances are not the only relations of reason, though they have that character in an eminent degree. Contrasts and comparisons are of the same sort. Resemblance is an identity of characters; and this is the same as to say that the mind gathers the resembling ideas together into one conception. Other relations of reason arise from ideas being connected by the mind in other ways; they consist in the relation between two parts of one complex concept, or, as we may say, in the relation of a complex concept to itself, in respect to two of its parts. This brings us to consider a sort of degenerate secondness that does not fulfill the definition of a relation of reason. Identity is the relation that everything bears to itself: Lucullus dines with Lucullus. Again, we speak of allurements and motives in the language of forces, as though a man suffered compulsion from within. So with the voice of conscience: and we observe our own feelings by a reflective sense. An echo is my own voice coming back to answer itself. So also, we speak of the abstract quality of a thing as if it were some second thing that the first thing possesses. But the relations of reason and these self-relations are alike in this, that they arise from the mind setting one part of a notion into relation to another. All degenerate seconds may be conveniently termed Internal, in contrast to External seconds, which are constituted by external fact, and are true actions of one thing upon another.

Among thirds, there are two degrees of degeneracy. The first is where there is in the fact itself no thirdness or mediation, but where there is true duality; the second degree is where there is not even true secondness in the fact itself.

Consider, first, the thirds degenerate in the first degree. A pin fastens two things together by sticking through one and also through the other: either might be annihilated, and the pin would continue to stick through the one which remained. A mixture brings its ingredients together by containing each. We may term these accidental thirds. "How did I slay thy son?" asked the merchant, and the genie replied, "When thou threwest away the date-stone, it smote my son who was passing at the time, on the breast, and he died forthright." Here there were two independent facts, first that the merchant threw away the date-stone, and second that the date-stone struck and killed the genie's son. Had it been aimed at him, the case would have been different; for then there would have been a relation of aiming which would have connected together the aimer, the thing aimed, and the object aimed at, in one fact. What monstrous injustice and inhumanity on the part of that genie to hold that poor merchant responsible for such an accident! I remember how I wept at it, as I lay in my father's arms and he first told me the story. It is certainly just that a man, even though he had no evil intention, should be held responsible for the immediate effects of his actions; but not for such as might result from them in a sporadic case here and there, but only for such as might have been guarded against by a reasonable rule of prudence. Nature herself often supplies the place of the intention of a rational agent in making a thirdness genuine and not merely accidental; as when a spark, as third, falling into a barrel of gunpowder, as first, causes an explosion, as second. But how does nature do this? By virtue of an intelligible law according to which she acts. If two forces are combined according to the parallelogram of forces, their resultant is a real third. Yet any force may, by the parallelogram of forces be mathematically resolved into the sum of two others, in an infinity of different ways. Such components, however, are mere creations of the mind. What is the difference? As far as one isolated event goes, there is none; the real forces are no more present in the resultant than any components that the mathematician may imagine. But what makes the real forces really there is the general law of nature which calls for them, and not for any other components of the resultant. Thus, intelligibility, or reason objectified, is what makes thirdness genuine.

We now come to thirds degenerate in the second degree. The dramatist Marlowe had something of that character of diction in which Shakespeare and Bacon agree. This is a trivial example; but the mode of relation is important. In natural history, intermediate types serve to bring out the resemblance between forms whose similarity might otherwise escape attention, or not be duly appreciated. In portraiture, photographs mediate between the original and the likeness. In science, a diagram or analogue of the observed fact leads on to a further analogy. The relations of reason which go to the formation of such a triple relation need not be all resemblances. Washington was eminently free from the faults in which most great soldiers resemble one another. A centaur is a mixture of a man and a horse. Philadelphia lies between New York and Washington. Such thirds may be called Intermediate thirds or Thirds of comparison.

Nobody will suppose that I wish to claim any originality in reckoning the triad important in philosophy. Since Hegel, almost every fanciful thinker has done the same. Originality is the last of recommendations for fundamental conceptions. On the contrary, the fact that the minds of men have ever been inclined to threefold divisions is one of the considerations in favor of them. Other numbers have been objects of predilection to this philosopher and that, but three has been prominent at all times and with all schools. My whole method will be found to be in profound contrast with that of Hegel; I reject his philosophy in toto.[14] Nevertheless, I have a certain sympathy with it, and fancy that if its author had only noticed a very few circumstances he would himself have been led to revolutionize his system. One of these is the double division or dichotomy of the second idea of the triad. He has usually overlooked external secondness, altogether. In other words, he has committed the trifling oversight of forgetting that there is a real world with real actions and reactions. Rather a serious oversight that. Then Hegel had the misfortune to be unusually deficient in mathematics. He shows this in the very elementary character of his reasoning. Worse still, while the whole burden of his song is that philosophers have neglected to take thirdness into account, which is true enough of the theological kind, with whom alone he was acquainted (for I do not call it acquaintance to look into a book without comprehending it), he unfortunately did not know, what it would have been of the utmost consequence for him to know, that the mathematical analysts had in great measure escaped this great fault, and that the thorough-going pursuit of the ideas and methods of the differential calculus would be sure to cure it altogether. Hegel's dialectical method is only a feeble and rudimentary application of the principles of the calculus to metaphysics. Finally Hegel's plan of evolving everything out of the abstractest conception by a dialectical procedure, though far from being so absurd as the experientialists think, but on the contrary representing one of the indispensible parts of the course of science, overlooks the weakness of individual man, who wants the strength to wield such a weapon as that.

CHAPTER III. THE TRIAD IN METAPHYSICS

I will run over all the conceptions that played an important [role] in the pre-Socratic philosophy and see how far they can be expressed in terms of one, two, three.

1. The first of all the conceptions of philosophy is that of a primal matter out of which the world is made.[15] Thales and the early Ionian philosophers busied themselves mainly with this. They called it the *arche*, the beginning; so that the conception of First was the quintessence of it. Nature was a wonder to them, and they asked its explanation; from what did it come? That was a good question, but it was rather stupid to suppose that they were going to learn much even if they could find out from what sort of matter it was made. But to ask how it had been formed, as they doubtless did, was not an exhaustive question, it would only carry them back a little way; they wished to go to the very beginning at once, and in the beginning there must have been a homogeneous something, for where there was variety they

supposed there must be always an explanation to be sought. The first must be indeterminate, and the indeterminate first of anything is the material of which it is formed. Besides, their idea was that they could not tell how the world was formed unless they knew from what to begin their account. The inductive /method/ of explaining phenomena by tracing them back step by step to their causes was foreign not only to them but to all ancient and medieval philosophy; that is the Baconian idea. Indeterminacy is really a character of the first. But not the indeterminacy of homogeneity. The first is full of life and variety. Yet that variety is only potential; it is not definitely there. Still, the notion of explaining the variety of the world, which was what they mainly wondered at, by non-variety was quite absurd. How is variety to come out of the womb of homogeneity; only by a principle of spontaneity, which is just that virtual variety that is the First.

CHAPTER IV. THE TRIAD IN PSYCHOLOGY

The line of reasoning which I propose to pursue is peculiar, and will need some careful study to estimate the strength of it. I shall review it critically in the last chapter, but meantime I desire to point out that the step I am about to take, which is analogous to others that will follow, is not so purely of the nature of a guess as might be supposed by persons expert in judging of scientific evidence. We have seen that the ideas of One, Two, Three, are forced upon us in logic, and really cannot be dispensed with. They meet us not once but at every turn. And we have found reason to think that they are equally important in metaphysics. How is the extraordinary prominence of these conceptions to be explained? Must it not be that they have their origin in the nature of the mind? This is the Kantian form of inference, which has been found so cogent in the hands of that hero of philosophy; and I do not know that modern studies have done anything to discredit it. It is true we no longer regard such a psychological explanation of a conception to be as final as Kant thought. It leaves further questions to be asked; but as far as it goes it seems to be satisfactory. We find the ideas of First, Second, Third, constant ingredients of our knowledge. It must then either be that they are continually given to us in the presentations of sense, or that it is the peculiar nature of the mind to mix them with our thoughts. Now we certainly cannot think that these ideas are given in sense. First, Second, and Third, are not sensations. They can only be given in sense by things appearing labelled as first, second, and third, and such labels things do not usually bear. They ought therefore to have a psychological origin. A man must be a very uncompromising partisan of the theory of the *tabula rasa* to deny that the ideas of first, second, and third are due to congenital tendencies of the mind. So far there is nothing in my argument to distinguish it from that of many a Kantian. The noticeable thing is that I do not rest here, but seek to put the conclusion to the test by an independent examination of the facts of psychology, to see whether we can find any traces of the existence of three parts or faculties of the soul or modes of consciousness, which might confirm the result just reached.

Now, three departments of the mind have been generally recognized since Kant; they are: Feeling, Knowing, and Willing. The unanimity with which this trisection of the mind has been accepted is, indeed, quite surprising. The division did not have its genesis in the peculiar ideas of Kant. On the contrary, it was borrowed by him from dogmatic philosophers, and his acceptance of it was, as has been well remarked, a concession to dogmatism. It has been allowed even by psychologists to whose general doctrines it seems positively hostile. This evidence that there is something true in it, is strengthened by the fact that it is impossible to make a critical examination of it, with /out/ coming to the conclusion that it is but a rough approximation to the truth, at best; and this has generally been conceded.

Where did this three-fold division of the functions of the mind come from? Kant took it ready made from the Leibnitzian writer Tetens. He drew a suggestion from the rhetoricians of the sixteenth century and they found it in an imperfect form in their idolized Plato. In Plato, it appears under a poetical garb and distorted mien which we cannot believe to have been the original one; and it is easy to credit the statement of Diogenes Laertius that it came from the school of Pythagoras. Now in the doctrine of Pythagoras everything was connected with number, which was taken to be the foundation of the world. There is a hint in its history, then, that the three-fold division of the mind may be connected with the ideas of one, two, three.

By feelings, as constituting one of the great classes of mental activities, are meant according to Kant and most psychologists feelings of pleasure and pain. This is not, however, the original doctrine of Tetens, who includes under this head all that is immediately present, or at least the subjective element of it. Kant's modification suits his peculiar system better than the truth of nature. There is no good reason for giving such a peculiar place to pleasure and pain; as if they had no resemblance to anything else that we can feel. Pleasure and pain are nothing but secondary sensations, or feelings produced by feelings, whenever the latter reach a certain degree of subjective intensity, that is, produce a certain amount of commotion in the organism. If we could pay attention enough, we should probably recognize that every exertion and every cognition produces pleasure or pain. There is pleasure in the contemplation of a theorem of geometry. Pain is perhaps essential to the consciousness of exertion; what we do without pain we do without effort. But that peculiarity of feelings which makes them one of the great branches of mental phenomena is that they form the sum total of all of which we have in immediate and instantaneous consciousness; they are what is present. We cannot be immediately conscious of what is past and gone; we only remember it, though it be past by but the hundredth of a second. No more can we be immediately conscious of what is yet to come, however close at hand it may be. We can only infer it. Of nothing but the fleeting instant can [we] have absolutely immediate consciousness, or feeling, whether much or little; and this instant is no sooner present than it is gone. In it we can be conscious of no change; because we do that by making a little rehearsal of the process or imitation of it, and that occupies time. We can draw no inference in an instant, nor can we recognize any inferential conclusion. We can neither divide nor synthetise; we can only feel. When an instant has once past, that immediate consciousness can never be recovered. It is totally and absolutely gone. We cannot compare any subsequent feeling with it, as immediate feeling, because we cannot have the second in our mind until the first has utterly gone from us. We remember it; that is to say, we have another cognition which professes to reproduce it; but we know that there is no resemblance between the memory and the sensation, because, in the first place, nothing can resemble an immediate feeling, for resemblance supposes a dismemberment and recomposition which is totally foreign to the immediate, and in the second place, memory is an articulated complex and worked-over product which differs infinitely and immeasurably from feeling. Look at a red surface, and try to feel what the sensation is, and then shut your eyes and remember it. No doubt different persons are different in this respect; to some the experiment will seem to yield an opposite result but I have convinced myself that there is nothing in my memory that is in the least like the vision of the red. When red is not before my eyes, I do not see it at all. Some people tell me they see it faintly;—a most inconvenient kind of memory, which would lead to remembering bright red as pale or dingy. I remember colours with unusual accuracy, because I have had much training in observing them; but my memory does not consist in any vision but in a habit by virtue of which I can recognize a newly presented colour as like or unlike one I had seen before. But even if the memory of some persons is of the nature of an hallucination, enough arguments remain to show that immediate consciousness or feeling is absolutely unlike anything else.

There are grave objections to making a whole third of the mind of the will alone. One great psychologist has said that the will is nothing but the strongest desire.[16] I cannot grant that; it seems to me to overlook that fact which of all that we observe is quite the most obtrusive, namely the difference between dreaming and doing. This is not a question of defining, but of noticing what we experience; and surely he who can confound desiring with willing must be a day-dreamer. The evidence, however, seems to be pretty strong that the consciousness of willing does not differ, at least not very much, from a sensation. The sense of hitting and of getting hit are nearly the same, and should be classed together. The common element is the sense of an actual occurrence, of actual action and reaction. There is an intense reality about this kind of experience, a sharp sundering of subject and object. While I am seated calmly in the dark, the lights are suddenly turned on, and at that instant I am conscious, not of a process of change, but yet of something more than can be contained in an instant. I have a sense of a saltus, of there being two sides to that instant. A consciousness of polarity would be a tolerably good phrase to describe what occurs. For will, then, as one of the great types of consciousness, we ought to substitute the polar sense.

But by far the most confused of the three members of the division, in its ordinary statement, is Cognition. In the first place every kind of consciousness enters into cognition. Feelings, in the sense in which alone they can be admitted as a great branch of mental phenomena form the warp and woof of cognition and even in the objectionable sense of pleasure and pain, they are constituents of cognition. The will, in the form of attention, constantly enters, and the sense of reality or objectivity, which is what we have found ought to take the place of will, in the division of consciousness, is even more essential yet, if possible. But that element of cognition which is neither feeling nor the polar sense, is the consciousness of a process, and this in the form of the sense of learning, of acquiring, of mental growth is eminently characteristic of cognition. This is a kind of consciousness which cannot be immediate, because it covers a time, and that not merely because it continues through every instant of that time, but because it cannot be contracted into an instant. It differs from immediate consciousness, as a melody does from one prolonged note. Neither can the consciousness of the two sides of an instant, of a sudden occurrence, in its individual reality, possibly embrace the consciousness of a process. This is the consciousness that binds our life together. It is the consciousness of synthesis.

Here then, we have indubitably three radically different elements of consciousness, these and no more. And they are evidently connected with the ideas of one-two-three. Immediate feeling is the consciousness of the first; the polar sense is the consciousness of the second; and synthetical consciousness is the consciousness of a Third or medium.

Note, too, that just as we have seen that there are two orders of secondness, so the polar sense splits into two, and that in two ways: for first, there is an active and a passive kind, or Will and Sense, and second, there are External Will and Sense, in opposition to Internal Will (self-control, inhibitory will) and Internal Sense (introspection). In like manner, just as there are three orders of thirdness, so there are three kinds of synthetical consciousness. The undegenerate and really typical form has not been made so familiar to us as the others, which have been more completely studied by psychologists; I shall therefore mention that last. Synthetical consciousness degenerate in the first degree, corresponding to accidental thirdness, is where there is an external compulsion upon us to think things together. Association by contiguity is an instance of this; but a still better instance is that in our first apprehension of our experiences, we cannot choose how we will arrange our ideas in reference to time and space, but are compelled to think certain things as nearer together than others. It would be putting the cart before the horse to say that we are compelled to think certain things together because they are together in time and space; the true way of stating it is that there is an exterior compulsion upon us to put them together in our construction of time and space, in our perspective. Synthetical consciousness degenerate in the second degree, corresponding to intermediate thirds, is where we think different feelings to be alike or different, which, since feelings in themselves cannot be compared and therefore cannot be alike, so that to say they are alike is merely to say that the synthetic consciousness regards them so, comes to this, that we are internally compelled to synthetise them or to sunder them. This kind of synthesis appears in a secondary form in association by resemblance. But the highest kind of synthesis is what the mind is compelled to make neither by the inward attractions of the feelings or representations themselves, nor by a transcendental force of haecceity, but in the interest of intelligibility, that is, in the interest of the synthetising "I think" itself; and this it does by introducing an idea not contained in the data, which gives connections which they would not otherwise have had. This kind of synthesis has not been sufficiently studied and especially the intimate relationship of its different varieties has not been duly considered. The work of the poet or novelist is not so utterly different from that of the scientific man. The artist introduces a fiction; but it is not an arbitrary one; it exhibits affinities to which the mind accords a certain approval in pronouncing them beautiful, which if it is not exactly the same as saying that the synthesis is true, is something of the same general kind. The geometer draws a diagram, which if not exactly a fiction, is at least a creation, and by means of observation of that diagram he is able to synthetise and show relations between elements which before seemed to have no necessary connection. The realities compel us to put some things into very close relation and others less so, in a highly complicated, and in the sense[17] itself unintelligible manner; but it is the genius of the mind, that takes up all these hints of sense, adds immensely to them, makes them precise, and shows them in intelligible form in the intuitions of space and time. Intuition is the regarding of the abstract in a concrete form, by the realistic hypostatisation of relations; that is the one sole method of valuable thought. Very shallow is the prevalent notion that this is something to be avoided. You might as well say at once that reasoning is to be avoided because it has led to so much error; quite in the same philistine line of thought would that be and so well in accord with the spirit of nominalism that I wonder some one does not put it forward. The true precept is not to abstain from hypostatisation, but to do it intelligently.

CHAPTER V. THE TRIAD IN PHYSIOLOGY

Granted that there are three fundamentally different kinds of consciousness, it follows as a matter of course that there must be something threefold in the physiology of the nervous system to account for them. No materialism is implied in this, further than that intimate dependence of the action of the mind upon the body, which every student of the subject must and does now acknowledge. Once more a prediction, as it were, is made by the theory; that is to say, certain consequences, not contemplated in the construction thereof, necessarily result from it; and these are of such a character that their truth or falsehood can be independently investigated. Were we to find them strikingly and certainly true, a remarkable confirmation of the theory would be afforded. So much as this, however, I cannot promise; I can only say that they are not certainly false; and we must be content to trace out these consequences, and see what they are, and leave them to the future judgment of physiologists.

Two of the three kinds of consciousness, indeed, the simple and dual, receive an instant physiological explanation. We know that the protoplasmic content of every nerve-cell has its active and passive conditions, and argument is unnecessary to show that Feeling, or immediate consciousness, arises in an active state of nerve-cells. Experiments on the effects of cutting the nerves show that there is no feeling after communication with the central nerve-cells is severed, so that the phenomenon has certainly some connection with the nerve-cells; and feeling is excited by just such stimuli as would be likely to throw protoplasm into an active condition. Thus, though we cannot say that every nerve-cell in its active condition has feeling (which we cannot deny, however), there is scarce room to doubt that the activity of nerve-cells is the main physiological requisite for consciousness. On the other hand, the sense of action and reaction, or the polar sense, as we agreed to call it, is plainly connected with the discharge of nervous energy through the nerve-fibres. External volition, the most typical case of it, involves such a discharge into muscle cells. In external sensation, where the polar sense enters in a lower intensity, there is a discharge from the terminal nerve-cell through the afferent nerve upon a cell or cells in the brain. In internal volition, or self-control, there is some inhibitory action of the nerves, which is also known to involve the movement of nervous force; and in internal observation, or visceral sensation, there are doubtless transfers of energy from one central cell to another. Remembering that the polar sense is the sense of the difference between what was before and what is after a dividing instant, or the sense of an instant as having sides, we see clearly that the physiological concomitant of it must be some event which happens very quickly and leaves a more abiding effect, and this description suits the passage of a nervous discharge over a nerve-fibre so perfectly, that I do not think we need hesitate to set this phenomenon down as the condition of dual consciousness.

Synthetic consciousness offers a more difficult problem. Yet the explanation of the genuine form of that consciousness, the sense of learning, is easy enough; it is only the degenerate modes, the sense of similarity, and the sense of real connection, which oblige us to hesitate. With regard to these two degenerate forms, I am driven to make hypotheses.

When two ideas resemble one another, we say that they have something in common; a part of the one is said to be identical with a part of the other. In what does that identity consist? Having closed both eyes, I open first one and then shut it and open the other, and I say that the two sensations are alike. How can the impressions of two nerves be judged to be alike? It appears to me that in order that that should become possible, the two nerve-cells must probably discharge themselves into one common nerve-cell. In any case, it seems to me that the first supposition to make, for scientific observation to confirm or reject, is that two ideas are alike so far as the same nerve-cells have been concerned in the production of them. In short, the hypothesis is that resemblance consists in the identity of a common element, and that that identity lies in a part of the one idea and a part of the other idea being the feeling peculiar to the excitation of one or more nerve-cells.

When we find ourselves under a compulsion to think that two elements of experience which do not particularly resemble one another are, nevertheless, really connected, that connection must, I think, be due in some way, to a discharge of nerve-energy; for the whole sense of reality is a determination of polar consciousness, which is itself due to such discharges. For example, I recognize that a certain surface, on one side of a certain boundary is red, and on the other side is blue; or that any two qualities are immediately contiguous in space or time. If the contiguity is in time, it is by the polar sense directly that we are conscious of a dividing instant with its difference on the two sides. If the contiguity is in space, I think we have at first a completely confused feeling of the whole, as yet unanalysed and unsynthetised, but afterward, when the analysis has been made, we find ourselves compelled, in recomposing the elements, to pass directly from what is on one side of the boundary to what is on the other. I suppose then that we are compelled to think the two feelings as contiguous because the nerve-cell whose excitation produces the feeling of one recalled sensation discharges itself into the nerve-cell whose excitation makes the feeling of the other recalled sensation.

The genuine synthetic consciousness, or the sense of the process of learning, which is the preeminent ingredient and quintessence of reason, has its physiological basis quite evidently in the most characteristic property of the nervous system, the power of taking habits. This depends on five principles, as follows. 1st, when a stimulus or irritation is continued for some time, the excitation spreads from the cells directly affected to those that are associated with it, and from those to others, and so on, and at the same time increases in intensity. 2nd, after a time, fatigue begins to set in. Now beside the utter fatigue which consists in the cell's losing all excitability, and the nervous system refusing to react to the stimulus at all, there is a gentler fatigue, which plays a very important part in adapting the brain to serving as an organ of reason, this form of fatigue consisting in the reflex action or discharge of the nerve-cell ceasing to go on one path and either beginning on a path where there had been no discharge, or increasing the intensity of the discharge along a path on which there had been previously only a slight discharge. For example, a frog whose cerebrum or brain has been removed, and whose hind leg has been irritated by putting a drop of acid upon it, after repeatedly rubbing the place with the other foot, as if to wipe off the acid, may at length be observed to give several hops, the first avenue of nervous discharge having become fatigued. 3rd, when from any cause the stimulus to a nerve-cell is removed, the excitation quickly subsides. That it does not do so instantly is well-known, and the phenomenon goes among physicists by the name of persistence of sensation. All noticeable feeling subsides in a fraction of a second, but a very small remnant continues for a much longer time. 4th, if the same cell which was once excited, and which by some chance had happened to discharge itself along a certain path or paths, comes to get excited a second time, it is more likely to discharge itself the second time along some or all of those paths along which it had previously discharged itself than it would have been had it not so discharged itself before. This is the central principle of habit; and the striking contrast of its modality to that of any mechanical law is most significant. The laws of physics know nothing of tendencies or probabilities; whatever they require at all they require absolutely and without fail, and they are never disobeyed. Were the tendency to take habits replaced by an absolute requirement that the cell should discharge itself always in the same way, or according to any rigidly fixed condition whatever, all possibility of habit developing into intelligence would be cut off at the outset; the virtue of thirdness would be absent. It is essential that there should be an element of chance in some sense as to how the cell shall discharge itself; and then that this chance or uncertainty shall not be entirely obliterated by the principle of habit, but only somewhat affected. 5th, when a considerable time has elapsed without a nerve having reacted in any particular way, there comes in a principle of forgetfulness or negative habit rendering it the less likely to react in that way. Now let us see what will be the result of these five principles taken in combination. When a nerve is stimulated, if the reflex activity is not at first of the right sort to remove the source of irritation, it will change its character again and again until the cause of irritation is removed, when the activity will quickly subside. When the nerve comes to be stimulated a second time in the same way, probably some of the other movements which had been made on the first occasion will be repeated; but, however this may be, one of them must ultimately be repeated, for the activity will continue until this does happen: I mean that movement which removes the source of irritation. On a third occasion, the process of forgetfulness will have been begun in regard to any tendency to repeat any of the actions of the first occasion which were not repeated on the second. Of those which were repeated, some will probably be repeated again, and some not; but always there remains that one which must be repeated before the activity comes to an end. The ultimate effect of this will inevitably be that a habit gets established of at once reacting in the way which removes the source of irritation; for this habit alone will be strengthened at each repetition of the experiment, while every other will tend to become weakened at an accelerated rate.

I have invented a little game or experiment with playing-cards to illustrate the working of these principles; and I can promise the reader that if he will try it half a dozen times he will be better able to estimate the value of the account of habit here proposed. The rules of this game are as follows. Take a good many cards of four suits, say a pack of 52, though fewer will do. The four suits are supposed to represent four modes in which a cell may react. Let one suit, say spades, represent that mode of reaction which removes the source of irritation and brings the activity to an end. In order readily to find a card of any suit as wanted, you had better lay all the cards down face up and distributed into four packets, each containing the cards of one suit only. Now take 2 spades, 2 diamonds, 2 clubs, and 2 hearts, to represent the original disposition of the nerve-cell, which is supposed to be equally likely to react in any of the four ways. You turn these 8 cards face down and shuffle them with extreme thoroughness.* Then turn up cards from the top of this pack, one by one until a spade is reached. This process represents the reaction of the cell. Take up the cards just dealt off, and add to the pack held in the hand one card of each of those suits that have just been turned up (for habit) and remove from the pack one card of each suit not turned up (for forgetfulness). Shuffle, and go through with this operation 13 times or until the spades are exhausted. It will then generally be found that you hold nothing but spades in your hand.

Thus we see how these principles not only lead to the establishment of habits, but to habits directed to definite ends, namely the removal of sources of irritation. Now it is precisely action according to final causes which distinguishes mental from mechanical action; and the general formula of all our desires may be taken as this: to remove a stimulus. Every man is busily working to bring to an end that state of things which now excites him to work.

But we are led yet deeper into physiology. The three fundamental functions of the nervous system, namely, 1st, the excitation of cells, 2nd, the transfer of excitation over fibres, 3rd, the fixing of definite tendencies under the influence of habit, are plainly due to three properties of the protoplasm or life-slime itself. Protoplasm has its active and its passive condition, its active state is transferred from one part of it to another, and it also exhibits the phenomena of habit. But these three facts do not seem to sum up the main properties of protoplasm, as our theory would lead us to expect them to do. Still, this may be because the nature of this strange substance is so little understood; and if we had the true secret of its constitution we might see that qualities that now appear unrelated really group themselves into one, so that it may be after all that it accords with our theory better than it seems to do. There have been at least two attempts to explain the properties of protoplasm by means of chemical suppositions; but inasmuch as chemical forces are as far as possible themselves from being understood, such hypotheses, even if they were known to be correct, would be of little avail. As for what a physicist would understand by a molecular explanation of protoplasm, such a thing seems hardly to have been thought of; yet I cannot see that it is any more difficult than the

---

*Cards are almost never shuffled enough to illustrate fairly the principles of probabilities; but if after being shuffled in any of the usual ways, they are dealt into three packs and taken up again, and then passed from one hand into the other one by one, every other one going to the top and every other to the bottom of the pack that thus accumulates in the second hand, and finally cut, the shuffling may be considered as sufficient for the purpose of this game. Whenever the direction is to shuffle, shuffling as thorough as this is meant.

constitution of inorganic matter. The properties of protoplasm are enumerated as follows: contractility, irritability, automatism, nutrition, metabolism, respiration, and reproduction; but these can all be summed up under the heads of sensibility, motion, and growth. These three properties are respectively first, second, and third. Let us, however, draw up a brief statement of the facts which a molecular theory of protoplasm would have to account for. In the first place, then, protoplasm is a definite chemical substance, or class of substances, recognizable by its characteristic reactions. "We do not at present," says Dr. Michael Foster (1879), "know anything definite about the molecular composition of active living protoplasm; but it is more than probable that its molecule is a large and complex one in which a proteid substance is peculiarly associated with a complex fat and with some representative of the carbohydrate group, i.e. that each molecule of protoplasm contains residues of each of these three great classes. The whole animal body is modified protoplasm."[18] The chemical complexity of the protoplasm molecule must be amazing. A proteid is only one of its constituents, and doubtless very much simpler. Yet chemists do not attempt to infer from their analyses the ultimate atomic constitution of any of the proteids, the number of atoms entering into them being so great as almost to nullify the law of multiple proportions. I do find in the book just quoted the following formula for nuclein, a substance allied to the proteids. It is $C_{29}H_{49}N_9P_3O_{22}$. But as the sum of the numbers of atoms of hydrogen, nitrogen, and phosphorus ought to be even, this formula must be multiplied by some even number; so that the number of atoms in nuclein must be 224 at the very least. We can hardly imagine, then, that the number of atoms in protoplasm is much less than a thousand, and if one considers the very minute proportions of some necessary ingredients of animal and vegetable organisms, one is somewhat tempted to suspect that 50000 might do better, or even come to /be/ looked upon in the future as a ridiculously small guess. Protoplasm combines with water in all proportions, the mode of combination being apparently intermediate between solution and mechanical mixture. According to the amount of water it contains, it passes from being brittle, to being pliable, then gelatinous, then slimy, then liquid. Generally, it has the character of being elastico-viscous; that is to say, it springs back partially after a long strain, and wholly after a short one; but its viscosity is much more marked than its elasticity. It is generally full of granules, by which we can see slow streaming motions in it, continuing for some minutes in one way and then generally reversed. The effect of this streaming is to cause protuberances in the mass, often very long and slender. They occasionally stick up against gravity; and their various forms are characteristic of the different kinds of protoplasm. When a mass of it is disturbed by a jar, a poke, an electric shock, heat, etc., the streams are arrested and the whole contracts into a ball; or if it were very much elongated sometimes breaks up into separate spheres. When the external excitation is removed, the mass sinks down into something like its former condition. Protoplasm also grows; it absorbs material and converts it into the like of its own substance; and in all its growth and reproduction, it preserves its specific characters.

Such are the properties that have to be accounted for. What first arrests our attention as likely to afford the key to the problem, is the contraction of the mass of protoplasm on being disturbed. This is obviously due to a vast and sudden increase of what the physicists call "surface tension," or the pulling together of the outer parts, which phenomenon is always observed in liquids, and is the cause of their making drops. This surface tension is due to the cohesion, or attraction between neighboring molecules. The question is, then, how can a body, on having its equilibrium deranged, suddenly increase the attractions between its neighboring molecules? These attractions must increase rapidly as the distance is diminished; and thus the answer suggests itself that the distance between neighboring molecules is diminished. True, the average distance must remain nearly the same, but if the distances which had previously been nearly equal are rendered unequal, the attractions between the molecules that are brought nearer to one another will be much more increased than those between those that are removed from one another will be diminished. We are thus led to the supposition that in the ordinary state of the substance, its particles are moving for the most part in complicated orbital or quasi-orbital systems, instead of in the chemical molecules or more definite systems of atoms of less complex substances, these particles thus moving in orbits not being, however, atoms but chemical molecules. But we must suppose that the forces between these particles are just barely sufficient to hold them in their orbits and that in fact, as long as the protoplasm is in an active condition, they are not all so held, but that one and another get occasionally thrown out of their orbits and wander about until they are drawn into some other system. We must suppose that these systems have some approximate composition, about so many of one kind of particles and so many of another kind, etc., entering into them. This is necessary to account for the nearly constant chemical composition of the whole. On the other hand, we cannot suppose that the number of the different kinds is rigidly exact; for in that case we should not know how to account for the power of assimilation. We must suppose then that there is considerable range in the numbers of particles that go to form an orbital system, and that the somewhat exact chemical composition of the whole is the exactitude of a statistical average; just as there is a close equality between the proportions of the two sexes in any nation or province, though there is considerable inequality in each of the different households. Owing to the complexity of this arrangement, the moment that there is any molecular disturbance, producing perturbations, large numbers of the particles are thrown out of their orbits, the systems are more or less deranged in the immediate neighborhood of the disturbance, and the harmonic relations between the different revolutions are somewhat broken up. In consequence of this, the distances between neighboring particles, which had presented a systematic regularity, now become extremely unequal, and their average attractions, upon which the cohesion depends, is increased. At the same time, the particles thrown out of their systems shoot into other systems and derange these in their turn, and so the disturbance is propagated throughout the entire mass. The source of disturbance, however, being removed, interchanges of energy take place, in which there is a tendency to equalise the vis viva[19] of the different particles, and they consequently tend to sink down into orbital motions again, and gradually something very like the original state of things is reestablished, the original orbital systems remaining, for the most part, and the wandering particles in large proportion finding places in these systems or forming new ones. Some of these particles will not find any places, and thus there will be a certain amount of wasting of the protoplasmic mass. If the same disturbance is repeated, so far as the orbital systems remain the same as they were before, there will /be/ a repetition of almost exactly the same events. The same kinds of particles (the same I mean in mass, velocities, directions of movement, attractions, etc.) which were thrown out of the different systems before will generally get thrown out again, until, if the disturbance is repeated several times, there gets to be rather a deficiency of those kinds of particles in the different systems, when some new kinds will begin to be thrown out. These new kinds will differently perturb the systems into which they fly, tending to cause classes of particles like themselves to be thrown out, and, in that way, the direction of propagation of the disturbance, as well as its velocity and intensity, may be altered, and, in short, the phenomenon of fatigue will be manifested. Even when the protoplasmic mass is left to itself, there will be some wandering of particles, producing regions of slight disturbance, and so inequalities of tension; and thus, streams will be set up, movements of the mass will take place, and slender processes will be formed. If, however, the mass be left to itself for a very long time, all the particles that are readily thrown out, will, in all the changes that are rung on the combinations of situations and velocities in the orbital systems, get thrown out; while the others will constantly tend to settle down into more stable relations; and so the protoplasm will gradually take a passive state from which its orbital systems are not easily deranged. The food for those kinds of protoplasm that are capable of marked reaction has to be presented in chemically complex form. It must doubtless present particles just like those that revolve in the orbital systems of the protoplasm. In order to be drawn into an orbital system, a particle whether of food matter or just thrown off from some other system, must have the right mass, must present itself at the right point, and move with the right velocity in the right direction and be subject to the right attraction. It will be right in all these respects, if it comes to take the place of a particle which has just been thrown off; and thus, particles taken in are particularly likely to be of the same material and masses and to take the same places in the orbits as those that have been shortly before thrown off. Now these particles being the exact representatives of those thrown off, will be likely to be thrown off by the same disturbances, in the same directions, and with the same results, as those which were thrown off before; and this accounts for the principle of habit. All the higher kinds of protoplasm, those for example which have any marked power of contraction, are fed with matter chemically highly complex.

CHAPTER VI. THE TRIAD IN BIOLOGICAL DEVELOPMENT

Whether the part played by natural selection and the survival of the fittest in the production of species be large or small, there remains little doubt that the Darwinian theory indicates a real cause, which tends to adapt animal and vegetable forms to their environment. A very remarkable feature of it is that it shows how merely fortuitous variations of individuals together with merely fortuitous mishaps to them would, under the action of heredity, result, not in mere irregularity, nor even in a statistical constancy, but in continual and indefinite progress toward a better adaptation of means to ends. How can this be? What, abstractly stated, is the peculiar factor in the conditions of the problem which brings about this singular consequence?

Suppose a million persons, each provided with one dollar, to sit down to play a simple and fair game of chance, betting for example on whether a die turns up an odd or even number. The players are supposed to make their bets independently of one another, and each to bet on the result of each throw one dollar against a dollar on the part of the bank. Of course, at the very first bet, one half of them would lose their only dollar and go out of the game, for it is supposed that no credit is allowed, while the other half would win each a dollar and so come to be worth $2. Of these 500000 players, after the second throw, 250000 would have lost, and so be worth only $1 each, while the other 250000 would have won, and so be worth $3. After the third throw, 125000, or one half of those who had had $1 each, would be ruined; 250000 would be worth $2 (namely one half the 250000 who had had $1 each, and one half the 250000 who had had $3 each) and 125000 would be worth $4 each. The further progress of the game is illustrated by the following table, where the numbers of players are given having each possible sum after the 1st, 2nd, 3rd, etc. throws.

	1st	2nd	3rd	4th	5th	6th	7th	8th	9th	10th	16th
$1		250000		125000		78125		$54687\frac{1}{2}$		$41015\frac{5}{8}$	21820
2	500000		250000		156250		109375		$82031\frac{1}{4}$		
3		250000		187500		140625		109375		$87890\frac{5}{8}$	52368
4			125000		125000		109375		93750		
5				62500		78125		78125		$73242\frac{3}{16}$	55542
6					31250		46875		$52734\frac{3}{8}$		
7						15625		$27343\frac{3}{4}$		$34179\frac{11}{16}$	38880
8							$7812\frac{1}{2}$		15625		
9								$3906\frac{1}{4}$		$8789\frac{1}{16}$	19226
10									$1953\frac{1}{8}$		
11										$976\frac{9}{16}$	6714
12											
13											1587
14											
15											229
16											
17											15

It will be seen by the table,[20] that at the end of the 4th throw, the most usual fortune is $3, at the end of the 9th $4, at the end of the 16th $5, and in like manner at the end of the 25th it would be $6, at the end of the 36th $7, and so forth. Here then, would be a continual increase of wealth, which is a sort of "adaptation to one's environment," produced by a survival of the fittest, that is, by the elimination from the game of every player who has lost his last dollar. It is easy to see that the increase of average and usual wealth comes about by the subtraction of all those small fortunes which would be in the hands of men who had once been bankrupt had they been allowed to continue betting.

Now the adaptation of a species to its environment consists, for the purposes of natural selection, in a power of continuing to exist, that is to say, in the power of one generation to bring forth another, for as long as another generation is brought forth the species will continue and as soon as this ceases it is doomed after one lifetime. This reproductive faculty, then, depending partly on direct fecundity, and partly on the animal's living through the age of procreation, is precisely what the Darwinian theory accounts for. This character plainly is one of those which has an absolute minimum, for no animal can produce fewer offspring than none at all and it has no apparent upper limit, so that it is quite analogous to the wealth of those players. It is to be remarked that the phrase "survival of the fittest" in the formula of the principle does not mean the survival of the fittest individuals, but the survival of the fittest types; for the theory does not at all require that individuals ill-adapted to their environment should die at an earlier age than others, so long only as they do not reproduce so many off-spring as others; and indeed it is not necessary that this should go so far as to extinguish the line of descent, provided there be some reason why the offspring of ill-adapted parents are less likely than others to inherit those parents' characteristics. It seems likely that the process, as a general rule, is something as follows. A given individual is in some respect ill-adapted to his environment, that is to say, he has characters which are generally unfavorable to the production of numerous off-spring. These characters will be apt to weaken the reproductive system of that individual, for various reasons, so that its offspring are not up to the average strength of the species. This second generation will couple with other individuals, but owing to their weakness, their offspring will be more apt to resemble the other parent, and so the unfavorable character will gradually be eliminated, not merely by diminished numbers of offspring, but also by the offspring more resembling the stronger parent. There are other ways in which the unfavorable characters will disappear. When the procreative power is weakened, there are many examples to show that the principle of heredity becomes relaxed, and the race shows more tendency to sport-ing. This sporting will go on until in the course of it the unfavorable character has become obliterated. The general power of reproduction thereupon becomes strengthened, with it the direct procreative force is reinforced, the hereditary transmission of characters again becomes more strict, and the improved type is hardened.

But all these different cases are but so many different modes of one and the same principle, which is, the elimination of unfavorable characters. We see then that there are just three factors in the process of natural selection; to wit: 1st, the principle of individual variation or sporting; 2nd, the principle of hereditary transmission, which wars against the first principle; and 3rd, the principle of the elimination of unfavorable characters.

Let us see how far these principles correspond with the triads that we have already met with. The principle of sporting is the principle of irregularity, indeterminacy, chance. It corresponds with the irregular and manifold wandering of particles in the active state of the protoplasm. It /is/ the bringing in of something fresh and first. The principle of heredity is the principle of the determination of something by what went before, the principle of compulsion, corresponding to will and sense. The principle of the elimination of unfavorable characters is the principle of generalization by a casting out of sporadic cases, corresponding particularly to the principle of forgetfulness in the action of the nervous system. We have, then, here, a somewhat imperfect reproduction of the same triad as before. Its imperfection may be the imperfection of the theory of development.

Chapter VII. The Triad in Physics

Metaphysical philosophy may almost be called the child of geometry. Of the three schools of early Greek philosophers, two, the Ionic and the Pythagorean, were all geometers, and the interest of the Eleatics in geometry is often mentioned. Plato was a great figure in the history of both subjects; and Aristotle derived from the study of space some of his most potent conceptions. Metaphysics depends in great measure on the idea of rigid demonstration from first principles; and this idea, as well in regard to the process as the axioms from which it sets out, bears its paternity on its face. Moreover, the conviction that any metaphysical philosophy is possible has been upheld at all times, as Kant well says, by the example in geometry of a similar science.

The unconditional surrender, then, by the mathematicians of our time of the absolute exactitude of the axioms of geometry cannot prove an insignificant event for the history of philosophy.[21] Gauss, the greatest of geometers, declares that "there is no reason to think that the sum of the three angles of a triangle is exactly equal to two right angles."[22] It is true, experience shows that the deviation of that sum from that amount is so excessively small that language must be ingeniously used to express the degree of approximation: but experience never can show any truth to be exact, nor so much as give the least reason to think it to be so, unless it be supported by some other considerations. We can only say that the sum of the three angles of any given triangle cannot be much greater or less than two right angles; but that exact value is only one among an infinite number of others each of which is as possible as that. So say the mathematicians with unanimity.

The absolute exactitude of the geometrical axioms is exploded; and the corresponding belief in the metaphysical axioms, considering the dependence of metaphysics on geometry, must surely follow it to the tomb of extinct creeds. The first to go must be the proposition that every event in the universe is precisely determined by causes according to inviolable law. We have no reason to think that this is absolutely exact. Experience shows that it is so to a wonderful degree of approximation, and that is all. This degree of approximation will be a value for future scientific investigation to determine; but we have no more reason to think that the error of the ordinary statement is precisely zero, than any one of an infinity of values in that neighborhood. The odds are infinity to one that it is not zero; and we are bound to think of it as a quantity of which zero is only one possible value. Phoenix, in his Lectures on Astronomy,[23] referring to Joshua's commanding the sun to stand still, said that he could not help suspecting that it might have wiggled a very little when Joshua was not looking directly at it. We know that when we try to verify any law of nature by experiment, we always find discrepancies between the observations and the theory. These we rightly refer to errors of observation; but why may there not be similar aberrations due to the imperfect obedience of the facts to law?

Grant that this is conceivable and there can be nothing in experience to negative it. Strange to say, there are many people who will have a difficulty in conceiving of an element of lawlessness in the universe, and who may perhaps be tempted to reckon the doctrine of the perfect rule of causality as one of the original instinctive beliefs, like that of space having three dimensions. Far from that, it is historically altogether a modern notion, a loose inference from the discoveries of science. Aristotle often lays it down that some things are determined by causes while others happen by chance.[24] Lucretius, following Democritus, supposes his primordial atoms to deviate from their rectilinear trajectories just fortuitously, and without any reason at all. To the ancients, there was nothing strange in such notions; they were matters of course; the strange thing would have been to have said that there was no chance. So we are under no inward necessity of believing /in/ perfect causality if we do not find any facts to bear it out.

I am very far from holding that experience is our only light; Whewell's views of scientific method seem to me truer than Mill's; so much so that I should pronounce the known principles of physics to be but a development of original instinctive beliefs. Yet I cannot help acknowledging that the whole history of thought shows that our instinctive beliefs, in their original condition are so mixed up with error, that they can never be trusted till they have been corrected by experiment. Now the only thing that the inference from experience can ever teach us is the approximate value of a ratio. It all rests on the principle of sampling; we take a handful of coffee from a bag, and we judge that there is about the same proportion of sound beans in the whole bag that there is in that sample. At this rate, every proposition which we can be entitled to make about the real world must be an approximate one; we never can have the right to hold any truth to be exact. Approximation must be the fabric out of which our philosophy has to be built.

I come now to another point. Most systems of philosophy maintain certain facts or principles as ultimate. In truth, any fact is in one sense ultimate,—that is to say, in its isolated aggressive stubbornness and individual reality. What Scotus calls the haecceities of things, the hereness and nowness of them, are indeed ultimate. Why this which is here is such as it is, how, for instance, if it happens to be a grain of sand it came to be so small and so hard, we can ask; we can also ask how it got carried here, but the explanation in this case merely carries us back to the fact that it was once in some other place, where similar things might naturally be expected to be. Why IT, independently of its general characters, comes to have any definite place in the world, is not a question to be asked; it is simply an ultimate fact. There is also another class of facts of which it is not reasonable to expect an explanation, namely, facts of indeterminacy or variety. Why one definite kind of event is frequent and another rare, is a question to be asked, but a reason for the general fact that of events some kinds are common and some rare, it would be unfair to demand. If all births took place on a given day of the week, or if there were always more on Sundays than on Mondays, that would be a fact to be accounted for, but that they happen in about equal proportions on all the days requires no particular explanation. If we were to find that all the grains of sand on a certain beach separated themselves into two or more sharply discrete classes, as spherical and cubical ones, there would be something to be explained, but that they are of various sizes and shapes, of no definable character, can only be referred to the general manifoldness of nature. Indeterminacy, then, or pure firstness, and haecceity, or pure secondness, are facts not calling for and not capable of explanation. Indeterminacy affords us nothing to ask a question about; haecceity is the *ultima ratio,* the brutal fact that will not be questioned. But every fact of a general or orderly nature calls for an explanation; and logic forbids us to assume in regard to any given fact of that sort that it is of its own nature absolutely inexplicable. This is what Kant* calls a regulative principle, that is to say, an intellectual hope.[25] The sole immediate purpose of thinking is to render things intelligible; and to think and yet in that very act to think a thing unintelligible is a self-stultification. It is as though a man furnished with a pistol to defend himself against an enemy were, on finding that enemy very redoubtable, to use his pistol to blow his own brains out to escape being killed by his enemy. Despair is insanity. True, there may be facts that will never get explained; but that any given fact is of the number, is what experience can never give us reason to think; far less can it show that any fact is of its own nature unintelligible. We must therefore be guided by the rule of hope, and consequently we must reject every philosophy or general conception of the universe, which could ever lead to the conclusion that any given general fact is an ultimate one. We must look

*After the scholastics. See Eckius in Petr. Hisp. 48 b nota 1.

forward to the explanation, not of all things, but of any given thing whatever. There is no contradiction here, any more than there is in our holding each one of our opinions, while we are ready to admit that it is probable that not all are true; or any more than there is in saying that any future time will sometime be passed, though there never will be a time when all time is past.

Among other regular facts that have to be explained is Law or regularity itself. We enormously exaggerate the part that law plays in the universe. It is by means of regularities that we understand what little we do understand of the world, and thus there is a sort of mental perspective which brings regular phenomena to the foreground. We say that every event is determined by causes according to law. But apart from the fact that this must not be regarded as absolutely true, it does not mean so much as it seems to do. We do not mean, for example, that if a man and his antipode both sneeze at the same instant, that event comes under any general law. That is merely what we call a coincidence. But what we mean is there was a cause for the first man's sneezing, and another cause for the second man's sneezing; and the aggregate of these two events make up the first event about which we began by inquiring. The doctrine is that the events of the physical universe are merely motions of matter, and that these obey the laws of dynamics. But this only amounts to saying that among the countless systems of relationship existing among things we have found one that is universal and at the same time is subject to law. There is nothing except this singular character which makes this particular system of relationship any more important than the others. From this point of view, uniformity is seen to be really a highly exceptional phenomenon. But we pay no attention to irregular relationships, as having no interest for us.

We are brought, then, to this: conformity to law exists only within a limited range of events and even there is not perfect, for an element of pure spontaneity or lawless originality mingles, or at least, must be supposed to mingle, with law everywhere. Moreover, conformity with law is a fact requiring to be explained; and since Law in general cannot be explained by any law in particular, the explanation must consist in showing how law is developed out of pure chance, irregularity, and indeterminacy.

To this problem we are bound to address ourselves; and it is particularly needful to do so in the present state of science. The theory of the molecular constitution of matter has now been carried as far as there are clear indications to direct us, and we are now in the mists. To develope the mathematical consequences of any hypothesis as to the nature and laws of the minute parts of matter, and then to test it by physical experiment, will take fifty years; and out of the innumerable hypotheses that might be framed, there seems to be nothing to make one more antecedently probable than another. At this rate how long will it take to make any decided advance? We need some hint as to how molecules may be expected to behave; whether for instance, they would be likely to attract or repel one another inversely as the fifth power of the distance, so that we may be saved from many false suppositions, if we are not at once shown the way to the true one. Tell us how the laws of nature came about, and we may distinguish in some measure between laws that might and laws that could not have resulted from such a process of development.

To find that out is our task. I will begin the work with this guess. Uniformities in the modes of action of things have come about by their taking habits. At present, the course of events is approximately determined by law. In the past that approximation was less perfect; in the future it will be more perfect. The tendency to obey laws has always been and always will be growing. We look back toward a point in the infinitely distant past when there was no law but mere indeterminacy; we look forward to a point in the infinitely distant future when there will be no indeterminacy or chance but a complete reign of law. But at any assignable date in the past, however early, there was already some tendency toward uniformity; and at any assignable date in the future there will be some slight aberrancy from law. Moreover, all things have a tendency to take habits. For atoms and their parts, molecules and groups of molecules, and in short every conceivable real object, there is a greater probability of acting as on a former like occasion than otherwise. This tendency itself constitutes a regularity, and is continually on the increase. In looking back into the past we are looking towards periods when it was a less and less decided tendency. But its own essential nature is to grow. It is a generalizing tendency; it causes actions in the future to follow some generalization of past actions; and this tendency is itself something capable of similar generalization; and thus, it is self-generative. We have therefore only to suppose the smallest spur of it in the past, and that germ would have been bound to develope into a mighty and over-ruling principle, until it supersedes itself by strengthening habits into absolute laws regulating the action of all things in every respect in the indefinite future.

According to this, three elements are active in the world, first, chance; second, law; and third, habit-taking.

Such is our guess of the secret of the sphinx. To raise it from the rank of a philosophical speculation to that of a scientific hypothesis, we must show that consequences can be deduced from it with more or less probability which can be compared with observation. We must show that there is some method of deducing the characters of the laws which could result in this way by the action of habit-taking on purely fortuitous occurrences, and a method of ascertaining whether such characters belong to the actual laws of nature.

The existence of things consists in their regular behaviour. If an atom had no regular attractions and repulsions, if its mass was at one instant nothing, at another a ton, at another a negative quantity, if its motion instead of being continuous, consisted in a series of leaps from one place to another without passing through any intervening places, and if there were no definite relations between its different positions, velocities and directions of displacement, if it were at one time in one place and at another time in a dozen, such a disjointed plurality of phenomena would not make up any existing thing. Not only substances, but events, too, are constituted by regularities. The flow of time, for example, in itself is a regularity. The original chaos, therefore, where there was no regularity, was in effect a state of mere indeterminacy, in which nothing existed or really happened.

Our conceptions of the first stages of the development, before time yet existed, must be as vague and figurative as the expressions of the first chapter of Genesis. Out of the womb of indeterminacy we must say that there would have come something by the principle of firstness, which we may call a flash. Then by the principle of habit there would have been a second flash. Though time would not yet have been, this second flash was in some sense after the first, because resulting from it. Then there would have come other successions ever more and more closely connected, the habits and the tendency to take them ever strengthening themselves, until the events would have been bound together into something like a continuous flow. We have no reason to think that even now time is quite perfectly continuous and uniform in its flow. The quasi-flow which would result would, however, differ essentially from time in this respect, that it would not necessarily be in a single stream. Different flashes might start different streams, between which there should be no relations of contemporaneity or succession. So one stream might branch into two, or two might coalesce. But the further result of habit would inevitably be to separate utterly those that were long separated, and to make those which presented frequent common points coalesce into perfect union. Those that were completely separated would be so many different worlds which would know nothing of one another; so that the effect would be just what we actually observe.

But secondness is of two types. Consequently, besides flashes genuinely second to others, so as to come after them, there will be pairs of flashes, or, since time is now supposed to be developed, we had better say pairs of states, which are reciprocally second, each member of the pair to the other. This is the first germ of spatial extension. These states will undergo changes; and habits will be formed of passing from certain states to certain others, and of not passing from certain states to certain others. Those states to which a state will immediately pass, will be adjacent to it; and thus habits will be formed which will constitute a spatial continuum, but differing from our space by being very irregular in its connections, having one number of dimensions in one place and another number in another place, and being different for one moving state from what it is for another.

Pairs of states will also begin to take habits, and thus each state having different habits with reference to the different other states, will give rise to bundles of habits, which will be substances.* Some of these states will chance to take habits of persistency, and will get to be less and less liable to disappear; while those that fail to take such habits will fall out of existence. Thus, substances will get to be permanent.

In fact, habits, from the mode of their formation necessarily consist in the permanence of some relation, and therefore on this theory, each law of nature would consist in some permanence, such as the permanence of mass, momentum, and energy. In this respect, the theory suits the facts admirably.

The substances carrying their habits with them in their motions through space, will tend to render the different parts of space alike. Thus, the dimensionality of space will tend gradually to uniformity; and multiple connections, except at infinity, where substances never go, will be obliterated. At the outset, the connections of space were probably different for one substance and part of a substance from what they were for another; that is to say, points adjacent or near one another for the motions of one body would not be so for another; and this may possibly have contributed to break substances into little pieces or atoms. But the mutual actions of bodies would have tended to reduce their habits to uniformity in this respect; and besides there must have arisen conflicts between the habits of bodies and the habits of parts of space, which would never have ceased till they were brought into conformity.

*I use substance, here, in the old sense of a thing, not in the modern chemical sense.

20

Trichotomic

MS 1600. [Previously unpublished.] Written (probably for oral presentation) in early 1888, shortly after the completion of item 19, this three-page typescript (found in one of the thirteen boxes of MS 1600) is a sort of summary of some of the main points of "A Guess at the Riddle." In addition, it includes a discussion of Peirce's categories applied to signs (a topic that had been projected for the unwritten second chapter of the "Guess") and a comparison of his views, on the subject of dramatic expression and the principles of being, with those of the New York playwright and theater manager Steele MacKaye. The title of the paper is one of the alternatives Peirce had considered for his projected "One, Two, Three," which then became "A Guess at the Riddle."

TRICHOTOMIC is the art of making three-fold divisions. Such division depends on the conceptions of 1st, 2nd, 3rd. First is the beginning, that which is fresh, original, spontaneous, free. Second is that which is determined, terminated, ended, correlative, object, necessitated, reacting. Third is the medium, becoming, developing, bringing about.

A thing considered in itself is a unit. A thing considered as a correlate or dependent, or as an effect, is second to something else. A thing which in any way brings one thing into relation with another is a third or medium between the two.

Firstness or freshness may have manifold varieties, or rather arbitrariness and variety is its essence, but it is absolute and unsusceptible of differences of degree. It may be present more or less, but it has no different orders of complication in itself. Secondness, on the other hand, may be genuine or degenerate. Degenerate secondness has two varieties, for a single object considered as second to itself is a degenerate second, and an object considered as second to another with which it has no real connection, so that were that other taken away it would still have those same characters which are implied in the relation, is also a degenerate second. Genuine secondness is dynamical connection; degenerate secondness is a relation of reason, as a mere resemblance. Thirdness has two different orders of degeneracy. Genuine thirdness is where of the three terms A, B, C, each is related to each of the others, but by a relation which only subsists by virtue of the third term, and each has a character which belongs to it only so long as the others really influence it. It would not be enough to say that the connection between the terms is dynamical, for forces only subsist between pairs of objects; we had better use the word "vital" to express the mode of connection, for wherever there is life, generation, growth, development, there and there alone is such genuine thirdness. Thirdness of the first order of degeneracy is where two of the three terms are identical, so that the other only mediates between two aspects of the same object or where in some other way there is no vital connection between A, B, and C, but only a dynamical connection between A and B, and another between B and C, thus bringing about a dynamical connection between A and C. The second order of degeneracy is where there is not even any dynamical connection between the terms, or at least where the thirdness does not consist in that [although it may be necessary for the establishment of the thirdness] but where all three terms are virtually identical or are connected by mere relations of reason.

Expression is a kind of representation or signification. A sign is a third mediating between the mind addressed and the object represented. If the thirdness is undegenerate, the relation of the sign to the thing signified is one which only subsists by virtue of the relation of the sign to the mind addressed; that is to say, the sign is related to its object by virtue of a mental association. Conventional modes of expression, and other modes dependent on the force of association, enter largely into every art. They make up the bulk of language. If the thirdness is degenerate in the first degree, the sign mediates between the object and the mind by virtue of dynamical connections with the object on the one hand and with the mind on the other. This is the only kind of sign which can demonstrate the reality of things, or distinguish between things exactly alike. As I am walking alone on a dark night, a man suddenly jumps out of a corner with a "Boh!" and thus brings his presence home to me in a particularly forcible manner. It would be impossible to follow a geometrical proof without the letters which are attached to the different parts of the figure and thus forcibly direct the attention to the right object. So a desired frame of mind on the part of the audience is often brought about by the dramatist in a forcible way by directly affecting the nervous system, without appealing to association; or the attention of the audience may be awakened, as a clergyman shouts out the commencement of a new head to his sermon, or may be directed to a particular part of the stage, as the jugglers do. If the thirdness is degenerate in the second[1] degree, the idea in the mind addressed, the object represented, and the representation of it, are only connected by a mutual resemblance. The sign is a likeness; and this is the main mode of representation in all art. Here there is no sharp discrimination between the sign and the thing signified, the mind floats in an ideal world and does not ask or care whether it be real or not. This character makes a striking point of difference between this kind of representation and the second; and that is why the use of the second mode of representation is so unartistic. Again, the third mode of representation is unanalytic, it presents the total object as it exists in the concrete, and not merely abstract relations and points in that object; and this constitutes a marked contrast from the first mode of representation; and this is what makes the first mode of representation unartistic. Mr. Mackaye divides dramatic expression into pantomime, voice, and language.[2] A person would at first glance make the division into speech and gesture, and this would doubtless answer some purposes better. But with reference to the value of the different instruments at our command it is important to make a division which shall correspond as nearly as may be with the different kinds of representation. Now language is in the main representation by the force of association; it involves the analysis of whatever is to be conveyed [on the part of the hearer as well as on the part of the author] and the separate expression of abstract points. Voice, on the other hand, awakes attention, directs it to particular channels, calls up feelings, and modifies consciousness generally, in a physiological way in the main; and is therefore a mode of expression of the second kind. Pantomime alone is mainly representation of the purely artistic kind, to be contemplated without analysis and without discrimination of the sign from the thing signified. Pantomime may itself be divided, on the same principle, into three varieties; artistic pantomime which merely exhibits the man, his general disposition and what there is uppermost in him at the moment, and is to be contemplated without analysis; dynamical pantomime, as where one points with finger or shakes or holds up the finger to impress what one is saying, or when one shakes the fist, or knocks the interlocutor down; and sign-language, mostly (owing to the peculiar nature of pantomime) of an imitative kind but yet involving analysis and being really rather language than pantomime proper.

CONSCIOUSNESS has three elements, Single, Dual, and Plural consciousness. Single or simple consciousness is consciousness as it can exist in a single instant, the consciousness of all that is immediately present, for which all that is not immediately present is an absolute blank. This is the pure Feeling which forms the warp and woof of consciousness, or in Kant's phrase its matter.[3] In this kind of consciousness subject and object are nowise discriminated, in fact there is no discrimination, no parts, no analysis, there is no considering a thing for anything else, no relation, no representation, but just a pure indescribable quale which is gone in the twinkling of an eye and which bears no resemblance to any memory of it. It is just the quality of the immediately present, which is continually pouring through us, always here but never stopping to be examined. It is always fresh, always new, sporting in unbounded manifoldness. Dual consciousness is a sense of another, not present, a sense of hitting and of getting hit, of action and reciprocal reaction, of energy. This is the most wide-awake kind of consciousness; it strenuously sets object over against subject, in place of the dreamy failure to recognize the situation which belongs to Feeling. Dual consciousness includes Will, but the consciousness of hitting and /that/ of being hit have been shown by conclusive experiments not to differ, and Sense in its direct reference to an object is likewise consciousness of action and reaction. It is the energetic and real character of the dual consciousness that principally distinguishes it. It consists of a sense of "can" which is at the same time a sense of "cannot." Force implies resistance, and power limitation. There is always an opposite, always a but, always a second, in the dual consciousness. It has nothing to do with may-be's; it is always right there. Plural or synthetic consciousness, is not the mere feeling of what is immediately present, nor yet the mere sense of something without, but is the being aware of the bridge which unites the present and the absent, of a Process as such. Zeno showed how motion is impossible if you refuse to open the eyes of the synthetic consciousness. It is the perception of motion and change. I am soundly asleep and my bed-clothes take fire. At first, the warmth merely tinges my consciousness, so to speak; that is pure Feeling; then I become energetically conscious of something and start up without knowing what it is; that is Dual consciousness, Sense with Will; last I begin to collect myself, I am aware of a process of learning, I put things together; that is Perception and Synthetic consciousness, which collects present and absent into a whole.

Dual consciousness, because it is consciousness of a second, has two degrees, the dynamical and the statical or degenerate form. Dynamical dual consciousness consists of outward action and reaction, External Sense and Volition; statical dual consciousness consists of inward action and reaction, Self-consciousness and Self-control. Plural consciousness because it is consciousness of a third, has two degrees of degeneracy. The genuine synthetic consciousness, the consciousness of that which has its being in its thirdness, is Reason. The dynamical variety is a consciousness of a coordination between acts of sense and will, it is the looking upon the phenomena of sense and will as rational, which we may call Desire, though that does not precisely define it. The statical variety is the comparison of feelings, and may be called esthetic understanding.

Mr. Mackaye's division of the principles of being has considerable resemblance with this. What he calls the vital or passional principle, which sustains life, seems to be nearly what I call the simple consciousness of Feeling; what he calls the affectional or impulsive principle is my dual consciousness plus Desire and minus Sense; what he calls Reflection is probably Reason with the esthetic understanding.[4]

The functions of the Nervous System are three, corresponding to the three kinds of consciousness. They are, first, Irritability, for the capacity of a nerve-cell to be thrown into an excited condition is undoubtedly the physiological ground of feeling; second, the power of conveying nervous disturbance over the nerve-fibres, for it is by this property of the nerves that we are placed in relation with the outward world; and third, power of acquiring habits, which is the ground of our faculty of learning.

The properties of protoplasm in general are three, first, its capacity of being thrown into a state in which it is more liquid and at the same time has a stronger cohesion and surface-tension; second, the tendency of this condition to spread throughout the entire mass; and third, its power, when passing into or out of this condition, of assimilating new material, provided this is presented so as to be subject to the same forces as that which is deranged,—in other words the power of growth with all that that implies.

21

The Architecture of Theories

P 439: The Monist *1 (January 1891):161–76. [Also published in CP 6.7–34.] This is the first of five papers (although at least one more had been projected, and "The Reply to the Necessitarians" mentioned in the headnote to item 22 should be considered a companion piece to that item) in the* Monist Metaphysical Series, *in which Peirce fully applied to metaphysical questions the evolutionary philosophy developed in "A Guess at the Riddle." (The chapter on metaphysics in item 19 is a mere outline.) The architectonic approach of the "Guess" is here explained and defended, and Peirce examines a number of conceptions to determine which ones "ought to form the brick and mortar of a philosophical system." He then reviews many of the essential ideas of the "Guess," again using his categories to organize his examination of different sciences, and demonstrates that philosophy requires thoroughgoing evolutionism, that mental phenomena fall into three classes (feelings, sensations of reaction, and general conceptions), that the fundamental law of mental action is that feelings and ideas tend to spread, and that "the one intelligible theory of the universe is that of objective idealism, that matter is effete mind." Peirce concludes that chance and continuity are two of the most fundamental ideas on which to build a philosophical theory that is compatible with modern science.*

Of the fifty or hundred systems of philosophy that have been advanced at different times of the world's history, perhaps the larger number have been, not so much results of historical evolution, as happy thoughts which have accidentally[1] occurred to their authors. An idea which has been found interesting and fruitful has been adopted, developed, and forced to yield explanations of all sorts of phenomena. The English have been particularly given to this way of philosophising; witness, Hobbes, Hartley, Berkeley, James Mill. Nor has it been by any means useless labor; it shows us what the true nature and value of the ideas developed are, and in that way affords serviceable materials for philosophy. Just as if a man, being seized with the conviction that paper was a good material to make things of, were to go to work to build a *papier mâché* house, with roof of roofing-paper, foundations of pasteboard, windows of paraffined paper, chimneys, bath tubs, locks, etc., all of different forms of paper, his experiment would probably afford valuable lessons to builders, while it would certainly make a detestable house, so those one-idea'd philosophies are exceedingly interesting and instructive, and yet are quite unsound.

The remaining systems of philosophy have been of the nature of reforms, sometimes amounting to radical revolutions, suggested by certain difficulties which have been found to beset systems previously in vogue; and such ought certainly to be in large part the motive of any new theory. This is like partially rebuilding a house. The faults that have been committed are, first, that the dilapidations have generally not been sufficiently thoroughgoing, and second, that not sufficient pains has been taken to bring the additions into deep harmony with the really sound parts of the old structure.

When a man is about to build a house, what a power of thinking he has to do, before he can safely break ground! With what pains he has to excogitate the precise wants that are to be supplied! What a study to ascertain the most available and suitable materials, to determine the mode of construction to which those materials are best adapted, and to answer a hundred such questions! Now without riding the metaphor too far, I think we may safely say that the studies preliminary to the construction of a great theory should be at least as deliberate and thorough as those that are preliminary to the building of a dwelling-house.

That systems ought to be constructed architectonically has been preached since Kant, but I do not think the full import of the maxim has by any means been apprehended. What I would recommend is that every person who wishes to form an opinion concerning fundamental problems, should first of all make a complete survey of human knowledge, should take note of all the valuable ideas in each branch of science, should observe in just what respect each has been successful and where it has failed, in order that in the light of the thorough acquaintance so attained of the available materials for a philosophical theory and of the nature and strength of each, he may proceed to the study of what the problem of philosophy consists in, and of the proper way of solving it. I must not be understood as endeavoring to state fully all that these preparatory studies should embrace; on the contrary, I purposely slur over many points, in order to give emphasis to one special recommendation, namely, to make a systematic study of the conceptions out of which a philosophical theory may be built, in order to ascertain what place each conception may fitly occupy in such a theory, and to what uses it is adapted.

The adequate treatment of this single point would fill a volume, but I shall endeavor to illustrate my meaning by glancing at several sciences and indicating conceptions in them serviceable for philosophy. As to the results to which long studies thus commenced have led me, I shall just give a hint at their nature.

We may begin with dynamics,—field in our day of perhaps the grandest conquest human science has ever made,—I mean the law of the conservation of energy. But let us revert to the first step taken by modern scientific thought,—and a great stride it was,—the inauguration of dynamics by Galileo. A modern physicist on examining Galileo's works is surprised to find how little experiment had to do with the establishment of the foundations of mechanics. His principal appeal is to common sense and *il lume naturale*. [2] He always assumes that the true theory will be found to be a simple and natural one. And we can see why it should indeed be so in dynamics. For instance, a body left to its own inertia, moves in a straight line, and a straight line appears to us the simplest of curves. In *itself*, no curve is simpler than another. A system of straight lines has intersections precisely corresponding to those of a system of like parabolas similarly placed, or to those of any one of an infinity of systems of curves. But the straight line appears to us simply, because, as Euclid says, it lies evenly between its extremities; that is, because viewed endwise it appears as a point. That is, again, because light moves in straight lines. Now, light moves in straight lines because of the part which the straight line plays in the laws of dynamics. Thus it is that our minds having been formed under the influence of phenomena governed by the laws of mechanics, certain conceptions entering into those laws become implanted in our minds, so that we readily guess at what the laws are. Without such a natural prompting, having to search blindfold for a law which would suit the phenomena, our chance of finding it would be as one to infinity. The further physical studies depart from phenomena which have directly influenced the growth of the mind, the less we can expect to find the laws which govern them "simple," that is, composed of a few conceptions natural to our minds.

The researches of Galileo, followed up by Huygens and others, led to those modern conceptions of *Force* and *Law*, which have revolutionised the intellectual world. The great attention given to mechanics in the seventeenth century soon so emphasised these conceptions as to give rise to the Mechanical Philosophy, or doctrine that all the phenomena of the physical universe are to be explained upon mechanical principles. Newton's great discovery imparted a new impetus to this tendency. The old notion that heat consists in an agitation of corpuscles was now applied to the explanation of the chief properties of gases. The first suggestion in this direction was that the pressure of gases is explained by the battering of the particles against the walls of the containing vessel, which explained Boyle's law of the compressibility of air.[3] Later, the expansion of gases, Avogadro's chemical law,[4] the diffusion and viscosity of gases, and the action of Crookes's radiometer[5] were shown to be consequences of the same kinetical theory; but other phenomena, such as the ratio of the specific heat at constant volume to that at constant pressure, require additional hypotheses, which we have little reason to suppose are simple, so that we find ourselves quite afloat. In like manner with regard to light, that it consists of vibrations was almost proved by the phenomena of diffraction, while those of polarisation showed the excursions of the particles to be perpendicular to the line of propagation; but the phenomena of dispersion, etc., require additional hypotheses which may be very complicated. Thus, the further progress of molecular speculation appears quite uncertain. If hypotheses are to be tried haphazard, or simply because they will suit certain phenomena, it will occupy the mathematical physicists of the world say half a century on the average to bring each theory to the test, and since the number of possible theories may go up into the trillions, only one of which can be true, we have little prospect of making further solid additions to the subject in our time. When we come to atoms, the presumption in favor of a simple law seems very slender. There is room for serious doubt whether the fundamental laws of mechanics hold good for single atoms, and it seems quite likely that they are capable of motion in more than three dimensions.

To find out much more about molecules and atoms, we must search out a natural history of laws of nature, which may fulfill that function which the presumption in favor of simple laws fulfilled in the early days of dynamics, by showing us what kind of laws we have to expect and by answering such questions as this: Can we with reasonable prospect of not wasting time,[6] try the supposition that atoms attract one another inversely as the seventh power of their distances, or can we not? To suppose universal laws of nature capable of being apprehended by the mind and yet having no reason for their special forms, but standing inexplicable and irrational, is hardly a justifiable position. Uniformities are precisely the sort of facts that need to be accounted for. That a pitched coin should sometimes turn up heads and sometimes tails calls for no particular explanation; but if it shows heads every time, we wish to know how this result has been brought about. Law is *par excellence* the thing that wants a reason.

Now the only possible way of accounting for the laws of nature and for uniformity in general is to suppose them results of evolution. This supposes them not to be absolute, not to be obeyed precisely. It makes an element of indeterminacy, spontaneity, or absolute chance in nature. Just as, when we attempt to verify any physical law, we find our observations cannot be precisely satisfied by it, and rightly attribute the discrepancy to errors of observation, so we must suppose far more minute discrepancies to exist owing to the imperfect cogency of the law itself, to a certain swerving of the facts from any definite formula.

Mr. Herbert Spencer wishes to explain evolution upon mechanical principles.[7] This is illogical, for four reasons. First, because the principle of evolution requires no extraneous cause; since the tendency to growth can be supposed itself to have grown from an infinitesimal germ accidentally started. Second, because law ought more than anything else to be supposed a result of evolution. Third, because exact law obviously never can produce heterogeneity out of homogeneity; and arbitrary heterogeneity is the feature of the universe the most manifest and characteristic. Fourth, because the law of the conservation of energy is equivalent to the proposition that all operations governed by mechanical laws are reversible; so that an immediate corollary from it is that growth is not explicable by those laws, even if they be not violated in the process of growth. In short, Spencer is not a philosophical evolutionist, but only a half-evolutionist,—or, if you will, only a semi-Spencerian.[8] Now philosophy requires thorough-going evolutionism or none.

The theory of Darwin was that evolution had been brought about by the action of two factors: first, heredity, as a principle making offspring nearly resemble their parents, while yet giving room for "sporting," or accidental variations,—for very slight variations often, for wider ones rarely; and, second, the destruction of breeds or races that are unable to keep the birth rate up to the death rate. This Darwinian principle is plainly capable of great generalisation. Wherever there are large numbers of objects, having a tendency to retain certain characters unaltered, this tendency, however, not being absolute but giving room for chance variations, then, if the amount of variation is absolutely limited in certain directions by the destruction of everything which reaches those limits, there will be a gradual tendency to change in directions of departure from them. Thus, if a million players sit down to bet at an even game, since one after another will get ruined, the average wealth of those who remain will perpetually increase.[9] Here is indubitably a genuine formula of possible evolution, whether its operation accounts for much or little in the development of animal and vegetable species.

The Lamarckian theory also supposes that the development of species has taken place by a long series of insensible changes, but it supposes that those changes have taken place during the lives of the individuals, in consequence of effort and exercise, and that reproduction plays no part in the process except in preserving these modifications.[10] Thus, the Lamarckian theory only explains the development of characters for which individuals strive, while the Darwinian theory only explains the production of characters really beneficial to the race, though these may be fatal to individuals.* But more broadly and philosophically conceived, Darwinian evolution is evolution by the operation of chance, and the destruction of bad results, while Lamarckian evolution is evolution by the effect of habit and effort.

A third theory of evolution is that of Mr. Clarence King.[11] The testimony of monuments and of rocks is that species are unmodified or scarcely modified, under ordinary circumstances, but are rapidly altered after cataclysms or rapid geological changes. Under novel circumstances, we often see animals and plants sporting excessively in reproduction, and sometimes even undergoing transformations during individual life, phenomena no doubt due partly to the enfeeblement of vitality from the breaking up of habitual modes of life, partly to changed food, partly to direct specific influence of the element in which the organism is immersed. If evolution has been brought about in this way, not only have its single steps not been insensible, as both Darwinians and Lamarckians suppose, but they are furthermore neither haphazard on the one hand, nor yet determined by an inward striving on the other, but on the contrary are effects of the changed environment, and have a positive general tendency to adapt the organism to that environment, since variation will particularly affect organs at once enfeebled and stimulated. This mode of evolution, by external forces and the breaking up of habits, seems to be called for by some of the broadest and most important facts of biology and paleontology; while it certainly has been the chief factor in the historical evolution of institutions as in that of ideas; and cannot possibly be refused a very prominent place in the process of evolution of the universe in general.

Passing to psychology, we find the elementary phenomena of mind fall into three categories. First, we have Feelings, comprising all that is immediately present, such as pain, blue, cheerfulness, the feeling that arises when we contemplate a consistent theory, etc. A feeling is a state of mind having its own living quality, independent of any other state of mind. Or, a feeling is an element of consciousness which might conceivably override every other state until it monopolised the mind, although such a rudimentary state cannot actually be realized, and would not properly be consciousness. Still, it is conceivable, or supposable, that the quality of blue should usurp the whole mind, to the exclusion of the ideas of shape, extension, contrast, commencement and cessation, and all other ideas, whatsoever. A feeling is necessarily perfectly simple, *in itself,* for if it had parts these would also be in the

*The neo-Darwinian, Weismann, has shown that mortality would almost necessarily result from the action of the Darwinian principle.[12]

mind, whenever the whole was present, and thus the whole could not monopolise the mind.*

Besides Feelings, we have Sensations of reaction; as when a person blindfold suddenly runs against a post, when we make a muscular effort, or when any feeling gives way to a new feeling. Suppose I had nothing in my mind but a feeling of blue, which were suddenly to give place to a feeling of red; then, at the instant of transition there would be a shock, a sense of reaction, my blue life being transmuted into red life. If I were further endowed with a memory, that sense would continue for some time, and there would also be a peculiar feeling or sentiment connected with it. This last feeling might endure (conceivably I mean) after the memory of the occurrence and the feelings of blue and red had passed away. But the *sensation* of reaction cannot exist except in the actual presence of the two feelings blue and red to which it relates. Wherever we have two feelings and pay attention to a relation between them of whatever kind, there is the sensation of which I am speaking. But the sense of action and reaction has two types: it may either be a perception of relation between two ideas, or it may be a sense of action and reaction between feeling and something out of feeling. And this sense of external reaction again has two forms; for it is either a sense of something happening to us, by no act of ours, we being passive in the matter, or it is a sense of resistance, that is, of our expending feeling upon something without. The sense of reaction is thus a sense of connection or comparison between feelings, either, *A*, between one feeling and another, or *B*, between feeling and its absence or lower degree; and under *B* we have, First, the sense of the access of feeling, and Second, the sense of remission of feeling.

Very different both from feelings and from reaction-sensations or disturbances of feeling are general conceptions. When we think, we are conscious that a connection between feelings is determined by a general rule, we are aware of being governed by a habit. Intellectual power is nothing but facility in taking habits and in following them in cases essentially analogous to, but in non-essentials widely remote from, the normal cases of connections of feelings under which those habits were formed.

The one primary and fundamental law of mental action consists in a tendency to generalisation. Feeling tends to spread; connections between feelings awaken feelings; neighboring feelings become assimilated; ideas are apt to reproduce themselves. These are so many formulations of the one law of the growth of mind. When a disturbance of feeling takes place, we have a consciousness of gain, the gain of experience; and a new disturbance will be apt to assimilate itself to the

---

*A feeling may certainly be compound, but only in virtue of a perception which is not that feeling nor any feeling at all.

one that preceded it. Feelings, by being excited, become more easily excited, especially in the ways in which they have previously been excited. The consciousness of such a habit constitutes a general conception.

The cloudiness of psychological notions may be corrected by connecting them with physiological conceptions. Feeling may be supposed to exist, wherever a nerve-cell is in an excited condition. The disturbance of feeling, or sense of reaction, accompanies the transmission of disturbance between nerve-cells or from a nerve-cell to a muscle-cell or the external stimulation of a nerve-cell. General conceptions arise upon the formation of habits in the nerve-matter, which are molecular changes consequent upon its activity and probably connected with its nutrition.

The law of habit exhibits a striking contrast to all physical laws in the character of its commands. A physical law is absolute. What it requires is an exact relation. Thus, a physical force introduces into a motion a component motion to be combined with the rest by the parallelogram of forces; but the component motion must actually take place exactly as required by the law of force. On the other hand, no exact conformity is required by the mental law. Nay, exact conformity would be in downright conflict with the law; since it would instantly crystallise thought and prevent all further formation of habit. The law of mind only makes a given feeling *more likely* to arise. It thus resembles the "non-conservative" forces of physics, such as viscosity and the like, which are due to statistical uniformities in the chance encounters of trillions of molecules.

The old dualistic notion of mind and matter, so prominent in Cartesianism, as two radically different kinds of substance, will hardly find defenders to-day. Rejecting this, we are driven to some form of hylopathy, otherwise called monism. Then the question arises whether physical laws on the one hand, and the psychical law on the other are to be taken—

(A) as independent, a doctrine often called *monism,* but which I would name *neutralism;* or,

(B) the psychical law as derived and special, the physical law alone as primordial, which is *materialism;* or,

(C) the physical law as derived and special, the psychical law alone as primordial, which is *idealism.*

The materialistic doctrine seems to me quite as repugnant to scientific logic as to common sense; since it requires us to suppose that a certain kind of mechanism will feel, which would be a hypothesis absolutely irreducible to reason,—an ultimate, inexplicable regularity; while the only possible justification of any theory is that it should make things clear and reasonable.

Neutralism is sufficiently condemned by the logical maxim known as Ockham's razor, i.e., that not more independent elements are to be supposed than necessary. By placing the inward and outward aspects of substance on a par, it seems to render both primordial.

The one intelligible theory of the universe is that of objective idealism, that matter is effete mind, inveterate habits becoming physical laws. But before this can be accepted it must show itself capable of explaining the tridimensionality of space, the laws of motion, and the general characteristics of the universe, with mathematical clearness and precision; for no less should be demanded of every Philosophy.

Modern mathematics is replete with ideas which may be applied to philosophy. I can only notice one or two. The manner in which mathematicians generalise is very instructive. Thus, painters are accustomed to think of a picture as consisting geometrically of the intersections of its plane by rays of light from the natural objects to the eye. But geometers use a generalised perspective. For instance, in the figure let O be the eye, let $A\ B\ C\ D\ E$ be the edgewise view of any plane, and let $a\ f\ e\ D\ c$ be the edgewise view of another plane. The geometers draw

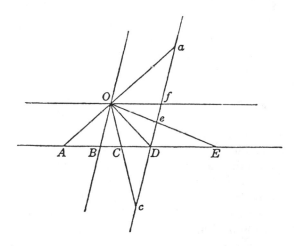

rays through O cutting both these planes, and treat the points of intersection of each ray with one plane as representing the point of intersection of the same ray with the other plane. Thus, e represents E, in the painter's way. D represents itself. C is represented by c, which is further from the eye; and A is represented by a which is on the other side of the eye. Such generalisation is not bound down to sensuous images. Further, according to this mode of representation every point on one plane represents a point on the other, and every point on the latter is represented by a point on the former. But how about the point f which is in a direction from O parallel to the represented plane, and how about the point B which is in a direction parallel to the representing plane? Some will say that these are exceptions; but modern mathematics does not allow exceptions which can be annulled by generalisation. As a point moves from C to D and thence to E and off toward infinity, the corresponding point on the other plane moves from c to D and thence to e and toward f. But this second point can pass through f to a, and when it is there the first point has arrived at A. We therefore say that the first point has passed *through infinity*, and that every line joins in to itself somewhat like an oval. Geometers talk of the parts of lines at an infinite distance as points. This is a kind of generalisation very efficient in mathematics.

Modern views of measurement have a philosophical aspect. There is an indefinite number of systems of measuring along a line; thus, a perspective representation of a scale on one line may be taken to measure another, although of course such measurements will not agree with what we call the distances of points on the latter line. To establish a system of measurement on a line we must assign a distinct number to each point of it, and for this purpose we shall plainly have to suppose the numbers carried out into an infinite number of places of decimals. These numbers must be ranged along the line in unbroken sequence. Further, in order that such a scale of numbers should be of any use, it must be capable of being shifted into new positions, each number continuing to be attached to a single distinct point. Now it is found that if this is true for "imaginary" as well as for real points (an expression which I cannot stop to elucidate), any such shifting will necessarily leave two numbers attached to the same points as before. So that when the scale is moved over the line by any continuous series of shiftings of one kind, there are two points which no numbers on the scale can ever reach, except the numbers fixed there. This pair of points, thus unattainable in measurement, is called the Absolute. These two points may be distinct and real, or they may coincide, or they may be both imaginary. As an example of a linear quantity with a double absolute we may take probability, which ranges from an unattainable absolute certainty *against* a proposition to an equally unattainable absolute certainty *for* it. A line, according to ordinary notions, we have seen is a linear quantity where the two points at infinity coincide. A velocity is another example. A train going with infinite velocity from Chicago to New York would be at all the points on the line at the very same instant, and if the time of transit were reduced to less than nothing it would be moving in the other direction. An angle is a familiar example of a mode of magnitude with no real immeasurable values. One of the questions philosophy has to consider is whether the development of the universe is like the increase of an angle, so that it proceeds forever without tending toward anything unattained, which I take to be the Epicurean view, or whether the universe sprang from a chaos in the infinitely distant past to tend toward something different in the infinitely distant future, or whether the universe sprang from nothing in the past to go on indefinitely toward a point in the infinitely distant future, which, were it attained, would be the mere nothing from which it set out.

The doctrine of the absolute applied to space comes to this, that either—

First, space is, as Euclid teaches, both *unlimited* and *immeasurable*, so that the infinitely distant parts of any plane seen in perspective appear as a straight line, in which case the sum of the three angles of a triangle amounts to 180°; or,

Second, space is *immeasurable* but *limited*, so that the infinitely distant parts of any plane seen in perspective appear as a circle, beyond which all is blackness, and in this case the sum of the three angles of a triangle is less than 180° by an amount proportional to the area of the triangle; or,

Third, space is *unlimited* but *finite* (like the surface of a sphere), so that it has no infinitely distant parts; but a finite journey along any straight line would bring one back to his original position, and looking off with an unobstructed view one would see the back of his own head enormously magnified, in which case the sum of the three angles of a triangle exceeds 180° by an amount proportional to the area.

Which of these three hypotheses is true we know not. The largest triangles we can measure are such as have the earth's orbit for base, and the distance of a fixed star for altitude. The angular magnitude resulting from subtracting the sum of the two angles at the base of such a triangle from 180° is called the star's *parallax*. The parallaxes of only about forty stars have been measured as yet. Two of them come out negative, that of Arided (α Cycni), a star of magnitude $1\frac{1}{2}$, which is $-0.''082$, according to C. A. F. Peters, and that of a star of magnitude $7\frac{3}{4}$, known as Piazzi III 422, which is $-0.''045$ according to R. S. Ball.[13] But these negative parallaxes are undoubtedly to be attributed to errors of observation; for the probable error of such a determination is about $\pm 0.''075$, and it would be strange indeed if we were to be able to see, as it were, more than half way round space, without being able to see stars with larger negative parallaxes. Indeed, the very fact that of all the parallaxes measured only two come out negative would be a strong argument that the smallest parallaxes really amount to $+0.''1$, were it not for the reflexion that the publication of other negative parallaxes may have been suppressed. I think we may feel confident that the parallax of the furthest star lies somewhere between $-0.''05$ and $+0.''15$, and within another century our grandchildren will surely know whether the three angles of a triangle are greater or less than 180°,—that they are *exactly* that amount is what nobody ever can be justified in concluding. It is true that according to the axioms of geometry the sum of the three angles of a triangle is[14] precisely 180°; but these axioms are now exploded, and geometers confess that they, as geometers, know not the slightest reason for supposing them to be precisely true. They are expressions of our inborn conception of space, and as such are entitled to credit, so far as their truth could have influenced the formation of the mind. But that affords not the slightest reason for supposing them exact.

Now, metaphysics has always been the ape of mathematics. Geometry suggested the idea of a demonstrative system of absolutely certain philosophical principles; and the ideas of the metaphysicians have at all times been in large part drawn from mathematics. The metaphysical axioms are imitations of the geometrical axioms; and now that the latter have been thrown overboard, without doubt the former will be sent after them. It is evident, for instance, that we can have no reason to think that every phenomenon in all its minutest details is precisely determined by law. That there is an arbitrary element in the universe we see,—namely, its variety. This variety must be attributed to spontaneity in some form.

Had I more space, I now ought to show how important for philosophy is the mathematical conception of continuity.[15] Most of what is true in Hegel is a darkling glimmer of a conception which the mathematicians had long before made pretty clear, and which recent researches have still further illustrated.

Among the many principles of Logic which find their application in Philosophy, I can here only mention one. Three conceptions are perpetually turning up at every point in every theory of logic, and in the most rounded systems they occur in connection with one another. They are conceptions so very broad and consequently indefinite that they are hard to seize and may be easily overlooked. I call them the conceptions of First, Second, Third. First is the conception of being or existing independent of anything else. Second is the conception of being relative to, the conception of reaction with, something else. Third is the conception of mediation, whereby a first and second are brought into relation. To illustrate these ideas, I will show how they enter into those we have been considering. The origin of things, considered not as leading to anything, but in itself, contains the idea of First, the end of things that of Second, the process mediating between them that of Third. A philosophy which emphasises the idea of the One, is generally a dualistic philosophy in which the conception of Second receives exaggerated attention; for this One (though of course involving the idea of First) is always the other of a manifold which is not one. The idea of the Many, because variety is arbitrariness and arbitrariness is repudiation of any Secondness, has for its principal component the conception of First. In psychology Feeling is First, Sense of reaction Second, General conception Third, or mediation. In biology, the idea of arbitrary sporting is First, heredity is Second, the process whereby the accidental characters become fixed is Third. Chance is First, Law is Second, the tendency to take habits is Third. Mind is First, Matter is Second, Evolution is Third.

Such are the materials out of which chiefly a philosophical theory ought to be built, in order to represent the state of knowledge to which the nineteenth century has brought us. Without going into other important questions of philosophical architectonic, we can readily foresee what sort of a metaphysics would appropriately be constructed from those conceptions. Like some of the most ancient and some of the most recent speculations it would be a Cosmogonic Philosophy. It would suppose that in the beginning,—infinitely remote,—there was a chaos of unpersonalised feeling, which being without connection or regularity would properly be without existence. This feeling, sporting here and there in pure arbitrariness, would have started the germ of a generalising tendency. Its other sportings would be evanescent, but this would have a growing virtue. Thus, the tendency to habit would be started; and from this with the other principles of evolution all the regularities of the universe would be evolved. At any time, however, an element of pure chance survives and will remain until the world becomes an absolutely perfect, rational, and symmetrical system, in which mind is at last crystallised in the infinitely distant future.

That idea has been worked out by me with elaboration. It accounts for the main features of the universe as we know it,—the characters of time, space, matter, force, gravitation, electricity, etc. It predicts many more things which new observations can alone bring to the test. May some future student go over this ground again, and have the leisure to give his results to the world.

22

The Doctrine of Necessity Examined

P 474: The Monist *2 (April 1892):321–37. [Also published in CP 6.35–65; see also the companion piece to this item, Peirce's lengthy "Reply to the Necessitarians" (6.588–618), a reply to two articles published in the July and October 1892 issues by Paul Carus, editor of the* Monist.*] In this paper, Peirce considers—and then rejects—the main arguments for determinism, and he concludes that an element of absolute chance prevails in the world. He names his anti-necessitarian doctrine 'tychism' and argues that "tychism must give birth to an evolutionary cosmology, in which all the regularities of nature and mind are regarded as products of growth."*

In *The Monist* for January 1891, I endeavored to show what elementary ideas ought to enter into our view of the universe.[1] I may mention that on those considerations I had already grounded a cosmical theory, and from it had deduced a considerable number of consequences capable of being compared with experience. This comparison is now in progress, but under existing circumstances must occupy many years.

I propose here to examine the common belief that every single fact in the universe is precisely determined by law. It must not be supposed that this is a doctrine accepted everywhere and at all times by all rational men. Its first advocate appears to have been Democritus the atomist, who was led to it, as we are informed, by reflecting upon the "impenetrability, translation, and impact of matter (ἀντιτυπία καὶ φορὰ καὶ πληγὴ τῆς ὕλης)."[2] That is to say, having restricted his attention to a field where no influence other than mechanical constraint could possibly come before his notice, he straightway jumped to the conclusion that throughout the universe that was the sole principle of action,—a style of reasoning so usual in our day with men not unreflecting as to be more than excusable in the infancy of thought. But Epicurus, in revising the atomic doctrine and repairing its defences, found himself obliged to suppose that atoms swerve from their courses by spontaneous chance; and thereby he conferred upon the theory life and entelechy.[3] For we now see clearly that the peculiar function of the molecular hypothesis in physics is to open an entry for the calculus of probabilities. Already, the prince of philosophers had repeatedly and emphatically condemned the dictum of Democritus (especially in the *Physics*, Book II, chapters iv, v, vi), holding that events come to pass in three ways, namely, (1) by external compulsion, or the action of efficient causes, (2) by virtue of an inward nature, or the influence of final causes, and (3) irregularly without definite cause, but just by absolute chance; and this doctrine is of the inmost essence of Aristotelianism. It affords, at any rate, a valuable enumeration of the possible ways in which anything can be supposed to have come about. The freedom of the will, too, was admitted both by Aristotle and by Epicurus.[4] But the Stoa, which in every department seized upon the most tangible, hard, and lifeless element, and blindly denied the existence of every other, which, for example, impugned the validity of the inductive method and wished to fill its place with the *reductio ad absurdum*, very naturally became the one school of ancient philosophy to stand by a strict necessitarianism, thus returning to the single principle of Democritus that Epicurus had been unable to swallow.[5] Necessitarianism and materialism with the Stoics went hand in hand, as by affinity they should. At the revival of learning, Stoicism met with considerable favor, partly because it departed just enough from Aristotle to give it the spice of novelty, and partly because its superficialities well adapted it for acceptance by students of literature and art who wanted their philosophy drawn mild. Afterwards, the great discoveries in mechanics inspired the hope that mechanical principles might suffice to explain the universe; and though without logical justification, this hope has since been continually stimulated by subsequent advances in physics. Nevertheless, the doctrine was in too evident conflict with the freedom of the will and with miracles to be generally acceptable, at first. But meantime there arose that most widely spread of philosophical blunders, the notion that associationalism belongs intrinsically to the materialistic family of doctrines; and thus was evolved the theory of motives; and libertarianism became weakened. At present, historical criticism has almost exploded the miracles, great and small; so that the doctrine of necessity has never been in so great vogue as now.

The proposition in question is that the state of things existing at any time, together with certain immutable laws, completely determine the state of things at every other time (for a limitation to *future* time is indefensible). Thus, given the state of the universe in the original nebula, and given the laws of mechanics, a sufficiently powerful mind could deduce from these data the precise form of every curlicue of every letter I am now writing.

Whoever holds that every act of the will as well as every idea of the mind is under the rigid governance of a necessity coördinated with that of the physical world, will logically be carried to the proposition that minds are part of the physical world in such a sense that the laws of mechanics determine everything that happens according to immutable attractions and repulsions. In that case, that instantaneous state of things from which every other state of things is calculable consists in the positions and velocities of all the particles at any instant. This, the usual and most logical form of necessitarianism, is called the mechanical philosophy.

When I have asked thinking men what reason they had to believe that every fact in the universe is precisely determined by law, the first answer has usually been that the proposition is a "presupposition" or postulate of scientific reasoning. Well, if that is the best that can be said for it, the belief is doomed. Suppose it be "postulated": that does not make it true, nor so much as afford the slightest rational motive for yielding it any credence. It is as if a man should come to borrow money, and when asked for his security, should reply he "postulated" the loan. To "postulate" a proposition is no more than to hope it is true. There are, indeed, practical emergencies in which we act upon assumptions of certain propositions as true, because if they are not so, it can make no difference how we act. But all such propositions I take to be hypotheses of individual facts. For it is manifest that no universal principle can in its universality be comprised[6] in a special case or can be requisite for the validity of any ordinary inference. To say, for instance, that the demonstration by Archimedes of the property of the lever would fall to the ground if men were endowed with free will, is extravagant; yet this is implied by those who make a proposition incompatible with the freedom of the will the postulate of all inference. Considering, too, that the conclusions of science make no pretence to being more than probable, and considering that a probable inference can at most only suppose something to be most frequently, or otherwise approximately, true, but never that anything is precisely true without exception throughout the universe, we see how far this proposition in truth is from being so postulated.

But the whole notion of a postulate being involved in reasoning appertains to a by-gone and false conception of logic. Non-deductive, or ampliative inference is of three kinds: induction, hypothesis, and analogy. If there be any other modes, they must be extremely unusual and highly complicated, and may be assumed with little doubt to be of the same nature as those enumerated. For induction, hypothesis, and analogy, as far as their ampliative character goes, that is, so far as they conclude something not implied in the premises, depend upon one principle and involve the same procedure. All are essentially inferences from sampling. Suppose a ship arrives in Liverpool laden with wheat in bulk. Suppose that by some machinery the whole cargo be stirred up with great thoroughness. Suppose that twenty-seven thimblefuls be taken equally from the forward, midships, and aft parts, from the starboard, centre, and larboard parts, and from the top, half depth, and lower parts of her hold, and that these being mixed and the grains counted, four-fifths of the latter are found to be of quality *A*. Then we infer, experientially and provisionally, that approximately four-fifths of all the grain in the cargo is of the same quality. I say we infer this *experientially* and *provisionally*. By saying that we infer it *experientially*, I mean that our conclusion makes no pretension to knowledge of wheat-in-itself, our ἀλήθεια, as the derivation of that word implies, has nothing to do with *latent* wheat. We are dealing only with the matter of possible experience,—experience in the full acceptation of the term as something not merely affecting the senses but also as the subject of thought. If there be any wheat hidden on the ship, so that it can neither turn up in the sample nor be heard of subsequently from purchasers,—or if it be half-hidden, so that it may, indeed, turn up, but is less likely to do so than the rest,—or if it can affect our senses and our pockets, but from some strange cause or causelessness cannot be reasoned about,—all such wheat is to be excluded (or have only its proportional weight) in calculating that true proportion of quality *A*, to which our inference seeks to approximate. By saying that we draw the inference *provisionally*, I mean that we do not hold that we have reached any assigned degree of approximation as yet, but only hold that if our experience be indefinitely extended, and if every fact of whatever nature, as fast as it presents itself, be duly applied, according to the inductive method, in correcting the inferred ratio, then our approximation will become indefinitely close in the long run; that is to say, close to the experience *to come* (not merely close by the exhaustion of a finite collection) so that if experience in general is to fluctuate irregularly to and fro, in a manner to deprive the ratio sought of all definite value, we shall be able to find out approximately within what limits it fluctuates, and if, after having one definite value, it changes and assumes another, we shall be able to find that out, and in short, whatever may be the variations of this ratio in experience, experience indefinitely extended will enable us to detect them, so as to predict rightly, at last, what its ultimate value may be, if it have any ultimate value, or what the ultimate law of succession of values may be, if there be any such ultimate law, or that it ultimately fluctuates irregularly within certain limits, if it do so ultimately fluctuate. Now our inference, claiming to be no more than thus experiential and provisional, manifestly involves no postulate whatever.

For what is a postulate? It is the formulation of a material fact which we are not entitled to assume as a premise, but the truth of which is requisite to the validity of an inference. Any fact, then, which might be supposed postulated, must either be such that it would ultimately present itself in experience, or not. If it will present itself, we need not postulate it now in our provisional inference, since we shall ultimately be entitled to use it as a premise. But if it never would present itself in experience, our conclusion is valid but for the possibility of this fact being otherwise than assumed, that is, it is valid as far as possible experience goes, and that is all that we claim. Thus, every postulate is cut off, either by the provisionality or by the experientiality of our inference. For instance, it has been said that induction postulates that, if an indefinite succession of samples be drawn, examined, and thrown back each before the next is drawn, then in the long run every grain will be drawn as often as any other, that is to say postulates that the ratio of the numbers of times in which any two are drawn will indefinitely approximate to unity. But no such postulate is made; for if, on the one hand, we are to have no other experience of the wheat than from such drawings, it is the ratio that presents itself in those drawings and not the ratio which belongs to the wheat in its latent existence that we are endeavoring to determine; while if, on the other hand, there is some other mode by which the wheat is to come under our knowledge, equivalent to another kind of sampling, so that after all our care in stirring up the wheat, some experiential grains will present themselves in the first sampling operation more often than others in the long run, this very singular fact will be sure to get discovered by the inductive method, which must avail itself of every sort of experience; and our inference, which was only provisional, corrects itself at last. Again, it has been said that induction postulates that under like circumstances like events will happen, and that this postulate is at bottom the same as the principle of universal causation. But this is a blunder, or *bevue*, due to thinking exclusively of inductions where the concluded ratio is either 1 or 0. If any such proposition were postulated, it would be that under like circumstances (the circumstances of drawing the different samples) different events occur in the same proportions in all the different sets,—a proposition which is false and even absurd. But in truth no such thing is postulated, the experiential character of the inference reducing the condition of validity to this, that if a certain result does not occur, the opposite result will be manifested, a condition assured by the provisionality of the inference. But it may be asked whether it is not conceivable that every instance of a certain class destined to be ever employed as a datum of induction should have one character, while every instance destined not to be so employed should have the opposite character. The answer is that in that case, the instances excluded from being subjects of reasoning would not be experienced in the full sense of the word, but would be among these *latent* individuals of which our conclusion does not pretend to speak.

To this account of the rationale of induction I know of but one objection worth mention: it is that I thus fail to deduce the full degree of force which this mode of inference in fact possesses; that according to my view, no matter how thorough and elaborate the stirring and mixing process had been, the examination of a single handful of grain would not give me any assurance, sufficient to risk money upon, that the next handful would not greatly modify the concluded value of the ratio under inquiry, while, in fact, the assurance would be very high that this ratio was not greatly in error. If the true ratio of grains of quality *A* were 0.80 and the handful contained a thousand grains, nine such handfuls out of every ten would contain from 780 to 820 grains of quality *A*. The answer to this is that the calculation given is correct when we know that the units of this handful and the quality inquired into have the normal independence of one another, if for instance the stirring has been complete and the character sampled for has been settled upon in advance of the examination of the sample. But in so far as these conditions are not known to be complied with, the above figures cease to be applicable. Random sampling and predesignation of the character sampled for should always be striven after in inductive reasoning, but when they cannot be attained, so long as it is conducted honestly, the inference retains some value. When we cannot ascertain how the sampling has been done or the sample-character selected, induction still has the essential validity which my present account of it shows it to have.

I do not think a man who combines a willingness to be convinced with a power of appreciating an argument upon a difficult subject can resist the reasons which have been given to show that the principle of universal necessity cannot be defended as being a postulate of reasoning. But then the question immediately arises whether it is not proved to be true, or at least rendered highly probable, by observation of nature.

Still, this question ought not long to arrest a person accustomed to reflect upon the force of scientific reasoning. For the essence of the necessitarian position is that certain continuous quantities have certain exact values. Now, how can observation determine the value of such a quantity with a probable error absolutely *nil?* To one who is behind the scenes, and knows that the most refined comparisons of masses, lengths, and angles, far surpassing in precision all other measurements, yet fall behind the accuracy of bank-accounts, and that the ordinary determinations of physical constants, such as appear from month to month in the journals, are about on a par with an upholsterer's measurements of carpets and curtains, the idea of mathematical exactitude being demonstrated in the laboratory will appear simply ridiculous. There is a recognised method of estimating the probable magnitudes of errors in physics,—the method of least squares. It is universally admitted that this method makes the errors smaller than they really are; yet even according to that theory an error indefinitely small is indefinitely improbable; so that any statement to the effect that a certain continuous quantity has a certain exact value, if well-founded at all, must be founded on something other than observation.

Still, I am obliged to admit that this rule is subject to a certain qualification. Namely, it only applies to continuous* quantity. Now, certain kinds of continuous quantity are discontinuous at one or at two limits, and for such limits the rule must be modified. Thus, the length of a line cannot be less than zero. Suppose, then, the question arises how long a line a certain person had drawn from a marked point on a piece of paper. If no line at all can be seen, the observed length is zero; and the only conclusion this observation warrants is that the length of the line is less than the smallest length visible with the optical power employed. But indirect observations,—for example, that the person supposed to have drawn the line was never within fifty feet of the paper,—may make it probable that no line at all was made, so that the concluded length will be strictly zero. In like manner, experience no doubt would warrant the conclusion that there is absolutely *no* indigo in a given ear of wheat, and absolutely *no* attar in a given lichen. But such inferences can only be rendered valid by positive experiential evidence, direct or remote, and cannot rest upon a mere inability to detect the quantity in question. We have reason to think there is no indigo in the wheat, because we have remarked that wherever indigo is produced it is produced in considerable quantities, to mention only one argument. We have reason to think there is no attar in the lichen, because essential oils seem to be in general peculiar to single species. If the question had been whether there was iron in the wheat or the lichen, though chemical analysis should fail to detect its presence, we should think some of it probably was there, since iron is almost everywhere. Without any such information, one way or the other, we could only abstain from any opinion as to the presence of the substance in question. It cannot, I conceive, be maintained that we are in any *better* position than this in regard to the presence of the element of chance or spontaneous departures from law in nature.

Those observations which are generally adduced in favor of mechanical causation simply prove that there is an element of regularity in nature, and have no bearing whatever upon the question of whether such regularity is exact and universal, or not. Nay, in regard to this *exactitude*, all observation is directly *opposed* to it; and the most that can be said is that a good deal of this observation can be explained away. Try to verify any law of nature, and you will find that the more precise your observations, the more certain they will be to show irregular

---

*Continuous is not exactly the right word, but I let it go to avoid a long and irrelevant discussion.

departures from the law. We are accustomed to ascribe these, and I do not say wrongly, to errors of observation; yet we cannot usually account for such errors in any antecedently probable way. Trace their causes back far enough, and you will be forced to admit they are always due to arbitrary determination, or chance.

But it may be asked whether if there were an element of real chance in the universe it must not occasionally be productive of signal effects such as could not pass unobserved. In answer to this question, without stopping to point out that there is an abundance of great events which one might be tempted to suppose were of that nature, it will be simplest to remark that physicists hold that the particles of gases are moving about irregularly, substantially as if by real chance, and that by the principles of probabilities there must occasionally happen to be concentrations of heat in the gases contrary to the second law of thermodynamics, and these concentrations, occurring in explosive mixtures, must sometimes have tremendous effects. Here, then, is in substance the very situation supposed; yet no phenomena ever have resulted which we are forced to attribute to such chance concentration of heat, or which anybody, wise or foolish, has ever dreamed of accounting for in that manner.

In view of all these considerations, I do not believe that anybody, not in a state of case-hardened ignorance respecting the logic of science, can maintain that the precise and universal conformity of facts to law is clearly proved, or even rendered particularly probable, by any observations hitherto made. In this way, the determined advocate of exact regularity will soon find himself driven to *a priori* reasons to support his thesis. These received such a socdolager from Stuart Mill in his *Examination of Hamilton,*[7] that holding to them now seems to me to denote a high degree of imperviousness to reason; so that I shall pass them by with little notice.

To say that we cannot help believing a given proposition is no argument, but it is a conclusive fact if it be true; and with the substitution of "I" for "we," it is true in the mouths of several classes of minds, the blindly passionate, the unreflecting and ignorant, and the person who has overwhelming evidence before his eyes. But that which has been inconceivable to-day has often turned out indisputable on the morrow. Inability to conceive is only a stage through which every man must pass in regard to a number of beliefs,—unless endowed with extraordinary obstinacy and obtuseness. His understanding is enslaved to some blind compulsion which a vigorous mind is pretty sure soon to cast off.

Some seek to back up the *a priori* position with empirical arguments. They say that the exact regularity of the world is a natural belief, and that natural beliefs have generally been confirmed by experience. There is some reason in this. Natural beliefs, however, if they generally have a foundation of truth, also require correction and purification from natural illusions. The principles of mechanics are undoubtedly natural beliefs; but, for all that, the early formulations of them were exceedingly erroneous. The general approximation to truth in natural beliefs is, in fact, a case of the general adaptation of genetic products to recognisable utilities or ends. Now, the adaptations of nature, beautiful and often marvellous as they verily are, are never found to be quite perfect; so that the argument is quite *against* the absolute exactitude of any natural belief, including that of the principle of causation.

Another argument, or convenient commonplace, is that absolute chance is *inconceivable*. This word has eight current significations. The *Century Dictionary* enumerates six.[8] Those who talk like this will hardly be persuaded to say in what sense they mean that chance is inconceivable. Should they do so, it would easily be shown either that they have no sufficient reason for the statement or that the inconceivability is of a kind which does not prove that chance is non-existent.

Another *a priori* argument is that chance is unintelligible; that is to say, while it may perhaps be conceivable, it does not disclose to the eye of reason the how or why of things; and since a hypothesis can only be justified so far as it renders some phenomenon intelligible, we never can have any right to suppose absolute chance to enter into the production of anything in nature. This argument may be considered in connection with two others. Namely, instead of going so far as to say that the supposition of chance can *never* properly be used to explain any observed fact, it may be alleged merely that no facts are known which such a supposition could in any way help in explaining. Or again, the allegation being still further weakened, it may be said that since departures from law are not unmistakably observed, chance is not a *vera causa*, and ought not unnecessarily to be introduced into a hypothesis.

These are no mean arguments, and require us to examine the matter a little more closely. Come, my superior opponent, let me learn from your wisdom. It seems to me that every throw of sixes with a pair of dice is a manifest instance of chance.

"While you would hold a throw of deuce-ace to be brought about by necessity?" [The opponent's supposed remarks are placed in quotation marks.]

Clearly one throw is as much chance as another.

"Do you think throws of dice are of a different nature from other events?"

I see that I must say that *all* the diversity and specificalness of events is attributable to chance.

"Would you, then, deny that there is any regularity in the world?"

That is clearly undeniable. I must acknowledge there is an approximate regularity, and that every event is influenced by it. But the diversification, specificalness, and irregularity of things I suppose is chance. A throw of sixes appears to me a case in which this element is particularly obtrusive.

"If you reflect more deeply, you will come to see that *chance* is only a name for a cause that is unknown to us."

Do you mean that we have no idea whatever what kind of causes could bring about a throw of sixes?

"On the contrary, each die moves under the influence of precise mechanical laws."

But it appears to me that it is not these *laws* which made the die turn up sixes; for these laws act just the same when other throws come up. The chance lies in the diversity of throws; and this diversity cannot be due to laws which are immutable.

"The diversity is due to the diverse circumstances under which the laws act. The dice lie differently in the box, and the motion given to the box is different. These are the unknown causes which produce the throws, and to which we give the name of chance; not the mechanical law which regulates the operation of these causes. You see you are already beginning to think more clearly about this subject."

Does the operation of mechanical law not increase the diversity?

"Properly not. You must know that the instantaneous state of a system of particles is defined by six times as many numbers as there are particles, three for the coördinates of each particle's position, and three more for the components of its velocity. This number of numbers, which expresses the amount of diversity in the system, remains the same at all times. There may be, to be sure, some kind of relation between the coördinates and component velocities of the different particles, by means of which the state of the system might be expressed by a smaller number of numbers. But, if this is the case, a precisely corresponding relationship must exist between the coördinates and component velocities at any other time, though it may doubtless be a relation less obvious to us. Thus, the intrinsic complexity of the system is the same at all times."

Very well, my obliging opponent, we have now reached an issue. You think all the arbitrary specifications of the universe were introduced in one dose, in the beginning, if there was a beginning, and that the variety and complication of nature has always been just as much as it is now. But I, for my part, think that the diversification, the specification, has been continually taking place. Should you condescend to ask me why I so think, I should give my reasons as follows:

1) Question any science which deals with the course of time. Consider the life of an individual animal or plant, or of a mind. Glance at the history of states, of institutions, of language, of ideas. Examine the successions of forms shown by paleontology, the history of the globe as set forth in geology, of what the astronomer is able to make out

concerning the changes of stellar systems. Everywhere the main fact is growth and increasing complexity. Death and corruption are mere accidents or secondary phenomena. Among some of the lower organisms, it is a moot point with biologists whether there be anything which ought to be called death. Races, at any rate, do not die out except under unfavorable circumstances. From these broad and ubiquitous facts we may fairly infer, by the most unexceptionable logic, that there is probably in nature some agency by which the complexity and diversity of things can be increased; and that consequently the rule of mechanical necessity meets in some way with interference.

2) By thus admitting pure spontaneity or life as a character of the universe, acting always and everywhere though restrained within narrow bounds by law, producing infinitesimal departures from law continually, and great ones with infinite infrequency, I account for all the variety and diversity of the universe, in the only sense in which the really *sui generis* and new can be said to be accounted for. The ordinary view has to admit the inexhaustible mulitudinous variety of the world, has to admit that its mechanical law cannot account for this in the least, that variety can spring only from spontaneity, and yet denies without any evidence or reason the existence of this spontaneity, or else shoves it back to the beginning of time and supposes it dead ever since. The superior logic of my view appears to me not easily controverted.

3) When I ask the necessitarian how he would explain the diversity and irregularity of the universe, he replies to me out of the treasury of his wisdom that irregularity is something which from the nature of things we must not seek to explain. Abashed at this, I seek to cover my confusion by asking how he would explain the uniformity and regularity of the universe, whereupon he tells me that the laws of nature are immutable and ultimate facts, and no account is to be given of them. But my hypothesis of spontaneity does explain irregularity, in a certain sense; that is, it explains the general fact of irregularity, though not, of course, what each lawless event is to be. At the same time, by thus loosening the bond of necessity, it gives room for the influence of another kind of causation, such as seems to be operative in the mind in the formation of associations, and enables us to understand how the uniformity of nature could have been brought about. That single events should be hard and unintelligible, logic will permit without difficulty: we do not expect to make the shock of a personally experienced earthquake appear natural and reasonable by any amount of cogitation. But logic does expect things *general* to be understandable. To say that there is a universal law, and that it is a hard, ultimate, unintelligible fact, the why and wherefore of which can never be inquired into, at this a sound logic will revolt; and will pass over at once to a method of philosophising which does not thus barricade the road of discovery.

4) Necessitarianism cannot logically stop short of making the whole action of the mind a part of the physical universe. Our notion that we decide what we are going to do, if as the necessitarian says, it has been calculable since the earliest times, is reduced to illusion. Indeed, consciousness in general thus becomes a mere illusory aspect of a material system. What we call red, green, and violet are in reality only different rates of vibration. The sole reality is the distribution of qualities of matter in space and time. Brain-matter is protoplasm in a certain degree and kind of complication,—a certain arrangement of mechanical particles. Its feeling is but an inward aspect, a phantom. For, from the positions and velocities of the particles at any one instant, and the knowledge of the immutable forces, the positions at all other times are calculable; so that the universe of space, time, and matter is a rounded system uninterfered with from elsewhere. But from the state of feeling at any instant, there is no reason to suppose the states of feeling at all other instants are thus exactly calculable; so that feeling is, as I said, a mere fragmentary and illusive aspect of the universe. This is the way, then, that necessitarianism has to make up its accounts. It enters consciousness under the head of sundries, as a forgotten trifle; its scheme of the universe would be more satisfactory if this little fact could be dropped out of sight. On the other hand, by supposing the rigid exactitude of causation to yield, I care not how little,—be it but by a strictly infinitesimal amount,—we gain room to insert mind into our scheme, and to put it into the place where it is needed, into the position which, as the sole self-intelligible thing, it is entitled to occupy, that of the fountain of existence; and in so doing we resolve the problem of the connection of soul and body.

5) But I must leave undeveloped the chief of my reasons, and can only adumbrate it. The hypothesis of chance-spontaneity is one whose inevitable consequences are capable of being traced out with mathematical precision into considerable detail. Much of this I have done and find the consequences to agree with observed facts to an extent which seems to me remarkable. But the matter and methods of reasoning are novel, and I have no right to promise that other mathematicians shall find my deductions as satisfactory as I myself do, so that the strongest reason for my belief must for the present remain a private reason of my own, and cannot influence others. I mention it to explain my own position; and partly to indicate to future mathematical speculators a veritable gold-mine, should time and circumstances and the abridger of all joys prevent my opening it to the world.

If now I, in my turn, inquire of the necessitarian why he prefers to suppose that all specification goes back to the beginning of things, he will answer me with one of those last three arguments which I left unanswered.

First, he may say that chance is a thing absolutely unintelligible, and therefore that we never can be entitled to make such a supposition. But does not this objection smack of naïve impudence? It is not mine, it is his own conception of the universe which leads abruptly up to hard, ultimate, inexplicable, immutable law, on the one hand, and to inexplicable specification and diversification of circumstances on the other. My view, on the contrary, hypothetises nothing at all, unless it be hypothesis to say that all specification came about in some sense, and is not to be accepted as unaccountable. To undertake to account for anything by saying baldly that it is due to chance would, indeed, be futile. But this I do not do. I make use of chance chiefly to make room for a principle of generalisation, or tendency to form habits, which I hold has produced all regularities. The mechanical philosopher leaves the whole specification of the world utterly unaccounted for, which is pretty nearly as bad as to boldly attribute it to chance. I attribute it altogether to chance, it is true, but to chance in the form of a spontaneity which is to some degree regular. It seems to me clear at any rate that one of these two positions must be taken, or else specification must be supposed due to a spontaneity which develops itself in a certain and not in a chance way, by an objective logic like that of Hegel. This last way I leave as an open possibility, for the present; for it is as much opposed to the necessitarian scheme of existence as my own theory is.

Secondly, the necessitarian may say there are, at any rate, no observed phenomena which the hypothesis of chance could aid in explaining. In reply, I point first to the phenomenon of growth and developing complexity, which appears to be universal, and which though it may possibly be an affair of mechanism perhaps, certainly presents all the appearance of increasing diversification. Then, there is variety itself, beyond comparison the most obtrusive character of the universe: no mechanism can account for this. Then, there is the very fact the necessitarian most insists upon, the regularity of the universe which for him serves only to block the road of inquiry. Then, there are the regular relationships between the laws of nature,—similarities and comparative characters, which appeal to our intelligence as its cousins, and call upon us for a reason. Finally, there is consciousness, feeling, a patent fact enough, but a very inconvenient one to the mechanical philosopher.

Thirdly, the necessitarian may say that chance is not a *vera causa*, that we cannot know positively there is any such element in the universe. But the doctrine of the *vera causa* has nothing to do with elementary conceptions. Pushed to that extreme, it at once cuts off belief in the existence of a material universe; and without that necessitarianism could hardly maintain its ground. Besides, variety is a fact which must be admitted; and the theory of chance merely consists in supposing this diversification does not antedate all time. Moreover, the avoidance of hypotheses involving causes nowhere positively known to act—is only a recommendation of logic, not a positive command. It cannot be formulated in any precise terms without at once betraying its untenable character,—I mean as rigid rule, for as a recommendation it is wholesome enough.

I believe I have thus subjected to fair examination all the important reasons for adhering to the theory of universal necessity, and have shown their nullity. I earnestly beg that whoever may detect any flaw in my reasoning will point it out to me, either privately or publicly; for if I am wrong, it much concerns me to be set right speedily.[9] If my argument remains unrefuted, it will be time, I think, to doubt the absolute truth of the principle of universal law; and when once such a doubt has obtained a living root in any man's mind, my cause with him, I am persuaded, is gained.

23

The Law of Mind

P 477: The Monist *2 (July 1892):533–59. [Also published in CP 6.102–63.] In this paper, Peirce develops his synechism, the doctrine that continuity is "of prime importance in philosophy" and, according to which, the one law of mind is that ideas tend to spread and to affect other ideas but that, in spreading, they lose intensity as they gain generality. From synechism, the doctrines of logical realism, objective idealism, and tychism follow. Peirce also considers continuity from the standpoint of mathematics (with reference to Cantor), and he isolates two fundamental properties of a continuous series: Aristotelicity (every continuum contains its limits) and Kanticity (every continuum is infinitely divisible); applying the former to philosophy, he finds that consciousness essentially occupies time. He also claims that the three principal types of mental action correspond to the three main classes of logical inference.*

In an article published in *The Monist* for January 1891, I endeavored to show what ideas ought to form the warp of a system of philosophy, and particularly emphasised that of absolute chance. In the number of April 1892, I argued further in favor of that way of thinking, which it will be convenient to christen *tychism* (from τύχη, chance).[1] A serious student of philosophy will be in no haste to accept or reject this doctrine; but he will see in it one of the chief attitudes which speculative thought may take, feeling that it is not for an individual, nor for an age, to pronounce upon a fundamental question of philosophy. That is a task for a whole era to work out. I have begun by showing that *tychism* must give birth to an evolutionary cosmology, in which all the regularities of nature and of mind are regarded as products of growth, and to a Schelling-fashioned idealism which holds matter to be mere specialised and partially deadened mind. I may mention, for the benefit of those who are curious in studying mental biographies, that I was born and reared in the neighborhood of Concord,—I mean in Cambridge,—at the time when Emerson, Hedge, and their friends were disseminating the ideas that they had caught from Schelling, and Schelling from Plotinus, from Boehm, or from God knows what minds stricken with the monstrous mysticism of the East. But the atmosphere of Cambridge held many an antiseptic against Concord transcendentalism; and I am not conscious of having contracted any of that virus. Nevertheless, it is probable that some cultured bacilli, some benignant form of the disease was implanted in my soul, unawares, and that now, after long incubation, it comes to the surface, modified by mathematical conceptions and by training in physical investigations.

The next step in the study of cosmology must be to examine the general law of mental action. In doing this, I shall for the time drop my tychism out of view, in order to allow a free and independent expansion to another conception signalised in my first *Monist*-paper as one of the most indispensible to philosophy, though it was not there dwelt upon; I mean the idea of continuity. The tendency to regard continuity, in the sense in which I shall define it, as an idea of prime importance in philosophy may conveniently be termed *synechism*. The present paper is intended chiefly to show what synechism is, and what it leads to. I attempted, a good many years ago, to develop this doctrine in the *Journal of Speculative Philosophy* (Vol. II.); but I am able now to improve upon that exposition, in which I was a little blinded by nominalistic prepossessions. I refer to it, because students may possibly find that some points not sufficiently explained in the present paper are cleared up in those earlier ones.[2]

WHAT THE LAW IS

Logical analysis applied to mental phenomena shows that there is but one law of mind, namely, that ideas tend to spread continuously and to affect certain others which stand to them in a peculiar relation of affectibility. In this spreading they lose intensity, and especially the power of affecting others, but gain generality and become welded with other ideas.

I set down this formula at the beginning, for convenience; and now proceed to comment upon it.

INDIVIDUALITY OF IDEAS

We are accustomed to speak of ideas as reproduced, as passed from mind to mind, as similar or dissimilar to one another, and, in short, as if they were substantial things; nor can any reasonable objection be raised to such expressions. But taking the word "idea" in the sense of an event in an individual consciousness, it is clear that an idea once past is gone forever, and any supposed recurrence of it is another idea. These two ideas are not present in the same state of consciousness, and therefore cannot possibly be compared. To say, therefore, that they are similar can only mean that an occult power from the depths of the soul forces us to connect them in our thoughts after they are both no more. We may note, here, in passing that of the two generally recognised principles of association, contiguity and similarity, the former is a connection due to a power without, the latter a connection due to a power within.

But what can it mean to say that ideas wholly past are thought of at all, any longer? They are utterly unknowable. What distinct meaning can attach to saying that an idea in the past in any way affects an idea in the future, from which it is completely detached? A phrase between the assertion and the denial of which there can in no case be any sensible difference is mere gibberish.

I will not dwell further upon this point, because it is a commonplace of philosophy.

CONTINUITY OF IDEAS

We have here before us a question of difficulty, analogous to the question of nominalism and realism. But when once it has been clearly formulated, logic leaves room for one answer only. How can a past idea be present? Can it be present vicariously? To a certain extent, perhaps; but not merely so; for then the question would arise how the past idea can be related to its vicarious representation. The relation, being between Ideas, can only exist in some consciousness: now that past idea was in no consciousness but that past consciousness that alone contained it; and that did not embrace the vicarious idea.

Some minds will here jump to the conclusion that a past idea cannot in any sense be present. But that is hasty and illogical. How extravagant, too, to pronounce our whole knowledge of the past to be mere delusion! Yet it would seem that the past is as completely beyond the bonds of possible experience as a Kantian thing-in-itself.

How can a past idea be present? Not vicariously. Then, only by direct perception. In other words, to be present, it must be *ipso facto* present. That is, it cannot be wholly past; it can only be going, infinitesimally past, less past than any assignable past date. We are thus brought to the conclusion that the present is connected with the past by a series of real infinitesimal steps.

It has already been suggested by psychologists that consciousness necessarily embraces an interval of time. But if a finite time be meant, the opinion is not tenable. If the sensation that precedes the present by half a second were still immediately before me, then, on the same principle, the sensation preceding that would be immediately present, and so on *ad infinitum*. Now, since there is a time, say a year, at the end of which an idea is no longer *ipso facto* present, it follows that this is true of any finite interval, however short.

But yet consciousness must essentially cover an interval of time; for if it did not, we could gain no knowledge of time, and not merely no veracious cognition of it, but no conception whatever. We are, therefore, forced to say that we are immediately conscious through an infinitesimal interval of time.

This is all that is requisite. For, in this infinitesimal interval, not only is consciousness continuous in a subjective sense, that is, considered as a subject or substance having the attribute of duration; but also, because it is immediate consciousness, its object is *ipso facto* continuous. In fact, this infinitesimally spread-out consciousness is a direct feeling of its contents as spread out. This will be further elucidated below. In an infinitesimal interval we directly perceive the temporal sequence of its beginning, middle, and end,—not, of course, in the way of recognition, for recognition is only of the past, but in the way of immediate feeling. Now upon this interval follows another, whose beginning is the middle of the former, and whose middle is the end of the former. Here, we have an immediate perception of the temporal sequence of its beginning, middle, and end, or say of the second, third, and fourth instants. From these two immediate perceptions, we gain a mediate, or inferential, perception of the relation of all four instants. This mediate perception is objectively, or as to the object represented, spread over the four instants; but subjectively, or as itself the subject of duration, it is completely embraced in the second moment. [The reader will observe that I use the word *instant* to mean a point of time, and *moment* to mean an infinitesimal duration.] If it is objected that, upon the theory proposed, we must have more than a mediate perception of the succession of the four instants, I grant it; for the sum of the two infinitesimal intervals is itself infinitesimal, so that it is immediately perceived. It is immediately perceived in the whole interval, but only mediately perceived in the last two-thirds of the interval. Now, let there be an indefinite succession of these inferential acts of comparative perception; and it is plain that the last moment will contain objectively the whole series. Let there be, not merely an indefinite succession, but a continuous flow of inference through a finite time; and the result will be a mediate objective consciousness of the whole time in the last moment. In this last moment, the whole series will be recognised, or known as known before, except only the last moment, which of course will be absolutely unrecognisable to itself. Indeed, even this last moment will be recognised like the rest, or, at least be just beginning to be so. There is a little *elenchus*, or appearance of contradiction, here, which the ordinary logic of reflection quite suffices to resolve.

INFINITY AND CONTINUITY, IN GENERAL

Most of the mathematicians who during the last two generations have treated the differential calculus have been of the opinion that an infinitesimal quantity is an absurdity; although, with their habitual caution, they have often added "or, at any rate, the conception of an infinitesimal is so difficult, that we practically cannot reason about it with confidence and security." Accordingly, the doctrine of limits has been invented to evade the difficulty, or, as some say, to explain the signification of the word "infinitesimal." This doctrine, in one form or another, is taught in all the text-books, though in some of them only as an alternative view of the matter; it answers well enough the purposes of calculation, though even in that application it has its difficulties.

The illumination of the subject by a strict notation for the logic of relatives had shown me clearly and evidently that the idea of an infinitesimal involves no contradiction, before I became acquainted with the writings of Dr. Georg Cantor (though many of these had already appeared in the *Mathematische Annalen* and in *Borchardt's Journal,* if not yet in the *Acta Mathematica,* all mathematical journals of the first distinction), in which the same view is defended with extraordinary genius and penetrating logic.[3]

The prevalent opinion is that finite numbers are the only ones that we can reason about, at least, in any ordinary mode of reasoning, or, as some authors express it, they are the only numbers that can be reasoned about mathematically. But this is an irrational prejudice. I long ago showed[4] that finite collections are distinguished from infinite ones only by one circumstance and its consequences, namely, that to them is applicable a peculiar and unusual mode of reasoning called by its discoverer, De Morgan, the "syllogism of transposed quantity."

Balzac, in the introduction of his *Physiologie du mariage,* remarks that every young Frenchman boasts of having seduced some Frenchwoman. Now, as a woman can only be seduced once, and there are no more Frenchwomen than Frenchmen, it follows, if these boasts are true, that no French women escape seduction. If their number be finite, the reasoning holds. But since the population is continually increasing, and the seduced are on the average younger than the seducers, the conclusion need not be true. In like manner, De Morgan, as an actuary, might have argued that if an insurance company pays to its insured on an average more than they have ever paid it, including interest, it must lose money. But every modern actuary would see a fallacy in that, since the business is continually on the increase. But should war, or other cataclysm, cause the class of insured to be a finite one, the conclusion would turn out painfully correct, after all. The above two reasonings are examples of the syllogism of transposed quantity.[5]

The proposition that finite and infinite collections are distinguished by the applicability to the former of the syllogism of transposed quantity ought to be regarded as the basal one of scientific arithmetic.

If a person does not know how to reason logically, and I must say that a great many fairly good mathematicians,—yea distinguished ones,—fall under this category, but simply uses a rule of thumb in blindly drawing inferences like other inferences that have turned out well, he will, of course, be continually falling into error about infinite numbers. The truth is such people do not reason, at all. But for the few who do reason, reasoning about infinite numbers is easier than about finite numbers, because the complicated syllogism of transposed quantity is not called for. For example, that the whole is greater than its part is not an axiom, as that eminently bad reasoner, Euclid, made it to be. It is a theorem readily proved by means of a syllogism of transposed quantity, but not otherwise. Of finite collections it is true, of infinite collections false. Thus, a part of the whole numbers are even numbers. Yet the even numbers are no fewer than all the numbers; an evident proposition since if every number in the whole series of whole numbers be doubled, the result will be the series of even numbers.

$$1, 2, 3, 4, 5, 6, \text{etc.}$$
$$2, 4, 6, 8, 10, 12, \text{etc.}$$

So for every number there is a distinct even number. In fact, there are as many distinct doubles of numbers as there are of distinct numbers. But the doubles of numbers are all even numbers.

In truth, of infinite collections there are but two grades of magnitude, the *endless* and the *innumerable*. Just as a finite collection is distinguished from an infinite one by the applicability to it of a special mode of reasoning, the syllogism of transposed quantity, so, as I showed in the paper last referred to, a numerable collection is distinguished from an innumerable one by the applicability to it of a certain mode of reasoning, the Fermatian inference, or, as it is sometimes improperly termed, "mathematical induction."[6]

As an example of this reasoning, Euler's demonstration of the binomial theorem for integral powers may be given. The theorem is that $(x + y)^n$, where n is a whole number, may be expanded into the sum of a series of terms of which the first is $x^n y^0$ and each of the others is derived from the next preceding by diminishing the exponent of x by 1 and multiplying by that exponent and at the same time increasing the exponent of y by 1 and dividing by that increased exponent. Now, suppose this proposition to be true for a certain exponent, $n = M$, then it must also be true for $n = M + 1$. For let one of the terms in the expansion of $(x + y)^M$ be written $Ax^p y^q$. Then, this term with the two following will be

$$Ax^p y^q + A\frac{p}{q+1}x^{p-1}y^{q+1} + A\frac{p}{q+1}\frac{p-1}{q+2}x^{p-2}y^{q+2}$$

Now, when $(x + y)^M$ is multiplied by $x + y$ to give $(x + y)^{M+1}$, we multiply first by x and then by y instead of by x and add the two results. When we multiply by x, the second of the above three terms will be the only one giving a term involving $x^p y^{q+1}$ and the third will be the only one giving a term in $x^{p-1}y^{q+2}$; and when we multiply by y, the first will be the only term giving a term in $x^p y^{q+1}$, and the second will be the only term giving a term in $x^{p-1}y^{q+2}$. Hence, adding like terms, we find that the coefficient of $x^p y^{q+1}$ in the expansion of $(x + y)^{M+1}$ will be the sum of the coefficients of the first two of the above three terms, and that the coefficient of $x^{p-1}y^{q+2}$ will be the sum of the coefficients of the last two terms. Hence, two successive terms in the expansion of $(x + y)^{M+1}$ will be

$$A\left(1 + \frac{p}{q+1}\right)x^p y^{q+1} + A\frac{p}{q+1}\left(1 + \frac{p-1}{q+2}\right)x^{p-1}y^{q+2}$$

$$= A\frac{p+q+1}{q+1}x^p y^{q+1} + A\frac{p+q+1}{q+1}\cdot\frac{p}{q+2}x^{p-1}y^{q+2}.$$

It is, thus, seen that the succession of terms follows the rule. Thus if any integral power follows the rule, so also does the next higher power. But the first power obviously follows the rule. Hence, all powers do so.

Such reasoning holds good of any collection of objects capable of being ranged in a series which though it may be endless, can be numbered so that each member of it receives a definite integral number. For instance, all the whole numbers constitute such a numerable collection. Again, all numbers resulting from operating according to any definite rule with any finite number of whole numbers form such a collection. For they may be arranged in a series thus. Let F be the symbol of operation. First operate on 1, giving $F(1)$. Then, operate on a second 1, giving $F(1,1)$. Next, introduce 2, giving 3rd, $F(2)$; 4th, $F(2,1)$; 5th, $F(1,2)$; 6th, $F(2,2)$. Next use a third variable giving 7th, $F(1,1,1)$; 8th, $F(2,1,1)$; 9th, $F(1,2,1)$; 10th, $F(2,2,1)$; 11th, $F(1,1,2)$; 12th, $F(2,1,2)$; 13th $F(1,2,2)$; 14th, $F(2,2,2)$. Next introduce 3, and so on, alternately introducing new variables and new figures; and in this way it is plain that every arrangement of integral values of the variables will receive a numbered place in the series.*

*This proposition is substantially the same as a theorem of Cantor, though it is enunciated in a much more general form.[7]

The class of endless but numerable collections (so called because they can be so ranged that to each one corresponds a distinct whole number) is very large. But there are collections which are certainly innumerable. Such is the collection of all numbers to which endless series of decimals are capable of approximating. It has been recognised since the time of Euclid that certain numbers are surd or incommensurable, and are not exactly expressible by any finite series of decimals, nor by a circulating decimal. Such is the ratio of the circumference of a circle to its diameter, which we know is nearly 3.1415926. The calculation of this number has been carried to over 700 figures without the slightest appearance of regularity in their sequence. The demonstrations that this and many other numbers are incommensurable are perfect. That the entire collection of incommensurable numbers is innumerable has been clearly proved by Cantor.[8] I omit the demonstration; but it is easy to see that to discriminate one from some other would, in general, require the use of an endless series of numbers. Now if they cannot be exactly expressed and discriminated, clearly they cannot be ranged in a linear series.

It is evident that there are as many points on a line or in an interval of time as there are of real numbers in all. These are, therefore, innumerable collections. Many mathematicians have incautiously assumed that the points on a surface or in a solid are more than those on a line. But this has been refuted by Cantor.[9] Indeed, it is obvious that for every set of values of coördinates there is a single distinct number. Suppose, for instance, the values of the coördinates all lie between 0 and +1. Then if we compose a number by putting in the first decimal place the first figure of the first coördinate, in the second the first figure of the second coördinate, and so on, and when the first figures are all dealt out go on to the second figures in like manner, it is plain that the values of the coördinates can be read off from the single resulting number, so that a triad or tetrad of numbers, each having innumerable values, has no more values than a single incommensurable number.

Were the number of dimensions infinite, this would fail; and the collection of infinite sets of numbers having each innumerable variations, might, therefore, be greater than the simple innumerable collection, and might be called *endlessly infinite.* The single individuals of such a collection could not, however, be designated, even approximately, so that this is indeed a magnitude concerning which it would be possible to reason only in the most general way, if at all.

Although there are but two grades of magnitudes of infinite collections, yet when certain conditions are imposed upon the order in which individuals are taken, distinctions of magnitude arise from that cause. Thus, if a simply endless series be doubled by separating each unit into two parts, the successive first parts and also the second parts being taken in the same order as the units from which they are derived, this double endless series will, so long as it is taken in that order, appear as twice as large as the original series. In like manner the product of two innumerable collections, that is, the collection of possible pairs composed of one individual of each, if the order of continuity is to be maintained, is, by virtue of that order, infinitely greater than either of the component collections.

We now come to the difficult question, What is continuity? Kant confounds it with infinite divisibility, saying that the essential character of a continuous series is that between any two members of it a third can always be found.[10] This is an analysis beautifully clear and definite; but unfortunately, it breaks down under the first test. For according to this, the entire series of rational fractions arranged in the order of their magnitude, would be an infinite series, although the rational fractions are numerable, while the points of a line are innumerable. Nay, worse yet, if from that series of fractions any two with all that lie between them be excised, and any number of such finite gaps be made, Kant's definition is still true of the series, though it has lost all appearance of continuity.

Cantor defines a continuous series as one which is *concatenated* and *perfect*.[11] By a concatenated series, he means such a one that if any two points are given in it, and any finite distance, however small, it is possible to proceed from the first point to the second through a succession of points of the series each at a distance from the preceding one less than the given distance. This is true of the series of rational fractions ranged in the order of their magnitude. By a perfect series, he means one which contains every point such that there is no distance so small that this point has not an infinity of points of the series within that distance of it. This is true of the series of numbers between o and 1 capable of being expressed by decimals in which only the digits o and 1 occur.

It must be granted that Cantor's definition includes every series that is continuous; nor can it be objected that it includes any important or indubitable case of a series not continuous. Nevertheless, it has some serious defects. In the first place, it turns upon metrical considerations; while the distinction between a continuous and a discontinuous series is manifestly non-metrical. In the next place, a perfect series is defined as one containing "every point" of a certain description. But no positive idea is conveyed of what all the points are: that is definition by negation, and cannot be admitted. If that sort of thing were allowed, it would be very easy to say, at once, that the continuous linear series of points is one which contains every point of the line between its extremities. Finally, Cantor's definition does not convey a distinct notion of what the components of the conception of continuity are. It ingeniously wraps up its properties in two separate parcels, but does not display them to our intelligence.

Kant's definition expresses one simple property of a continuum;[12] but it allows of gaps in the series. To mend the definition, it is only necessary to notice how these gaps can occur. Let us suppose, then, a linear series of points extending from a point, A, to a point, B, having a gap from B to a third point, C, and thence extending to a final limit, D; and let us suppose this series conforms to Kant's definition. Then, of the two points, B and C, one or both must be excluded from the series; for otherwise, by the definition, there would be points between them. That is, if the series contains C, though it contains all the points up to B, it cannot contain B. What is required, therefore, is to state in non-metrical terms that if a series of points up to a limit is included in a continuum the limit is included. It may be remarked that this is the property of a continuum to which Aristotle's attention seems to have been directed when he defines a continuum as something whose parts have a common limit.[13] The property may be exactly stated as follows: If a linear series of points is continuous between two points, A and D, and if an endless series of points be taken, the first of them between A and D and each of the others between the last preceding one and D, then there is a point of the continuous series between all that endless series of points and D, and such that every other point of which this is true lies between this point and D. For example, take any number between 0 and 1, as 0.1; then, any number between 0.1 and 1, as 0.11; then any number between 0.11 and 1, as 0.111; and so on, without end. Then, because the series of real numbers between 0 and 1 is continuous, there must be a *least* real number, greater than every number of that endless series. This property, which may be called the Aristotelicity of the series, together with Kant's property, or its Kanticity, completes the definition of a continuous series.

The property of Aristotelicity may be roughly stated thus: a continuum contains the end point belonging to every endless series of points which it contains. An obvious corollary is that every continuum contains its limits. But in using this principle it is necessary to observe that a series may be continuous except in this, that it omits one or both of the limits.

Our ideas will find expression more conveniently if, instead of points upon a line, we speak of real numbers. Every real number is, in one sense, the limit of a series, for it can be indefinitely approximated to. Whether every real number is a limit of a *regular* series may perhaps be open to doubt. But the series referred to in the definition of Aristotelicity must be understood as including all series whether regular or not. Consequently, it is implied that between any two points an innumerable series of points can be taken.

Every number whose expression in decimals requires but a finite number of places of decimals is commensurable. Therefore, incommensurable numbers suppose an infinitieth place of decimals. The word infinitesimal is simply the Latin form of infinitieth; that is, it is an ordinal formed from *infinitum*, as centesimal from *centum*. Thus, continuity supposes infinitesimal quantities. There is nothing contradictory about the idea of such quantities. In adding and multiplying them the continuity must not be broken up, and consequently they are precisely like any other quantities, except that neither the syllogism of transposed quantity nor the Fermatian inference applies to them.

If A is a finite quantity and i an infinitesimal, then in a certain sense we may write $A + i = A$. That is to say, this is so for all purposes of measurement. But this principle must not be applied except to get rid of *all* the terms in the highest order of infinitesimals present. As a mathematician, I prefer the method of infinitesimals to that of limits, as far easier and less infested with snares.[14] Indeed, the latter, as stated in some books, involves propositions that are false; but this is not the case with the forms of the method used by Cauchy, Duhamel, and others.[15] As they understand the doctrine of limits, it involves the notion of continuity, and therefore contains in another shape the very same ideas as the doctrine of infinitesimals.

Let us now consider an aspect of the Aristotelical principle which is particularly important in philosophy. Suppose a surface to be part red and part blue; so that every point on it is either red or blue, and, of course, no part can be both red and blue. What, then, is the color of the boundary line between the red and the blue? The answer is that red or blue, to exist at all, must be spread over a surface; and the color of the surface is the color of the surface in the immediate neighborhood of the point. I purposely use a vague form of expression. Now, as the parts of the surface in the immediate neighborhood of any ordinary point upon a curved boundary are half of them red and half blue, it follows that the boundary is half red and half blue. In like manner, we find it necessary to hold that consciousness essentially occupies time; and what is present to the mind at any ordinary instant, is what is present during a moment in which that instant occurs. Thus, the present is half past and half to come. Again, the color of the parts of a surface at any finite distance from a point, has nothing to do with its color just at that point; and, in the parallel, the feeling at any finite interval from the present has nothing to do with the present feeling, except vicariously. Take another case: the velocity of a particle at any instant of time is its mean velocity during an infinitesimal instant in which that time is contained. Just so my immediate feeling is my feeling through an infinitesimal duration containing the present instant.

ANALYSIS OF TIME

One of the most marked features about the law of mind is that it makes time to have a definite direction of flow from past to future. The relation of past to future is, in reference to the law of mind, different from the relation of future to past. This makes one of the great contrasts between the law of mind and the law of physical force, where there is no more distinction between the two opposite directions in time than between moving northward and moving southward.

In order, therefore, to analyse the law of mind, we must begin by asking what the flow of time consists in. Now, we find that in reference to any individual state of feeling, all others are of two classes, those which affect this one (or have a tendency to affect it, and what this means we shall inquire shortly), and those which do not. The present is affectible by the past but not by the future.

Moreover, if state A is affected by state B, and state B by state C, then A is affected by state C, though not so much so. It foliows, that if A is affectible by B, B is not affectible by A.

If, of two states, each is absolutely unaffectible by the other, they are to be regarded as parts of the same state. They are contemporaneous.

To say that a state is *between* two states means that it affects one and is affected by the other. Between any two states in this sense lies an innumerable series of states affecting one another; and if a state lies between a given state and any other state which can be reached by inserting states between this state and any third state, these inserted states not immediately affecting or being affected by either, then the second state mentioned immediately affects or is affected by the first, in the sense that in the one the other is *ipso facto* present in a reduced degree.

These propositions involve a definition of time and of its flow. Over and above this definition they involve a doctrine, namely, that every state of feeling is affectible by every earlier state.

THAT FEELINGS HAVE INTENSIVE CONTINUITY

Time with its continuity logically involves some other kind of continuity than its own. Time, as the universal form of change, cannot exist unless there is something to undergo change, and to undergo a change continuous in time, there must be a continuity of changeable qualities. Of the continuity of intrinsic qualities of feeling we can now form but a feeble conception. The development of the human mind has practically extinguished all feelings, except a few sporadic kinds, sound, colors, smells, warmth, etc., which now appear to be disconnected and disparate. In the case of colors, there is a tridimensional spread of feelings. Originally, all feelings may have been connected in the same way, and the presumption is that the number of dimensions was endless. For development essentially involves a limitation of possibilities. But given a number of dimensions of feeling, all possible varieties are obtainable by varying the intensities of the different elements. Accordingly, time logically supposes a continuous range of intensity in feeling. It follows, then, from the definition of continuity, that when any particular kind of feeling is present, an infinitesimal continuum of all feelings differing infinitesimally from that is present.

That Feelings Have Spatial Extension

Consider a gob of protoplasm, say an amœba or a slime-mold. It does not differ in any radical way from the contents of a nerve-cell, though its functions may be less specialised. There is no doubt that this slime-mold, or this amœba, or at any rate some similar mass of protoplasm feels. That is to say, it feels when it is in its excited condition. But note how it behaves. When the whole is quiescent and rigid, a place upon it is irritated. Just at this point, an active motion is set up, and this gradually spreads to other parts. In this action, no unity nor relation to a nucleus, or other unitary organ can be discerned. It is a mere amorphous continuum of protoplasm, with feeling passing from one part to another. Nor is there anything like a wave-motion. The activity does not advance to new parts just as fast as it leaves old parts. Rather, in the beginning, it dies out at a slower rate than that at which it spreads. And while the process is going on, by exciting the mass at another point, a second quite independent state of excitation will be set up. In some places, neither excitation will exist, in others each separately, in still other places, both effects will be added together. Whatever there is in the whole phenomenon to make us think there is feeling in such a mass of protoplasm,—*feeling*, but plainly no *personality*,—goes logically to show that that feeling has a subjective, or substantial, spatial extension, as the excited state has. This is, no doubt, a difficult idea to seize, for the reason that it is a subjective, not an objective, extension. It is not that we have a feeling of bigness; though Professor James, perhaps rightly, teaches that we have.[16] It is that the feeling, as a subject of inhesion, is big. Moreover, our own feelings are focused in attention to such a degree that we are not aware that ideas are not brought to an absolute unity; just as nobody not instructed by special experiment has any idea how very, very little of the field of vision is distinct. Still, we all know how the attention wanders about among our feelings; and this fact shows that those feelings that are not coördinated in attention have a reciprocal externality, although they are present at the same time. But we must not tax introspection to make a phenomenon manifest which essentially involves externality.

Since space is continuous, it follows that there must be an immediate community of feeling between parts of mind infinitesimally near together. Without this, I believe it would have been impossible for minds external to one another, ever to become coördinated, and equally impossible for any coördination to be established in the action of the nerve-matter of one brain.

AFFECTIONS OF IDEAS

But we are met by the question what is meant by saying that one idea affects another. The unravelment of this problem requires us to trace out phenomena a little further.

Three elements go to make up an idea. The first is its intrinsic quality as a feeling. The second is the energy with which it affects other ideas, an energy which is infinite in the here-and-nowness of immediate sensation, finite and relative in the recency of the past. The third element is the tendency of an idea to bring along other ideas with it.

As an idea spreads, its power of affecting other ideas gets rapidly reduced; but its intrinsic quality remains nearly unchanged. It is long years now since I last saw a cardinal in his robes;[17] and my memory of their color has become much dimmed. The color itself, however, is not remembered as dim. I have no inclination to call it a dull red. Thus, the intrinsic quality remains little changed; yet more accurate observation will show a slight reduction of it. The third element, on the other hand, has increased. As well as I can recollect, it seems to me the cardinals I used to see wore robes more scarlet than vermilion is, and highly luminous. Still, I know the color commonly called cardinal is on the crimson side of vermilion and of quite moderate luminosity, and the original idea calls up so many other hues with it, and asserts itself so feebly, that I am unable any longer to isolate it.

A finite interval of time generally contains an innumerable series of feelings; and when these become welded together in association, the result is a general idea. For we have just seen how by continuous spreading an idea becomes generalised.

The first character of a general idea so resulting is that it is living feeling. A continuum of this feeling, infinitesimal in duration, but still embracing innumerable parts, and also, though infinitesimal, entirely unlimited, is immediately present. And in its absence of boundedness a vague possibility of more than is present is directly felt.

Second, in the presence of this continuity of feeling, nominalistic maxims appear futile. There is no doubt about one idea affecting another, when we can directly perceive the one gradually modified and shaping itself into the other. Nor can there any longer be any difficulty about one idea resembling another, when we can pass along the continuous field of quality from one to the other and back again to the point which we had marked.

Third, consider the insistency of an idea. The insistency of a past idea with reference to the present is a quantity which is less the further back that past idea is, and rises to infinity as the past idea is brought up into coincidence with the present. Here we must make one of those

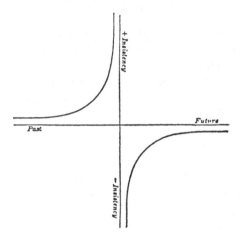

inductive applications of the law of continuity which have produced such great results in all the positive sciences. We must extend the law of insistency into the future. Plainly, the insistency of a future idea with reference to the present is a quantity affected by the minus sign; for it is the present that affects the future, if there be any effect, not the future that affects the present. Accordingly, the curve of insistency is a sort of equilateral hyperbola. [See the figure.] Such a conception is none the less mathematical, that its quantification cannot now be exactly specified.

Now consider the induction which we have here been led into. This curve says that feeling which has not yet emerged into immediate consciousness is already affectible and already affected. In fact, this is habit, by virtue of which an idea is brought up into present consciousness by a bond that had already been established between it, and another idea while it was still *in futuro*.

We can now see what the affection of one idea by another consists in. It is that the affected idea is attached as a logical predicate to the affecting idea as subject. So when a feeling emerges into immediate consciousness, it always appears as a modification of a more or less general object already in the mind. The word suggestion is well adapted to expressing this relation. The future is suggested by, or rather is influenced by the suggestions of, the past.

Ideas Cannot Be Connected Except By Continuity

That ideas can nowise be connected without continuity is sufficiently evident to one who reflects upon the matter. But still the opinion may be entertained that after continuity has once made the connection of ideas possible, then they may get to be connected in other modes than through continuity. Certainly, I cannot see how anyone can deny that the infinite diversity of the universe, which we call chance, may bring ideas into proximity which are not associated in one general idea. It may do this many times. But then the law of continuous spreading will produce a mental association; and this I suppose is an abridged statement of the way the universe has been evolved. But if I am asked whether a blind ἀνάγκη cannot bring ideas together, first I point out that it would not remain blind. There being a continuous connection between the ideas, they would infallibly become associated in a living, feeling, and perceiving general idea. Next, I cannot see what the mustness or necessity of this ἀνάγκη would consist in. In the absolute uniformity of the phenomenon, says the nominalist. Absolute is well put in; for if it merely happened so three times in succession, or three million times in succession, in the absence of any reason, the coincidence could only be attributed to chance. But absolute uniformity must extend over the whole infinite future; and it is idle to talk of that except as an idea. No; I think we can only hold that wherever ideas come together they tend to weld into general ideas; and wherever they are generally connected, general ideas govern the connection; and these general ideas are living feelings spread out.

Mental Law Follows the Forms of Logic

The three main classes of logical inference are Deduction, Induction, and Hypothesis. These correspond to three chief modes of action of the human soul. In deduction the mind is under the dominion of a habit or association by virtue of which a general idea suggests in each case a corresponding reaction. But a certain sensation is seen to involve that idea. Consequently, that sensation is followed by that reaction. That is the way the hind legs of a frog, separated from the rest of the body, reason, when you pinch them. It is the lowest form of psychical manifestation.

By induction, a habit becomes established. Certain sensations, all involving one general idea, are followed each by the same reaction; and an association becomes established, whereby that general idea gets to be followed uniformly by that reaction.

Habit is that specialisation of the law of mind whereby a general idea gains the power of exciting reactions. But in order that the general idea should attain all its functionality, it is necessary, also, that it should become suggestible by sensations. That is accomplished by a psychical process having the form of hypothetic inference. By hypothetic inference, I mean, as I have explained in other writings, an induction from qualities. For example, I know that the kind of man known and classed as a "mugwump" has certain characteristics. He has a high self-respect and places great value upon social distinction. He laments the great part that rowdyism and unrefined good-fellowship play in the dealings of American politicians with their constituency. He thinks that the reform which would follow from the abandonment of the system by which the distribution of offices is made to strengthen party organisations and a return to the original and essential conception of office-filing would be found an unmixed good. He holds that monetary considerations should usually be the decisive ones in questions of public policy. He respects the principle of individualism and of *laisser-faire* as the greatest agency of civilisation. These views, among others, I know to be obtrusive marks of a "mugwump." Now, suppose I casually meet a man in a railway-train, and falling into conversation find that he holds opinions of this sort; I am naturally led to suppose that he is a "mugwump." That is hypothetic inference. That is to say, a number of readily verifiable marks of a mugwump being selected, I find this man has these, and infer that he has all the other characters which go to make a thinker of that stripe. Or let us suppose that I meet a man of a semi-clerical appearance and a sub-pharisaical sniff, who appears to look at things from the point of view of a rather wooden dualism. He cites several texts of scripture and always with particular attention to their logical implications; and he exhibits a sternness, almost amounting to vindictiveness, toward evil-doers, in general. I readily conclude that he is a minister of a certain denomination. Now the mind acts in a way similar to this, every time we acquire a power of coördinating reactions in a peculiar way, as in performing any act requiring skill. Thus, most persons have a difficulty in moving the two hands simultaneously and in opposite directions through two parallel circles nearly in the medial plane of the body. To learn to do this, it is necessary to attend, first, to the different actions in different parts of the motion, when suddenly a general conception of the action springs up and it becomes perfectly easy. We think the motion we are trying to do involves this action, and this, and this. Then, the general idea comes which unites all those actions, and thereupon the desire to perform the motion calls up the general idea.

The same mental process is many times employed whenever we are learning to speak a language or are acquiring any sort of skill.

Thus, by induction, a number of sensations followed by one reaction become united under one general idea followed by the same reaction; while by the hypothetic process, a number of reactions called for by one occasion get united in a general idea which is called out by the same occasion. By deduction, the habit fulfils its function of calling out certain reactions on certain occasions.

Uncertainty of Mental Action

The inductive and hypothetic forms of inference are essentially probable inferences, not necessary; while deduction may be either necessary or probable.

But no mental action seems to be necessary or invariable in its character. In whatever manner the mind has reacted under a given sensation, in that manner it is the more likely to react again; were this, however, an absolute necessity, habits would become wooden and ineradicable, and no room being left for the formation of new habits, intellectual life would come to a speedy close. Thus, the uncertainty of the mental law is no mere defect of it, but is on the contrary of its essence. The truth is, the mind is not subject to "law," in the same rigid sense that matter is. It only experiences gentle forces which merely render it more likely to act in a given way than it otherwise would be. There always remains a certain amount of arbitrary spontaneity in its action, without which it would be dead.

Some psychologists think to reconcile the uncertainty of reactions with the principle of necessary causation by means of the law of fatigue. Truly for a *law,* this law of fatigue is a little lawless. I think it is merely a case of the general principle that an idea in spreading loses its insistency. Put me tarragon into my salad, when I have not tasted it for years, and I exclaim "What nectar is this!" But add it to every dish I taste for week after week, and a habit of expectation has been created; and in thus spreading into habit, the sensation makes hardly any more impression upon me; or, if it be noticed, it is on a new side from which it appears as rather a bore. The doctrine that fatigue is one of the primordial phenomena of mind I am much disposed to doubt. It seems a somewhat little thing to be allowed as an exception to the great principle of mental uniformisation. For this reason, I prefer to explain it in the manner here indicated, as a special case of that great principle. To consider it as something distinct in its nature, certainly somewhat strengthens the necessitarian position; but even if it be distinct, the hypothesis that all the variety and apparent arbitrariness of mental action ought to be explained away in favor of absolute determinism does not seem to me to recommend itself to a sober and sound judgment, which seeks the guidance of observed facts and not that of prepossessions.

RESTATEMENT OF THE LAW

Let me now try to gather up all these odds and ends of commentary and restate the law of mind, in a unitary way.

First, then, we find that when we regard ideas from a nominalistic, individualistic, sensualistic way, the simplest facts of mind become utterly meaningless. That one idea should resemble another or influence another, or that one state of mind should so much as be thought of in another is, from that standpoint, sheer nonsense.

Second, by this and other means we are driven to perceive, what is quite evident of itself, that instantaneous feelings flow together into a continuum of feeling, which has in a modified degree the peculiar vivacity of feeling and has gained generality. And in reference to such general ideas, or continua of feeling, the difficulties about resemblance and suggestion and reference to the external, cease to have any force.

Third, these general ideas are not mere words, nor do they consist in this, that certain concrete facts will every time happen under certain descriptions of conditions; but they are just as much, or rather far more, living realities than the feelings themselves out of which they are concreted. And to say that mental phenomena are governed by law does not mean merely that they are describable by a general formula; but that there is a living idea, a conscious continuum of feeling, which pervades them, and to which they are docile.

Fourth, this supreme law, which is the celestial and living harmony, does not so much as demand that the special ideas shall surrender their peculiar arbitrariness and caprice entirely; for that would be self-destructive. It only requires that they shall influence and be influenced by one another.

Fifth, in what measure this unification acts, seems to be regulated only by special rules; or, at least, we cannot in our present knowledge say how far it goes. But it may be said that, judging by appearances, the amount of arbitrariness in the phenomena of human minds is neither altogether trifling nor very prominent.

PERSONALITY

Having thus endeavored to state the law of mind, in general, I descend to the consideration of a particular phenomenon which is remarkably prominent in our own consciousnesses, that of personality. A strong light is thrown upon this subject by recent observations of double and multiple personality. The theory which at one time seemed plausible that two persons in one body corresponded to the two halves of the brain will, I take it, now be universally acknowledged to be insufficient. But that which these cases make quite manifest is that personality is some kind of coördination or connection of ideas. Not much to say, this, perhaps. Yet when we consider that, according to the principle which we are tracing out, a connection between ideas is itself a general idea, and that a general idea is a living feeling, it is plain that we have at least taken an appreciable step toward the understanding of personality. This personality, like any general idea, is not a thing to be apprehended in an instant. It has to be lived in time; nor can any finite time embrace it in all its fulness. Yet in each infinitesimal interval it is present and living, though specially colored by the immediate feelings of that moment. Personality, so far as it is apprehended in a moment, is immediate self-consciousness.

But the word coördination implies somewhat more than this; it implies a teleological harmony in ideas, and in the case of personality this teleology is more than a mere purposive pursuit of a predeterminate end; it is a developmental teleology. This is personal character. A general idea, living and conscious now, it is already determinative of acts in the future to an extent to which it is not now conscious.

This reference to the future is an essential element of personality. Were the ends of a person already explicit, there would be no room for development, for growth, for life; and consequently there would be no personality. The mere carrying out of predetermined purposes is mechanical. This remark has an application to the philosophy of religion. It is that a genuine evolutionary philosophy, that is, one that makes the principle of growth a primordial element of the universe, is so far from being antagonistic to the idea of a personal creator, that it is really inseparable from that idea; while a necessitarian religion is in an altogether false position and is destined to become disintegrated. But a pseudo-evolutionism which enthrones mechanical law above the principle of growth, is at once scientifically unsatisfactory, as giving no possible hint of how the universe has come about, and hostile to all hopes of personal relations to God.

COMMUNICATION

Consistently with the doctrine laid down in the beginning of this paper, I am bound to maintain that an idea can only be affected by an idea in continuous connection with it. By anything but an idea, it cannot be affected at all. This obliges me to say, as I do say, on other grounds, that what we call matter is not completely dead, but is merely mind hide-bound with habits. It still retains the element of diversification; and in that diversification there is life. When an idea is conveyed from one mind to another, it is by forms of combination of the diverse elements of nature, say by some curious symmetry, or by some union of a tender color with a refined odor. To such forms the law of mechanical energy has no application. If they are eternal, it is in the spirit they embody; and their origin cannot be accounted for by any mechanical necessity. They are embodied ideas; and so only can they convey ideas. Precisely how primary sensations, as colors and tones, are excited, we cannot tell, in the present state of psychology. But in our ignorance, I think that we are at liberty to suppose that they arise in essentially the same manner as the other feelings, called secondary. As far as sight and hearing are in question, we know that they are only excited by vibrations of inconceivable complexity; and the chemical senses are probably not more simple. Even the least psychical of peripheral sensations, that of pressure, has in its excitation conditions which, though apparently simple, are seen to be complicated enough when we consider the molecules and their attractions. The principle with which I set out requires me to maintain that these feelings are communicated to the nerves by continuity, so that there must be something like them in the excitants themselves. If this seems extravagant, it is to be remembered that it is the sole possible way of reaching any explanation of sensation, which otherwise must be pronounced a general fact absolutely inexplicable and ultimate. Now absolute inexplicability is a hypothesis which sound logic refuses under any circumstances to justify.

I may be asked whether my theory would be favorable or otherwise to telepathy. I have no decided answer to give to this. At first sight, it seems unfavorable. Yet there may be other modes of continuous connection between minds other than those of time and space.

The recognition by one person of another's personality takes place by means to some extent identical with the means by which he is conscious of his own personality. The idea of the second personality, which is as much as to say that second personality itself, enters within the field of direct consciousness of the first person, and is as immediately perceived as his ego, though less strongly. At the same time, the opposition between the two persons is perceived, so that the externality of the second is recognised.

The psychological phenomena of intercommunication between two minds have been unfortunately little studied. So that it is impossible to say, for certain, whether they are favorable to this theory or not. But the very extraordinary insight which some persons are able to gain of others from indications so slight that it is difficult to ascertain what they are, is certainly rendered more comprehensible by the view here taken.

A difficulty which confronts the synechistic philosophy is this. In considering personality, that philosophy is forced to accept the doctrine of a personal God; but in considering communication, it cannot but admit that if there is a personal God, we must have a direct perception of that person and indeed be in personal communication with him. Now, if that be the case, the question arises how it is possible that the existence of this being should ever have been doubted by anybody. The only answer that I can at present make is that facts that stand before our face and eyes and stare us in the face are far from being, in all cases, the ones most easily discerned. That has been remarked from time immemorial.

Conclusion

I have thus developed as well as I could in a little space the *synechistic* philosophy, as applied to mind. I think that I have succeeded in making it clear that this doctrine gives room for explanations of many facts which without it are absolutely and hopelessly inexplicable; and further that it carries along with it the following doctrines: 1st, a logical realism of the most pronounced type; 2nd, objective idealism; 3rd, tychism, with its consequent thorough-going evolutionism. We also notice that the doctrine presents no hindrances to spiritual influences, such as some philosophies are felt to do.

24

Man's Glassy Essence

P 480: The Monist *3 (October 1892):1–22. [Also published in
CP 6.238–71.] In this paper, Peirce applies his synechistic philosophy to the mind-body problem or "the relation between the
psychical and physical aspects of a substance." In order to
carry out his purpose of developing a philosophy that ade-
quately represents the state of knowledge in the nineteenth
century, he discusses at length, and in elaborate technical
detail, the constitution of matter and the molecular theory of
protoplasm. He associates the main physical properties of
protoplasm with the three main types of mental action, and
he suggests that—as "matter is effete mind," as "physical
events are but degraded or undeveloped forms of psychical
events," and as "mechanical laws are nothing but acquired
habits, like all the regularities of mind"—"the idealist has no
need to dread a mechanical theory of life." Peirce ends his
paper with a discussion of the life of ideas and the self-
consciousness of groups of individuals.*

In *The Monist* for January 1891, I tried to show what conceptions
ought to form the brick and mortar of a philosophical system. Chief
among these was that of absolute chance for which I argued again in
last April's number.* In July, I applied another fundamental idea, that
of continuity, to the law of mind.[2] Next in order, I have to elucidate,
from the point of view chosen, the relation between the psychical and
physical aspects of a substance.

The first step towards this ought, I think, to be the framing of a
molecular theory of protoplasm. But before doing that, it seems indispensible to glance at the constitution of matter, in general. We shall,
thus, unavoidably make a long detour; but, after all, our pains will not

---

*I am rejoiced to find, since my last paper was printed, that a philosopher as subtle
and profound as Dr. Edmund Montgomery has long been arguing for the same element
in the universe. Other world-renowned thinkers, as M. Renouvier and M. Delboeuf,
appear to share this opinion.[1]

be wasted, for the problems of the papers that are to follow in the series will call for the consideration of the same question.

All physicists are rightly agreed the evidence is overwhelming which shows all sensible matter is composed of molecules in swift motion and exerting enormous mutual attractions, and perhaps repulsions, too. Even Sir William Thomson, Lord Kelvin, who wishes to explode action at a distance and return to the doctrine of a plenum, not only speaks of molecules, but undertakes to assign definite magnitudes to them.[3] The brilliant Judge Stallo, a man who did not always rightly estimate his own qualities in accepting talks for himself, declared war upon the atomic theory in a book well worth careful perusal.[4] To the old arguments in favor of atoms which he found in Fechner's monograph,[5] he was able to make replies of considerable force, though they were not sufficient to destroy those arguments. But against modern proofs he made no headway at all. These set out from the mechanical theory of heat. Rumford's experiments showed that heat is not a substance.[6] Joule demonstrated that it was a form of energy.[7] The heating of gases under constant volume, and other facts instanced by Rankine, proved that it could not be an energy of strain.[8] This drove physicists to the conclusion that it was a mode of motion. Then it was remembered that John Bernoulli had shown that the pressure of gases could be accounted for by assuming their molecules to be moving uniformly in rectilinear paths.[9] The same hypothesis was now seen to account for Avogadro's law, that in equal volumes of different kinds of gases exposed to the same pressure and temperature are contained equal numbers of molecules.[10] Shortly after, it was found to account for the laws of diffusion and viscosity of gases, and for the numerical relation between these properties. Finally, Crookes's radiometer furnished the last link in the strongest chain of evidence which supports any physical hypothesis.[11]

Such being the constitution of gases, liquids must clearly be bodies in which the molecules wander in curvilinear paths, while in solids they move in orbits or quasi-orbits. (See my definition *solid* II, 1, in the *Century Dictionary*.)[12]

We see that the resistance to compression and to interpenetration between sensible bodies is, by one of the prime propositions of the molecular theory, due in large measure to the kinetical energy of the particles, which must be supposed to be quite remote from one another, on the average, even in solids. This resistance is no doubt influenced by finite attractions and repulsions between the molecules. All the impenetrability of bodies which we can observe is, therefore, a limited impenetrability due to kinetic and positional energy. This being the case, we have no logical right to suppose that absolute impenetrability, or the exclusive occupancy of space, belongs to molecules or to atoms. It is an unwarranted hypothesis, not a *vera causa*.* Unless we are to give up the theory of energy, finite positional attractions and repulsions between molecules must be admitted. Absolute impenetrability would amount to an infinite repulsion at a certain distance. No analogy of known phenomena exists to excuse such a wanton violation of the principle of continuity as such a hypothesis is. In short, we are logically bound to adopt the Boscovichian idea that an atom is simply a distribution of component potential energy throughout space (this distribution being absolutely rigid), combined with inertia.[13] The potential energy belongs to two molecules, and is to be conceived as different between molecules A and B from what it is between molecules A and C. The distribution of energy is not necessarily spherical. Nay, a molecule may conceivably have more than one centre; it may even have a central curve, returning into itself. But I do not think there are any observed facts pointing to such multiple or linear centres. On the other hand, many facts relating to crystals, especially those observed by Voigt,† go to show that the distribution of energy is harmonical but not concentric. We can easily calculate the forces which such atoms must exert upon one another by considering‡ that they are equivalent to aggregations of pairs of electrically positive and negative points infinitely near to one another. About such an atom there would be regions of positive and of negative potential, and the number and distribution of such regions would determine the valency of the atom, a number which it is easy to see would in many cases be somewhat indeterminate. I must not dwell further upon this hypothesis, at present. In another paper, its consequences will be further considered.[14]

I cannot assume that the students of philosophy who read this magazine are thoroughly versed in modern molecular physics, and therefore it is proper to mention that the governing principle in this branch of science is Clausius's law of the virial. I will first state the law, and then explain the peculiar terms of the statement. This statement is that the total kinetic energy of the particles of a system in stationary motion is equal to the total virial. By a *system* is here meant a number of particles acting upon one another.** Stationary motion is a quasi-

---

*By a *vera causa*, in the logic of science, is meant a state of things known to exist in some cases and supposed to exist in other cases, because it would account for observed phenomena.

†Wiedemann, *Annalen*, 1887–1889 [30:190; 31:141, 544; 32:526; 34:981; 35:76, 370; 36:743; 38:573].

‡See Maxwell on Spherical Harmonics, in his *Electricity and Magnetism* [2:179].

**The word *system* has three peculiar meanings in mathematics. (*A.*) It means an orderly exposition of the truths of astronomy, and hence a theory of the motions of the stars; as the Ptolemaic *system;* the Copernican *system.* This is much like the sense in which we speak of the Calvinistic *system* of theology, the Kantian *system* of philosophy, etc. (*B.*) It means the aggregate of the planets considered as all moving in somewhat the orbital motion among a system of particles so that none of them are removed to indefinitely great distances nor acquire indefinitely great velocities. The kinetic energy of a particle is the work which would be required to bring it to rest, independently of any forces which may be acting upon it. The virial of a pair of particles is half the work which the force which actually operates between them would do if, being independent of the distance, it were to bring them together. The equation of the virial is

$$\tfrac{1}{2}\Sigma mv^2 = \tfrac{1}{2}\Sigma\Sigma Rr.$$

Here m is the mass of a particle, v its velocity, R is the attraction between two particles, and r is the distance between them. The sign Σ on the left-hand side signifies that the values of mv^2 are to be summed for all the particles, and $\Sigma\Sigma$ on the right-hand side signifies that the values of Rr are to be summed for all the pairs of particles. If there is an external pressure P (as from the atmosphere) upon the system, and the volume of vacant space within the boundary of that pressure is V, then the virial must be understood as including $\tfrac{3}{2}PV$, so that the equation is

$$\tfrac{1}{2}\Sigma mv^2 = \tfrac{3}{2}PV + \tfrac{1}{2}\Sigma\Sigma Rr.$$

There is strong (if not demonstrative) reason for thinking that the temperature of any body above the absolute zero ($-273°C.$), is proportional to the average kinetic energy of its molecules, or say $a\theta$, where a is a constant and θ is the absolute temperature. Hence, we may write the equation

$$a\theta = \tfrac{1}{2}\overline{mv^2} = \tfrac{3}{2}P\overline{V} + \tfrac{1}{2}\Sigma\overline{Rr}$$

where the heavy lines above the different expressions signify that the average values for single molecules are to be taken. In 1872, a student in the University of Leyden, Van der Waals, propounded in his thesis for the doctorate a specialisation of the equation of the virial which has since attracted great attention.[15] Namely, he writes it

$$a\theta = \left(P + \frac{c}{v^2}\right)(V - b).$$

The quantity b is the volume of a molecule, which he supposes to be an impenetrable body, and all the virtue of the equation lies in this term which makes the equation a cubic in V, which is required to

---

same way, as the solar *system;* and hence any aggregate of particles moving under mutual forces. (*C.*) It means a number of forces acting simultaneously upon a number of particles.

account for the shape of certain isothermal curves.* But if the idea of an impenetrable atom is illogical, that of an impenetrable molecule is almost absurd. For the kinetical theory of matter teaches us that a molecule is like a solar system or star-cluster in miniature. Unless we suppose that in all heating of gases and vapors internal work is performed upon the molecules, implying that their atoms are at considerable distances, the whole kinetical theory of gases falls to the ground. As for the term added to P, there is no more than a partial and roughly approximative justification for it. Namely, let us imagine two spheres described round a particle as their centre, the radius of the larger being so great as to include all the particles whose action upon the centre is sensible, while the radius of the smaller is so large that a good many molecules are included within it. The possibility of describing such a sphere as the outer one implies that the attraction of the particles varies at some distances inversely as some higher power of the distance than the cube, or, to speak more clearly, that the attraction multiplied by the cube of the distance diminishes as the distance increases; for the number of particles at a given distance from any one particle is proportionate to the square of that distance and each of these gives a term of the virial which is the product of the attraction into the distance. Consequently unless the attraction multiplied by the cube of the distance diminished so rapidly with the distance as soon to become insensible, no such outer sphere as is supposed could be described. However, ordinary experience shows that such a sphere is possible; and consequently there must be distances at which the attraction does thus rapidly diminish as the distance increases. The two spheres, then, being so drawn, consider the virial of the central particle due to the particles between them. Let the density of the substance be increased, say, N times. Then, for every term, Rr, of the virial before the condensation, there will be N terms of the same magnitude after the condensation. Hence, the virial of each particle will be proportional to the density, and the equation of the virial becomes

$$a\theta = P\bar{V} + \frac{c}{v}.$$

This omits the virial within the inner sphere, the radius of which is so taken that within that distance the number of particles is not proportional to the number in a large sphere. For Van der Waals this radius is the diameter of his hard molecules, which assumption gives his equation. But it is plain that the attraction between the molecules must to a certain extent modify their distribution, unless some pecu-

---

*But, in fact, an inspection of these curves is sufficient to show that they are of a higher degree than the third. For they have the line $V = 0$, or some line V a constant for an asymptote, while for small values of P, the values of $d^2P/(dV)^2$ are positive.

liar conditions are fulfilled. The equation of Van der Waals can be approximately true therefore only for a gas. In a solid or liquid condition, in which the removal of a small amount of pressure has little effect on the volume, and where consequently the virial must be much greater than $P\bar{V}$, the virial must increase with the volume. For suppose we had a substance in a critical condition in which an increase of the volume would diminish the virial more than it would increase $\frac{3}{2}P\bar{V}$. If we were forcibly to diminish the volume of such a substance, when the temperature became equalised, the pressure which it could withstand would be less than before, and it would be still further condensed, and this would go on indefinitely until a condition were reached in which an increase of volume would increase $\frac{3}{2}P\bar{V}$ more than it would decrease the virial. In the case of solids, at least, P may be zero; so that the state reached would be one in which the virial increases with the volume, or the attraction between the particles does not increase so fast with a diminution of their distance as it would if the attraction were inversely as the distance.

Almost contemporaneously with Van der Waals's paper, another remarkable thesis for the doctorate was presented at Paris by Amagat.[16] It related to the elasticity and expansion of gases, and to this subject the superb experimenter, its author, has devoted his whole subsequent life. Especially interesting are his observations of the volumes of ethylene and of carbonic acid at temperatures from 20° to 100° and at pressures ranging from an ounce to 5000 pounds to the square inch. As soon as Amagat had obtained these results, he remarked that the "coefficient of expansion at constant volume," as it is absurdly called, that is, the rate of variation of the pressure with the temperature, was very nearly constant for each volume. This accords with the equation of the virial, which gives

$$\frac{dp}{d\theta} = \frac{a}{V} - \frac{d\Sigma\bar{R}r}{d\theta}.$$

Now, the virial must be nearly independent of the temperature, and therefore the last term almost disappears. The virial would not be quite independent of the temperature, because if the temperature (i.e. the square of the velocity of the molecules) is lowered, and the pressure correspondingly lowered, so as to make the volume the same, the attractions of the molecules will have more time to produce their effects, and consequently, the pairs of molecules the closest together will be held together longer and closer; so that the virial will generally be increased by a decrease of temperature. Now, Amagat's experiments do show an excessively minute effect of this sort, at least, when the volumes are not too small. However, the observations are well enough satisfied by assuming the "coefficient of expansion at constant volume" to consist wholly of the first term, $a/\bar{V}$. Thus, Amagat's experiments enable us to determine the values of a and thence to calculate the virial; and this we find varies for carbonic acid gas nearly inversely to $\bar{V}^{0.9}$. There is, thus, a rough approximation to satisfying Van der Waals's equation. But the most interesting result of Amagat's experiments, for our purpose at any rate, is that the quantity a, though nearly constant for any one volume, differs considerably with the volume, nearly doubling when the volume is reduced five-fold. This can only indicate that the mean kinetic energy of a given mass of the gas for a given temperature is greater the more the gas is compressed. But the laws of mechanics appear to enjoin that the mean kinetic energy of a moving particle shall be constant at any given temperature. The only escape from contradiction, then, is to suppose that the mean mass of a moving particle diminishes upon the condensation of the gas. In other words, many of the molecules are dissociated, or broken up into atoms or sub-molecules. The idea that dissociation should be favored by diminishing the volume will be pronounced by physicists, at first blush, as contrary to all our experience. But it must be remembered that the circumstances we are speaking of, that of a gas under fifty or more atmospheres pressure, are also unusual. That the "coefficient of expansion under constant volume" when multiplied by the volumes should increase with a decrement of the volume is also quite contrary to ordinary experience; yet it undoubtedly takes place in all gases under great pressure. Again, the doctrine of Arrhenius[*] is now generally accepted, that the molecular conductivity of an electrolyte is proportional to the dissociation of ions. Now the molecular conductivity of a fused electrolyte is usually superior to that of a solution. Here is a case, then, in which diminution of volume is accompanied by increased dissociation.

The truth is that several different kinds of dissociation have to be distinguished. In the first place, there is the dissociation of a chemical molecule to form chemical molecules under the regular action of chemical laws. This may be a double decomposition, as when iodhydric acid is dissociated, according to the formula

$$HI + HI = HH + II;$$

or, it may be a simple decomposition, as when pentachloride of phosphorus is dissociated according to the formula

$$PCl_5 = PCl_3 + ClCl.$$

All these dissociations require, according to the laws of thermochemistry, an elevated temperature. In the second place, there is the dissociation of a physically polymerous molecule, that is, of several chemical

[*]Anticipated by Clausius as long ago as 1857; and by Williamson in 1851.[17]

molecules joined by physical attractions. This I am inclined to suppose is a common concomitant of the heating of solids and liquids; for in these bodies there is no increase of compressibility with the temperature at all comparable with the increase of the expansibility. But, in the third place, there is the dissociation with which we are now concerned, which must be supposed to be a throwing off of unsaturated sub-molecules or atoms from the molecule. The molecule may, as I have said, be roughly likened to a solar system. As such, molecules are able to produce perturbations of one another's internal motions; and in this way a planet, i.e. a sub-molecule, will occasionally get thrown off and wander about by itself, till it finds another unsaturated sub-molecule with which it can unite. Such dissociation by perturbation will naturally be favored by the proximity of the molecules to one another.

Let us now pass to the consideration of that special substance, or rather class of substances, whose properties form the chief subject of botany and of zoölogy, as truly as those of the silicates form the chief subject of mineralogy: I mean the life-slimes, or protoplasm. Let us begin by cataloguing the general characters of these slimes. They one and all exist in two states of aggregation, a solid or nearly solid state and a liquid or nearly liquid state; but they do not pass from the former to the latter by ordinary fusion. They are readily decomposed by heat, especially in the liquid state; nor will they bear any considerable degree of cold. All their vital actions take place at temperatures very little below the point of decomposition. This extreme instability is one of numerous facts which demonstrate the chemical complexity of protoplasm. Every chemist will agree that they are far more complicated than the albumens. Now, albumen is estimated to contain in each molecule about a thousand atoms; so that it is natural to suppose that the protoplasms contain several thousands. We know that while they are chiefly composed of oxygen, hydrogen, carbon, and nitrogen, a large number of other elements enter into living bodies in small proportions; and it is likely that most of these enter into the composition of protoplasms. Now, since the numbers of chemical varieties increase at an enormous rate with the number of atoms per molecule, so that there are certainly hundreds of thousands of substances whose molecules contain twenty atoms or fewer, we may well suppose that the number of protoplasmic substances runs into the billions or trillions. Professor Cayley has given a mathematical theory of "trees," with a view of throwing a light upon such questions;[18] and in that light the estimate of trillions (in the English sense) seems immoderately moderate. It is true that an opinion has been emitted, and defended among biologists, that there is but one kind of protoplasm; but the observations of biologists, themselves, have almost exploded that hypothesis, which from a chemical standpoint appears utterly incredible. The anticipation of the chemist would decidedly be that enough different chemical substances having protoplasmic characters might be formed to account, not only for the differences between nerve-slime and muscle-slime, between whale-slime and lion-slime, but also for those minuter pervasive variations which characterise different breeds and single individuals.

Protoplasm, when quiescent, is, broadly speaking, solid; but when it is disturbed in an appropriate way, or sometimes even spontaneously without external disturbance, it becomes, broadly speaking, liquid. A moner in this state is seen under the microscope to have streams within its matter; a slime-mold slowly flows by force of gravity. The liquefaction starts from the point of disturbance and spreads through the mass. This spreading, however, is not uniform in all directions; on the contrary it takes at one time one course, at another another, through the homogeneous mass, in a manner that seems a little mysterious. The cause of disturbance being removed, these motions gradually (with higher kinds of protoplasm, quickly) cease, and the slime returns to its solid condition.

The liquefaction of protoplasm is accompanied by a mechanical phenomenon. Namely, some kinds exhibit a tendency to draw themselves up into a globular form. This happens particularly with the contents of muscle-cells. The prevalent opinion, founded on some of the most exquisite experimental investigations that the history of science can show, is undoubtedly that the contraction of muscle-cells is due to osmotic pressure; and it must be allowed that that is a factor in producing the effect. But it does not seem to me that it satisfactorily accounts even for the phenomena of muscular contraction; and besides, even naked slimes often draw up in the same way. In this case, we seem to recognise an increase of the surface-tension. In some cases, too, the reverse action takes place, extraordinary pseudopodia being put forth, as if the surface-tension were diminished in spots. Indeed, such a slime always has a sort of skin, due no doubt to surface-tension, and this seems to give way at the point where a pseudopodium is put forth.

Long-continued or frequently repeated liquefaction of the protoplasm results in an obstinate retention of the solid state, which we call fatigue. On the other hand repose in this state, if not too much prolonged, restores the liquefiability. These are both important functions.

The life-slimes have, further, the peculiar property of growing. Crystals also grow; their growth, however, consists merely in attracting matter like their own from the circumambient fluid. To suppose the growth of protoplasm of the same nature, would be to suppose this substance to be spontaneously generated in copious supplies wherever food is in solution. Certainly, it must be granted that protoplasm is but a chemical substance, and that there is no reason why it should not be formed synthetically like any other chemical substance. Indeed, Clifford has clearly shown that we have overwhelming evidence that it is so formed.[19] But to say that such formation is as regular and frequent as the assimilation of food is quite another matter. It is more consonant with the facts of observation to suppose that assimilated protoplasm is formed at the instant of assimilation, under the influence of the protoplasm already present. For each slime in its growth preserves its distinctive characters with wonderful truth, nerve-slime growing nerve-slime and muscle-slime muscle-slime, lion-slime growing lion-slime, and all the varieties of breeds and even individual characters being preserved in the growth. Now it is too much to suppose there are billions of different kinds of protoplasm floating about wherever there is food.

The frequent liquefaction of protoplasm increases its power of assimilating food; so much so, indeed, that it is questionable whether in the solid form it possesses this power.

The life-slime wastes as well as grows; and this too takes place chiefly if not exclusively in its liquid phases.

Closely connected with growth is reproduction; and though in higher forms this is a specialised function, it is universally true that wherever there is protoplasm, there is, will be, or has been a power of reproducing that same kind of protoplasm in a separated organism. Reproduction seems to involve the union of two sexes; though it is not demonstrable that this is always requisite.

Another physical property of protoplasm is that of taking habits. The course which the spread of liquefaction has taken in the past is rendered thereby more likely to be taken in the future; although there is no absolute certainty that the same path will be followed again.

Very extraordinary, certainly, are all these properties of protoplasm; as extraordinary as indubitable. But the one which has next to be mentioned, while equally undeniable, is infinitely more wonderful. It is that protoplasm feels. We have no direct evidence that this is true of protoplasm universally, and certainly some kinds feel far more than others. But there is a fair analogical inference that all protoplasm feels. It not only feels but exercises all the functions of mind.

Such are the properties of protoplasm. The problem is to find a hypothesis of the molecular constitution of this compound which will account for these properties, one and all.

Some of them are obvious results of the excessively complicated constitution of the protoplasm molecule. All very complicated substances are unstable; and plainly a molecule of several thousand atoms may be separated in many ways into two parts in each of which the polar chemical forces are very nearly saturated. In the solid protoplasm, as in other solids, the molecules must be supposed to be moving as it were in orbits, or, at least, so as not to wander indefinitely. But this solid cannot be melted, for the same reason that starch cannot be melted; because an amount of heat insufficient to make the entire molecules wander is sufficient to break them up completely and cause them to form new and simpler molecules. But when one of the molecules is disturbed, even if it be not quite thrown out of its orbit at first, sub-molecules of perhaps several hundred atoms each are thrown off from it. These will soon acquire the same mean kinetic energy as the others, and therefore velocities several times as great. They will naturally begin to wander, and in wandering will perturb a great many other molecules and cause them in their turn to behave like the one originally deranged. So many molecules will thus be broken up, that even those that are intact will no longer be restrained within orbits, but will wander about freely. This is the usual condition of a liquid, as modern chemists understand it; for in all electrolytic liquids there is considerable dissociation.

But this process necessarily chills the substance, not merely on account of the heat of chemical combination, but still more because the number of separate particles being greatly increased, the mean kinetic energy must be less. The substance being a bad conductor, this heat is not at once restored. Now the particles moving more slowly, the attractions between them have time to take effect, and they approach the condition of equilibrium. But their dynamic equilibrium is found in the restoration of the solid condition, which therefore takes place, if the disturbance is not kept up.

When a body is in the solid condition, most of its molecules must be moving at the same rate, or, at least, at certain regular sets of rates; otherwise the orbital motion would not be preserved. The distances of neighboring molecules must always be kept between a certain maximum and a certain minimum value. But if, without absorption of heat, the body be thrown into a liquid condition, the distances of neighboring molecules will be far more unequally distributed, and an effect upon the virial will result. The chilling of protoplasm upon its liquefaction must also be taken into account. The ordinary effect will no doubt be to increase the cohesion and with that the surface-tension, so that the mass will tend to draw itself up. But in special cases, the virial will be increased so much that the surface-tension will be diminished at points where the temperature is first restored. In that case, the outer film will give way and the tension at other places will aid in causing the general fluid to be poured out at those points, forming pseudopodia.

When the protoplasm is in a liquid state, and then only, a solution of food is able to penetrate its mass by diffusion. The protoplasm is then considerably dissociated; and so is the food, like all dissolved matter. If then the separated and unsaturated sub-molecules of the food happen to be of the same chemical species as sub-molecules of the protoplasm, they may unite with other sub-molecules of the protoplasm to form new molecules, in such a fashion that when the solid state is resumed, there may be more molecules of protoplasm than there were at the beginning. It is like the jack-knife whose blade and handle, after having been severally lost and replaced, were found and put together to make a new knife.

We have seen that protoplasm is chilled by liquefaction, and that this brings it back to the solid state, when the heat is recovered. This series of operations must be very rapid in the case of nerve-slime and even of muscle-slime, and may account for the unsteady or vibratory character of their action. Of course, if assimilation takes place, the heat of combination, which is probably trifling, is gained. On the other hand, if work is done, whether by nerve or by muscle, loss of energy must take place. In the case of the muscle, the mode by which the instantaneous part of the fatigue is brought about is easily traced out. If when the muscle contracts it be under stress, it will contract less than it otherwise would do, and there will be a loss of heat. It is like an engine which should work by dissolving salt in water and using the contraction during the solution to lift a weight, the salt being recovered afterwards by distillation. But the major part of fatigue has nothing to do with the correlation of forces. A man must labor hard to do in a quarter of an hour the work which draws from him enough heat to cool his body by a single degree. Meantime, he will be getting heated, he will be pouring out extra products of combustion, perspiration, etc., and he will be driving the blood at an accelerated rate through minute tubes at great expense. Yet all this will have little to do with his fatigue. He may sit quietly at his table writing, doing practically no physical work at all, and yet in a few hours be terribly fagged. This seems to be owing to the deranged sub-molecules of the nerve-slime not having had time to settle back into their proper combinations. When such sub-molecules are thrown out, as they must be from time to time, there is so much waste of material.

In order that a sub-molecule of food may be thoroughly and firmly assimilated into a broken molecule of protoplasm, it is necessary not only that it should have precisely the right chemical composition, but also that it should be at precisely the right spot at the right time and should be moving in precisely the right direction with precisely the right velocity. If all these conditions are not fulfilled, it will be more loosely retained than the other parts of the molecule; and every time it comes round into the situation in which it was drawn in, relatively to the other parts of that molecule and to such others as were near enough to be factors in the action, it will be in special danger of being thrown out again. Thus, when a partial liquefaction of the protoplasm takes place many times to about the same extent, it will, each time, be pretty nearly the same molecules that were last drawn in that are now thrown out. They will be thrown out, too, in about the same way, as to position, direction of motion, and velocity, in which they were drawn in; and this will be in about the same course that the ones last before them were thrown out. Not exactly, however; for the very cause of their being thrown off so easily is their not having fulfilled precisely the conditions of stable retention. Thus, the law of habit is accounted for, and with it its peculiar characteristic of not acting with exactitude.

It seems to me that this explanation of habit, aside from the question of its truth or falsity, has a certain value as an addition to our little store of mechanical examples of actions analogous to habit. All the others, so far as I know, are either statical or else involve forces which, taking only the sensible motions into account, violate the law of energy. It is so with the stream that wears its own bed. Here, the sand is carried to its most stable situation and left there. The law of energy forbids this; for when anything reaches a position of stable equilibrium, its momentum will be at a maximum, so that it can according to this law only be left at rest in an unstable situation. In all the statical illustrations, too, things are brought into certain states and left there. A garment receives folds and keeps them; that is, its limit of elasticity is exceeded. This failure to spring back is again an apparent violation of the law of energy; for the substance will not only not spring back of itself (which might be due to an unstable equilibrium being reached) but will not even do so when an impulse that way is applied to it. Accordingly, Professor James says "the phenomena of habit . . . are due to the plasticity of the . . . materials."[20] Now, plasticity of materials means the having of a low limit of elasticity. (See the *Century Dictionary*, under *solid*.)[21] But the hypothetical constitution of protoplasm here proposed involves no forces but attractions and repulsions strictly following the law of energy. The action here, that is, the throwing of an atom out of its orbit in a molecule, and the entering of a new atom into nearly, but not quite the same orbit, is somewhat similar to the molecular actions which may be supposed to take place in a solid strained beyond its limit of elasticity. Namely, in that case certain molecules must be thrown out of their orbits, to settle down again shortly after into new orbits. In short, the plastic solid resembles protoplasm in being partially and temporarily liquefied by a slight mechanical force. But the taking of a set by a solid body has but a moderate resemblance to the taking of a habit, inasmuch as the characteristic feature of the latter, its inexactitude and want of complete determinacy, is not so marked in the former, if it can be said to be present there, at all.

The truth is that though the molecular explanation of habit is pretty vague on the mathematical side, there can be no doubt that systems of atoms having polar forces would act substantially in that manner, and the explanation is even too satisfactory to suit the convenience of an advocate of tychism. For it may fairly be urged that since the phenomena of habit may thus result from a purely mechanical arrangement, it is unnecessary to suppose that habit-taking is a primordial principle of the universe. But one fact remains unexplained mechanically, which concerns not only the facts of habit, but all cases of actions apparently violating the law of energy; it is that all these phenomena depend upon aggregations of trillions of molecules in one and the same condition and neighborhood; and it is by no means clear how they could have all been brought and left in the same place and state by any conservative forces. But let the mechanical explanation be as perfect as it may, the state of things which it supposes presents evidence of a primordial habit-taking tendency. For it shows us like things acting in like ways because they are alike. Now, those who insist on the doctrine of necessity will for the most part insist that the physical world is entirely individual. Yet law involves an element of generality. Now to say that generality is primordial, but generalisation not, is like saying that diversity is primordial but diversification not. It turns logic upside down. At any rate, it is clear that nothing but a principle of habit, itself due to the growth by habit of an infinitesimal chance tendency toward habit-taking is the only bridge that can span the chasm between the chance-medley of chaos and the cosmos of order and law.

I shall not attempt a molecular explanation of the phenomena of reproduction, because that would require a subsidiary hypothesis, and carry me away from my main object. Such phenomena, universally diffused though they be, appear to depend upon special conditions; and we do not find that all protoplasm has reproductive powers.

But what is to be said of the property of feeling? If consciousness belongs to all protoplasm, by what mechanical constitution is this to be accounted for? The slime is nothing but a chemical compound. There is no inherent impossibility in its being formed synthetically in the laboratory, out of its chemical elements; and if it were so made, it would present all the characters of natural protoplasm. No doubt, then, it would feel. To hesitate to admit this would be puerile and ultra-puerile. By what element of the molecular arrangement, then, would that feeling be caused? This question cannot be evaded or pooh-poohed. Protoplasm certainly does feel; and unless we are to accept a weak dualism, the property must be shown to arise from some peculiarity of the mechanical system. Yet the attempt to deduce it from the three laws of mechanics, applied to never so ingenious a mechanical contrivance, would obviously be futile. It can never be explained, unless we admit that physical events are but degraded or undeveloped forms of psychical events. But once grant that the phenomena of matter are but the result of the sensibly complete sway of habits upon mind, and it only remains to explain why in the protoplasm these habits are to some slight extent broken up, so that according to the law of mind, in that special clause of it sometimes called the principle of accommodation,* feeling becomes intensified. Now the manner in which habits generally get broken up is this. Reactions usually terminate in the removal of a stimulus; for the excitation continues as long as the stimulus is present. Accordingly, habits are general ways of behavior which are associated with the removal of stimuli. But when the expected removal of the stimulus fails to occur, the excitation continues and increases, and non-habitual reactions take place; and these tend to weaken the habit. If, then, we suppose that matter never does obey its ideal laws with absolute precision, but that there are almost insensible fortuitous departures from regularity, these will produce, in general, equally minute effects. But protoplasm is in an excessively unstable condition; and it is the characteristic of unstable equilibrium, that near that point excessively minute causes may produce startlingly large effects. Here then, the usual departures from regularity will be followed by others that are very great; and the large fortuitous departures from law so produced, will tend still further to break up the laws, supposing that these are of the nature of habits. Now, this breaking up of habit and renewed fortuitous spontaneity will, according to the law of mind, be accompanied by an intensification of feeling. The nerve-protoplasm is, without doubt, in the most unstable condition of any kind of matter; and consequently, there the resulting feeling is the most manifest.

Thus we see that the idealist has no need to dread a mechanical theory of life. On the contrary, such a theory, fully developed, is bound to call in a tychistic idealism as its indispensible adjunct. Wherever chance-spontaneity is found, there, in the same proportion, feeling exists. In fact, chance is but the outward aspect of that which within itself is feeling. I long ago showed that real existence, or thing-ness, consists in regularities.[22] So, that primeval chaos in which there was no regularity was mere nothing, from a physical aspect. Yet it was not a blank zero; for there was an intensity of consciousness there in comparison with which all that we ever feel is but as the struggling of a molecule or two to throw off a little of the force of law to an endless and innumerable diversity of chance utterly unlimited.

But after some atoms of the protoplasm have thus become partially emancipated from law, what happens next to them? To understand

*"Physiologically, . . . accommodation means the breaking up of a habit. . . . Psychologically, it means reviving consciousness." Baldwin, *Psychology*, Part III, ch. i., §5.

this, we have to remember that no mental tendency is so easily strengthened by the action of habit as is the tendency to take habits. Now, in the higher kinds of protoplasm, especially, the atoms in question have not only long belonged to one molecule or another of the particular mass of slime of which they are parts; but before that, they were constituents of food of a protoplasmic constitution. During all this time, they have been liable to lose habits and to recover them again; so that now, when the stimulus is removed, and the foregone habits tend to reassert themselves, they do so in the case of such atoms with great promptness. Indeed, the return is so prompt that there is nothing but the feeling to show conclusively that the bonds of law have ever been relaxed.

In short, diversification is the vestige of chance-spontaneity; and wherever diversity is increasing, there chance must be operative. On the other hand, wherever uniformity is increasing, habit must be operative. But wherever actions take place under an established uniformity, there so much feeling as there may be takes the mode of a sense of reaction. That is the manner in which I am led to define the relation between the fundamental elements of consciousness and their physical equivalents.

It remains to consider the physical relations of general ideas. It may be well here to reflect that if matter has no existence except as a specialisation of mind, it follows that whatever affects matter according to regular laws is itself matter. But all mind is directly or indirectly connected with all matter, and acts in a more or less regular way; so that all mind more or less partakes of the nature of matter. Hence, it would be a mistake to conceive of the psychical and the physical aspects of matter as two aspects absolutely distinct. Viewing a thing from the outside, considering its relations of action and reaction with other things, it appears as matter. Viewing it from the inside, looking at its immediate character as feeling, it appears as consciousness. These two views are combined when we remember that mechanical laws are nothing but acquired habits, like all the regularities of mind, including the tendency to take habits, itself; and that this action of habit is nothing but generalisation, and generalisation is nothing but the spreading of feelings. But the question is, how do general ideas appear in the molecular theory of protoplasm?

The consciousness of a habit involves a general idea. In each action of that habit certain atoms get thrown out of their orbit, and replaced by others. Upon all the different occasions it is different atoms that are thrown off, but they are analogous from a physical point of view, and there is an inward sense of their being analogous. Every time one of the associated feelings recurs, there is a more or less vague sense that there are others, that it has a general character, and of about what this general character is. We ought not, I think, to hold that in protoplasm habit never acts in any other than the particular way suggested above. On the contrary, if habit be a primary property of mind, it must be equally so of matter, as a kind of mind. We can hardly refuse to admit that wherever chance motions have general characters, there is a tendency for this generality to spread and to perfect itself. In that case, a general idea is a certain modification of consciousness which accompanies any regularity or general relation between chance actions.

The consciousness of a general idea has a certain "unity of the ego" in it, which is identical when it passes from one mind to another. It is, therefore, quite analogous to a person; and, indeed, a person is only a particular kind of general idea. Long ago, in the *Journal of Speculative Philosophy* (Vol. II, p. 156), I pointed out that a person is nothing but a symbol involving a general idea;[23] but my views were, then, too nominalistic to enable me to see that every general idea has the unified living feeling of a person.

All that is necessary, upon this theory, to the existence of a person is that the feelings out of which he is constructed should be in close enough connection to influence one another. Here we can draw a consequence which it may be possible to submit to experimental test. Namely, if this be the case, there should be something like personal consciousness in bodies of men who are in intimate and intensely sympathetic communion. It is true that when the generalisation of feeling has been carried so far as to include all within a person, a stopping-place, in a certain sense, has been attained; and further generalisation will have a less lively character. But we must not think it will cease. *Esprit de corps*, national sentiment, sym-pathy, are no mere metaphors. None of us can fully realise what the minds of corporations are, any more than one of my brain-cells can know what the whole brain is thinking. But the law of mind clearly points to the existence of such personalities, and there are many ordinary observations which, if they were critically examined and supplemented by special experiments, might, as first appearances promise, give evidence of the influence of such greater persons upon individuals. It is often remarked that on one day half a dozen people, strangers to one another, will take it into their heads to do one and the same strange deed, whether it be a physical experiment, a crime, or an act of virtue. When the thirty thousand young people of the society for Christian Endeavor were in New York, there seemed to me to be some mysterious diffusion of sweetness and light.[24] If such a fact is capable of being made out anywhere, it should be in the church. The Christians have always been ready to risk their lives for the sake of having prayers in common, of getting together and praying simultaneously with great energy, and especially for their common body, for "the whole state of Christ's church militant here in earth," as one of the missals has it. This practice they have been keeping up everywhere, weekly, for many centuries. Surely, a personality ought to have developed in that church, in that "bride of Christ," as they call it, or else there is a strange break in the action of mind, and I shall have to acknowledge my views are much mistaken. Would not the societies for psychical research be more likely to break through the clouds, in seeking evidences of such corporate personality, than in seeking evidences of telepathy, which, upon the same theory, should be a far weaker phenomenon?

25

Evolutionary Love

P 521: The Monist 3 (January 1893):176–200. [Also published in CP 6.287–317.] In this fifth (and last) Monist *paper, Peirce develops his agapism, the doctrine that the law of love is operative in the world. He argues that of the three kinds of evolution (by fortuitous variation, by mechanical necessity, and by creative love) the third is the most fundamental: "Love, recognizing germs of loveliness in the hateful, gradually warms it into life, and makes it lovely. That is the sort of evolution which every careful student of my essay 'The Law of Mind' must see that* synechism *calls for." Peirce delivers a polemic against the "gospel of greed" and laments the fact that* sentiment *seems to have lost favor; sentimentalism, he says, is "the doctrine that great respect should be paid to the natural judgments of the sensible heart," and he entreats his readers "to consider whether to contemn it is not of all blasphemies the most degrading." He compares some of the views expressed here with those of Christianity, and ends with a discussion of the continuity of mind and the caution that we should not overestimate the importance of the individual.*

AT FIRST BLUSH. COUNTER-GOSPELS

Philosophy, when just escaping from its golden pupa-skin, mythology, proclaimed the great evolutionary agency of the universe to be Love. Or, since this pirate-lingo, English, is poor in such-like words, let us say Eros, the exuberance-love. Afterwards, Empedocles set up passionate-love and hate as the two coördinate powers of the universe.[1] In some passages, kindness is the word. But certainly, in any sense in which it has an opposite, to be senior partner of that opposite, is the highest position that love can attain. Nevertheless, the ontological gospeller, in whose days those views were familiar topics, made the One Supreme Being, by whom all things have been made out of nothing, to be cherishing-love. What, then, can he say to hate? Never mind, at this time, what the scribe of the apocalypse, if he were John, stung at length by persecution into a rage unable to distinguish suggestions of evil from visions of heaven, and so become the Slanderer of God to men, may have dreamed. The question is rather what the sane John thought, or ought to have thought, in order to carry out his idea consistently. His statement that God is love seems aimed at that saying of Ecclesiastes that we cannot tell whether God bears us love or hatred. "Nay," says John, "we can tell, and very simply! We know and have trusted the love which God hath in us. God is love." There is no logic in this, unless it means that God loves all men. In the preceding paragraph, he had said, "God is light and in him is no darkness at all." We are to understand, then, that as darkness is merely the defect of light, so hatred and evil are mere imperfect stages of $\dot{\alpha}\gamma\dot{\alpha}\pi\eta$ and $\dot{\alpha}\gamma\alpha\theta\dot{o}\nu$, love and loveliness. This concords with that utterance reported in John's Gospel: "God sent not the Son into the world to judge the world; but that the world should through him be saved. He that believeth on him is not judged: he that believeth not hath been judged already. . . . And this is the judgment, that the light is come into the world, and that men loved darkness rather than the light." That is to say, God visits no punishment on them; they punish themselves, by their natural affinity for the defective. Thus, the love that God is, is not a love of which hatred is the contrary; otherwise Satan would be a coördinate power; but it is a love which embraces hatred as an imperfect stage of it, an Anteros—yea, even needs hatred and hatefulness as its object. For self-love is no love; so if God's self is love, that which he loves must be defect of love; just as a luminary can light up only that which otherwise would be dark. Henry James, the Swedenborgian, says: "It is no doubt very tolerable finite or creaturely love to love one's own in another, to love another for his conformity to one's self: but nothing can be in more flagrant contrast with the creative Love, all whose tenderness *ex vi termini* must be reserved only for what intrinsically is most bitterly hostile and negative to itself." This is from *Substance and Shadow: an Essay on the Physics of Creation.*[2] It is a pity he had not filled his pages with things like this, as he was able easily to do, instead of scolding at his reader and at people generally, until the physics of creation was wellnigh forgot. I must deduct, however, from what I just wrote: obviously no genius could make his every sentence as sublime as one which discloses for the problem of evil its everlasting solution.

The movement of love is circular, at one and the same impulse projecting creations into independency and drawing them into harmony. This seems complicated when stated so; but it is fully summed up in the simple formula we call the Golden Rule. This does not, of course, say, Do everything possible to gratify the egoistic impulses of others, but it says, Sacrifice your own perfection to the perfectionment of your neighbor. Nor must it for a moment be confounded with the

Benthamite, or Helvetian, or Beccarian motto, Act for the greatest
good of the greatest number. Love is not directed to abstractions but
to persons; not to persons we do not know, nor to numbers of people,
but to our own dear ones, our family and neighbors. "Our neighbor,"
we remember, is one whom we live near, not locally perhaps, but in
life and feeling.

Everybody can see that the statement of St. John is the formula of
an evolutionary philosophy, which teaches that growth comes only
from love, from—I will not say self-*sacrifice*, but from the ardent impulse to fulfil another's highest impulse. Suppose, for example, that I
have an idea that interests me. It is my creation. It is my creature; for
as shown in last July's *Monist*,[3] it is a little person. I love it; and I will
sink myself in perfecting it. It is not by dealing out cold justice to the
circle of my ideas that I can make them grow, but by cherishing and
tending them as I would the flowers in my garden. The philosophy we
draw from John's gospel is that this is the way mind develops; and as
for the cosmos, only so far as it yet is mind, and so has life, is it capable
of further evolution. Love, recognising germs of loveliness in the hateful, gradually warms it into life, and makes it lovely. That is the sort
of evolution which every careful student of my essay "The Law of
Mind"[4] must see that *synechism* calls for.

The nineteenth century is now fast sinking into the grave, and we
all begin to review its doings and to think what character it is destined
to bear as compared with other centuries in the minds of future historians. It will be called, I guess, the Economical Century; for political
economy has more direct relations with all the branches of its activity
than has any other science. Well, political economy has its formula of
redemption, too. It is this: Intelligence in the service of greed ensures
the justest prices, the fairest contracts, the most enlightened conduct
of all the dealings between men, and leads to the *summum bonum*, food
in plenty and perfect comfort. Food for whom? Why, for the greedy
master of intelligence. I do not mean to say that this is one of the
legitimate conclusions of political economy, the scientific character of
which I fully acknowledge. But the study of doctrines, themselves
true, will often temporarily encourage generalisations extremely false,
as the study of physics has encouraged necessitarianism. What I say,
then, is that the great attention paid to economical questions during
our century has induced an exaggeration of the beneficial effects of
greed and of the unfortunate results of sentiment, until there has
resulted a philosophy which comes unwittingly to this, that greed is
the great agent in the elevation of the human race and in the evolution
of the universe.

I open a handbook of political economy,[5]—the most typical and
middling one I have at hand,—and there find some remarks of which
I will here make a brief analysis. I omit qualifications, sops thrown to

Cerberus, phrases to placate Christian prejudice, trappings which serve to hide from author and reader alike the ugly nakedness of the greed-god. But I have surveyed my position. The author enumerates "three motives to human action:

The love of self;

The love of a limited class having common interests and feelings with one's self;

The love of mankind at large."[6]

Remark, at the outset, what obsequious title is bestowed on greed,—"the love of self." Love! The second motive *is* love. In place of "a limited class" put "certain persons," and you have a fair description. Taking "class" in the old-fashioned sense, a weak kind of love is described. In the sequel, there seems to be some haziness as to the delimitation of this motive. By the love of mankind at large, the author does not mean that deep, subconscious passion that is properly so called; but merely public-spirit, perhaps little more than a fidget about pushing ideas. The author proceeds to a comparative estimate of the worth of these motives. Greed, says he, but using, of course, another word, "is not so great an evil as is commonly supposed. . . . Every man can promote his own interests a great deal more effectively than he can promote any one else's, or than any one else can promote his." Besides, as he remarks on another page, the more miserly a man is, the more good he does. The second motive "is the most dangerous one to which society is exposed." Love is all very pretty: "no higher or purer source of human happiness exists." (Ahem!) But it is a "source of enduring injury," and, in short, should be overruled by something wiser. What is this wiser motive? We shall see.

As for public spirit, it is rendered nugatory by the "difficulties in the way of its effective operation." For example, it might suggest putting checks upon the fecundity of the poor and the vicious; and "no measure of repression would be too severe," in the case of criminals. The hint is broad. But unfortunately, you cannot induce legislatures to take such measures, owing to the pestiferous "tender sentiments of man towards man." It thus appears, that public-spirit, or Benthamism, is not strong enough to be the effective tutor of love (I am skipping to another page), which must therefore be handed over to "the motives which animate men in the pursuit of wealth," in which alone we can confide, and which "are in the highest degree beneficent."* Yes, in the "highest degree" without exception are they beneficent to the being upon whom all their blessings are poured out, namely, the Self, whose "sole object," says the writer, in accumulating wealth is his individual

---

*How can a writer have any respect for science, as such, who is capable of confounding with the scientific propositions of political economy, which have nothing to say concerning what is "beneficent," such brummagem generalisations as this?

"sustenance and enjoyment." Plainly, the author holds the notion that some other motive might be in a higher degree beneficent even for the man's self to be a paradox wanting in good sense. He seeks to gloze and modify his doctrine; but he lets the perspicacious reader see what his animating principle is; and when, holding the opinions I have repeated, he at the same time acknowledges that society could not exist upon a basis of intelligent greed alone, he simply pigeon-holes himself as one of the eclectics of inharmonious opinions. He wants his mammon flavored with a *soupçon* of god.

The economists accuse those to whom the enunciation of their atrocious villainies communicates a thrill of horror of being *sentimentalists*. It may be so: I willingly confess to having some tincture of sentimentalism in me, God be thanked! Ever since the French Revolution brought this leaning of thought into ill-repute,—and not altogether undeservedly, I must admit, true, beautiful, and good as that great movement was,—it has been the tradition to picture sentimentalists as persons incapable of logical thought and unwilling to look facts in the eyes. This tradition may be classed with the French tradition that an Englishman says *godam* at every second sentence, the English tradition that an American talks about "Britishers," and the American tradition that a Frenchman carries forms of etiquette to an inconvenient extreme, in short with all those traditions which survive simply because the men who use their eyes and ears are few and far between. Doubtless some excuse there was for all those opinions in days gone by; and sentimentalism, when it was the fashionable amusement to spend one's evenings in a flood of tears over a woeful performance on a candle-litten stage, sometimes made itself a little ridiculous. But what after all is sentimentalism? It is an *ism,* a doctrine, namely, the doctrine that great respect should be paid to the natural judgments of the sensible heart. This is what sentimentalism precisely is; and I entreat the reader to consider whether to contemn it is not of all blasphemies the most degrading. Yet the nineteenth century has steadily contemned it, because it brought about the Reign of Terror. That it did so is true. Still, the whole question is one of *how much.* The reign of terror was very bad; but now the Gradgrind banner has been this century long flaunting in the face of heaven, with an insolence to provoke the very skies to scowl and rumble. Soon a flash and quick peal will shake economists quite out of their complacency, too late. The twentieth century, in its latter half, shall surely see the deluge-tempest burst upon the social order,—to clear upon a world as deep in ruin as that greed-philosophy has long plunged it into guilt. No post-thermidorian high jinks then!

So a miser is a beneficent power in a community, is he? With the same reason precisely, only in a much higher degree, you might pronounce the Wall Street sharp to be a good angel, who takes money from heedless persons not likely to guard it properly, who wrecks feeble enterprises better stopped, and who administers wholesome lessons to unwary scientific men, by passing worthless checks upon them,—as you did, the other day, to me, my millionaire Master in glomery, when you thought you saw your way to using my process without paying for it, and of so bequeathing to your children something to boast of their father about,—and who by a thousand wiles puts money at the service of intelligent greed, in his own person.[7] Bernard Mandeville, in his *Fable of the Bees*, maintains that private vices of all descriptions are public benefits, and proves it, too, quite as cogently as the economist proves his point concerning the miser.[8] He even argues, with no slight force, that but for vice civilisation would never have existed. In the same spirit, it has been strongly maintained and is to-day widely believed that all acts of charity and benevolence, private and public, go seriously to degrade the human race.

The *Origin of Species* of Darwin merely extends politico-economical views of progress to the entire realm of animal and vegetable life. The vast majority of our contemporary naturalists hold the opinion that the true cause of those exquisite and marvellous adaptations of nature for which, when I was a boy, men used to extol the divine wisdom, is that creatures are so crowded together that those of them that happen to have the slightest advantage force those less pushing into situations unfavorable to multiplication or even kill them before they reach the age of reproduction. Among animals, the mere mechanical individualism is vastly reënforced as a power making for good by the animal's ruthless greed. As Darwin puts it on his title-page, it is the struggle for existence; and he should have added for his motto: Every individual for himself, and the Devil take the hindmost! Jesus, in his Sermon on the Mount, expressed a different opinion.

Here, then, is the issue. The gospel of Christ says that progress comes from every individual merging his individuality in sympathy with his neighbors. On the other side, the conviction of the nineteenth century is that progress takes place by virtue of every individual's striving for himself with all his might and trampling his neighbor under foot whenever he gets a chance to do so. This may accurately be called the Gospel of Greed.

Much is to be said on both sides. I have not concealed, I could not conceal, my own passionate predilection. Such a confession will probably shock my scientific brethren. Yet the strong feeling is in itself, I think an argument of some weight in favor of the agapastic theory of evolution,—so far as it may be presumed to bespeak the normal judgment of the Sensible Heart. Certainly, if it were possible to believe in agapasm without believing it warmly, that fact would be an argument against the truth of the doctrine. At any rate, since the warmth of feeling exists, it should on every account be candidly confessed; especially since it creates a liability to one-sidedness on my part against which it behooves my readers and me to be severally on our guard.

SECOND THOUGHTS. IRENICA

Let us try to define the logical affinities of the different theories of evolution. Natural selection, as conceived by Darwin, is a mode of evolution in which the only positive agent of change in the whole passage from moner to man is fortuitous variation. To secure advance in a definite direction chance has to be seconded by some action that shall hinder the propagation of some varieties or stimulate that of others. In natural selection, strictly so called, it is the crowding out of the weak. In sexual selection, it is the attraction of beauty, mainly.

The *Origin of Species* was published toward the end of the year 1859. The preceding years since 1846 had been one of the most productive seasons,—or if extended so as to cover the great book we are considering, *the* most productive period of equal length in the entire history of science from its beginnings until now. The idea that chance begets order, which is one of the corner-stones of modern physics (although Dr. Carus considers it "the weakest point in Mr. Peirce's system,")[9] was at that time put into its clearest light. Quételet had opened the discussion by his *Letters on the Application of Probabilities to the Moral and Political Sciences*, a work which deeply impressed the best minds of that day, and to which Sir John Herschel had drawn general attention in Great Britain.[10] In 1857, the first volume of Buckle's *History of Civilisation* had created a tremendous sensation, owing to the use he made of this same idea. Meantime, the "statistical method" had, under that very name, been applied with brilliant success to molecular physics. Dr. John Herapath, an English chemist, had in 1847 outlined the kinetical theory of gases in his *Mathematical Physics;* and the interest the theory excited had been refreshed in 1856 by notable memoirs by Clausius and Krönig.[11] In the very summer preceding Darwin's publication, Maxwell had read before the British Association the first and most important of his researches on this subject.[12] The consequence was that the idea that fortuitous events may result in a physical law, and further that this is the way in which those laws which appear to conflict with the principle of the conservation of energy are to be explained, had taken a strong hold upon the minds of all who were abreast of the leaders of thought. By such minds, it was inevitable that the *Origin of Species,* whose teaching was simply the application of the same principle to the explanation of another "non-conservative" action, that of organic development, should be hailed and welcomed. The sublime discovery of the conservation of energy by Helmholtz in 1847, and that of the mechanical theory of heat by Clausius and by Rankine, independently, in 1850, had decidedly overawed all those who might have been inclined to sneer at physical science.[13] Thereafter a belated poet still harping upon "science peddling with the names of things" would fail of his effect. Mechanism was now known to be all, or very nearly so. All this time, utilitarianism,—that improved substitute for the Gospel,—was in its fullest feather; and was a natural ally of an individualistic theory. Dean Mansel's injudicious advocacy had led to mutiny among the bondsmen of Sir William Hamilton, and the nominalism of Mill had profited accordingly;[14] and although the real science that Darwin was leading men to was sure some day to give a death-blow to the sham-science of Mill, yet there were several elements of the Darwinian theory which were sure to charm the followers of Mill. Another thing: an æsthetics had been in use for thirteen years. Already, people's acquaintance with suffering had dropped off very much; and as a consequence, that unlovely hardness by which our times are so contrasted with those that immediately preceded them, had already set in, and inclined people to relish a ruthless theory. The reader would quite mistake the drift of what I am saying if he were to understand me as wishing to suggest that any of those things (except perhaps Malthus) influenced Darwin himself. What I mean is that his hypothesis, while without dispute one of the most ingenious and pretty ever devised, and while argued with a wealth of knowledge, a strength of logic, a charm of rhetoric, and above all with a certain magnetic genuineness that was almost irresistible, did not appear, at first, at all near to being proved; and to a sober mind its case looks less hopeful now than it did twenty years ago; but the extraordinarily favorable reception it met with was plainly owing, in large measure, to its ideas being those toward which the age was favorably disposed, especially, because of the encouragement it gave to the greed-philosophy.

Diametrically opposed to evolution by chance, are those theories which attribute all progress to an inward necessary principle, or other form of necessity. Many naturalists have thought that if an egg is destined to go through a certain series of embryological transformations, from which it is perfectly certain not to deviate, and if in geological time almost exactly the same forms appear successively, one replacing another in the same order, the strong presumption is that this latter succession was as predeterminate and certain to take place as the former. So, Nägeli, for instance, conceives that it somehow follows from the first law of motion and the peculiar, but unknown, molecular constitution of protoplasm, that forms must complicate themselves more and more. Kölliker makes one form generate another after a certain maturation has been accomplished. Weismann, too, though he calls himself a Darwinian, holds that nothing is due to chance, but that all forms are simple mechanical resultants of the heredity from two parents.*[15] It is very noticeable that all these different sectaries seek to import into their science a mechanical necessity to which the facts that come under their observation do not point. Those geologists who think that the variation of species is due to cataclasmic alterations of climate or of the chemical constitution of the air and water are also making mechanical necessity chief factor of evolution.

Evolution by sporting and evolution by mechanical necessity are conceptions warring against one another. A third method, which supersedes their strife, lies enwrapped in the theory of Lamarck.[16] According to his view, all that distinguishes the highest organic forms from the most rudimentary has been brought about by little hypertrophies or atrophies which have affected individuals early in their lives, and have been transmitted to their offspring. Such a transmission of acquired characters is of the general nature of habit-taking, and this is the representative and derivative within the physiological domain of the law of mind. Its action is essentially dissimilar to that of a physical force; and that is the secret of the repugnance of such necessitarians as Weismann to admitting its existence. The Lamarckians further suppose that although some of the modifications of form so transmitted were originally due to mechanical causes, yet the chief factors of their first production were the straining of endeavor and the overgrowth superinduced by exercise, together with the opposite actions. Now, endeavor, since it is directed toward an end, is essentially psychical, even though it be sometimes unconscious; and the growth due to exercise, as I argued in my last paper,[17] follows a law of a character quite contrary to that of mechanics.

Lamarckian evolution is thus evolution by the force of habit.— That sentence slipped off my pen while one of those neighbors whose function in the social cosmos seems to be that of an Interrupter, was asking me a question. Of course, it is nonsense. Habit is mere inertia, a resting on one's oars, not a propulsion. Now it is energetic projaculation (lucky there is such a word, or this untried hand might have been put to inventing one) by which in the typical instances of Lamarckian evolution the new elements of form are first created. Habit, however, forces them to take practical shapes, compatible with the structures they affect, and in the form of heredity and otherwise, gradually replaces the spontaneous energy that sustains them. Thus, habit plays a double part; it serves to establish the new features, and also to bring them into harmony with the general morphology and function of the animals and plants to which they belong. But if the reader will now kindly give himself the trouble of turning back a page or two, he will

*I am happy to find that Dr. Carus, too, ranks Weismann among the opponents of Darwin, notwithstanding his flying that flag.

see that this account of Lamarckian evolution coincides with the general description of the action of love, to which, I suppose, he yielded his assent.

Remembering that all matter is really mind, remembering, too, the continuity of mind, let us ask what aspect Lamarckian evolution takes on within the domain of consciousness. Direct endeavor can achieve almost nothing. It is as easy by taking thought to add a cubit to one's stature, as it is to produce an idea acceptable to any of the Muses by merely straining for it, before it is ready to come. We haunt in vain the sacred well and throne of Mnemosyne; the deeper workings of the spirit take place in their own slow way, without our connivance. Let but their bugle sound, and we may then make our effort, sure of an oblation for the altar of whatsoever divinity its savor gratifies. Besides this inward process, there is the operation of the environment, which goes to break up habits destined to be broken up and so to render the mind lively. Everybody knows that the long continuance of a routine of habit makes us lethargic, while a succession of surprises wonderfully brightens the ideas. Where there is a motion, where history is a-making, there is the focus of mental activity, and it has been said that the arts and sciences reside within the temple of Janus, waking when that is open, but slumbering when it is closed. Few psychologists have perceived how fundamental a fact this is. A portion of mind abundantly commissured to other portions works almost mechanically. It sinks to the condition of a railway junction. But a portion of mind almost isolated, a spiritual peninsula, or *cul-de-sac*, is like a railway terminus. Now mental commissures are habits. Where they abound, originality is not needed and is not found; but where they are in defect, spontaneity is set free. Thus, the first step in the Lamarckian evolution of mind is the putting of sundry thoughts into situations in which they are free to play. As to growth by exercise, I have already shown, in discussing "Man's Glassy Essence," in last October's *Monist*, [18] what its *modus operandi* must be conceived to be, at least, until a second equally definite hypothesis shall have been offered. Namely, it consists of the flying asunder of molecules, and the reparation of the parts by new matter. It is, thus, a sort of reproduction. It takes place only during exercise, because the activity of protoplasm consists in the molecular disturbance which is its necessary condition. Growth by exercise takes place also in the mind. Indeed, that is what it is to *learn*. But the most perfect illustration is the development of a philosophical idea by being put into practice. The conception which appeared, at first, as unitary, splits up into special cases; and into each of these new thought must enter to make a practicable idea. This new thought, however, follows pretty closely the model of the parent conception; and thus a homogeneous development takes place. The parallel between this and the course of molecular occurrences is apparent. Patient attention will be able to trace all these elements in the transaction called learning.

Three modes of evolution have thus been brought before us; evolution by fortuitous variation, evolution by mechanical necessity, and evolution by creative love. We may term them *tychastic* evolution, or *tychasm, anancastic* evolution, or *anancasm,* and *agapastic* evolution, or *agapasm.* The doctrines which represent these as severally of principal importance, we may term *tychasticism, anancasticism,* and *agapasticism.* On the other hand the mere propositions that absolute chance, mechanical necessity, and the law of love, are severally operative in the cosmos, may receive the names of *tychism, anancism,* and *agapism.*

All three modes of evolution are composed of the same general elements. Agapasm exhibits them the most clearly. The good result is here brought to pass, first, by the bestowal of spontaneous energy by the parent upon the offspring, and, second, by the disposition of the latter to catch the general idea of those about it and thus to subserve the general purpose. In order to express the relation that tychasm and anancasm bear to agapasm, let me borrow a word from geometry. An ellipse crossed by a straight line is a sort of cubic curve; for a cubic is a curve which is cut thrice by a straight line; now a straight line might cut the ellipse twice and its associated straight line a third time. Still the ellipse with the straight line across it would not have the characteristics of a cubic. It would have, for instance, no contrary flexure, which no true cubic wants; and it would have two nodes, which no true cubic has. The geometers say that it is a *degenerate* cubic. Just so, tychasm and anancasm are degenerate forms of agapasm.

Men who seek to reconcile the Darwinian idea with Christianity will remark that tychastic evolution, like the agapastic, depends upon a reproductive creation, the forms preserved being those that use the spontaneity conferred upon them in such wise as to be drawn into harmony with their original, quite after the Christian scheme. Very good! This only shows that just as love cannot have a contrary, but must embrace what is most opposed to it, as a degenerate case of it, so tychasm is a kind of agapasm. Only, in the tychastic evolution progress is solely owing to the distribution of the napkin-hidden talent of the rejected servant among those not rejected, just as ruined gamesters leave their money on the table to make those not yet ruined so much the richer. It makes the felicity of the lambs just the damnation of the goats, transposed to the other side of the equation. In genuine agapasm, on the other hand, advance takes place by virtue of a positive sympathy among the created springing from continuity of mind. This is the idea which tychasticism knows not how to manage.

The anancasticist might here interpose, claiming that the mode of evolution for which he contends agrees with agapasm at the point at which tychasm departs from it. For it makes development go through certain phases, having its inevitable ebbs and flows, yet tending on the whole to a foreordained perfection. Bare existence by this its destiny betrays an intrinsic affinity for the good. Herein, it must be admitted, anancasm shows itself to be in a broad acception a species of agapasm. Some forms of it might easily be mistaken for the genuine agapasm. The Hegelian philosophy is such an anancasticism. With its revelatory religion, with its synechism (however imperfectly set forth), with its "reflection," the whole idea of the theory is superb, almost sublime. Yet, after all, living freedom is practically omitted from its method. The whole movement is that of a vast engine, impelled by a *vis a tergo*, with a blind and mysterious fate of arriving at a lofty goal. I mean that such an engine it *would* be, if it really worked; but in point of fact, it is a Keely motor.[19] Grant that it really acts as it professes to act, and there is nothing to do but accept the philosophy. But never was there seen such an example of a long chain of reasoning,—shall I say with a flaw in every link?—no, with every link a handful of sand, squeezed into shape in a dream. Or say, it is a pasteboard model of a philosophy that in reality does not exist. If we use the one precious thing it contains, the idea of it, introducing the tychism which the arbitrariness of its every step suggests, and make that the support of a vital freedom which is the breath of the spirit of love, we may be able to produce that genuine agapasticism, at which Hegel was aiming.

A Third Aspect. Discrimination

In the very nature of things, the line of demarcation between the three modes of evolution is not perfectly sharp. That does not prevent its being quite real; perhaps it is rather a mark of its reality. There is in the nature of things no sharp line of demarcation between the three fundamental colors, red, green, and violet. But for all that they are really different. The main question is whether three radically different evolutionary elements have been operative; and the second question is what are the most striking characteristics of whatever elements have been operative.

I propose to devote a few pages to a very slight examination of these questions in their relation to the historical development of human thought. I first formulate for the reader's convenience the briefest possible definitions of the three conceivable modes of development of thought, distinguishing also two varieties of anancasm and three of agapasm. The tychastic development of thought, then, will consist in slight departures from habitual ideas in different directions indifferently, quite purposeless and quite unconstrained whether by outward circumstances or by force of logic, these new departures being followed by unforeseen results which tend to fix some of them as habits more than others. The anancastic development of thought will consist of new ideas adopted without foreseeing whither they tend, but having a character determined by causes either external to the mind, such as changed circumstances of life, or internal to the mind as logical developments of ideas already accepted, such as generalisations. The agapastic development of thought is the adoption of certain mental tendencies, not altogether heedlessly, as in tychasm, nor quite blindly by the mere force of circumstances or of logic, as in anancasm, but by an immediate attraction for the idea itself, whose nature is divined before the mind possesses it, by the power of sympathy, that is, by virtue of the continuity of mind; and this mental tendency may be of three varieties, as follows. First, it may affect a whole people or community in its collective personality, and be thence communicated to such individuals as are in powerfully sympathetic connection with the collective people, although they may be intellectually incapable of attaining the idea by their private understandings or even perhaps of consciously apprehending it. Second, it may affect a private person directly, yet so that he is only enabled to apprehend the idea, or to appreciate its attractiveness, by virtue of his sympathy with his neighbors, under the influence of a striking experience or development of thought. The conversion of St. Paul may be taken as an example of what is meant. Third, it may affect an individual, independently of his human affections, by virtue of an attraction it exercises upon his mind, even before he has comprehended it. This is the phenomenon which has been well called the *divination* of genius; for it is due to the continuity between the man's mind and the Most High.

Let us next consider by means of what tests we can discriminate between these different categories of evolution. No absolute criterion is possible in the nature of things, since in the nature of things there is no sharp line of demarcation between the different classes. Nevertheless, quantitative symptoms may be found by which a sagacious and sympathetic judge of human nature may be able to estimate the approximate proportions in which the different kinds of influence are commingled.

So far as the historical evolution of human thought has been tychastic, it should have proceeded by insensible or minute steps; for such is the nature of chances when so multiplied as to show phenomena of regularity. For example, assume that of the native-born white adult males of the United States in 1880, one-fourth part were below 5 feet 4 inches in stature and one-fourth part above 5 feet 8 inches. Then by the principles of probability, among the whole population, we should expect

	216 under 4 feet 6 inches,					216 above 6 feet 6 inches.				
	48	"	4	"	5	"	48	"	6	"	7	"
	9	"	4	"	4	"	9	"	6	"	8	"
less than	2	"	4	"	3	"	less than	2	"	6	"	9	"

I set down these figures to show how insignificantly few are the cases in which anything very far out of the common run presents itself by chance. Though the stature of only every second man is included within the four inches between 5 feet 4 inches and 5 feet 8 inches, yet if this interval be extended by thrice four inches above and below, it will embrace all our 8 millions odd of native-born adult white males (of 1880), except only 9 taller and 9 shorter.

The test of minute variation, if *not* satisfied, absolutely negatives tychasm. If it *is* satisfied, we shall find that it negatives anancasm but not agapasm. We want a positive test, satisfied by tychasm, only. Now wherever we find men's thought taking by imperceptible degrees a turn contrary to the purposes which animate them, in spite of their highest impulses, there, we may safely conclude, there has been a tychastic action.

Students of the history of mind there be of an erudition to fill an imperfect scholar like me with envy edulcorated by joyous admiration, who maintain that ideas when just started are and can be little more than freaks, since they cannot yet have been critically examined, and further that everywhere and at all times progress has been so gradual that it is difficult to make out distinctly what original step any given man has taken. It would follow that tychasm has been the sole method of intellectual development. I have to confess I cannot read history so; I cannot help thinking that while tychasm has sometimes been operative, at others great steps covering nearly the same ground and made by different men independently, have been mistaken for a succession of small steps, and further that students have been reluctant to admit a real entitative "spirit" of an age or of a people, under the mistaken and unscrutinised impression that they should thus be opening the door to wild and unnatural hypotheses. I find, on the contrary, that, however it may be with the education of individual minds, the historical development of thought has seldom been of a tychastic nature, and exclusively in backward and barbarising movements. I desire to speak with the extreme modesty which befits a student of logic who is required to survey so very wide a field of human thought that he can cover it only by a reconnaisance, to which only the greatest skill and most adroit methods can impart any value at all; but, after all, I can only express my own opinions and not those of anybody else; and in my humble judgment, the largest example of tychasm is afforded by the history of Christianity, from about its establishment by Constantine, to, say, the time of the[20] Irish monasteries, an era or eon of about 500 years. Undoubtedly the external circumstance which more than all others at first inclined men to accept Christianity in its loveliness and tenderness, was the fearful extent to which society was broken up into units by the unmitigated greed and hard-heartedness into which the Romans had seduced the world. And yet it was that very same fact, more than any other external circumstance, that fostered that bitterness against the wicked world of which the primitive Gospel of Mark contains not a single trace. At least, I do not detect it in the remark about the blasphemy against the Holy Ghost, where nothing is said about vengeance, nor even in that speech where the closing lines of Isaiah are quoted, about the worm and the fire that feed upon the "carcasses of the men that have transgressed against me."[21] But little by little the bitterness increases until in the last book of the New Testament, its poor distracted author represents that all the time Christ was talking about having come to save the world, the secret design was to catch the entire human race, with the exception of a paltry 144000, and souse them all in brimstone lake, and as the smoke of their torment went up for ever and ever, to turn and remark, "There is no curse any more." Would it be an insensible smirk or a fiendish grin that should accompany such an utterance? I wish I could believe St. John did not write it; but it is his gospel which tells about the "resurrection unto condemnation,"—that is of men's being resuscitated just for the sake of torturing them;—and, at any rate, the Revelation is a very ancient composition. One can understand that the early Christians were like men trying with all their might to climb a steep declivity of smooth wet clay; the deepest and truest element of their life, animating both heart and head, was universal love; but they were continually, and against their wills, slipping into a party spirit, every slip serving as a precedent, in a fashion but too familiar to every man. This party feeling insensibly grew until by about A.D. 330 the lustre of the pristine integrity that in St. Mark reflects the white spirit of light was so far tarnished that Eusebius (the Jared Sparks[22] of that day), in the preface to his *History*, could announce his intention of exaggerating everything that tended to the glory of the church and of suppressing whatever might disgrace it.[23] His Latin contemporary Lactantius is worse, still;[24] and so the darkling went on increasing until before the end of the century the great library of Alexandria was destroyed by Theophilus,* until Gregory the Great, two centuries later, burnt the great library of Rome, proclaiming that "Ignorance is the mother of devotion"[25] (which is true, just as oppression and injustice is the mother of spirituality), until a sober description of the state of the church would be a thing our not too nice newspapers would treat as "unfit for publication." All this movement is shown by the application of the test given above to have been tychastic. Another very much like it on a small scale, only a hundred times swifter, for the study of which there are documents by the library-full, is to be found in the history of the French Revolution.

---

*See [John William] Draper's *History of Intellectual Development* [1862], chap. x.

Anancastic evolution advances by successive strides with pauses between. The reason is that in this process a habit of thought having been overthrown is supplanted by the next strongest. Now this next strongest is sure to be widely disparate from the first, and as often as not is its direct contrary. It reminds one of our old rule of making the second candidate vice-president. This character, therefore, clearly distinguishes anancasm from tychasm. The character which distinguishes it from agapasm is its purposelessness. But external and internal anancasm have to be examined separately. Development under the pressure of external circumstances, or cataclasmine evolution, is in most cases unmistakable enough. It has numberless degrees of intensity, from the brute force, the plain war, which has more than once turned the current of the world's thought, down to the hard fact of evidence, or what has been taken for it, which has been known to convince men by hordes. The only hesitation that can subsist in the presence of such a history is a quantitative one. Never are external influences the only ones which affect the mind, and therefore it must be a matter of judgment for which it would scarcely be worth while to attempt to set rules, whether a given movement is to be regarded as principally governed from without or not. In the rise of medieval thought, I mean scholasticism and the synchronistic art developments, undoubtedly the crusades and the discovery of the writings of Aristotle were powerful influences. The development of scholasticism from Roscellin to Albertus Magnus closely follows the successive steps in the knowledge of Aristotle. Prantl thinks that that is the whole story, and few men have thumbed more books than Carl Prantl.[26] He has done good solid work, notwithstanding his slap-dash judgments. But we shall never make so much as a good beginning of comprehending scholasticism until the whole has been systematically explored and digested by a company of students regularly organised and held under rule for that purpose. But as for the period we are now specially considering, that which synchronised the Romanesque architecture, the literature is easily mastered. It does not quite justify Prantl's dicta as to the slavish dependence of these authors upon their authorities. Moreover, they kept a definite purpose steadily before their minds, throughout all their studies. I am, therefore, unable to offer this period of scholasticism as an example of pure external anancasm, which seems to be the fluorine of the intellectual elements. Perhaps the recent Japanese reception of western ideas is the purest instance of it in history. Yet in combination with other elements, nothing is commoner. If the development of ideas under the influence of the study of external facts be considered as external anancasm,—it is on the border between the external and the internal forms,—it is, of course, the principal thing in modern learning. But Whewell, whose masterly comprehension of the history of science critics have been too ignorant properly to appreciate, clearly shows that it is far from being the overwhelmingly preponderant influence, even there.[27]

Internal anancasm, or logical groping, which advances upon a predestined line without being able to foresee whither it is to be carried nor to steer its course, this is the rule of development of philosophy. Hegel first made the world understand this; and he seeks to make logic not merely the subjective guide and monitor of thought, which was all it had been ambitioning before, but to be the very mainspring of thinking, and not merely of individual thinking but of discussion, of the history of the development of thought, of all history, of all development. This involves a positive, clearly demonstrable error. Let the logic in question be of whatever kind it may, a logic of necessary inference or a logic of probable inference (the theory might perhaps be shaped to fit either), in any case it supposes that logic is sufficient of itself to determine what conclusion follows from given premises; for unless it will do so much, it will not suffice to explain why an individual train of reasoning should take just the course it does take, to say nothing of other kinds of development. It thus supposes that from given premises, only one conclusion can logically be drawn, and that there is no scope at all for free choice. That from given premises only one conclusion can logically be drawn, is one of the false notions which have come from logicians' confining their attention to that Nantucket of thought, the logic of non-relative terms. In the logic of relatives, it does not hold good.

One remark occurs to me. If the evolution of history is in considerable part of the nature of internal anancasm, it resembles the development of individual men; and just as 33 years is a rough but natural unit of time for individuals, being the average age at which man has issue, so there should be an approximate period at the end of which one great historical movement ought to be likely to be supplanted by another. Let us see if we can make out anything of the kind. Take the governmental development of Rome as being sufficiently long and set down the principal dates.

B.C.   753, Foundation of Rome.
B.C.   510, Expulsion of the Tarquins.
B.C.   27, Octavius assumes title Augustus.
A.D.   476, End of Western Empire.
A.D.   962, Holy Roman Empire.
A.D. 1453, Fall of Constantinople.

The last event was one of the most significant in history, especially for Italy. The intervals are 243, 483, 502, 486, 491 years. All are rather curiously near equal, except the first which is half the others. Successive reigns of kings would not commonly be so near equal. Let us set down a few dates in the history of thought.

B.C.   585, Eclipse of Thales. Beginning of Greek philosophy.
A.D.   30, The crucifixion.
A.D.   529, Closing of Athenian schools. End of Greek philosophy.
A.D. 1125, (Approximate) Rise of the Universities of Bologna and
       Paris.
A.D. 1543, Publication of the *De Revolutionibus* of Copernicus. Be-
       ginning of Modern Science.

The intervals are 615, 499, 596, 418 years. In the history of metaphysics,
we may take the following:

B.C.   322, Death of Aristotle.
A.D. 1274, Death of Aquinas.
A.D. 1804, Death of Kant.

The intervals are 1595 and 530 years. The former is about thrice the
latter.

From these figures, no conclusion can fairly be drawn. At the same
time, they suggest that perhaps there may be a rough natural era of
about 500 years. Should there be any independent evidence of this, the
intervals noticed may gain some significance.

The agapastic development of thought should, if it exists, be distinguished by its purposive character, this purpose being the development of an idea. We should have a direct agapic or sympathetic comprehension and recognition of it, by virtue of the continuity of
thought. I here take it for granted that such continuity of thought has
been sufficiently proved by the arguments used in my paper on the
"Law of Mind" in *The Monist* of last July. Even if those arguments are
not quite convincing in themselves, yet if they are reënforced by an
apparent agapasm in the history of thought, the two propositions will
lend one another mutual aid. The reader will, I trust, be too well
grounded in logic to mistake such mutual support for a vicious circle
in reasoning. If it could be shown directly that there is such an entity
as the "spirit of an age" or of a people, and that mere individual
intelligence will not account for all the phenomena, this would be
proof enough at once of agapasticism and of synechism. I must acknowledge that I am unable to produce a cogent demonstration of this;
but I am, I believe, able to adduce such arguments as will serve to
confirm those which have been drawn from other facts. I believe that
all the greatest achievements of mind have been beyond the powers of
unaided individuals; and I find, apart from the support this opinion
receives from synechistic considerations, and from the purposive character of many great movements, direct reason for so thinking in the
sublimity of the ideas and in their occurring simultaneously and independently to a number of individuals of no extraordinary general
powers. The pointed Gothic architecture in several of its develop-

ments appears to me to be of such a character. All attempts to imitate it by modern architects of the greatest learning and genius appear flat and tame, and are felt by their authors to be so. Yet at the time the style was living, there was quite an abundance of men capable of producing works of this kind of gigantic sublimity and power. In more than one case, extant documents show that the cathedral chapters, in the selection of architects, treated high artistic genius as a secondary consideration, as if there were no lack of persons able to supply that; and the results justify their confidence. Were individuals in general, then, in those ages possessed of such lofty natures and high intellect? Such an opinion would break down under the first examination.

How many times have men now in middle life seen great discoveries made independently and almost simultaneously! The first instance I remember was the prediction of a planet exterior to Uranus by Leverrier and Adams.[28] One hardly knows to whom the principle of the conservation of energy ought to be attributed, although it may reasonably be considered as the greatest discovery science has ever made. The mechanical theory of heat was set forth by Rankine and by Clausius during the same month of February, 1850;[29] and there are eminent men who attribute this great step to Thomson.* The kinetical theory of gases, after being started by John Bernoulli and long buried in oblivion, was reinvented and applied to the explanation not merely of the laws of Boyle, Charles, and Avogadro,[30] but also of diffusion and viscosity, by at least three modern physicists separately. It is well known that the doctrine of natural selection was presented by Wallace and by Darwin at the same meeting of the British Association; and Darwin in his "Historical Sketch" prefixed to the later editions of his book shows that both were anticipated by obscure forerunners. The method of spectrum analysis was claimed for Swan as well as for Kirchhoff, and there were others who perhaps had still better claims. The authorship of the Periodical Law of the Chemical Elements is disputed between a Russian, a German, and an Englishman;[31] although there is no room for doubt that the principal merit belongs to the first. These are nearly all the greatest discoveries of our times. It is the same with the inventions. It may not be surprising that the telegraph should have been independently made by several inventors, because it was an easy corollary from scientific facts well made out before. But it was not so with the telephone and other inventions. Ether, the first anæsthetic, was introduced independently by three different New England physicians.[32] Now ether had been a common article for a century. It had been in one of the pharmacopœias three centuries before. It is quite incredible that its anæsthetic property

*Thomson, himself, in his article *Heat* in the *Encyclopedia Britannica*, never once mentions the name of Clausius.

should not have been known; it was known. It had probably passed from mouth to ear as a secret from the days of Basil Valentine;[33] but for long it had been a secret of the Punchinello kind.[34] In New England, for many years, boys had used it for amusement. Why then had it not been put to its serious use? No reason can be given, except that the motive to do so was not strong enough. The motives to doing so could only have been desire for gain and philanthropy. About 1846, the date of the introduction, philanthropy was undoubtedly in an unusually active condition. That sensibility, or sentimentalism, which had been introduced in the previous century, had undergone a ripening process, in consequence of which, though now less intense than it had previously been, it was more likely to influence unreflecting people than it had ever been. All three of the ether-claimants had probably been influenced by the desire for gain; but nevertheless they were certainly not insensible to the agapic influences.

I doubt if any of the great discoveries ought, properly, to be considered as altogether individual achievements; and I think many will share this doubt. Yet, if not, what an argument for the continuity of mind, and for agapasticism is here! I do not wish to be very strenuous. If thinkers will only be persuaded to lay aside their prejudices and apply themselves to studying the evidences of this doctrine, I shall be fully content to await the final decision.

NOTES

These notes, numbered consecutively within each of the twenty-five items in the present volume, provide biographical, historical, bibliographic, explanatory, and other relevant information (including translations) not contained in Peirce's footnotes in the text. For some of the better known works by some of the better known philosophers (such as Hume's *Treatise [of Human Nature]*, Kant's *Critique [of the Pure Reason]*, or Locke's *Essay [Concerning Human Understanding]*), we have used abbreviated titles. We have also used a number of standard abbreviations (including those for books of the Bible) and a few somewhat less than standard: among these are aph. (aphorism), art. (article), pt. (part), qu. (question), sec. (section), and tract. (tractatus). Again, MS references are to Peirce's manuscripts in Harvard's Houghton Library, P references to his publications (as listed in Ketner et al., *A Comprehensive Bibliography*), W references to the *Writings of Charles S. Peirce*, and CP references to the *Collected Papers*.

1. On a New List of Categories

1. See book 1 of the Transcendental Analytic in Kant's *Critique*.

2. In note 12 in MS 785, Peirce made the following comment upon this statement: "It may be doubted whether it was philosophical to rest this matter on empirical psychology. The question is extremely difficult" (W2:94).

3. Johann Friedrich Herbart, *Lehrbuch zur Einleitung in die Philosophie* (vol. 1 of *Sämmtliche Werke* [Leipzig, 1850]), p. 77: "All our thoughts may be considered from two points of view; partly as activities of our mind, partly in relation to what is thought through them. In the latter respect they are called *concepts*, which term, by signifying *what is conceived*, requires us to abstract from the mode and manner in which we might receive, produce, or reproduce the thought."

4. See "Upon Logical Comprehension and Extension" (W2:70–86).

2. Questions Concerning Certain Faculties

1. St. Anselm, *Monologium et proslogion*, chs. 66 and 70. St. Paul's saying ("For now we see in a mirror, darkly; but then face to face") is quoted from the Vulgate, 1 Cor. 13:12.

2. Berengarius is quoted from Carl Prantl, *Geschichte der Logik im Abendlande* (Leipzig, 1855–67), 2:72–75: "Clearly it is characteristic of a great soul to take refuge in dialectic in all circumstances, because to take refuge in it is to take refuge in reason, and whoever does not take refuge there, since it is in respect of reason that he is made in the image of God, gives up his honor; nor can he be renewed from day to day in the image of God."

3. Peirce read Fredegisus (d. 834), an English monk who succeeded Alcuin at Charlemagne's court, in Prantl's *Geschichte*, 2:17–19.

4. Peter Abelard, *Ouvrages inédits* (Paris, 1836), p. 179.

5. *De generibus et speciebus* is included in Abelard's *Ouvrages inédits*; see pp. 528, 517, 535.

6. John of Salisbury, *Metalogicon,* bk. 4, ch. 27: "Although there are many mistakes in Aristotle, as is evident from the writings of Christians and pagans alike, his equal in logic has yet to be found."

7. Abelard, *Ouvrages inédits,* pp. 293 and 204: "But nothing against Aristotle" and "But if we can find fault with Aristotle the prince of the Peripatetics, what *can* we trust in this art?"

8. Almost certainly, this is J. M. Macallister, a New England magician.

9. *An Essay Towards a New Theory of Vision* (1709).

10. Peirce gives the following definition in the *Century Dictionary:* "the smallest angular measure of which the eye can distinguish the parts. It is about half a minute."

11. See Berkeley's *Principles of Human Knowledge,* secs. 1–6.

3. SOME CONSEQUENCES OF FOUR INCAPACITIES

1. Aristotle, *Prior Analytics,* 68b15–17 or 69a16–19.

2. There is no such published objection, but people like Chauncey Wright or F. E. Abbot might have objected to Peirce's argument when he presented his paper, "On the Natural Classification of Arguments" (W2:23–48), before the American Academy of Arts and Sciences on 9 April 1867.

3. This is the second volume of Dugald Stewart's *Elements of the Philosophy of the Human Mind,* where in addition to the four authors mentioned, he also discusses Bacon, Fontenelle, D'Alembert, Reid, and Prevost.

4. Aristotle, *Posterior Analytics,* 1.2.72a15.

5. Peirce did not know that this is a translation, by George Scholarios (1400–1464), of Petrus Hispanus's *Summulae logicales.*

6. "An hypothesis is a proposition that is assumed in order to test the truth of what is not yet known to be true. Many demand that for an hypothesis to be identified as being true, no matter how true it appears before, other things must be deducible from it. But others say that for an hypothesis to be true, this one thing is required; namely, that such things must be deducible from it as correspond to phenomena and as satisfy all the difficulties encountered, on the one hand, in the thing itself and, on the other, in such as arise from it."

7. "I have thus far explained the phenomena of the heavens and sea by the force of gravity, but have not yet assigned the cause of gravity. . . . I have not yet been able to deduce from the phenomena the reason for these properties of gravity, and I do not invent hypotheses. Whatever cannot be deduced from the phenomena should be called an *hypothesis.* . . . In this philosophy, propositions are deduced from phenomena and are rendered general by induction." (General Scholium.)

8. This is Peirce's short title for Herbart's book cited on p. 8 (and in note 3 to item 1).

9. The reference is to J. S. Mill, *Logic,* bk. 2, ch. 3, sec. 3.

10. Ermolao Barbaro (1454–1493), Italian poet and savant and translator of Aristotle.

11. Berkeley, *Principles of Human Knowledge,* sec. 10 of Introduction.

12. Locke, *Essay,* vol. 3, bk. 4, ch. 7, sec. 9.

13. Hume, *Enquiry,* sec. 2.

14. Henry Longueville Mansel, *Prolegomena Logica,* 2nd ed. (Oxford, 1860), p. 9n.

15. See his doctoral dissertation, *De mundi sensibilis atque intelligibilis forma et principiis.*

16. See note 10 to item 2.

17. "It is the same nature that in existence is determinate through the grade of singularity and that in the intellect, that is as having to the intellect the relation of known to knower, is indeterminate."

18. See *Ockham's Theory of Terms: Part I of the "Summa Logicae,"* tr. Michael J. Loux (Notre Dame, IN: University of Notre Dame Press, 1974), pp. 82–84.

19. Shakespeare, *Measure for Measure*, 2.2.117–20. Peirce usually leaves out l. 118 ("Drest in a little brief authority").

4. GROUNDS OF VALIDITY

1. See item 3.

2. In MS 593, "are" has been changed to "may be."

3. See items 2 and 3, as well as "Nominalism *versus* Realism" and "What Is Meant by 'Determined' " (W2:144–54 and 155–58).

4. This and the following quotation is from Petrus Hispanus, *Summulae logicales*, tract. 6. (1) Signification is "the representation, established by convention, of a thing by an utterance" and (2) "Signification is thus prior to supposition, and they differ in that signification belongs to the word, whereas supposition belongs to the term already composed of the word and its signification."

5. See item 3.

6. In MS 593, "and" has been changed to "*plus.*"

7. In MS 593, the word "possibility" is underlined.

8. In MS 593, Peirce has added the following footnote: "That is, in the Kantian sense. See the discussion of the nature of continuity in Essay XVII" (of the "Search for a Method"); the reference is to "The Law of Mind" (item 23).

9. See item 3.

10. Locke, *Essay*, bk. 4, ch. 17, sec. 4.

11. *Logic*, bk. 2, ch. 3.

12. *Gulliver's Travels*, pt. 3, ch. 5.

13. For example, his *Wissenschaft der Logik*, pt. 2, sec. 1, ch. 3.

14. In MS 593, "This . . . contradict" has been changed to "This, however, does not, in the least, contradict"; and "everything . . . future" has been changed to "it is possible to cognize everything,[1] that is, that at some time all things will be known" (with the corresponding footnote: "The difference between the two statements is like that between 'Every man is the son of some woman,' and 'Some woman is the mother of every man.' ").

15. In MS 593, Peirce has added the following footnote: "So far as there is any validity in this conception."

16. See his *Wissenschaft der Logik*, pt. 2, sec. 1, ch. 3.

17. For the Achilles and the Tortoise argument, see Aristotle's *Physics*, 6.9.239b5, or Plutarch's *Moralia*, ch. 43.

18. In MS 593, "is . . . fact" has been changed to "is supposed to follow from the undoubted fact."

19. In MS 593, Peirce has added the following footnote: "Again the distinction is analogous to that between 'Every man is the son of some woman or other,' and 'Some one woman is the mother of all men.' "

20. In MS 593, "seems" has been changed to "in 1869 seemed."

21. Hobbes, *Leviathan*, ch. 11. Peirce reiterates the statement a few pages later (p. 81) and also in item 7 (p. 119).

22. Whenever Peirce refers to the soporific power, or somnific virtue, of opium (as he often does when explaining his theory of hypostatic abstraction), he has in mind the final scene of Molière's *Le Malade Imaginaire*.

23. Kant, *Critique*, B19.
24. See Matthew 16:26, Mark 8:36, or Luke 9:25.
25. See note 22 above.

5. FRASER'S *BERKELEY*

1. Aristotle, *Posterior Analytics*, 83a33–34 ("they are mere prattle or twitterings, and even if they exist, they are irrelevant").
2. Edward reigned 1272–1307.
3. Henry Hallam, *View of the State of Europe during the Middle Ages*, 4th ed. (London, 1869), p. 684.
4. See note 22 in item 4.
5. Kant, *Critique*, B16, 22n2.
6. This long paragraph summarizes Duns Scotus's views expressed in *Ordinatio*, bk. 2, dist. 3, pt. 1, qu. 1–6, or *Quaestiones subtilissimae*, bk. 7, qu. 18.
7. Ockham, *Summa logicae*, pt. 1, ch. 13.
8. Hobbes, *Elements of Philosophy*, in *The English Works* (London, 1839), 1:36.
9. Ibid., 1:118–19.
10. Locke, *Essay*, vol. 3, bk. 4, ch. 7, sec. 9.
11. *Principles of Human Knowledge*, sec. 14 of Introduction.
12. "Commonplace Book of Occasional Metaphysical Thoughts," in *Works*, 4:448.
13. *Second Dialogue between Hylas and Philonous*, in *Works*, 1:304.
14. For Berkeley's views on reality, existence, and experience (expressed in this long paragraph), see his *Principles of Human Knowledge*, sec. 89, and his "Commonplace Book," secs. 29–33.
15. The reference is to David Hartley's "white medullary substance" (and the related theories on sensation and imagination), in his *Observations on Man, His Frame, His Duty and His Expectations* (London, 1749).
16. *Principles of Human Knowledge*, secs. 102, 106, 107.
17. Archer Butler (in an article in the *Dublin University Magazine* 7:538–39), as quoted in Fraser's "Life and Letters of George Berkeley," in *Works*, 4:407.
18. In Fraser's preface to Berkeley's *Theory of Vision*.
19. Hermann Helmholtz, *Handbuch der physiologischen Optik* (Leipzig, 1867), sec. 33, p. 796.

6. ON A NEW CLASS OF OBSERVATIONS

1. For further discussion of the views of Scotus and Ockham, see pp. 92–95 (item 5).
2. The Harvard folder for this manuscript (MS 1104) contains a dark grey envelope, with this inscription: "74 Scraps of Ribbon—Numbered in order of apparent brightness of light by CSP on a dark day."
3. Reported by Alexander Aphrodisiensis, in his commentary upon *Topics*, 149.9–17, as having been said in Aristotle's *Protrepticus*. See *The Works of Aristotle* (Oxford, 1952), 12:27: "since even to inquire whether we ought to philosophize or not is to philosophize."

7. THE FIXATION OF BELIEF

1. Roger Bacon, *Opus Majus*, tr. R. B. Burke (Philadelphia, 1928), pt. 6.
2. In MS 334, Peirce has expanded this sentence by adding "as Harvey, a

genuine man of science, said." See William Harvey's comment to John Aubrey, in the latter's *Brief Lives* (Oxford, 1898), 1:299.

3. In MS 334, Peirce has added "and Harvey."

4. In MS 334, Peirce has changed "Mars;* and" to "Mars and to state the times occupied by the planet in describing the different parts of that curve; but perhaps" (and has deleted the footnote).

5. In MS 334, Peirce has deleted the phrase "in the . . . us)."

6. In MS 334, Peirce has changed the phrase "written; and each" to "Written. Each."

7. "Read, read, read, work, pray, and read again" is a sentiment frequently expressed in the old alchemical texts.

8. In MS 334, Peirce has added "veritable" before "instruments."

9. In MS 334, Peirce has added "but he had been more particularly impressed by Malthus's book on Population."

10. In MS 334, Peirce has changed "were yet able" to read "had yet been able, eight years before the publication of Darwin's immortal work."

11. In MS 334, Peirce has added "relative" before "number."

12. In MS 334, Peirce has changed "A . . . conclusion" to "A being the fact stated in the premisses and B that concluded."

13. In MS 334, Peirce has added "(if this be understood, not in the old sense, but as consisting in a wise union of security with fruitfulness of reasoning)."

14. In MS 334, Peirce has changed "whether . . . follows" to "why a certain conclusion is thought to follow."

15. A Syrian religious and military order founded in 1090 in Persia and finally subdued in Lebanon in 1272. The Holy Spirit was said to reside in Sheik al Jebal (Old Man of the Mountain), whose will was followed in blind obedience. Notorious for their wide-spread acts of terror, the Assassins numbered over 50,000 during the time of the Crusades.

16. In MS 334, Peirce has changed "effect of this sort" to "such active effect," and "action" to "inquiry."

17. In MS 334, Peirce has changed "secondary" to "accidental," and "produced by" to "superinduced by reflexion or."

18. In MS 334, Peirce has changed "any . . . which . . . and" to "as . . . any . . . and then."

19. From the beginning to the present, that is. Numa Pompilius was the legendary second king of Rome (715–672 B.C.), and Pius IX, or Giovanni Mastai Ferretti, was pope from 1846 until his death in 1878. He was the prime mover in the acceptance, on 18 July 1870, of the doctrine of papal infallibility, an event that deeply impressed Peirce.

20. See his *Timaeus*, 35–39, or *Epinomis*, 990–92.

21. See p. 72n.

22. In MS 334, Peirce has added this sentence: "Indeed, as long as no better method can be applied, it ought to be followed, since it is then the expression of instinct which must be the ultimate cause of belief in all cases." The following "But" has been changed to "Nevertheless."

23. Francis Bacon, *Novum Organum*, bk. 1, aphs. 19 and 21.

24. In MS 334, Peirce has added to "ceases" "in some degree at least." In the following sentence, he has changed "caused" to "determined."

25. In MS 334, Peirce has changed "realities, or" to "realities; for."

26. In MS 334, Peirce has changed "uses" to "does use."

27. In MS 334, Peirce has changed "me" to "us."

28. In MS 334, Peirce has changed "that" to "his."

29. In MS 407, Peirce has revised this sentence to read: "Not that the first

three methods of settling opinions are every way at a disadvantage compared with that of experience."

8. How to Make Our Ideas Clear

1. See Descartes, *Principia philosophiae*, pt. 1, sec. 45. In MS 422, Peirce has deleted "one sees that."

2. In MS 422, Peirce has changed "whether it be" to "be it," and "help doing" to "but do." In the following sentence, he has expanded "formulas . . . self-contradiction" to read "two classes, those which cannot be denied without self-contradiction, and those which result from the principle of sufficient reason (of which more anon)."

3. See Leibniz's Eighth Letter to Burnet; also his *Opera omnia* (Geneva, 1768), 6:267.

4. An apparent veiled allusion to his (first) wife, Harriet Melusina Fay Peirce, from whom Peirce had separated two years earlier.

5. See item 7. In MS 422, Peirce has changed "principles . . . papers" to "principles already set forth."

6. In MS 422, Peirce has added "among themselves" and "as" after the first and second "arranged," respectively.

7. In MS 422, Peirce has added "—no matter if contrary to all previous experience."

8. In MS 422, Peirce has inserted "conceivably" before "practical."

9. In MS 422, Peirce has changed "or" to "and."

10. In MS 422, Peirce has added two handwritten pages, for which see CP 5.402n2.

11. In MS 422, Peirce has changed "Let . . . examples" to "Now let us illustrate our rule for attaining clearness of thought by some examples."

12. Gustav Kirchhoff, *Vorlesungen über mathematische Physik: Mechanik* (Leipzig, 1876), Preface.

13. In MS 422, Peirce has deleted "approach . . . and," and changed "it" to "logic."

14. In MS 422, Peirce has changed "scientific" to "experiential."

15. Although the passage has not been located, it is almost certainly in his *De divisione naturae.*

16. In MS 422, Peirce has added (in commas) "as for the 'born missionary' of today" after "whom."

17. A record of Abelard's life from 1119 until 1132, composed in or soon after the latter year. For a modern translation, see Betty Radice's *The Letters of Abelard and Heloise* (Baltimore, 1974).

18. In MS 422, Peirce has changed "fully persuaded" to "animated by a cheerful hope"; "every" to "each"; "can be applied" to "apply it."

19. In MS 422, Peirce has changed "will move" to "are found to move."

20. In MS 422, Peirce has changed "law" to "hope."

21. This is the first line of stanza 9 of William Cullen Bryant's "The Battle-Field." The entire stanza runs as follows:

> Truth struck to earth shall rise again
> The eternal years of God are hers
> While error . . . writhes in pain
> And dies amidst her worshippers.

22. Thomas Gray, "Elegy Written in a Country Churchyard," stanza 14.

23. In MS 422, Peirce has crossed out the remainder of the typewritten page and has substituted a new, four-page handwritten conclusion to the paper.

9. The Doctrine of Chances

1. In MS 703, Peirce has added the following footnote: "This characterization of chemistry now sounds antiquated indeed; and yet it was justified by the general state of mind of chemists at that day, as is shown by the fact that only a few months before van 't Hoff had put forth a statement of the law of mass-action as something absolutely new to science. I am satisfied by considerable search after pertinent facts that no distinction between different allied sciences can represent any truth of fact other than a difference between what habitually passes in the minds, and moves the investigations of the two general bodies of the cultivators of those sciences at the time to which the distinction refers."

2. Francis Bacon, *Novum Organum*, bk. 2, aph. 27.

3. See Adolphe Quételet, *Théorie des probabilités* (Brussels, 1853), and Francis Galton, *Hereditary Genius* (London, 1869).

4. See item 8.

5. Locke, *Essay*, bk. 4, ch. 15, sec. 1.

6. See item 7.

7. See note 5.

8. Peirce found Parmenides' statement in Hegel's *Wissenschaft der Logik*, bk. 1, pt. 1, ch. 1, sec. C1, n. 1.

9. See item 8.

10. For Peirce's review of Venn's book, see W2:98–102.

11. See 1 Cor. 13.

10. The Probability of Induction

1. John Venn, *The Logic of Chance*, Preface.

2. In the *Century Dictionary*, Peirce gives the following definition of the law: "as the physical force of excitation of a nerve increases geometrically the sensation increases arithmetically, so that the sensation is proportional to the logarithm of the excitation. . . . According to Fechner, the total sensation varies directly with the logarithm of the stimulus divided by the stimulus just sufficient to give an appreciable sensation." For Peirce's (and Joseph Jastrow's) experimental refutation of the law, see W5:122–35.

3. Adolphe Quételet, *Théorie des probabilités*, pt. 2, ch. 1.

4. Kant, *Critique*, B19.

5. See Gratry's *Logique*, introduction; bk. 1, ch. 1; bk. 3, ch. 4; and bk. 4, ch. 7.

11. The Order of Nature

1. Etienne Vacherot, *La religion* (Paris, 1869), bk. 2, ch. 5.

2. See Pierre Simon de Laplace's *Exposition du système du monde*. The anecdote of his answer to Napoleon is told in James R. Newman, *The World of Mathematics* (New York, 1956), 4:2376–77.

3. John Tillotson, *Works* (London, 1820), 1:346.

4. Ibid., 1:347.

5. See item 10.

6. See Mill's *Logic*, bk. 3, ch. 3, sec. 1.

7. Ibid., sec. 3.

8. See item 10.

9. Berkeley, *Theory of Vision*, secs. 2 and 3 (in *Works*, 1:35–36).

12. Deduction, Induction, and Hypothesis

1. Peirce provides the proof in the 1880 "On the Algebra of Logic" (item 13, although in the later part not included here) and in his *Century Dictionary* definition of "syllogism."

2. Peirce stopped in Turkey, in August/September 1870, on his way to explore observation sites in Southern Europe for an eclipse of the sun that he observed in Sicily on 22 December.

3. For Mill's four methods (of agreement, difference, residues, and concomitant variations), see his *Logic*, vol. 1, bk. 3, ch. 8.

4. Francis Bacon, *Novum Organum*, bk. 1, aph. 10.

5. In the *Century Dictionary*, Peirce gives the following definition: "in *physics*, the law that at any given temperature the volume of a given mass of gas varies inversely as the pressure which it bears. It was discovered by Robert Boyle, and published by him about 1662; but Edme Mariotte having published a book concerning it (about 1679), the law was for a long time called *Mariotte's law.*"

6. See his *Hydrodynamica*.

7. For the 1866 Lowell Lectures, see W1:358–514; for the 1867 "On the Natural Classification of Arguments," see W2:23–48.

13. On the Algebra of Logic (1880)

1. This is based on Joseph John Murphy, *Habit and Intelligence* (London, 1869), 1:169, which reads: "The definition of habit, and its primary law, is that all vital actions tend to repeat themselves; or, if they are not such as can repeat themselves, they tend to become easier on repetition." Murphy (1827–1894) was an Irish writer on religion, psychology, and logic.

2. The logical principle which, in Peirce's translation in Baldwin's *Dictionary of Philosophy and Psychology* (1901–1902), says that "The predicate of the predicate is the predicate of the subject." Peirce traces the principle back to Aristotle, although the Latin phrase first occurred in Kant. His use of the principle in the argument that follows suggests "The mark of a mark is the mark of the thing itself."

3. See W2:359–429.

4. De Morgan presented five papers on the syllogism before the Cambridge Philosophical Society (in 1846, 1850, 1858, 1860, 1863), which were subsequently published in the Society's *Transactions* (in 1849, 1856, and [the last three] 1864); throughout this article, Peirce gives the dates of presentation. De Morgan introduced the terms "universe" and "universe of a proposition" on p. 380 of his first paper (see also his *Formal Logic*, pp. 40–41, 55). The term "universe of discourse" was first used in Boole's *Laws of Thought*.

5. Boole, *Laws of Thought*, p. 63; the example is "Some men are not wise."

6. See William Stanley Jevons, *The Principles of Science* (London, 1874), 1:49.

7. See William Hamilton's theory of quantification of the predicate, in his *Lectures on Logic* (Boston, 1860), app. 5.

8. The attempt to answer this question led Peirce and his student Christine Ladd-Franklin to investigate second-order truth-functions, and it led to the first known publication of a full sixteen-place second-order truth table in

Ladd-Franklin's "On the Algebra of Logic," in *Studies in Logic* (1883), pp. 17–71. See also W4:569–71 (note 173.6–8).

14. LECTURE ON THE STUDY OF LOGIC

1. The lecture proper is preceded by the following two paragraphs: "Professor C. S. Peirce began his instruction for the current session by a lecture in Hopkins Hall, on the underlying methods of modern logic. It was attended by instructors as well as students. In compliance with a request for an abstract of his address, which was delivered without notes, the speaker has given the following outline.

"Mr. Peirce said that he had requested the instructors to do him the favor to listen to his observations, because he thought that a clear understanding of the purpose of the study of logic might remove some prejudices by leading to a true estimate of its nature."

2. The two references are, respectively, to the *Port-Royal Logic,* 2nd ed. (Edinburgh, 1851) and to Friedrich Ueberweg's *System der Logik* (Bonn, 1857); in the latter, logic is defined as "the science of normative or ideal laws of human cognition."

3. This is the first sentence in Petrus Hispanus's *Summulae logicales* (to which Peirce has added "aliarum scientiarum" from the second sentence). Peirce translated the sentence as "Logic is the art relating to arts, the science relating to sciences, which holds the road to the principles of all methods" (W4:400).

4. The unit of electrical resistance named after Georg Simon Ohm.

5. See his *On Methods of Inference,* defending Epicurean empirical methods against the Stoics.

6. This is Peirce's paraphrase of Matthew 3:3.

7. The classical economists Adam Smith and David Ricardo who developed the concept of free trade.

8. The neogrammarians, notably Friedrich Karl Brugmann, who applied methods of the natural sciences to linguistics.

9. Those astronomers who apply the spectroscopic method, especially Lewis Morris Rutherfurd in the United States; Sir George Stokes illustrated phenomena of emission and absorption of heat radiation by the resonance in sound; Wilhelm Wundt applied to psychology the experimental methods of the natural sciences.

10. For an outline of this part of the course, see item 13.

11. For one of these—namely, the first successful axiomatization of arithmetic—see "On the Logic of Number" (W4:299–309).

12. For Peirce's general theory of induction at this time, see his "A Theory of Probable Inference" (W4:408–50).

13. *De Motibus* is a part of Kepler's *Astronomia Nova.*

15. DESIGN AND CHANCE

1. *On the Origin of Species.*

2. William Edward Story (1850–1930), American mathematician who taught at the Johns Hopkins and at Harvard.

3. William Crookes (1832–1919), English chemist and physicist, and Johann Karl Friedrich Zöllner (1834–1882), German physicist and astronomer. (For Crookes, see also note 5 in item 21.)

4. For three of Peirce's critical discussions of psychical research, see P 347, 352, and 354; the first of these is in CP 6.548–56.

5. J. S. Mill, *Logic*, bk. 3, ch. 3, sec. 1.

6. William Kingdon Clifford, "Cosmic Emotion," in his *Lectures and Essays* (London, 1879), 2:253–85.

7. For Boyle's law, see note 5 in item 12; Jacques Charles's law says that, at a constant pressure, the volume of a gas is directly proportional to the temperature.

8. Although the ellipsis in italic brackets indicates a missing manuscript page, it is possible that only the word "chance" is missing.

16. On the Algebra of Logic (1885)

1. These are not the *tokens* in Peirce's well-known type-token division, but what are more generally known as his *symbols*, that is signs that represent their objects by convention or habit.

2. John Venn, "On the Diagrammatic and Mechanical Representations of Propositions and Reasoning," *Philosophical Magazine* 10 (1880):1–15.

17. An American Plato

1. *Religious Aspect*, especially bk. 2, ch. 12.

2. The reference is to Hegel's absolute idealism (especially in his *Phänomenologie des Geistes*) and to Schelling's pantheistic idealism (in his *Vorlesungen über die Methode des academischen Studium*).

3. Peirce refers to himself; see item 8 (sec. IV, pp. 136–41).

4. *Religious Aspect*, p. 426; the rhetor Thrasymachus appears in the first book of *The Republic* and in *Phaedrus*.

5. *Religious Aspect*, p. 427.

6. Ibid., p. 4.

7. This is the argument of "The Fixation of Belief" (item 7).

8. Peirce probably had in mind Schelling, Fichte, and Hegel, among others.

9. See the chapter on Transcendental Logic, *Critique*, A50–64 (B74–88).

10. Hermann Günther Grassmann (1809–1877), German mathematician and Orientalist, best known for his contributions to algebra and algebraic mathematical logic.

11. *Critique*, A71ff. (B96ff.) or A598f. (B626f.).

12. For O. H. Mitchell's study, see the footnote on p. 227.

13. The reference is to Kant's conception of space and time as forms of sensible intuition; see his *Critique*, A22–36 (B37–53).

14. Peirce later used the word "molition" which, in a 17 December 1909 letter to William James, he defined as "volition minus all desire and purpose, the mere consciousness of *exertion* of any kind" (CP 8.303).

15. *Critique*, A22–23 (B37–38).

16. Hegel, *Encyclopädie*, sec. 7.

17. *Religious Aspect*, p. 427.

18. See note 3.

19. *Religious Aspect*, p. 430.

20. Roger Bacon, *Compendium studii philosophiae*, in *Opera inedita* (London, 1859), ch. 1; see also note 1 in item 7.

21. The original reads "second."

22. For more on feigned and real doubt, see item 3 (pp. 28–29).

23. See J. S. Mill, *Logic*, bk. 3, ch. 3, sec. 1.

24. See *The Logic of Hegel* (Oxford, 1874), sec. 82.

25. Royce actually has "ethical realist" and "moral idealist" (*Religious Aspect*, pp. 21–22).

26. Ibid., ch. 3.

27. Ibid., p. 48.

28. Ibid., pp. 82ff., which refer to Spencer's "Data of Ethics," in pt. 1 of his *Principles of Ethics* (1879).

29. Royce mentions (pp. 135–36) Alexander Bain's conception of memory and Francis Galton's investigation of word associations.

30. Ibid., p. 138.

31. *Critique*, A5 (B8–9).

32. *Religious Aspect*, pp. 140–41.

33. Ibid., p. 144.

34. John Phoenix was the pseudonym of George Horatio Derby (1823–1862), American soldier and humorist. The story is given in his "Official Report . . . of a Military Survey and Reconnaissance of the Route from San Francisco to the *Mission of Dolores,*" in his *Phoenixiana; or, Sketches and Burlesques* (New York, 1856), p. 21. The original has 184 rather than 365 solar compasses.

35. *Religious Aspect*, pp. 181–82, 187, and 196–97.

36. For Apollo's lute, see Plato, *Republic,* 3.399e.

18. ONE, TWO, THREE

1. Peirce had first proposed this hypothesis in his January 1884 lecture on "Design and Chance" (item 15); it recurs throughout the *Monist* Metaphysical Series (items 21–25).

2. The hypothesis set out in this paragraph is an early statement of "A Guess at the Riddle" (item 19), and it is a preview of the evolutionary cosmology developed in items 21–25.

3. See chapter 7 in item 19, pp. 273–79.

19. A GUESS AT THE RIDDLE

1. The reference is not to the first chapter that follows below, but to item 35 or one of the chapters in items 47–50 in W5 (pp. 242–47 and 292–308), all chapters for the projected book entitled "One, Two, Three."

2. Although Peirce probably never wrote this chapter, its substance can be readily deduced from the five papers to which he refers (and which are identified in the next five notes). For this chapter, the editors of the *Collected Papers* used part of MS 901 (W5:242–47).

3. See item 16.

4. See item 1.

5. See "A Theory of Probable Inference" (W4:408–50).

6. See "On the Natural Classification of Arguments" (W2:23–48).

7. See "Description of a Notation for the Logic of Relatives" (W2:359–429).

8. The next two paragraphs, one of three such typewritten opening statements for Peirce's book, are taken from CP 1.1–2, where they serve as Preface to the *Collected Papers;* the original typescript is no longer extant.

9. Shakespeare, *The Merchant of Venice,* 2.6.15–18.

10. See item 14, where Peirce discusses this point in greater detail.

11. In the original, the number is IV.

12. For an explication of this statement, see Max H. Fisch, "Peirce's Arisbe," in his *Peirce, Semeiotic, and Pragmatism* (Bloomington, 1986), pp. 229ff.

13. Benjamin Franklin and Benjamin Thompson (afterward Count Rumford), whom Peirce mentions in his (Paris) July Fourth Address "On the State of Science in America" (W4:152ff.); in the original, "one another" is "each another."

14. For the fact that Peirce exaggerates here, or later changed his mind, see Max H. Fisch, "Hegel and Peirce," in his *Peirce, Semeiotic, and Pragmatism*, pp. 261ff.

15. For a somewhat earlier treatment of the subject matter of this chapter, see W5:295–98.

16. The reference is probably to Thomas Hobbes.

17. In the original, the preceding "in the" is lacking.

18. Not verified, but probably in his *Physiology* (New York, 1879).

19. In the *Century Dictionary*, Peirce gives the following definition: "in older writers, the mass into the square of the velocity, or the measure of the mass multiplied by the square of that of the velocity: but recent writers frequently use the phrase to denote one half of the above quantity."

20. The table contains a number of corrections by the editors.

21. See the beginning of item 15, pp. 215–16.

22. Karl Friedrich Gauss, *General Investigations of Curved Surfaces* (Princeton, 1902), art. 20.

23. See note 34 in item 17; for the "Lectures on Astronomy," see *Phoenixiana*, pp. 51–66.

24. *Physics*, 195b31–198a13.

25. See the appendix to the Transcendental Dialectic, *Critique*, A642ff. (B670ff.).

20. TRICHOTOMIC

1. The original reads "third."

2. The reference here, as on p. 284, is to Steele MacKaye (1842–1894), a New York playwright, actor, theater manager, and inventor, and (with his wife) a friend of the Peirces. MacKaye's divisions of dramatic expression and of the principles of being probably were made either in a public address or in a journal or newspaper, which have not been identified.

3. See ch. 1 of the Transcendental Aesthetic, *Critique*, A19–22 (B33–36).

4. See note 2.

21. THE ARCHITECTURE OF THEORIES

1. In the original, the word is "accidently."

2. Of "the natural light" (of reason), Peirce says in MS S104, that it "is no *evidence* of truth, yet this is the *one* way of distinguishing the truth which alone is quite indispensible. It must not be *relied upon* in the least degree; but it has to be *used.*"

3. See note 5 in item 12.

4. Named after Amedeo Avogadro (1776–1856), Italian chemist and physicist; for his law, see p. 335.

5. See William Crookes's article in the *Philosophical Transactions of the Royal Society* 165 (1875):519.

6. This was one of Peirce's concerns in his famous "Note on the Theory of the Economy of Research" (W4:72–78).

7. Herbert Spencer, *First Principles*, 5th ed. (New York, 1880), pt. 2, ch. 18.

8. For Peirce's contributions (signed "Outsider") to the controversy regarding Spencer's synthetic philosophy, which lasted for several weeks in March/April 1890 in the *New York Times*, see P 402 and 416.

9. For more elaborate discussions of this example, see item 15 (pp. 220–21) and item 19 (pp. 270–71).

10. Jean Baptiste Lamarck, *Philosophie zoologique* (Paris, 1873), pt. 1, ch. 7.

11. Clarence King, *Catastrophism and the Evolution of Environment* (1877).

12. August Weismann, "The Duration of Life," in his *Essays upon Heredity* (Oxford, 1889).

13. Christian August Friedrich Peters (1806–1880), German astronomer, and Robert Stawell Ball (1840–1913), Irish mathematician, astronomer, and scientific writer (both popular and technical).

14. In the original, the preceding phrase reads "the sum of the three sides of a triangle are."

15. Peirce demonstrates this importance in item 23.

22. The Doctrine of Necessity

1. See item 21.

2. See Hermann Diels, *Die Fragmente der Vorsokratiker* (Berlin, 1906), c. 55, A66.

3. See Aetius, *Placita* (in Migne, vol. 19), I, 12 and 15.

4. See *De Interpretatione*, 18b31, 19a7, and *Ethica Nicomachea*, 1112a7–10, and Epicurus' 3rd Epistle.

5. See (Cleanthes in) Epictetus, *Manual*, ch. 53, and Seneca, *De Providentia*, V, 8.

6. In the original, the word is "compromised."

7. *Examination of Sir William Hamilton's Philosophy* (Boston, 1865), ch. 16.

8. According to his inter-leaf copy of the *Century Dictionary*, Peirce himself wrote the six definitions.

9. As indicated in the headnote on p. 298, Paul Carus responded to the plea with two articles, to which Peirce offered his "Reply to the Necessitarians."

23. The Law of Mind

1. See items 21 and 22.

2. See items 2–4; in the original, the parenthetical number is "III."

3. See Cantor's *Gesammelte Abhandlungen mathematischen und philosophischen Inhalts* (Berlin, 1932), pp. 139–40. Peirce became acquainted with Cantor's writings in the mid-1880s.

4. See "On the Logic of Number" (W4:299–309, the last three pages).

5. See De Morgan's *Formal Logic* (1847), pp. 165ff.

6. See Pierre de Fermat, *Opera Omnia* (Leipzig, 1911), vol. 1, secs. 340–51.

7. See Cantor, *Gesammelte Abhandlungen*, pp. 115ff.

8. Ibid., p. 278.

9. Ibid., p. 289 (13, 14).

10. Kant, *Critique*, A169 (B211).

11. Cantor, *Gesammelte Abhandlungen*, p. 194.

12. See note 10.

13. Aristotle, *Physics*, 227a10, and *Metaphysics*, 1069a5.

14. For a brief account of Peirce's anticipation of the importance of infinitesimals in mathematics, see Carolyn Eisele, ed., *The New Elements of Mathematics* (The Hague, 1976), 3:ix–x.

15. See Augustin Louis Cauchy, *Leçons sur les applications du calcul infinitésimal à la géométrie* (Paris, 1826–28), and Jean Marie Constant Duhamel, *Eléments de calcul infinitésimal* (Paris, 1856).

16. See William James, *Principles of Psychology* (1890), vol. 2, ch. 20.

17. This was probably during his visits to Rome, in December 1870 and January 1871.

24. MAN'S GLASSY ESSENCE

1. Edmund Montgomery, "The Dependence of Quality on Specific Energies," *Mind* 5 (1880):1–29; Charles Bernard Renouvier, *Essais de critique générale* (Paris, 1875), app. 9; Joseph R. L. Delboeuf, "Déterminisme et liberté," *Revue Philosophique* 13 (1882):453–80, 608–38 and 14 (1882):158–89.

2. See items 21, 22, and 23. The "papers that are to follow in the series" mentioned in the next paragraph provide one of the several bits of evidence that Peirce had projected more than five papers for the series; see also the headnote to item 21.

3. William Thomson, "The Size of Atoms," in his *Popular Lectures and Addresses* (London, 1889), p. 218.

4. John Bernard Stallo, *The Concepts and Theories of Modern Physics* (New York, 1882), ch. 7.

5. Gustav Theodor Fechner, *Über die physikalische und philosophische Atomenlehre* (Leipzig, 1864).

6. Benjamin Thompson Rumford, *Complete Works* (Boston, 1870–75), 1:471–93; 2:1–22, 166–87, 208–21.

7. James Prescott Joule, *Scientific Papers* (London, 1884–87), 1:149ff.

8. William J. M. Rankine, *Transactions of the Royal Society of Edinburgh* 20 (1850):192.

9. See Daniel Bernoulli, *Hydrodynamica* (1738), sec. 10.

10. See also note 4 in item 21.

11. See note 5 in item 21 (and note 3 in item 15).

12. "A body which throughout its mass (and not merely at its surface) resists for an indefinite time a sufficiently small force that tends to alter its equilibrium figure, always springing back into shape after the force is removed; a body possessing elasticity of figure. Every such body has limits of elasticity, and, if subjected to a strain exceeding these limits, it takes a set and does not return to its original shape on being let go. This property is called *plasticity*. The minimum energy required to give a set to a body of definite form and size measures its resilience. When the resilience of a body is small and masks its springiness, the body is called *soft*. Even fluids transmit shearing forces if time be allowed, and many substances will yield indefinitely to very small (but not indefinitely small) forces applied for great lengths of time. So solids that have received a small set will sometimes partially recover their figures after a long time. This property in fluids is called *viscosity*, in solids *after-effect* (German *nachwirkung*). The phenomenon is connected with a regrouping of the molecules, and indicates the essential difference between a solid and a liquid. In fluids diffusion is continually active, and in gases it produces phenomena of viscosity. In liquids it is not rapid enough to give rise to sensible viscosity, but

the free motion of the molecules makes the body fluid, while the tendency of sets of molecules to continue for a while associated makes the fluidity imperfect. In solids, on the other hand (at least when not under strain), there is no diffusion, and the molecules are consequently in stationary motion or describing quasi-orbits. They thus become grouped in the mode in which they have least positional energy consistent with their kinetic energy. When this grouping is slightly disturbed, it tends to restore itself; but when the disturbance is greater, some of the molecules will tend to return to their old places and others to move on to new situations, and this may give rise to a new permanent grouping, and exhibit the phenomenon of plasticity. But if not quite sufficient for this, disturbances of the molecular motions somewhat similar to the secular perturbations of the planets will result, from which there will be no restoration for a very long time. Solid bodies are very strongly cohesive, showing that the molecules attract one another on the whole; and they are generally capable of crystallization, showing that the attractions of the molecules are different in different directions."

13. See R. J. Boscovich, *Theoria philosophiae naturalis* (Venice, 1763), secs. 8, 81, 132.

14. This is the paper mentioned in the headnote on p. 285, which Peirce seems not to have written.

15. "Over de continuitet van den gas en vloeistof-toestand," *Academisch Proefschrift* (Leiden, 1873).

16. Emile Hilaire Amagat, "Mémoire sur la compressibilité des gaz à des pressions élevées," *Annales de Chimie et de Physique* 19 (1880).345–85.

17. Svante August Arrhenius, "Über die Diffusion der in Wasser gelösten Stoffe," *Zeitschrift für physikalische Chemie* 1 (1887):631–48; Rudolf J. E. Clausius, "Über die Elektricitätsleitung in Elektrolyten," *Poggendorff's Annalen* 101 (1857):338–60; Alexander W. Williamson, "Über die Theorie der Aetherbildung," *Annalen der Chemie und Pharmacie* 77 (1851):37–49.

18. Arthur Cayley, "On the Theory of the Analytical Forms called Trees," *American Journal of Mathematics* 4 (1881):266–68.

19. William Kingdon Clifford, *Lectures and Essays* (London, 1879), 2:311–16.

20. William James, *Principles of Psychology* (1890), 1:105.

21. See note 12 above.

22. See item 3, p. 52.

23. See item 3, p. 54. (In the original, the volume number is "III.")

24. The opening session of this event was held in Madison Square Garden on 7 July 1892.

25. EVOLUTIONARY LOVE

1. See Hermann Diels, *Die Fragmente der Vorsokratiker* (Berlin, 1906), 1:21B.

2. See p. 442.

3. See item 24.

4. See item 23.

5. Simon Newcomb, *Principles of Political Economy* (New York, 1886).

6. Ibid., p. 534.

7. Peirce is speaking quite personally here. About the incident, he said in a 20 September 1892 letter to Augustus Lowell: "I lately reported on a chemical process for a man in Wall St. who was to pay me $500 cash and a share in the patents. He duly gave me a check and the bank returned it as 'no good.'" The "Master in glomery" was Thomas J. Montgomery.

8. Bernard Mandeville, *The Fable of the Bees* (London, 1806), remark G.

9. Paul Carus, "Mr. Charles S. Peirce's Onslaught on the Doctrine of Necessity," *Monist* 2 (1892):576.

10. O. G. Downes's translation of Quételet was published in London in 1849, and John Herschel's "Quételet on Probabilities" appeared in the *Edinburgh Review* (42:1–57) the following year.

11. Rudolf J. E. Clausius, "Über die Art der Bewegung welche wir Wärme nennen," *Poggendorff's Annalen* 100 (1857):365, and August Karl Krönig, "Grundzüge einer Theorie der Gase," *Poggendorff's Annalen* 99 (1856):315.

12. James Clerk Maxwell, "Illustrations of the Dynamical Theory of Gases," *Philosophical Magazine* 4 (1860):22. (Also in his *Collected Papers*, 1:377.)

13. Hermann Helmholtz, "Über die Erhaltung der Kraft," introduction to a series of lectures given in Karlsruhe in 1862–63, in his *Popular Scientific Lectures* (New York, 1885), 1:316–62; Rudolf J. E. Clausius, "Über die bewegende Kraft der Wärme," *Poggendorff's Annalen* 79 (1850):368; for W. J. M. Rankine, see note 8 in item 24.

14. Henry Longueville Mansel (1820–1871), English metaphysician and follower of Hamilton; see also note 14 in item 3.

15. Karl Wilhelm Nägeli, *Mechanisch-physiologische Theorie der Abstammungslehre* (Munich and Leipzig, 1884), Introduction; Albert von Kölliker, *Entwicklungsgeschichte des Menschen und der höheren Tiere* (Leipzig, 1879), sec. 1 of Introduction; August Weismann, *Essays on Heredity* (Oxford, 1889), vol. 1, essay 2.

16. Jean Baptiste Lamarck, *Philosophie zoologique* (Paris, 1873).

17. See item 24.

18. Ibid.

19. Invented by J. E. W. Keely in 1874, it was supposed to produce power by responding to the intermolecular vibrations of the ether.

20. In the original, "of the" is "the of."

21. See Mark 3:29, 9:48, and Isaiah 66:24.

22. Jared Sparks (1789–1866), American historian and editor, and president of Harvard College.

23. Eusebius Pamphili, *Ecclesiastical History* (London, 1876), 8:2.

24. Lactantius, "Of the False Wisdom of Philosophers," in *The Works* (Edinburgh, 1871), bk. 3.

25. See John of Salisbury, *Polycraticus*, 2:26, 8:19.

26. See Prantl's *Geschichte der Logik im Abendlande* (Leipzig, 1867), vol. 3, sec. 17, p. 2.

27. See William Whewell, *Novum Organon Renovatum*, 3rd ed. (London, 1858).

28. Urbain J. J. Leverrier, "Recherches sur les mouvements de la planète Herschel, dite Uranus," in *Connaissances des temps* (1849); J. C. Adams, *Nautical Almanac*, 1851, p. 3.

29. For Rankine, see note 8 in item 24; for Clausius, see note 13; for Thomson, see note 2 in item 24.

30. For Bernoulli, see note 9 in item 24; for Boyle, see note 5 in item 12; for Charles, see note 7 in item 15; for Avogadro, see p. 335 and note 4 in item 21.

31. Mendeleef, Lothar Meyer, and J. A. R. Newlands.

32. W. T. G. Morton, C. T. Jackson, and J. C. Warren.

33. According to Peirce's "Note on the Age of Basil Valentine" (P 674), Basil Valentine is reputed to have been one of the earliest scientific chemists, in fifteenth-century Germany; but Peirce goes on to say that he may have been the creation of Johann Thölde, who published several works attributed to Basil Valentine around 1600.

34. Originating in the Italian *commedia dell'arte*, Punchinello is a sort of rustic clown or buffoon (and the prototype of Punch).

INDEX